AF758297

# Macroeconomic Policy Environment

## Second Edition

*An Analytical Guide for Managers*

# CFM-MHE Series in Finance

*Honorary Consulting Editor: Dr. Prasanna Chandra*

The CFM-MHE Series in Finance, a joint initiative of the Centre for Financial Management and McGraw Hill Education (India), seeks to synthesise the findings of financial research with the concerns of practitioners. The aim of the books in this series is to convey the important developments in the theory and practice of finance in a rigorous, but relatively non-technical manner for the benefit of: (a) finance practitioners and (b) students of MBA.

***Titles in the Series***

| | |
|---|---|
| • *Macroeconomic Policy Environment* | **Shyamal Roy** |
| • *Projects: Planning, Analysis, Selection, Financing, Implementation, and Review* | **Prasanna Chandra** |
| • *Finance Sense: Finance for Non-finance Executives* | **Prasanna Chandra** |
| • *Behavioural Finance* | **Prasanna Chandra** |
| • *Financial Management: Theory and Practice* | **Prasanna Chandra** |
| • *Investment Analysis and Portfolio Management* | **Prasanna Chandra** |
| • *Corporate Valuation: A Guide to Analysts, Managers, and Investors* | **Prasanna Chandra** |
| • *Strategic Financial Management: Managing for Value Creation* | **Prasanna Chandra** |
| • *International Financial Management* | **Prakash G Apte, Sanjeevan Kapshe** |
| • *Investment Banking: Concepts, Analyses and Cases* | **Pratap G Subramanyam** |
| • *Corporate Governance and Stewardship: Emerging Role and Responsibilities of Corprate Boards and Directors* | **N Balasubramanian** |

# Macroeconomic Policy Environment

Second Edition

*An Analytical Guide for Managers*

**Shyamal Roy**

*Professor*
*Indian Institute of Management*
*Bangalore*

McGraw Hill Education (India) Private Limited

Published by McGraw Hill Education (India) Private Limited,
Anjana Complex No: 5/90 A, Butt Road, St. Thomas Mount, Chennai – 600016

Copyright © 2010, by McGraw Hill Education (India) Private Limited

21st reprint 2023

No part of this publication may be reproduced or distributed in any form or by any means, electronic, mechanical, recording, or otherwise or stored in a database retrieval system without the prior written permission of the publishers. The program listings (if any) may entered, stored and executed in a computer system, but they may not be reproduced for publication

This edition can be exported from India only by the publishers,
McGraw Hill Education (India) Private Limited

Print Edition
**ISBN-13: 978-0-07-070374-2**
**ISBN-10: 0-07-070374-4**

EBook Edition
**ISBN-13: 978-1-259-00083-6**
**ISBN-10: 1-259-00083-4**

**22 23 24 25 26 APO 27 26 25 24 23**

Information contained in this work has been obtained by McGraw-Hill Education (India), from sources believed to be reliable. However, neither McGraw-Hill Education (India) nor its authors guarantee the accuracy or completeness of any information published herein, and neither McGraw-Hill Education (India) nor its authors shall be responsible for any errors, omissions, or damages arising out of use of this information. This work is published with the understanding that McGraw-Hill Education (India) and its authors are supplying information but are not attempting to render professional services. If such services are required, the assistance of an appropriate professional should be sought.

Typeset at DigiConv Technologies, J-6, Street No. 3, Near Vijay Chowk, Laxmi Nagar, Delhi 110 092 and Printed and bound in India at A.P. Offset Pvt. Ltd. New Delhi 110 095

Cover Design: Kapil Gupta, Delhi

Visit us at: www.mheducation.co.in; Phone (Toll free in India): **1800 103 5875**
Write to us at: support.india@mheducation.com

CIN: U22200TN1970PTC111531

**To**

***the memory of my Father***

# Preface to the Second Edition

A sea change has taken place in our understanding of macroeconomics since the first edition of this book was published in 2005. The severity and depth of the global economic and financial meltdown, in the wake of the sub-prime crisis in USA, has given rise to several questions, mostly related to the efficacy of macroeconomic policies. Should financial stability be a key objective of monetary policy? Should monetary policy track asset price movements as well? What is the role of fiscal policy in a period of slowdown? Is fiscal deficit a concern? When and when not? Are controls on movement of certain types of capital undesirable? Should Central bank intervention in foreign exchange market to stabilize the exchange rate be discouraged? These are some of the issues that will occupy the interest of economists and policymakers across the globe in the years to come.

While Indian macroeconomic policies have come out relatively unscathed in the wake of global economic slowdown and have, in fact, been praised for their cautious approach, India has its own set of problems which throw up new challenges for our policy makers. How do we interpret these challenges? What are their business implications?

The second edition of the book attempts to focus on some of these emerging issues. Chapter 1 sets the stage by highlighting why in today's rapidly changing business environment, should a manager have exposure to how macroeconomic policies are framed and how certain events take effect. Chapter 2 introduces the key concepts in macroeconomics. Chapter 3 provides the analytical basis for understanding why, at times, macroeconomic policies may be rendered ineffective. Chapter 4 describes fiscal policy and all its dimensions. Chapter 5 discusses monetary policy and the dilemmas faced by the Central bank in the conduct of this policy. Chapter 6 discusses external sector developments, including the recent events. Chapter 7 brings out the implications for managerial decision making. Throughout the book, as in the first edition, every chapter has a section on Indian macroeconomic policies. And, each chapter relates to business environment.

Specific changes made in the second edition are:

1. All the data and analysis have been updated to 2008–09 and, in some cases, 2009–10.
2. Some of the topical issues have been put in the form of a box for ready reference.
3. Current topics like the global economic and financial meltdown, the Union Budget 2010–11, the crisis in Greece and others have been discussed in detail.
4. Annexure in Chapter 5 explains the IS-LM model.
5. Annexure at the end of Chapter 7 highlights changes in macroeconomics thinking in the light of recent happenings.
6. An instructor's manual is being made available separately.

While the second edition remains highly relevant to practicing managers and policy makers, the changes introduced also makes it an ideal choice as a first-level macroeconomics textbook in an MBA programme.

To enhance the utility of this book, powerpoint slides for instructors are available at https://connect.mheducation.com/.

I hope readers will receive the second edition as enthusiastically as the first. I will look forward to comments for future improvements.

**Shyamal Roy**

# Preface to the First Edition

This book is written for professional managers, both in public and private sectors, who have little or no background in Economics; but have to face, on a regular basis, the challenges posed by a rapidly changing macroeconomic policy environment. The book attempts to provide an understanding of how macroeconomic policies work and, in turn, how they impact the business environment. I have deliberately kept away from jargons, diagrams and equations in explaining the policy changes and policy impacts. The approach has been to explain the issues in a 'story' mode. And, I have developed this approach from my experience of teaching this subject in Executive Development Programmes, both at IIMB and outside, for over 20 years.

For MBA students the book will be useful in two respects. First, they will get a practical view of macroeconomics without losing the underlying theoretical foundation. Those management schools that follow a less quantitative approach to teaching macroeconomics will find this book useful as a textbook. Second, in my view, perhaps for the first time, they will get an exposure to Indian macroeconomic policy issues in an integrated fashion.

Policy makers in government will get a decent exposure to various policy issues and conflicts involved in the framing and conduct of macroeconomic policies.

Needless to say, in writing this book I have drawn from some excellent textbooks available on the subject. But I have also supplemented those with my own interpretation and research. I welcome comments from both colleagues and practicing managers/students on the book.

**Shyamal Roy**
Bangalore
June, 2005

ACKNOWLEDGEMENTS

While planning the second edition of this book I benefited from valuable suggestions provided by colleagues in academia, industry and government. I am deeply indebted to all of them. I will like to make particular mention of Professor Vasant Sukhatme of Macalester College, Minneapolis, Minnesota, for his detailed comments. I am equally indebted to my students at IIMB for putting forward their ideas on the content as well as the approach taken in the book. Interactive sessions, both within and outside the classroom, have helped me to a large extent in planning and structuring the new edition.

**Shyamal Roy**

# Contents

CHAPTER

1

# Introduction

## 1.1 Background

You must have wondered, at times, why the leading figures in the corporate world watch, with more than passing interest, what the Finance Minister announces on the day of the annual budget presentation or what the Reserve Bank of India (RBI) Governor has to state during the quarterly monetary policy announcements. What are these leading managers of industry looking for from the Finance Minister or the RBI Governor in these announcements? Certainly they do not want to hear words of wisdom on how to run their business. They know their businesses better than any Finance Minister or RBI Governor. Then what is it?

Managers have to cope with the economic environment at two levels. First, it is at the firm level where the business environment is driven primarily by the structure of the market. The economic principles, which guide decision making at the firm level, are the following:

1. The more competitive the market structure, the less influence a firm will have on prices, as a means to improve the bottom line growth. A lowering of price will result in similar moves by the competitors, thus, nullifying any price advantage for the firm. Any attempt to increase

prices will result in loss of customers in favour of competitors, once again, defeating the main purpose.

2. In a highly competitive market structure, a firm thus must endeavour to achieve cost advantage by lowering its per unit cost of production vis-à-vis competitors', and/or
3. Be able to differentiate its product or service so that in the customers' perception, the product or service of the firm offers more value than the competitors and are thereby willing to pay a higher price or, at a given price, willing to buy more of the firm's product/service.

Firms today are investing heavily towards points 2 and 3 above. Those who are able to play their cards well are doing well while others are lagging behind.

However, there is a second level at which the managers have to cope with the economic environment. This is not at a firm level but at a macro level.

When a firm takes decisions about new investments, there are certain assumptions. These are the following:

1. Demand will grow at a stable rate. This is crucial for deciding on the capacity and arriving at the revenue stream.
2. Interest rates will be stable. This is important to get a hold on the cost of money.
3. There will be stability in prices, i.e. rate of inflation. This is necessary for getting an accurate estimate of costs and returns.
4. Tax rates will be stable. This again will determine costs and prices, and
5. Exchange rate fluctuations will be minimum. This is another cost variable.

Stability in the above five variables is key to a conducive business environment. Any unpredictable change in any of these variables can upset the revenue and cost calculations, which formed the basis for undertaking new investments. The bottom lines of even the best-managed companies can get badly eroded.

Ironically, no company can influence these variables. Stability of these variables is dictated by how macroeconomic policies are formulated. It is, therefore, important, for managers, as a "second best", to at least, have a basic understanding of what macroeconomic policies are and how they impact business. More specifically, an understanding of macroeconomics and macroeconomic policies is of utmost importance to the manager for the following reasons:

1. To understand how an economy functions. What causes fluctuations in demand? What leads to instability in interest rates, tax rates, exchange rates, and prices?
2. To come to a judgment about the direction of government policies.
3. To arrive at a decision on timing of fresh investments, takeovers, penetration to new markets etc. and, ultimately,
4. To get the best return on investment.

Managers need to carefully monitor what the Finance Minister and the RBI Governor, in their policy announcements, have to indicate about the stability of the macroeconomic variables. Macroeconomic stability is an essential prerequisite for a sustained growth of business in an economy.

In the next section, we will get a feel of what macroeconomic policies do. We will unrealistically start with an industry example to understand the issues. Then realistically blow it up for the economy to see how the issues change.

## 1.2 What Do Macroeconomic Policies Do?

### 1.2.1 Understanding the Problem (1): An Industry Example

Take the case of cement industry. To keep the arithmetic simple, assume that the cement industry has an annual capacity to manufacture 100 tons of cement. For the time being, let us further assume that the desired level of inventories is zero; hence, this 100 tons is all for sale. But, the industry finds that the actual sale is only 80 tons. That is, on the one hand, a 100-ton capacity, which obviously is based on certain estimate of market demand, is set up. On the other hand, the actual sale, reflective of actual market demand, is only 80 tons. How do we explain this discrepancy? The answer clearly is that this situation has arisen because demand turned out, for whatever reason, to be deficient.

Under these circumstances, what is the cement industry likely to do? First, it may lower the prices to clear the excess inventory. The law of demand in economics states that as the price of a commodity falls, the quantity demanded of that commodity goes up and as the price of a commodity rises, the quantity demanded of that commodity goes down. Quantity demanded is, thus, inversely related to its price. A reduction in price, of cement will, therefore, increase the quantity demanded of cement. At a lower price demand will equal supply.

However, prices cannot be fixed below the average cost of production. It will render the business unviable. A sharp reduction in prices may also not be desirable from the point of brand equity. It is easy to lose brand equity but very difficult to gain it back. Obviously, then, there are limits to how much price reduction has to be arrived at.

Along with price cutting measures, the industry is, therefore, likely to resort to cost cutting measures. Since, in the short run, it is not possible to cut down the size of the plant, this may take the form of rendering some of the factors of production unemployed, i.e. some machines may not be used, workers may be laid off etc. These will save costs.

Now turn the story around. Assume, as before, that the cement industry's capacity to manufacture cement is still 100 tons, but the demand now is 120 tons. What is the industry likely to do? In a short span of time, it is going to be difficult to increase capacity to meet the increased demand. Setting up a new plant takes time.[1] In the short run, therefore, when the capacity is fixed, the most likely response to this kind of a situation will be to increase prices. Law of demand will work again. A rise in the price of cement will reduce quantity demanded of cement. At a higher price, demand will equal to supply.

Let us now list out the learning from this story. Make sure you can relate each point below to the story above. What we have seen is that in the short run is the following:

1. When actual demand is below capacity output (80 tons as against a capacity of 100 tons, in our example) we have, what is called, a slowdown. Recession is a deeper slowdown. And, depression is a deeper recession.

[1] Even if it were possible to put up another plant in a short period of time, firms may like to wait and watch to make sure that the increase in demand is durable and not a transitory phenomenon.

2. When actual demand exceeds capacity output (120 tons against a capacity of 100 tons, in our example), we have a boom, also referred to as overheating.
3. In a period of slowdown, prices fall. More likely, the rate of price rise falls. Or, inflation comes down. Also, some factors of production are rendered unemployed.
4. In a period of boom or, overheating, prices rise at a faster pace. Or, inflation goes up.
5. Both slowdowns and booms are caused by fluctuations in demand.

This is the story of a particular industry. The economy, of course, involves all the industries, which is obviously bigger. Let us see how the above learning can be used to understand the management problems of an economy.

## 1.2.2 Understanding the Problem (2): Now Consider the Entire Economy

The main points to be noted in the transition from the cement industry example to the description of the economy as a whole are the following:

First, as in the case of cement industry, so in the case of an economy, there is a capacity output. Indian economy's capacity to grow is presently estimated at 9% per annum.

Second, when we refer to an economy, we do not talk in terms of demand for a particular commodity like cement. We have to think in terms of all goods and services demanded in an economy. Hence, instead of cement demand, we use the term *aggregate demand* (AD) for goods and services.

Third, as in the case of demand, in the case of supply also, we need to consider the supply of all goods and services produced in an economy. Hence, we replace the word cement supply with *aggregate supply* (AS) of goods and services.

Finally, in an economy, where a large number of goods and services are produced and demanded, there is no concept of price of a commodity or a service. In an economy, some prices will rise, others will fall; our concern is what happens to the weighted average price level. We, therefore, consider *general price level* (GPL), and not just price of a product or a service.

Otherwise, the management problem of an economy, in the short run, is not different from the management problem of the cement industry, which can be explained as follows:

1. If the *aggregate demand* (AD) increases at a slower pace than the *aggregate supply* (AS) capacity in the economy, we have a slowdown/recession.[2] This manifests itself in a slower growth of general price level (GPL), or, inflation and/or unemployment of resources, including labour.
2. If the *aggregate demand* (AD) outpaces the *aggregate supply* (AS) capacity of the economy, we have a boom, followed by a rise in the inflation.
3. Both slowdowns and booms, in the short run, are caused by fluctuations in demand.[3]

How is the capacity to produce goods and services in an economy arrived at? This is an important question. Let us, therefore, first approach the answer from a firm's perspective. If a firm wants to add to its capacity, where will it find the money to invest in new capacity? There are several possibilities. It can use its retained earnings; it can borrow from the domestic market; or, it can borrow from the international market. Note that in each case, the firm is tapping somebody's savings. In the first case, the firm is using its own savings; in the second case, it is tapping the savings of the public; in the last case, it is tapping foreigner's savings. Therefore, the first prerequisite for investment and growth is availability of savings. Without savings, investment is not possible and without investment, the supply capacity of an economy cannot grow.

Is that all? No. A lot also depends on how the investment, made possible by savings, is translated into output growth. Consider two companies, A and B, producing similar products. Company A invests Rs. 10 and generates an increase of Rs. 5 in the output, but the same size of investment by company B results in an increase of only Re. 1 in the output. How do we explain the difference in performance between companies A and B? The answer is that company A is more efficient than company B. What constitutes this efficiency? "Efficiency" is an all-encompassing word. It could mean

---

[2] A slowdown becomes recession if for two consecutive quarters, output growth is negative. Recession turns into depression if each quarter of negative growth is more than 10%.

[3] If the economy is integrated with the world economy, slowdown can be delayed as the domestic deficient demand could be, at least, partially made up by higher exports. Similarly, the inflationary effect of domestic demand outpacing domestic production can also, to some extent, be arrested through imports. But the basic management problem spelled out earlier remains, more so, because in a highly integrated world both slowdowns and inflation, globally, will have a tendency to converge.

managerial efficiency, technological superiority and host of many other factors. Thus, the more endowed a production unit is with these qualities, the higher will be its output response to investment. The output response to investment is called the incremental capital–output ratio. In company A, the incremental capital–output ratio is 10:5. In Company B, the same is 10:1. *Other things being equal, as efficiency increases, incremental capital–output ratio falls.*

We can now see how India's 9% growth potential is arrived at. India's savings rate (which gives the size of investment) is estimated at about 36% of income or output and the incremental capital–output ratio (which measures the productivity of investment) at 4:1, thereby giving a potential growth of 9%. It clearly is not a fixed number. With no change in saving-investment rate, India's potential growth can be higher than 9% if incremental capital–output ratio comes down.[4] Similarly, with no change in incremental capital–output ratio, a higher rate of saving-investment can generate a higher rate of growth of output and vice versa. The 9% growth rate was arrived at on the basis of an elaborate exercise carried out at the Planning Commission at the time of launching of the Eleventh Five Year Plan covering the period from 2007 to 2012.

## 1.2.3 Macroeconomic Policy Objectives

The objectives of macroeconomic policies are two-fold: (a) sustained growth in output, and (b) stability in general price level. Sustained growth in output is achieved when the actual growth (i.e. the reported growth) each year is close, if not equal to potential growth. In India, for example, if the capacity of the economy to grow is 9% per annum, we would like to see the actual growth as close to this capacity growth as possible on a sustained basis. Stability in prices refers to a rate of increase in general price level, which is low and stable enough not to pose any uncertainty to the investor in terms of estimating costs and returns. Stability of prices is usually benchmarked against an acceptable rate of inflation. In India, as of now, an acceptable rate of inflation is considered as 5% per annum. Sustained growth and price stability are the twin objectives of the economy. Taking both together, what it means for India, for example, is that we would like to achieve a growth of 9% per annum on a sustained basis but within the constraint of 5% inflation.

[4] This can happen through technological progress (which pushes out the frontiers of an economy) and by improvements in the quality of human capital.

The actual growth of output in an economy is captured by the reported growth of Gross Domestic Product (GDP). The actual rate of growth is derived from the growth of aggregate demand for goods and services in an economy. Stability in the general price level is measured from the movements in Wholesale Price Indices (WPI) or Consumer Price Indices (CPI). In India, inflation is measured based on the changes in the WPI. If this inflation is contained at around 5% per annum, we consider prices to be stable.

Macroeconomic policy tools, which restrain demand, are: (a) fiscal policy and (b) monetary policy. Both policies aim to ensure that actual growth of GDP (AD) does not deviate too much from the potential (capacity) GDP either way so as to cause a slowdown or a higher rate of inflation. Fiscal policy formulation in India is primarily the responsibility of the Ministry of Finance. For devising the monetary policy, the primary responsibility rests with the Reserve Bank of India, the central bank of the country. The objective of fiscal policy is to achieve its target by changing government expenditure and tax rates. Monetary policy ensures that by changing money supply and thereby interest rates and credit availability, the broader objectives set forth in the economy are achieved. Thus, in order to give a boost to aggregate demand, for example, through fiscal policy, the government itself can increase its spending on goods and services or lower taxes to enable people to spend more. Monetary policy, through an increase in money supply, and thereby a decrease in interest rates, similarly can stimulate demand by inducing consumers and businesses to borrow more and spend more. The exact manner in which fiscal and monetary policy changes impact aggregate demand will be discussed in later chapters.

Macroeconomic policies not only impact aggregate demand for goods and services in an economy but, through demand, also exert an influence on the interest rates, exchange rates, tax rates, and prices. Interest rate, e.g., is the price of money. An increase in the demand for goods and services will also increase the demand for money. Other things being equal, this will put an upward pressure on interest rates. Similarly, exchange rate is the price of domestic currency vis-à-vis the foreign currency. An increase in aggregate demand, emanating from foreigners, will increase the demand for the Indian currency (the rupee). Again, other things being equal, this will push up the price of rupees vis-à-vis the foreign currency. Finally, general price level captures the price of goods and services in the economy, as a whole. As the aggregate demand for goods and services rise, with a given supply, the general price level will also rise. All these changes impact the business environment in an economy.

Figure 1.1 shows the relationship between macroeconomic policies and business environment. We will look at each relationship more closely in the subsequent chapters. To summarize, macroeconomic policies have two objectives: (a) sustained growth in GDP (aggregate demand) and (b) stability in general price level. The macroeconomic policy tools to achieve these objectives are two-fold: (a) fiscal policy and (b) monetary policy. Fiscal policy influences GDP and prices through changes in government expenditure and taxes and monetary policy impacts GDP and prices through change in money supply. How macroeconomic policies are formulated affect the growth of aggregate demand for goods and services and the interest rates, exchange rates, prices and tax rates in an economy. These in turn, affect the business environment.

## 1.3 Plan of the Book

The main focus of the book will be on short-term demand management. Not that increasing production potential in the long run is unimportant. But

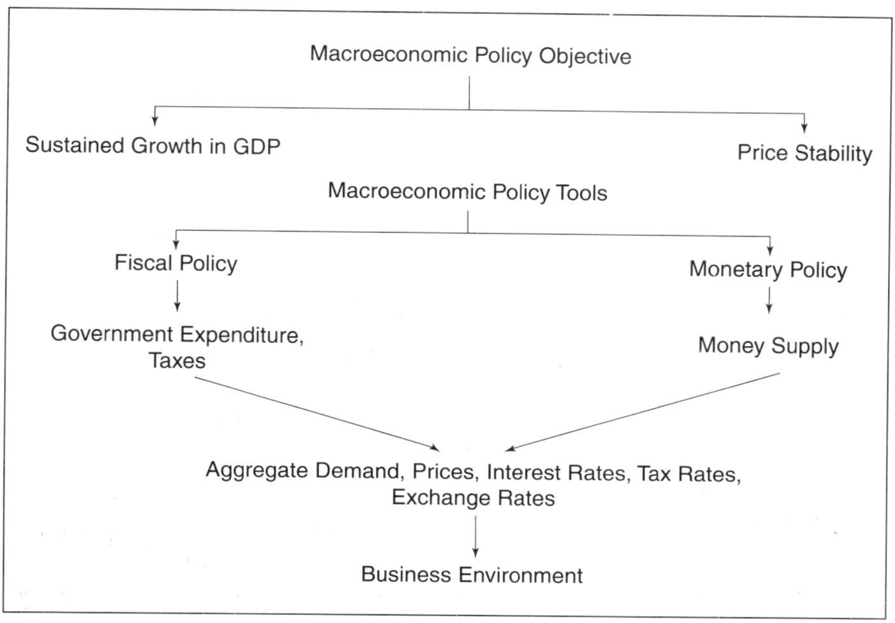


**Figure 1.1** *Understanding the Macroeconomic Policy Environment*

it is heavily contingent on creating a right type of business environment in the short run. Today, we are witnessing an economic slowdown globally. The real challenge is short-term demand management of the economy. New paradigms are emerging. The book will address all these concerns.

Chapter 2 will discuss concepts related to definition and measurement of GDP, general price level and other key macroeconomic aggregates. This chapter thus will give a conceptual understanding of the important variables that macroeconomic policies try to influence.

Chapter 3 will concentrate on aggregate demand. It will discuss the various components of demand, identify the factors that influence each component and then examine why demand behaves in the manner as it does.

Chapter 4 will be devoted to a discussion of fiscal policy. This will include discussion on the components of fiscal policy, the role and formulation of fiscal policy and the interrelationships between fiscal policy and other macroeconomic variables like demand, interest rates, exchange rates, prices and tax rates.

Chapter 5 will focus on monetary policy. This chapter will cover the monetary transmission mechanism, money supply process, the interrelationships between monetary policy and other macroeconomic variables and issues in the formulation of monetary policy.

Chapter 6 will look at the external sector and its role in stimulating demand. Some of the challenges in the formulation of macroeconomic policies in an open economy will be discussed in this chapter.

Chapter 7 will conclude and draw implications for managerial decision-making. The chapter will end by utilizing the learnings of the previous chapters in analyzing the current global economic scenario.

# REVIEW QUESTIONS

1. What are the macroeconomic policy objectives that an economy aims to achieve? Why attaining these objectives is important?
2. What is a slowdown? How does it manifest itself?
3. What is a boom? How does it manifest itself?
4. How do we arrive at capacity of an economy to grow?
5. Briefly describe how conduct of macroeconomic policies affects important revenue and cost variables facing business?
6. How can a manager benefit from learning macroeconomics?

CHAPTER

2

# GDP, General Price Level and Related Concepts

The two important objectives of macroeconomic policies, as we mentioned in the previous chapter, are: (a) sustained growth in GDP and (b) price stability. In this chapter, we will look at the definition and measurement of GDP and general price level, and certain related concepts.

## 2.1 Gross Domestic Product (GDP)

### 2.1.1 GDP Definition

GDP refers to the *market value* of *final* goods and services *produced* in an economy in a given *period of time*. There are four key words, shown in italics, in the definition of GDP.

First is *market value*. We take market value because the number of goods and services produced in an economy are both large and diverse. They cannot be reduced to a common unit of measurement. For example, an economy produces apples and also manufactures airplanes. Can we add the two? Clearly, we cannot. We, therefore, find out the total quantity of apples produced in an economy and multiply that with the price of apples to get the market value of apples. Then we take the total number of airplanes manufactured in an economy and multiply that with the price of airplanes to get the market value of airplanes. And, finally, add the two. In an economy, therefore, each good and service is valued at its market price and then aggregated to arrive at the total market value. There is no other way to arrive at the composite production.

Second is *produced*. GDP always refers to what is produced and, not necessarily, what is sold. Also, what is actually produced is equal to what is demanded. In other words, the actual production of goods and services is a mirror image of aggregate demand for goods and services in an economy. How do we conceptualize this? Let us go back to the cement industry example. We said that the cement production capacity was 100 tons per annum. Assume the production in the first year was to its full capacity, i.e., 100 tons. But the actual sale turned out to be only 80 tons. How does the production equal demand then? In this example, production equals demand because the unsold inventory of 20 tons is actually considered as bought/demanded by the cement industry. The total demand, therefore, consists of 80 tons of, what we commonly understand as market demand and, 20 tons of inventory demand, *albeit* unintended. Addition to stock of inventories from current year's production is, therefore, treated as inventory demand. But you may ask if actual production is equal to demand, where the slowdown is? It signals a slowdown, because next year, if 80 tons is projected to be the actual demand, the cement industry will cut production to 60 tons and meet the 80 tons demand from 60 tons of new production and 20 tons of unsold inventories from last year's production (a negative inventory demand this year). Actual production will be below capacity output, which is the definition of a slowdown.

The third key word is *final*. GDP considers the final value of goods and services produced in an economy in order to avoid double counting. Let us take the example of a car. There is a market value attached to the car given by the price of the car. Now, certain amount of steel, along with various other intermediate goods, has gone into the manufacturing of the car. Should we value those also? The answer is in the negative because the price of the final product, that is, the car, already includes the price of intermediate products that have gone into the making of the car. If we value them again, that will lead to double counting. Thus, all intermediate goods are excluded and only value of goods and services produced for final use, in a given period of time, enter into GDP.

The fourth and last key word is *period of time*. This is to emphasize that GDP is not a stock concept but a measure of the total flow of goods and services in an economy. And, if we are measuring the flow, it has to be over a specified time period. Normally, the time period is a year or a quarter.

## 2.1.2 Nominal vs. Real GDP

The manager's interest in monitoring the growth of GDP is to assess what is happening to the growth of demand for goods and services in an economy. Is this a growing economy? Is this a stagnant economy? Or, is it a declining economy? This information, among others, will go as an input in deciding whether to invest in an economy or not. The manager's interest, therefore, is in knowing the trends in quantities of goods and services produced/demanded in an economy. Unfortunately, as mentioned earlier, in the absence of a common unit of measurement, it is not possible to add up quantities of all goods and services produced in an economy. We, therefore, take the value of each good and service and then arrive at an aggregate measure.

What is the problem in looking at the trends in the value of goods and services produced rather than quantity? Let's go back to the definition of GDP. GDP is the value of final goods and services produced in an economy in a given period. Value is the price of the final good and service. Therefore, GDP is price times quantity of final goods and services produced. Or, GDP = $P \times Q$ aggregated over all goods and services produced in an economy. The problem begins here. If you look at the above relationship, you will see that it is quite possible for GDP to grow at an impressive pace with no change in $Q$. The entire increase can be due to $P$. Is that what the manager wants to know? No. His interest is in knowing to what extent GDP growth reflects growth in $Q$. How do we get over this problem? We can solve this problem, if we can hold $P$ constant at certain level. Because, if $P$ is held constant, any change in GDP has to be due to $Q$, which is of interest to the manager.

When $P$ is held constant at a certain level and only change in $Q$ is considered in arriving at GDP, this is called 'real GDP'. If, on the other hand, $P$ is not held constant and we multiply each year's $P$ with that year's $Q$, to arrive at the GDP, we will get 'nominal GDP'. As already mentioned, nominal GDP is of little interest to the manager.[1]

[1] In extreme situations when prices are falling absolutely (deflation), as it happened in Japan, of course, nominal GDP determines the rate of growth in profits and the ability of firms to service the debt.

Let us get a feel for how real and nominal GDPs are calculated with the help of data in Table 2.1.

*Table 2.1 Calculation of real GDP, an example*

| Good or service (Items) | Base year (P | Q) | Current year (P | Q) |
|---|---|---|---|---|
| $X_1$ | 2 | 40 | 3 | 60 |
| $X_2$ | 8 | 90 | 10 | 150 |
| $X_3$ | 80 | 100 | 90 | 110 |
| $X_4$ | 70 | 120 | 80 | 130 |

In this hypothetical economy, only four goods or services are produced. These are: $X_1$, $X_2$, $X_3$ and $X_4$. We are trying to find out the growth of GDP in this economy in the current period over the base period. The base period GDP is the sum of base year quantities and base year prices: i.e., (40 × 2) + (90 × 8) + (100 × 80) + (120 × 70) = 17,200. If we want to estimate the current year's GDP in nominal terms, then the methodology is the same. We take the current year quantities and multiply each item by its current year price and aggregate. This will give us (60 × 3) + (150 × 10) + (110 × 90) + (130 × 80) = 21,980. However, when we want to know the real GDP, we hold the prices constant at the base level. We, thus, multiply current year quantities with their base year prices and not with their current year prices. The real GDP, then, will work out to be: (60 × 2) + (150 × 8) + (110 × 80) + (130 × 70) = 19,220.

We are now ready to calculate the growth rate of GDP in the current period over the base period and interpret it. The growth in the nominal GDP is (21,980 – 17,200)/(17,200 × 100) = 27.79%, and this is partly due to increase in *Q* and partly to increase in *P*. The growth in real GDP, which is given as (19,220 – 17,200)/(17,200 × 100), is less at 11.74%. This reflects the increase in *Q* alone. By holding price constant at the base level, we have eliminated the impact of any change in price during this period in the estimation of real GDP growth. What was the increase in price during this period that we eliminated? The GDP deflator gives this and is obtained as: (Nominal GDP/Real GDP) × 100. In the case of our hypothetical economy, the GDP deflator works out to be (21,980/19,220) × 100 = 114.36. Or, we can say that the increase in prices during this period, which we eliminated in the real GDP growth calculation, was 14.36%.

By way of revision, then:

- Real GDP = Value of final goods and services in constant prices
- Nominal GDP = Value of final goods and services in current prices
- GDP deflator = (Nominal GDP/Real GDP) × 100
- A manager's interest is in real GDP growth. Real GDP values allow direct comparison of physical output from one year to the next, because a constant measuring device has been used.

A final point before we close this section. How are we going to get the real GDP measure if we have a product in the current period, say $X_5$, which did not exist in the base period, and therefore, we do not have a corresponding base year price? The answer is we cannot. We simply do not take $X_5$ into consideration in the estimation of real GDP. If the size of $X_5$ is inconsequential it probably does not matter. But if it is not, then there is a need to change the base period to adequately reflect the contribution of $X_5$ in the GDP. For a few years in the 1990s, when the base year for GDP calculation in India was still 1980/81, we were not able to adequately capture the contribution of IT sector in our GDP because there was no IT in the base period. Our base year for GDP calculation has since been changed. Hence, IT is properly represented. It is, therefore, important that the base year is a representative year.

### 2.1.3 Gross Domestic Product (GDP) vs. Gross National Product (GNP)

GDP refers to the value of final goods and services produced within the geographical area of a country, say, India. It does not matter if the producers of these goods and services are residents or non-residents. They just have to have a physical presence in the country. GNP, on the other hand, focuses on production of goods and services by the country's residents only, irrespective of the geographical area. In case of GNP, therefore, it does not matter where in the world the production is taking place; the producers of goods and services have to be Indian residents.

Let us try to establish a distinction between GDP and GNP. First, let us understand what a resident means? A resident of an economy could be an individual or an organization. Resident or non-resident status of individuals and organizations depend on the center of their economic interests. Infosys, whose center of economic interest is in India, if it invests in the United States, will be treated as an Indian resident organization and people working in this organization from Infosys India, will be treated as Indian residents. Similarly, IBM, whose center of economic interest is in the United States, when it invests in India, will be treated as a non-resident organization and the people working in this organization from IBM USA, will be treated as non-residents. Secondly, let us define a concept called factor incomes. Factor incomes are incomes accrued to various factors of production, i.e., rent for land; wages for labour; interest for capital and profit for organization. Factor incomes from abroad are incomes (profits, interest and wages that accrue to the residents, i.e., individuals and organizations through their investments in the rest of the world).

The relationship between GNP and GDP can now be seen as follows: the factor incomes earned by Infosys in the United States are a part of US GDP by virtue of the fact that production of goods and services has taken place within the geographical area of the United States, but they are not a part of U.S. GNP because the incomes do not accrue to U.S. residents but to Indian residents. Similarly, factor incomes accrued to IBM in India are a part of Indian GDP because production of goods and services have taken place within our geographical boundaries, but they are not a part of India's GNP because they have not accrued to our residents. The fundamental difference between GNP and GDP thus lies in the treatment of factor incomes from the rest of the world. Factor incomes of our residents from abroad are a part of India's GNP but not GDP; factor incomes earned by non-residents in India is a part of India's GDP but not GNP.

We now define a term called net factor income from abroad (NFIA). NFIA is defined as factor incomes earned by our residents from the rest of the world *minus* factor incomes earned by non-residents from our country. Then, you should be able to see that GNP = GDP + NFIA and GDP = GNP – NFIA. In India, GNP is slightly less than GDP, which means that NFIA in India is negative.

GDP and GNP are both measures of economic activity. GDP measures the overall level of economic activity and does not consider whether the economic activity (employment, industrial production) are enabled by non-resident or resident investments. GNP, on the other hand, focuses more on incomes of residents. More countries are moving towards GDP to fall in line with United Nation's System of National Accounts, which emphasizes GDP as a measure of economic activity. International comparisons become easier when all countries follow same standards. But the starting point of measure of a country's national income is clearly the GNP.

## 2.1.4 GDP Measurement[2]

GDP has been defined as market value of final goods and services produced in an economy, in a given period of time. There are three ways of measuring GDP: the expenditure method, the production method and, the income method. Theoretically, all should give the same results.

### *Expenditure Method*

Expenditure method measures the expenditure or total spending on domestically produced final goods and services in an economy. The idea here is that expenditure incurred on the purchase of a final good or service also captures the market value of the final good or service, which is the definition of GDP. For example, if I want to know the contribution of Tata Indica to India's GDP, I can find out what is the expenditure incurred on the purchase of the car, which is nothing but its market value.

Expenditure on final goods and services has four components:

1. Expenditure on consumption goods and services by the private sector usually referred to as 'C'. This includes consumer non-durables (food, clothing), consumer durables (air conditioners, TVs, cars) and consumption of various services (haircut, laundry and host of other services);
2. Expenditure on investment goods and services by the private sector usually referred to as 'I'. This includes addition to stock of capital (machineries, equipments), addition to structures (factories, buildings), addition to stock of inventories from current year's production and, investment in services (consultancy services, financial services);
3. Expenditure on final consumption and investment of goods and services, as defined above, by the government, usually referred to as 'G'; and,

[2] Our discussion, henceforth, will be in terms of GDP; if the interest of the reader is in GNP, all that is needed is to convert GDP into GNP by using the formula, GNP = GDP + NFIA, derived in Section 2.3. The rest of the analysis is the same in both cases.

4. Expenditure on final goods and services by the foreigners, which are our exports and usually referred to as 'X'.

There is, however, one adjustment that we need to make in the expenditure stream described above. To the extent that some of our actual purchases of goods and services may have some imported component, they are not a part of our GDP, as they are not domestically produced. We must, therefore, take out from our spending the component, which has gone towards the purchase of imported products, usually referred to as 'M'. Now we have the total picture: Expenditure method of estimating GDP is given as sum of $C + I + G + X - M$.

GDP measured through the expenditure method is reported as GDP at market prices ($GDP_{mp}$), which can be expressed in current market prices (nominal GDP) or, in constant market prices (real GDP).

## *Output Method*

Conceptually, this method adds up the value, expressed in market prices, of all goods and services produced in the economy. In reality, however, as we have mentioned earlier, adding up the value of all goods and services produced in an economy can lead to double counting. We cited an example that in the production of a car, certain quantity of steel, paint and a whole lot of other products are used, but we do not add up the value of production of all these products separately because the value of the car already reflects the value of all the products that has gone as inputs into the making of the car. If we did so, that would amount to double counting.

The output method, thus, arrives at the true value of goods and services produced in the economy not by adding up the total value of production, but the *value added* at each stage of production. How does it work? Suppose company A produces some raw materials for Rs. 1,000 and sells it to company B. Company B uses the raw material to produce a finished product and sells it to a retailer for Rs. 1,500. The retailer sells the product to the consumer at Rs. 2,000. What is the contribution to GDP? The answer, for reasons mentioned in the preceding paragraph, is that we do not add up the total value but the extra value or value added by each firm to the item under consideration. In this example, the value added by company A is Rs. 1,000; that by company B is Rs. 500 and that by company C is another Rs. 500, giving us a total value of Rs. 2,000 as the items' contribution to GDP. You will notice that this is nothing but the market value of the final good produced. Expenditure and output methods of measuring GDP, therefore, give identical results.

GDP arrived at through output or value-added method is also reported as GDP at market prices ($GDP_{mp}$), which once again can be expressed in current market prices (nominal GDP) or constant market prices (real GDP).

## *Income Method*

The idea for calculating GDP by income method is as follows: suppose the GDP of a country is Rs. 1,000. If we are estimating it through the expenditure method, this amount reflects total spending on domestically produced final goods and services. The use of the word 'final', it may be recalled, means that the value of Rs. 1,000, which is the GDP of the country in this hypothetical example, includes the value of all the intermediate products that have gone into the production of goods and services in the economy. Again, let us suppose we are estimating the GDP through the output method. In that case the GDP of Rs. 1,000 will reflect the sum of the value added at each stage of production by various goods and services in the economy. Value added, as we have seen earlier, is arrived at as total value (or, total revenue) minus the cost of intermediate products. Thus, the GDP of Rs. 1,000 in this hypothetical economy, irrespective of whether we use the expenditure or output method gives identical results and, is arrived at after allowing for the cost of all intermediate products.

In the income method we are asking the question: What happens to Rs. 1,000, which is arrived at after taking into consideration the value of all intermediate products? Who gets it? The answer is that it is paid as income to those who helped in producing the output. Those who help in the production of output are called factors of production and these, as earlier mentioned, are land, labour, capital and organization. Payment for the use of land, say for setting up a factory or a shop, is rent ($r$); payment for labour is wages ($w$); payment for capital is interest ($i$) and, finally, payment for organization is profit ($p$). The income method of estimating GDP, therefore, adds up the total income that accrues to the various factors of production. And, this is reported as GDP at factor cost ($GDP_{fc}$)[3] and can be expressed in current prices (nominal GDP) or constant prices (real GDP). Table 2.2 summarizes the relationship between expenditure, output and income methods of measuring GDP.

[3] That is, how much has each factor of production cost, which is another way of saying how much you paid to each factor of production?

In Table 2.2, we are looking at the contribution of bread in GDP. Different stages of production in bread are wheat, flour, dough and bread, which is the final product. Using the expenditure method, GDP is the value of the final product, equal to 90. This is nothing but the sum of sales.

*Table 2.2 Relationship between expenditure, output and income methods of measuring GDP*

| Stage of production (1) | Sales receipts (2) | Cost of intermediate products (3) | Value added (4) | Factor incomes (5) |
|---|---|---|---|---|
| Wheat | 24 | 0 | 24 | $r + w + i + p$ |
| Flour | 33 | 24 | 9 | $r + w + i + p$ |
| Dough | 60 | 33 | 27 | $r + w + i + p$ |
| Bread | 90 | 60 | 30 | $r + w + i + p$ |

Receipts (column 2), which is 207 minus the sum of costs of intermediate products (column 3), which are 117. Using the output method, we find out the value added at each stage of production (column 4) and add them up. This also comes to 90. Once again, this is nothing but the total revenue (value) at each stage of production (column 2) minus the cost of intermediate produce at that stage of production (column 3), aggregated over all stages. Finally, the GDP of 90 is paid out to the various factors of production (column 5) in the form of rent ($r$), wages ($w$), interest ($i$) and profit ($p$).

The relationship, thus, emerges as follows:

1. Total sales receipt = Cost of intermediate products = $r + w + i + p$
2. Total sales receipt – Cost of intermediate products = Final expenditure
3. Total revenue – Cost of intermediate products = Value added
4. Final expenditure = Value added = $r + w + i + p$
5. Expenditure method = Output method = Income method

## *From Conceptualization to Reality*

Conceptually, as we have seen above, the three measures of GDP, i.e., the expenditure method ($GDP_{mp}$), the output method (also $GDP_{mp}$) and the income method ($GDP_{fc}$) are the same. In reality, however, $GDP_{mp}$ need not be equal to $GDP_{fc}$. This is because, when we purchase a final product, the market price of that product also captures the indirect taxes (say, excise duty) on that product, which is not available for distribution to the factors of production in the form of rent ($r$), wages ($w$), interest ($i$) and profits ($p$). For example, let us say, the value of the final product, measured at its market price is Rs. 100. Also, assume that the excise duty on this product is Rs. 20. Then, what is available for distribution to the factors of production is not Rs. 100 but Rs. 100 – Rs. 20 = Rs. 80. The reverse is true in case of a subsidy (negative indirect tax), which is revenue to the firm and available for distribution to the factors of production but does not show up in the posted market price. In other words, if the price of Rs. 100 for our product has a subsidy component of Rs. 10, then for all practical purposes, the market value of the product (in the absence of the subsidy) is Rs. 110 and so the value of the subsidy has to be added as incomes to the factors of production. We can now see the relationship between GDP at market prices ($GDP_{mp}$) and GDP at factor cost ($GDP_{fc}$). $GDP_{mp}$ – (indirect taxes – subsidies) = $GDP_{fc}$. Let us define indirect taxes *minus* subsidies as net indirect taxes. Then, $GDP_{mp}$ – net indirect taxes = $GDP_{fc}$.

In Table 2.2, both indirect taxes and subsidies were assumed to be zero. Under the circumstances, understandably, all the three methods of measuring GDP turned out to be the same.

In reality, do all the three measures give identical results, even after market price and factor cost adjustments as discussed above are carried out? The answer is that these estimates are similar but not identical. The differences are due primarily to statistical discrepancies, as each method relies on an independent source of data. The Statistical Office reconciles these differences through a balancing process such that the end result is identical. Finally, which method is more appropriate as a measure of GDP? Clearly, the question of appropriateness does not arise as all the three methods give identical results. Nevertheless, output method may be used while comparing sectoral growth rates, i.e., what is the value added by manufacturing, agriculture or service sectors to India's GDP and how each is changing over time. Similarly, expenditure method is used to arrive at estimate of aggregate demand, i.e., to find out the trends in different components of demand ($C + I + G + X - M$) and how each may be affecting GDP. In subsequent chapters, our focus will primarily be in understanding the causes of fluctuations in demand; we will, therefore, use the expenditure method as the starting point. Lastly, the income method may come in handy when the objective is to find out how the income is distributed to each factor of production, i.e., what is the per centage going to labour as wages, how much is profit, what is the outgo towards payment of interest, rent, and so on. These data may form the basis for some policy announcements with regard to these factors of production. Income method is also essential in estimating national income and per-capita income.

### *Summary*

The main points from this section can now be summarized as follows:

- GDP can be measured using three different methods: expenditure, output and income methods. The first two are expressed as GDP at market prices and the last one as GDP at factor cost. Conceptually, all three methods are same.
- In reality, however, GDP at factor cost is different from GDP at market prices by the amount of net indirect taxes (indirect taxes – subsidies).
- Also, in reality, because of different data sources and estimation errors involved, the GDP arrived at through the three different methods give similar but not identical results. Some adjustments usually are carried out to arrive at a common measure.
- Though the end result of all the three methods is a common measure of GDP for the economy, each method has a specific use depending on the purpose of analysis of GDP data.

## 2.1.5 Gross Domestic Product (GDP) vs. Net Domestic Product (NDP)

We have said earlier that the actual growth of GDP, in real terms, is a mirror image of actual growth of demand for goods and services in the economy. When the aggregate demand increases, this induces more production of goods and services and the GDP grows, assuming production potential exists. We have also discussed the source of this sustained growth of GDP.[4] We have said that the source is two-fold: new investments and the rate at which the new investment translates into increased production.

[4] Here, we are talking about sustained growth. For a short period of time it is possible for GDP to grow impressively without additional investment, if there is excess existing capacity in the economy.

The former depends on availability of savings and the latter on incremental capital–output ratio. The important point to note here is that investment is a necessary prerequisite for growth and improved efficiency in production, which results in a reduction in incremental capital– output ratio and contributes to getting more out of a given investment.

The relevance of GDP vs. NDP discussion can now be appreciated. The investment figure that we consider in the estimation of GDP refers to gross investment. Gross investment only considers the amount of capital added each year; it does not consider the fact that each year some capital also gets used up or depreciated. Suppose Rs. 100 crores worth of investment goods (say, machines and tools) are added in the current year, but Rs. 25 crores of investment goods have been used up or have depreciated in the production of current year's output. What is the net addition to investment goods this year? It is not Rs. 100 crores but Rs. 75 crores, the difference being depreciation. The difference between GDP and NDP is the difference between gross investment and net investment, which is depreciation. In other words, GDP – Depreciation = NDP.

Why do we look at NDP? Since the difference between GDP and NDP is depreciation, and is arrived at by calculating the difference between gross and net investment, the size of depreciation also determines the size of net investment in the economy. If depreciation is greater than gross investment, net investment is negative; if depreciation is equal to gross investment, net investment is zero and, if depreciation is less than gross investment, net investment is positive. And, for sustained growth of an economy, what matters is net and not gross investment. In other words, an economy where net investment is negative is a declining economy; an economy where net investment is zero is a stagnant economy and an economy where net investment is positive is a growing economy.

Macroeconomics is concerned with the overall level of economic activity and uses 'gross' concepts. We, therefore, do not see frequent reference to NDP. Another reason why we do not see frequent reference to NDP is because depreciation figures are difficult to estimate or may not be available on time. But NDP, indeed, is a more accurate measure of level of economic activity in an economy. Of course, if NDP, over a period of time, turns out to be a fixed proportion of GDP, implying thereby that depreciation rate is stable, GDP growth can be used as a reliable proxy for NDP growth also.

## 2.1.6 National Income (NI) and Per-Capita Income (PCI)

National income is defined as factor incomes accrued to the residents of a country. How do we arrive at that? Let us go step by step.

From our discussion of GDP vs. GNP in Section 2.1.3, it should be clear that if we are talking about the incomes accruing to our residents, the starting point is GNP and not GDP. In Step 1, therefore, we convert GDP into GNP, i.e., GNP = GDP + NFIA.

In Step 2, we ask: should we take GNP at market prices ($GNP_{mp}$) or GNP at factor costs ($GNP_{fc}$)? Again, in Section 2.1.4, we saw that $GNP_{mp}$ would include net indirect taxes that do not accrue to the factors of production; hence, a correct point to measure of what accrues to the factors of production would be $GNP_{fc}$.

In the final step, we ask: does $GNP_{fc}$ accurately reflect what accrues to the factors of production? Or, is some more adjustment called for? We refer to Section 2.1.5 and note $GNP_{fc}$ would include depreciation, which is not a factor payment. If we take out depreciation from $GNP_{fc}$, we end up with $NNP_{fc}$. $NNP_{fc}$, indeed, accurately reflects what is paid out as factor incomes to our residents. $NNP_{fc}$, thus, is what is defined as national income (NI).

In other words, national income equals $GNP_{mp}$ *minus* net indirect taxes (which gives us $GNP_{fc}$) *minus* depreciation (which gives us $NNP_{fc}$). Let us now summarize all the steps:

1. Convert $GDP_{mp}$ to $GNP_{mp} \Rightarrow GNP_{mp} = GDP_{mp}$ + NFIA
2. Convert $GNP_{mp}$ to $GNP_{fc} \Rightarrow GNP_{fc} = GNP_{mp}$ – Net Indirect Taxes
3. Convert $GNP_{fc}$ to $NNP_{fc} \Rightarrow NNP_{fc} = GNP_{fc}$ – Depreciation
4. NI = $NNP_{fc}$

Once the concept of national income is clear, per-capita income (PCI) is straightforward. Just divide national income ($NNP_{fc}$) each year by each year's population and we have the per capita income figure for that year. Per-capita income signifies the average standard of living of the people.

## 2.1.7 Personal Income (PI) and Disposable Income (DI)

National income, of course, is all earned. This income is earned by the resident factors of production for their contribution to current year's output. However, all earned income is not received by the factors of production in the same year. For example, profits earned may not be fully received by the owners in the form of dividends because part of it may go out in the form of corporate income taxes; another part may be retained in the form of undistributed profits. Similarly, wages received may vary from wages earned by the amount of deductions towards pension. While this is true, it is also true that factors of production receive incomes that are not earned. What could these be? For example, these could be gifts, welfare payments and pensions. These are called transfer payments and are payments that are not in lieu of any current factor services performed. These are, therefore, income received but not earned. Now, we have the definition of personal income (PI):

Personal Income = National income – Income earned but not received + Income received but not earned.

The concept of PI, by itself, may not assume much significance to the manager but it is an important interim step to arrive at disposable income (DI), to which we turn now.

Disposable income (DI) is defined as Personal income (PI) – Personal taxes.

This is the income that goes either towards consumption (*C*) or saving (*S*). Consumption is a measure of current consumption while saving indicates future consumption. The amount that is consumed adds directly to increased current sales and revenue; the amount that is saved provides funds for investment, which is necessary for future production, income and consumption. Thus, if *C* is disproportionately high, future consumption growth may be assumed to be moderate and, if it is the other way round, one can assume a higher consumption at a future date. Disposable income is a key indicator of economic activity to the manager.

## 2.1.8 Putting the Whole Thing Together

In this section, we will bring together the important relationships developed so far in this chapter. You should be able to see through the relationships clearly. Else, read the previous sections again.

1. GDP/GNP measures are expressed in real terms
2. GDP/GNP can be measured using three different methods
3. GDP + NFIA = GNP

4. $GDP/GNP_{mp}$ – Net indirect taxes = $GDP/GNP_{fc}$
5. $GDP/GNP_{fc}$ – Depreciation = $NDP/NNP_{fc}$
6. $NNP_{fc}$ = NI
7. NI ÷ Population = Per-capita income
8. NI – Income earned but not received + Income received but not earned = PI
9. PI – Personal taxes = DI
10. DI = $C + S$

## 2.1.9 GDP, Omissions

Omissions in measurement of GDP are of three types. First, sets of activities which, by definition, are not a part of GDP should be excluded. Second are those which, perhaps, should be included in GDP but get left out because of measurement problems. Third are sets of considerations related to the welfare of the people, which are not captured by the manner in which GDP is calculated. These omissions need to be highlighted in order to get a perspective on what GDP is and what it is not.

Let us begin with the first sets of activities, which do not form a part of GDP and are, therefore, deliberate omissions. The simple rule of thumb to get a hold on these activities, which need to be deliberately left out of GDP, is to understand that GDP refers to payments received in lieu of goods and services produced in the current period. Clearly, therefore, the following activities are not a part of GDP. For example, transfer payments such as pension and other social security payments are not a part of GDP because these payments are received not in lieu of current production of goods and services. For the same reason, gifts received from various sources are not a part of GDP. Again, second hand transactions are not a part of GDP because such goods and services are not produced in the current period. As an example, if I bought a new house last year and sold it this year, it is not a part of this year's GDP. But, if I hired the services of a broker to sell the house, the payment made to the broker is a part of this year's GDP because this payment is in lieu of service performed in the current period. Finally, an increase in the price of a company's share does not represent any current production of goods and services and, thus, is not a part of GDP.

The second set of omissions, as we mentioned, is not deliberate. Ideally, they should have been a part of GDP, but because of measurement and other problems, they are not. For example, all non-market transactions are not a part of GDP, though a sizeable amount of economic activity takes place outside the market. If I teach my students, it is a part of GDP because I get paid in the market place for the services performed, the salary being the market value of the service rendered. But if I teach my children, it is not a part of GDP, as it is a non-market transaction. All the work that spouses do in their homes is not a part of GDP, but if they do the same work for a wage, it becomes a part of GDP.

Again, consider another area. A large part of economic activity in India takes place in the unorganized sector. These are small firms or petty shopkeepers from whom the income data is difficult to obtain. The statistical office conducts periodical surveys and extrapolates the results to arrive at the incomes generated through the unorganized sector. But, given the characteristics of the sector, surveys may not be very accurate. In fact, a much of the economic activity in the unorganized sector gets left out of GDP calculation. The problem is more severe in India, but exists in other countries as well.

Another major omission in this category is failure to account for certain types of investments that contribute to growth. The definition of investment in the GDP identity is restricted to creation of durable assets, which add to further production of goods and services. But what about investment in R&D or investment in training and education (investment in human capital)? Do not these activities also augment GDP growth? Unfortunately, these expenditures currently are treated as part of consumption expenditure. Under these circumstances, therefore, the prevailing growth of the economy, as reflected in investment spending, could be understating the strength of the economy.

Finally, in all countries, a large amount of economic transaction takes place through illegal means. Here, the problem is a deliberate attempt to conceal income through generation of what is known as black money. The size of black money is believed to be high in countries where taxes are high and bureaucracy is smothering. In India, black money is estimated to be quite high.

The net result of all the above exclusions is that the reported GDP data is an underestimate. Unofficially, it is stated that Indian GDP data is underestimated to the extent of 33% or more. Therefore, the final question is: if GDP data is unreliable why worry about GDP? The answer is that if we give too much of importance to absolute numbers that may not, indeed, throw up much. But assuming that error has crept into each year's data and is a stable function of time, the year-to-year changes, or growth rates, in GDP will still be a good indicator of what is happening to production of goods and services over time. No wonder we all the time talk about GDP growth rather than the absolute value.

A third aspect of GDP relates to its impact on welfare. GDP, being a pure measure of economic activity in a country, does not consider certain factors that affect the welfare of the people. For example, GDP growth does not assume anything about the distribution of income. An impressive growth in output or income is perfectly compatible with a situation where a large segment of the population remains poor. Again, with enhanced economic activity, industrialization, urbanization and so on, also comes traffic congestion, pollution, which adversely affect the quality of life. GDP will look only at the market value of goods and services produced and will pay no heed to the adverse lifestyles, which result from the increased economic activity. Also, in the process of production, certain key resources of a country may face depletion. GDP will not assign any cost to such irreplaceable resources. Similarly, if a pay commission recommends in favour of a salary rise for the government servants, the service of the government staff will be valued in the GDP according to the expenditure incurred on salaries, however inefficient the staff may be. GDP, thus, does not account for inefficiency. Lastly, just as GDP does not account for inefficiency, it also fails to account for qualitative improvements. A personal computer today may be technologically far superior to the one you owned five years back, but GDP will treat the better computer as just another computer.

The broader question that arises is that if GDP does not recognize the finer aspects of life like the value of leisure, enjoyment from listening to music, satisfaction from reciting poetry; if GDP is indifferent to health and resource implications of increased economic activity; if GDP is unable to either reprimand inefficiency or reward technological change; if GDP does not assume participation of all sections of population in the growth process, what is GDP good for? The immediate answer is that GDP serves a different purpose. It focuses exclusively on the production of goods and services in an economy (i.e., what is the level of economic activity?), which has its own uses. Questions raised above do not directly fall within the definition of GDP. It is also true that countries that have achieved a high level of economic activity through sustained growth in GDP are also the ones that have been able to attend to the welfare related concerns of its population better. What this means is that higher level of GDP is perhaps necessary to enable a higher quality of life, though it may not be sufficient.

## 2.1.10 Getting a Feel for the Data

We now look at the actual data on GDP and related aggregates for India. These are shown in Table 2.3. You should be able to figure out the following from the data:

1. Column 2 refers to nominal GDP
2. Column 3 refers to real GDP where prices are held constant at 1999/00 levels.
3. GDP deflator = Column 2 ÷ Column 3 × 100
4. Column 4 = Column 3 + NFIA
5. Column 5 = Column 4 – Net indirect taxes
6. Column 6 = Column 5 – Depreciation, which is = NI and,
7. Column 7 = Column 6 ÷ Population

What can we do with this data? We can do the following:

1. Calculate the GDP deflator for each year and then see the annual rate of inflation, as captured by the GDP deflator.
2. Find out the annual increase in real GDP, which mirrors the annual increase in demand for goods and services in the economy. We can look at the trend growth.
3. Notice that the difference between GNP and GDP, or NFIA, in India, is small. Hence, growth in GNP can be used as a proxy for growth in GDP.
4. Also, notice that $NNP_{fc}$ is almost a fixed proportion of $GNP_{fc}$. Alternatively, the difference between gross investment and net investment is stable.
5. We can also estimate the trends in national income and,
6. We can see how per-capita income is growing over time and get a first approximation of what is happening to living standards in the country vis-à-vis other countries.

Of course, we also need to have a closer look at sectoral growth rates. From the output method of measuring GDP, we can find out how each sector is doing and how balanced the overall growth has been. Similarly, we can also analyze the trends in total spending using the expenditure method of measuring GDP to find out how each component of demand is changing from year to year. We will do that as we move along.

*Table 2.3 India, GDP statistics: 1999/00 to 2008/09*
*(Rupees in crores)*

| Year (1) | $GDP_{mp}$ (current prices) (2) | $GDP_{mp}$ (1999/00 prices)[a] (3) | $GNP_{mp}$ (1999/00 prices) (4) | $GNP_{fc}$ (1999/00 prices) (5) | $NNP_{fc}$ (1999/00 prices) (6) | Per-capita income[b] (1999/00 prices) (7) |
|---|---|---|---|---|---|---|
| 1999/00 | 19,52,035 | 19,52,035 | 19,36,604 | 17,71,094 | 15,89,672 | 15,881 |
| 2000/01 | 21,02,314 | 20,30,710 | 20,08,165 | 18,41,755 | 16,47,903 | 16,172 |
| 2001/02 | 22,78,952 | 21,36,651 | 21,15,980 | 19,51,935 | 17,43,466 | 16,764 |
| 2002/03 | 24,54,561 | 22,17,134 | 21,98,329 | 20,29,482 | 18,05,830 | 17,101 |
| 2003/04 | 27,54,621 | 24,02,727 | 23,84,883 | 22,04,913 | 19,63,544 | 18,317 |
| 2004/05 | 31,49,412 | 26,01,630 | 25,80,132 | 23,66,886 | 21,04,520 | 19,325 |
| 2005/06 | 35,80,344 | 28,41,967 | 28,22,280 | 25,93,160 | 23,06,894 | 20,858 |
| 2006/07 | 41,29,173 | 31,20,031 | 30,98,767 | 28,49,838 | 25,33,432 | 22,580 |
| 2007/08 | 47,23,400 | 34,02,716 | 33,87,863 | 31,14,864 | 27,64,795 | 24,295 |
| 2008/09 | 53,21,753 | 36,09,425 | N.A | 33,23,648 | 29,41,971 | 25,494 |

[a] The Indian GDP base period has been changed to 2004–05 = 100. GDP at constant 2004–05 prices are available for the period starting with the first quarter of 2007–08.

[b] In rupees.

*Source*: Reserve Bank of India, *Handbook of Statistics on Indian Economy*, http://www.rbi.org.in

## 2.1.11 International Comparisons of GDP

International comparisons of GDP are made to get a sense of how standard of living of the people varies across countries. Table 2.4 clearly brings out India's status in this regard. India's poor standing in the world is not because of overall GDP. India ranks 12th and 4th in the world in respect of overall GDP (columns 3 and 4) depending on whether comparisons are on the basis of nominal GDP or GDP adjusted for purchasing power parity (see below for definitions). However, India is relegated to the background when we compare per-capita GDP across countries.

Various methods have evolved to capture this difference. One way to compare, across countries, is to take the average per-capita GDP (or GNP) in each country in nominal terms, convert that into a common currency, say, U.S. dollars, at the going exchange rate and, then, see the relative position. There are two problems with this methodology. First, exchange rates are scarcely stable. Depending on the variation in the exchange rate, the per-capita GDP of a country will, therefore, vary though nothing may have changed in the level of economic activity in that country. The comparison, thus, can be misleading. The World Bank has attempted to mitigate the problem by using averaging devices, such as the Atlas method employed by the Bank,[5] but that does not eliminate the problem particularly if exchange rates change frequently. A second problem, and, perhaps, a more serious one, with this methodology is that it fails to capture the differences in prices for the same goods and services across countries. A haircut in India, for example, may cost 60 cents, but the same service in the U.S. may cost 20 dollars. Under the circumstances, are comparisons of average per-capita GDP across countries, as a measure of standard of living, meaningful? They are not. What is, therefore, needed is a measure, which takes into consideration price differences across countries, such that in the reported per-capita GDP figures one dollar has the same purchasing power in the domestic economy of a country as one dollar has in the U.S. economy.

A second method of comparing standard of living across countries, called the purchasing power parity (PPP) method, addresses the above concern. The PPP method adjusts for the different relative prices among countries before making comparisons in a common currency. PPPs between currencies are calculated using the prices collected in the different countries for a basket of comparable and representative goods and services. The prices, thus collected, are used to derive price ratios for individual goods and services. The price ratios are then aggregated and averaged to obtain PPPs for various levels of aggregation up to the level of GDP.

The PPP method changes both the levels of per-capita GDP across countries and their rankings. Thus, according to the World Bank data for 2007 (Table 2.4), per-capita GDP for India, calculated by the average GDP per-capita method, was 1042 dollars and India's ranking was 122 among 170 odd countries considered. When the average GNP per-capita was adjusted for differences in the price levels and PPP method was adopted, India's per capita GNP improved to 2753 dollars and ranking to 115. What this means is that the average purchasing power of a dollar in India is 2.7 times more than the purchasing power of the same dollar in the United States. In other words, the standard of living of an average Indian is better than what simple per-capita GNP comparisons will show.

---

[5] For details see under "data and statistics" in http://www.worldbank.org/

While PPP method of comparing GDP per-capita across countries is an improvement over the unadjusted simple per-capita GDP comparisons, GDP figures do not say how the income is distributed or and how the income is spent. The income could be cornered by only a small section of the population leaving a large section poor. The income could also be spent on military rather than education or health for the masses. In other words, as we mentioned earlier, GDP measure does not capture the welfare of the

***Table 2.4 Development indicators, 2007 (Select countries)***

| Country (1) | Nominal GDP (US trillion $) (2) | GDP adjusted for PPP (US trillion $) (3) | Per-capita nominal GDP (US$) (4) | Per-capita GDP (US$) adjusted for PPP (5) | Human development index rank (2006) (6) |
|---|---|---|---|---|---|
| United States | 13.81 (1) | 13.81 (1) | 45,790 (10) | 45,790 (4) | 15 |
| China | 3.28 (4) | 7.05 (2) | 2,485 (99) | 5,345 (90) | 94 |
| Japan | 4.37 (2) | 4.28 (3) | 34,254 (20) | 33,525 (17) | 8 |
| Germany | 3.29 (3) | 2.72 (5) | 40,079 (16) | 33,154 (19) | 23 |
| India | 1.17 (12) | 3.09 (4) | 1,042 (122) | 2,753 (115) | 132 |
| UK | 2.72 (5) | 2.04 (8) | 44,693 (12) | 33,535 (16) | 21 |
| France | 2.56 (6) | 2.06 (7) | 41,523 (14) | 33,414 (18) | 11 |
| Russia | 1.29 (11) | 2.08 (6) | 9,115 (44) | 14,743 (42) | 73 |
| Italy | 2.10 (7) | 1.77 (10) | 35,494 (18) | 29,934 (23) | 19 |
| Brazil | 1.31 (10) | 1.84 (9) | 6,859 (53) | 9,570 (66) | 70 |

*Note*: Figures in parenthesis are ranks.

*Source*: Columns 2–5 World Bank; Column 6 UNDP. All data downloaded from Wikipedia, the free Encyclopedia.

people. In international comparisons, it is perhaps useful to focus, in addition to average standard of living, on the level of human development as well. United Nations Development Program (UNDP), therefore, prepares a set of Indices for each country, which takes into consideration not only GDP per-capita through PPP method, but also life expectancy and education. The combined effect is the human development index (HDI). A quick look at the HDI for various countries (Table 2.4, column 6) put up by UNDP supports what we said earlier that countries with higher per-capita GDP are also the ones with a high HDI, the relationship is not one to one.

## 2.1.12 Saving, Investment and National Accounts

Saving is what is set aside from income for future consumption and investment is what is produced for future consumption. The national accounts concepts developed in this chapter can be used to derive important relationships between saving and investment in an economy and how the economy is being managed. To the extent proper management of the economy is important for a sustained growth of output, the manager must also look at these relationships to arrive at a judgment on the health of the economy.

We begin with some simplifying assumptions to make our point. Note that dropping any of these assumptions will not invalidate our conclusions. Only it will make the presentation somewhat more cumbersome. We will assume that GDP = GNP = NI. In other words, we are disregarding NFIA, depreciation and net indirect taxes and using GDP, GNP and NI interchangeably. Then we can define NI – Taxes = Disposable Income. We are now ready to derive the relationship between saving and investment from the national income accounts. We denote NI (also = GNP = GDP) as $Y$.

Then we have:

$Y = C + I + G + X - M$ ........................(1)

$Y - C = I + G + X - M$ ........................(2)

$S + T = I + G + X - M$ ........................(3)

$S + (T - G) + (M - X) = I$ ..................(4)

Therefore

$I = S_p + S_g + S_{row}$ ................................(5)

In this, equation (1) is an estimate of national income through the expenditure method. Equation (2) shows what is left out of income after consumption. Equation (3) brings out the income = expenditure identity. Thus, on the income side (the left hand side), it tells us that what is left of income after consumption goes towards savings ($S$) and taxes ($T$) and, on the expenditure side (the right hand side), it tells us that the sum of savings plus taxes is used to meet the expenditure on domestic investment ($I$), government spending ($G$) and net investment abroad ($X - M$). $X - M$ is called net investment abroad because the country is selling more to foreigners than it is buying from foreigners. In other words, it is investing the excess value of net exports abroad. The country can use the foreign exchange, thus earned, to buy stocks or bonds of foreign companies or governments, businesses or, simply leave them in the bank for future use. Equation (4) is another identity and just rearranges equation (3) to express domestic investment ($I$) as being dependent on private savings ($S$), government savings ($T - G$), i.e., excess of tax revenue over government expenditure and foreign savings ($M - X$). The latter can be understood as follows: when a country imports, it is an outgo of foreign exchange and is, therefore, a debit item in the external balance. Similarly, when a country exports, it is an inflow of foreign exchange and this is a credit item in the external balance. When $M$ is greater than $X$, a country is a net debtor. It shows that the country is drawing on the resources of other countries to meet the requirements of current consumption and investment. How does the country finance this excess of investment in goods and services? Foreign savings flowing into the country is financing the gap. Just as $X - M$, we said, is our net investment abroad, foreign savings into the country to finance $M - X$ is also net foreign investment into the country. Equation (5) summarizes the main relationships, i.e., investment in a country is a sum of private savings ($S_p$), government savings ($S_g$) and savings from the rest of the world ($S_{row}$).

## *Twin Deficit*

We are ready to do some analysis. But before that, let us introduce some terminologies. ($T - G$) is called the fiscal balance and ($M - X$) is called the current account balance.[6] If ($T - G$) is positive, there is a fiscal surplus and if ($T - G$) is negative, there is a fiscal deficit. Also note that when ($M - X$) is

[6] We will discuss both fiscal balance and current account balance in greater detail in later chapters. For the time being the current terminologies will suffice.

positive, we have a current account deficit and when $(M - X)$ is negative, we have a current account surplus. What equation (5) says, is that, if there is a fiscal deficit, i.e., government expenditure ($G$) is greater than the tax revenue ($T$) and the government is dis-saving, then one of the following must happen: (a) $S_p$ has to go up, which means people must reduce their consumption, (b) $S_{row}$ has to go up which means current account deficit $(M - X)$, must widen or (c) $I$ must come down. If we assume $I$ and $S_p$ to be constant, then we have a relationship between fiscal deficit and current account deficit. Higher the fiscal deficit, more it will spill over to the current account deficit. This is the famous "twin deficit" that economists talk about. In simple language, what it means is that, holding $S_p$ and $I$ constant, if the government dis-saves, then foreign savings must go up.

What is the problem with "twin deficit"? How does the presence of twin deficit reflect a management problem? If the economy utilizes the foreign savings productively, current account deficit need not be a problem. With a rise in productivity, exports may rise and pay for the deficit. But if foreign savings are not utilized properly, it may be difficult to service the foreign liability. A country may have to draw from foreign exchange reserves to finance the deficit; as a result, currency may become unstable[7] and a host of economic problems may crop up. The actual fear is that when the current account deficit is propelled by a fiscal deficit, given the way governments spend the money, the economy may not be able to utilize the savings productively and economic crisis may ensue. A manager, thus, has to closely monitor such developments. Particularly, with industrial revival well in place in India, as private sector investment demand picks up, a continued high fiscal deficit, holding private savings constant means that either current account deficit has to rise or, private sector investment plans have to slow down.

In fact, the Indian economic crisis in 1991, which forced us to liberalize, was to a great extent, due to a large fiscal deficit, which spilled over to the current account deficit. Hence, the size of the current account deficit became unsustainable.

## *Global Economic Imbalances*

The concept of current account deficit introduced above can also be used to develop an understanding of the phenomenon of global economic imbalances, frequently referred to in current economic debates. Global

[7] We will develop this relationship in later chapters.

economic imbalances arise when an economy exhibits persistently large current account deficit or surplus, or large domestic saving-investment gaps (equation (5)). This becomes a matter of concern if large deficits and surpluses prevail, on a sustained basis, in large economies. Thus the reference to global imbalances in today's context is to large and increasing current account deficits (CAD) of the United States and correspondingly large surpluses in other regions, particularly in Asia.

Table 2.5 provides the data on saving–investment gaps across a select group of countries in the world. What the data shows is that United States, the largest economy in the world has a very large current account deficit (excess of investment over saving), which is being financed largely by current account surplus in the Asian economies (excess of saving over investment).

***Table 2.5 Saving–investment gap: global imbalances, 2007***

| Country | X – M (US million $) |
|---|---|
| United States | –7,31,200 |
| China | 3,71,800 |
| Hong Kong | 19,870 |
| India | –18,530 |
| Indonesia | 10,210 |
| Korea | 3,700 |
| Malaysia | 25,930 |
| Singapore | 41,390 |
| Thailand | 8,619 |

*Source*: http://en.wikipedia.org/wiki/List_of_countries_by_current_account_balance

There is nothing wrong, per se, with this as long as foreigners are willing to invest in the United States. In fact, United States has put up with large current account deficits for many years. However, the fear is that, in view of the U.S. economic meltdown,[8] or even otherwise, if foreign investors lose confidence in the U.S. economy and pull out abruptly, then the U.S. economy may get into deeper slowdown, taking many other countries along with it. Alternately, if United States wants to correct this imbalance, in its own

[8] Some ascribe US meltdown to this culture of heavy indebtedness of the US, which resulted in a housing bubble and its eventual crash.

strategic interest, by increasing domestic savings and reducing dependence on foreign savings, it may seriously impact the growth of countries that invest abroad. The current debate, thus, revolves around how to correct the global imbalances in an orderly manner without causing disruption to the affected economies.

## 2.2 Money: The Basics

In this section we will provide a basic understanding of money and its role in an economy. This basic understanding will prepare the reader for a more rigorous analysis that will follow in the later chapters.

The first question we ask is: What is money? Money is primarily[9] a medium of exchange. It is what we use to make payments. We use money to pay for various goods and services that we buy. There is a distinction between money and income. What we earn is income. What we earn is not money. Money is used only to pay the income. We need money because it serves as a common item in which the prices of all goods and services can be set. Exchange then becomes easier.

Next question is: If money is what we use to make payments, what is money supply? Ask yourself what is it that we use to make payments? The answer is that we use currency and we use cheques to make payments. We also use credit cards to make payments but those are just deferred cheque payments. Now we have the definition of money supply. It consists of currency and cheque deposits with the banks. This is the narrow definition of money and denoted by M1 in our monetary statistics. There is also a broad definition of money. Broad money includes, in addition to M1, fixed or time deposits with banks, which are not usually available for spending until the end of the term, but, nevertheless, can be converted into saving or cheque deposits in no time, with some loss of interest. Broad money, therefore, is defined as currency + *all* bank deposits and is denoted by M3 in our monetary statistics. When we talk of money supply, we usually refer to M3.

Next question is: Why do we demand money? Before we answer this question, let us get two points clarified. First, what do we mean by demand for money? An individual's wealth can be held, broadly, in two forms: (a) interest bearing assets and (b) non-interest-bearing assets or, money. For

[9] It should also be acceptable, must also be a store of value, and should also serve as a unit of measurement.

analytical convenience, let us say that all interest bearing assets are bonds. So, when we are asking why do we demand money, we are essentially asking why anyone would like to keep his or her wealth in the form of money, which either yielded no interest (currency) or which yielded very low interest (cheque deposits)? Secondly, when we are talking about demand for money we are referring to real money demand. For example, if the price level doubled overnight, then the amount of money people would want to hold would also double. In this case, however, there is no increase in real demand for money because the increase in demand for money is proportional to the level of prices. In other words, if we define real money demand, as quantity of money demanded ($M^d$) divided by the price level ($P$), i.e., $M^d/P$, then for the money demand to increase $M^d/P$ must increase.

Let us now answer the question we posed in the beginning. We demand money for three reasons. First, we demand money to buy goods and services. This is called the transaction demand for money. This is the primary motive. The demand for money to transact in goods and services is a positive function of income (GDP). Higher the income greater will be the need to buy goods and services and higher will be the transaction demand for money. But it is also a negative function of interest rates. If interest rate rises, we are foregoing a higher return by holding money. So the temptation may be to hold less money at any point of time. For example, instead of drawing money for the whole month, I may draw money fortnightly and let the balance money earn interest in the mean time. A second reason for holding money is precautionary. Individuals and firms hold money with a precautionary motive for unforeseen contingencies. Of course, how much money we can set aside for precautionary purposes will depend on our income. It will also depend on how much interest we are foregoing on this money held. Thus, precautionary demand for money is also a positive function of income and a negative function of interest rates. And finally, we demand money for speculation. The argument goes as follows: Let us say, an individual holding bond thinks that the present price of bonds is ruling low and expects the price to rise. What will he do? Will he hold money or bonds? Clearly, he will hold less money and buy more bonds with the intention of making a capital gain. Alternatively, if the individual feels that the ruling price of bonds is high and, therefore, expects the price to fall, he will increase his holding of money to avoid a capital loss. The speculative demand for money, thus, arises because people think that by holding a certain stock of money, they can make capital gains or avoid capital losses.

You will also notice that there is an inverse relationship between bond prices and interest rates. Let us say that at some point in the past, an individual had bought a perpetual bond at a price of Rs. 100 with a fixed coupon rate (interest payment) of Rs. 10 every year. Now, suppose this bond is trading at Rs. 105. Obviously, the yield from the bond is no longer 10%, the coupon rate. Instead it is 9.52%, because now he is getting Rs. 10 on Rs. 105 and not on Rs. 100. Similarly, if this bond is trading at Rs. 95, the yield from the bond is now 10.52% and not the coupon rate of 10%. Since the rate of interest (yield) varies inversely with the bond price,[10] the speculative demand for money varies inversely with the interest rate. When the prevailing bond prices are low (interest rates are high), and people expect bond prices to go up (interest rates to come down), speculative demand for money is low. When the prevailing bond prices are high (interest rates are low), and people expect bond prices to fall (interest rates to go up), speculative demand for money is high. Of course, speculative demand for money is also a positive function of income to the extent the more income you have the more you can afford to speculate. We can conclude, then, that demand for money is an increasing function of income and a decreasing function of interest rate.

A final question we ask is: How does money supply affect GDP? This is a much more involved question. The exact transmission mechanism between money supply and GDP will be discussed later but the basic relationship can be explained as follows: GDP is the total production of goods and services in the economy and money refers to a stock of liquid assets, which can be exchanged for goods and services. A given stock of money flows through the economy a number of times (called, the velocity of circulation), each time resulting in a new transaction, and the value of the GDP is nothing but the sum total of all these transactions over a period of time. GDP, therefore, depends on the stock of money multiplied by the speed with which the money changes hands. If the number of times money changes hands, or the velocity of circulation, is assumed to be stable, then there is a close relationship between the stock of money and GDP. As the stock of money increases, more goods and services will be exchanged and the GDP will rise. However, there is a catch. If the economy is already operating at close

---

[10] The inverse relationship between bond prices and interest rates can also be seen as follows: Suppose the par value of bond is Rs. 100 and it carries a coupon rate of 10%. Interest rate in the economy goes up to 11%. No one will buy this bond for Rs. 100 and get Rs. 10 as interest. The price of the bond must fall to Rs. 99.1. Similarly, if the interest rate in the economy falls to 9%, bond price must increase to Rs. 101 to reflect that return.

to full capacity, and the money supply continues to grow, we have a situation where the money supply is rising but the supply of goods and services, which can be exchanged for this money, is not rising correspondingly. There is more money chasing few goods and services. As a result, prices will increase more than the increase in output and the policy maker may have to carefully weigh the trade offs, considering the fact that price stability is one of the paramount objectives of macroeconomic policies. On the other hand, if the actual GDP is below the capacity of the economy to produce, an increase in the money stock can play a stimulating role in the economy by increasing output with little rise in prices. Therefore, while money at all times provides the necessary lubricant to keep the wheels of the economy running, a change in money supply has to be assessed in terms of its impact on prices vs. output.

This much of exposure to money will suffice for a basic understanding at this stage. Clearly, the relationships are not cut and dry. We will deal with the complications in actual policy making and their implications for business, when we come to Chapter 5 on Monetary Policy. We will also introduce some more rigour into some of the concepts developed above, in addition to developing in detail the money supply process and the issues related to central bank's control over monetary policy.

## 2.3 Interest Rates: The Basics

Interest rate is the price money. It depends on the supply of money and demand for money. If the money available in the economy is greater than what individuals and businesses need on account of the three motives for holding money discussed above, the interest rate falls and if the demand for money of individuals and businesses is greater than the money available in the economy, the interest rate rises. While demand for money comes from individuals and businesses wanting to borrow and spend, the supply of money depends on the monetary authorities. As in the other markets, the price of money (interest rate) is set by the interaction of demand for and supply of money.

Interest rate is a very powerful tool of demand management. Since both consumers and investors rely on money for the purchase of goods and services, the monetary authorities can augment aggregate demand or contain aggregate demand in an economy by changing money supply and, thereby, interest rates. For example, if RBI chooses to follow an easy monetary policy (money supply growth increases), resulting in softening of the interest rates, we know that demand for money, being a negative function of interest rates, will increase spending on goods and services. Similarly, if RBI opts for a tight monetary policy (money supply growth falls), thereby hardening interest rates, demand for money will fall and so will spending on goods and services.

The rate of interest actually observed is called the nominal interest rate. This is different from real interest rate. And, the distinction is crucial. For example, if I expect inflation to be 5% per annum, then the money borrowed or lent can be expected to lose value by 5% per annum. The lender will lose and the borrower will gain. Real interest rate, therefore, takes out the expected loss in value, given by the expected inflation, i.e., 5% in our example, to arrive at what the borrower or lender will really return or receive. We can then, symbolically, put the relationship between real and nominal interest rate as: $r = i - \pi^e$ where $r$ is the real interest rate, $i$ is the nominal interest rate and $\pi^e$ is the expected inflation. Investment decisions are based on real interest rates. However, since expected rate of inflation is difficult to measure, the current rate of inflation is often used as a proxy.

There are certain features of interest rates, which may be useful to keep in mind:

1. Long-term interest rates (more than one year) are usually higher than short-term interest rates (less than one year). This is because longer the period of the loan greater is the risk.
2. Inflation is one reason why interest rates exist. Lenders want to be compensated for the decrease in the purchasing power of what they lend. So, rates generally are high when inflationary expectations are high.
3. In a period of slowdown interest rates are usually low as the demand for money comes down.

Finally, which interest rates do we refer to when we say that interest rate has gone up or down? In financial markets (which bring together the supply of money and demand for money), there are many interest rates. These vary depending on maturity, risk and tax status. Key interest rates in the Indian money markets are shown in Table 2.6 below for the purpose of illustration.

Call money market rates are rates at which one bank borrows from the other for a short term, ranging from call (repayable on demand) to

72 hours or, slightly longer. Rates on Treasury bills (T- Bills) and long-term government securities refer to yields (interest rates) on short-term and long-term government securities. In the table, long-term refers to yields (interest rates) on 10-year government bonds. Deposit rates are averages of what five major banks pay for term deposits of more than one-year maturity. Prime lending rate (PLR) is the rate at which banks lend to their favoured customers. The PLR figures in the table 2.6 are the average rates charged by five major banks. Finally, the last row in the table shows the annual inflation rate to enable calculation of real interest rates.

***Table 2.6 Key interest rates in India, 2005/06 to 2008/09***

(Percentages)

| Interest rates | 2005/06 | 2006/07 | 2007/08 | 2008/09 |
|---|---|---|---|---|
| 1. Call money market rate | 5.60 | 7.22 | 6.07 | 7.06 |
| 2. Short-term government securities | 2.84-8.57 | 6.23-11.37 | 6.95-9.93 | 4.6-11.09 |
| 3. Medium-term government securities | 6.48-7.92 | 6.61-8.67 | 6.87-10.55 | 5.5-10.69 |
| 4. Long-term government securities | 7.08-7.85 | 7.47-10 | 6.17-8.88 | 6.27-8.26 |
| 5. Deposit Rate | 6.0-7.00 | 7.5-9.00 | 8.25-9.00 | 7.75-8.5 |
| 6. Prime lending rate | 9.50-13.00 | 9.00-14.50 | 9.50-15.00 | N.A |
| 7. Inflation Rate | 4.4 | 5.4 | 4.7 | 8.33 |

*Source*: Compiled from Reserve Bank of India, *Handbook of Statistics on Indian Economy*, http://www.rbi.org.in

The differences in rates reflect different maturities, risks and tax status. Out of these, government securities are least risky; their maturity values are also fixed. Usually, therefore, the yields on long-term government securities are used as a reference point to assess the interest rate scenario in an economy. Economists monitor the yield trends over time by plotting the yields of government securities of various maturities, also called the yield curve. Typically, as we mentioned earlier, the relationship is positive; the longer the maturity period, higher will be the yield. But it need not always be so. In certain situations, if the yield on long-term government securities is lower than those on short-term government securities, this can mean that investors think that the economy will slowdown in the future. A lower yield (interest rate) on long term bonds may be viewed as sluggish demand for money, which is a sign of slowdown.

## 2.4 Exchange Rates: The Basics

Exchange rate, in its simplest form, is the amount of one currency needed to buy another currency. If Rs. 45 is needed to buy 1$, then the rupee–dollar exchange rate is Rs. 45 to a dollar. It is, thus, the price at which one currency is exchanged for the other. Like any other price, exchange rate is also determined by demand for and supply of foreign exchange. The supply of foreign exchange is given by the inflow of foreign exchange into the country. This, in turn, depends on: (a) supply of foreign exchange coming out of exports of goods and services and (b) supply of foreign exchange coming out of inflow of capital (money). Demand for foreign exchange similarly is given by the outflow of foreign exchange from the country and this depends on: (a) demand for foreign exchange emanating from demand for imports of goods and services, and (b) demand for foreign exchange to pay back a foreign loan, provide credit or give a grant to another country, which broadly fall under capital outflow. For example, if the price of dollar is falling vis-à-vis Indian rupee (or, the price of Indian rupee is going up in relation to dollar), it is because supply (inflow) of dollar is outpacing the demand (outflow) of dollar and vice versa.

Having stated the fundamentals of exchange rates and exchange rate determination, let us introduce certain caveats. The exchange rate that we usually observe in the market place is the *nominal exchange rate*, i.e., it is expressed simply as price of one currency in terms of another. Let us say that rupee–dollar exchange rate is Rs. 45 to a dollar. What does it mean? It means that an American can buy Rs. 45 worth of Indian goods and services and assets by paying one dollar and an Indian can buy one dollar worth of American goods and services and assets by paying Rs. 45. Let us suppose that rupee appreciates by 5% to Rs. 42.75 to a dollar. Does it necessarily mean that Indian products have become more costly (less competitive) to the Americans and American products have become less costly (more competitive) to the Indians? That will depend on the rate of price rise (inflation) in the United States relative to the rate of price rise (inflation) in India. Let us say, prices in the United States also increase by 5%, while Indian prices remain at the same level. In that case, despite a nominal appreciation of rupee by 5%, nothing has changed in real terms. Indian products have lost competitiveness by 5% because of rupee appreciation but have gained it back by way of cost competitiveness because of 5% higher increase in American domestic prices relative to Indian domestic prices, which essentially means that Indian products have become 5% cheaper relative to American products. There is no net loss in competitiveness to Indian products. Similarly, while the American products have gained in competitiveness because of relative appreciation of rupee, they have lost by the same amount on the cost front. Again, there is no net gain. *Real exchange rate* takes into account the impact of relative change in prices between countries and is defined as the nominal exchange rate times the foreign price level divided by the domestic price level. For a given nominal rate (say Rs. 45/dollar), if the ratio of foreign price level to domestic price level rises, then in real terms, the exchange rate is no longer Rs. 45/dollar but more than Rs. 45, or, in real terms, rupee has depreciated. In other words, Indian products have become more competitive and vice versa.

If we want to know the overall competitiveness of a product, we must focus on real and not just nominal exchange rates. A real depreciation of the currency, other things being equal, is a gain in competitiveness and a real appreciation of the currency, other things being equal, is a loss in competitiveness. One more concept is real effective exchange rate (REER). This concept is to be understood as follows: a country trades in different currencies like dollar, euro or yen. Suppose, rupee has appreciated against dollar in real terms, does it mean that overall India's exports are becoming less competitive? The answer will depend, also, on what is happening to the rupee vis-à-vis euro and yen and, therefore, what is the weighted average effect. For example, suppose rupee appreciates against dollar by 5%, but remains unchanged against euro and yen. Also assume that dollar accounts for 75% of India's trade. Then rupee's effective exchange rate has risen by 3.75% (5 × 75 + 0 × 25) and not by 5%. *Real effective exchange rate* (REER), thus, is a weighted average of bilateral real exchange rates with weights equal to trade shares. REER is the most effecting measure of international competitiveness. Many economists believe that between 2002/03 and 2007/08, despite an appreciation of the rupee against the U.S. dollar, Indian export growth did not do badly because, in terms of real effective exchange rate, Indian exports were still competitive.

Exchange rates can be determined in the market place based purely on the market demand for and supply of foreign exchange, as explained in the beginning of this section. This is called the *flexible exchange rate system.* However, at the other extreme, exchange rates can also be fixed, whereby the price of the currency of a country in relation to the other country's currency is fixed by the central bank of the country. This is called the *fixed exchange rate system*. In between, there are different variants, but the most common one is a system of managed float. Under this system, the exchange rate is, initially, determined in the market place but, from time to time, the central bank influences the demand and supply of foreign exchange to manage the exchange rate at a desired level. The exchange rate regime in India can be characterized as a managed float system.

The exchange rate regime followed by a country is crucial for the formulation of the macroeconomic policies in the country. The relationships that emerge between exchange rates, interest rates, prices and output, the various policy prescriptions that may ensue to deal with particular circumstances are all important for a manager to understand and analyze. We will discuss them in Chapters 5 and 6.

## 2.5 General Price Level: Measurement

There are three different measures of general price level. These are: (a) consumer price index (CPI), (b) wholesale price index (WPI), and (c) GDP deflator. Each is a weighted average of several prices and is presented in the form of index numbers. CPI signals changes in prices facing the consumer; WPI signals changes in prices facing the producer and GDP deflator signals overall national price changes. Each in its own way provides a measure of inflation in the economy. None is a perfect measure. We will first describe with the help of an example how CPI is constructed. We will then describe how WPI is constructed. Method of estimation of GDP deflator is already explained in Section 2.1.2. We will only bring out the highlights. The section will end with a comparison of different measures of general price level.

## 2.5.1 Consumer Price Index (CPI)

Consider Table 2.7. The numbers and items in the table are illustrative. However, the steps involved in the construction of CPI can be explained with the help of the table as follows:

1. Find the typical consumption basket in the base year (column 1). This will include both goods and services. In the table we have considered only 5 items for illustration; in reality there are many more.
2. For each item[11] in the consumption basket, find the base year quantity consumed (column 2) and base year retail prices (column 3). Data on items in the basket, quantity consumed of each item and its price can be obtained from the comprehensive consumption surveys conducted by the Central Statistical Organization and reported approximately every five years.
3. Find out the weight of each item in the consumption basket in the base year (column 4). First, find out the total expenditure on the basket (Rs. 910) by multiplying the quantity of each item (column 2) by its price (column 3) and then summing it up. Then see the share (weight) of each item's expenditure in the total expenditure. Thus, the weight of rice in the consumption basket, obtained as Rs. 150/Rs. 910, is 0.16, and similarly, for other items. The sum of the weights must add to 1.
4. Assume the base year weights hold in the current year also. This is a crucial assumption in the construction of the CPI. What it means is that the consumption basket and the proportionate share of each item in the basket do not change from the base year to the current year. Once we assume that all we need to do, for each item, is to divide the current year prices (column 5) with the base year prices (column 3) and multiply by 100 and obtain column 6. The ratio of prices is called the price relative.
5. Column 6 tells us the increase in price of each item in the consumption basket between the base year and the current year. For example, an index of 150 in case of rice tells us that between 1990/91 and 2007/08, the price of rice has gone up by 50%, and so on for other items. We, however, need a composite index to know what the

[11] In reality, it may not be possible to get data on each item. Data may, therefore, be presented in groups of commodities whose prices move in the same direction, like fruits and vegetables or petrol and lubricants etc.

increase in the cost of the basket is in 2007/08, compared to 1990/91. Since quantity weights (column 4) are constant, we multiply each item's index in the current period (column 6) by its weight (column 4) and add those up to obtain a weighted average for the entire basket. This gives us an index of 165.3.[12] What this means is that, between the base year and current year, the cost of the entire basket has gone up by 65.3%.

In summary, there are four points to keep in mind in CPI: (a) CPI covers goods and services (including imported) that enter the consumption basket, (b) the relevant price is the retail price and (c) the quantity weights are constant. Symbolically, CPI = $\Sigma p_t q_0 / \Sigma p_0 q_0$, where $p$ stands for price and $q$ for quantity and the subscripts '$t$' and '0' stand for current and base year[13] respectively. (d) It is reported in India with a one month time lag.

*Table 2.7 Construction of CPI: An example*

| Item (1) | Base year (1990/91) quantity (2) | Base year (1990/91) prices (3) | Base year (1990/91) weights (4) | Current year (2007/08) prices (5) | Price relatives, (Col. 5/Col. 3 × 100) (6) |
|---|---|---|---|---|---|
| Rice | 15 kg | Rs. 10/kg | 0.16 | Rs.15/kg | 150 |
| Wheat | 10 kg | Rs. 8/kg | 0.09 | Rs.10/kg | 125 |
| Milk | 40 l | Rs. 5/l | 0.22 | Rs.7/l | 140 |
| Cloth | 10 m | Rs.8/m | 0.09 | Rs.10/m | 125 |
| House | Two room | Rs. 200 | 0.44 | Rs. 400 | 200 |

## 2.5.2 Wholesale Price Index (WPI)

The methodology used for the construction of WPI is same as for CPI: only the data changes. Again, consider Table 2.7. For WPI, the information contained in each column will change as follows: Column 1 will now

[12] 150 × 0.16) +(125 × 0.09) +(140 × 0.22) +(125 × 0.09) +(200 × 0.44) = 165.3

[13] Those familiar with index numbers will note that here we are talking about Laspeyre kind of index.

consist of a much larger basket,[14] which will include items like fertilizers, minerals, industrial raw materials and semi-finished goods, machinery and equipment, in addition to goods contained in CPI. Unlike CPI, WPI considers only goods and all services are excluded. In column 2, WPI will consider the transaction of each item in the wholesale market. In column 3, WPI will take wholesale prices into consideration and not retail prices, as in CPI. In column 4, weights are based on value of transaction in the various items in the base year. Like in CPI, the base year weights are fixed. Once, the data is entered in columns 1–4, the method of calculation of column 5 and 6 in WPI is the same as in CPI.

In summary, in WPI also, there are four points to keep in mind: (a) WPI covers only goods (including intermediate goods) and no services. (b) The relevant price is the wholesale price. (c) The quantity weights are constant. Symbolically, the last point has the same methodological implication as CPI, i.e., WPI = $\Sigma p_t q_0 / \Sigma p_0 q_0$, where $p$ stands for price and $q$ for quantity and the subscripts '$t$' and '0' stand for current and base year respectively. (d) It is reported in India with a two-week time lag. In India, movements in WPI are used to measure inflation and CPI is used to measure cost of living changes of in the economy.

## 2.5.3 GDP Deflator

GDP deflator was discussed in Section 2.1.2 of this chapter. It is nominal GDP divided by real GDP. Recall that nominal GDP is obtained by multiplying current year price with current year quantity and real GDP is obtained by multiplying base year price with current year quantity. Symbolically, GDP deflator = $\Sigma p_t q_{t/} \Sigma p_0 q_t$. Note the difference between GDP deflator and WPI/CPI. In the estimation of GDP deflator quantity weights are not fixed. They vary each year. We come to know of the quantity of goods and services produced each year only at the end of the year. GDP deflator, therefore, comes with a one-year time lag. Otherwise, it is perhaps the most comprehensive measure of changes in the general price level as it considers all domestically produced final goods and services.

Table 2.8 summarizes the salient features of each measure of general price level discussed in this section. It can be seen from the table that none

[14] About 435 selected items currently. At the time of going to the press, a new series of WPI with a wider and updated basket of products (about 850 items) and a more recent base year (2004–05) has been introduced, making it more reliable, current and representative.

of the methods is without limitation. The CPI time lag is 1 month. Besides, considering the rapidity with which consumption habits are changing, using a fixed quantity weight for an extended period of time may be questionable. Also, there is no composite CPI covering the whole of India. WPI suffers from a major flaw in that it does not consider services. With service sector accounting for more than half of India's GDP, this omission is serious.[15] The inclusion of intermediate goods also leads to cascading effect on prices. WPI scores over both CPI and GDP deflator as it is available with the least time lag of two weeks. GDP deflator is the broadest indicator of changes in the domestic price level. But it is an implicit measure and comes with a longer lag. Also, the data is subject to frequent revisions with revision in GDP figures.

*Table 2.8 Price indices: A comparison*

| Price Index (1) | Basis (2) | Prices (3) | Basket (4) | Weights (5) | Lag (6) |
|---|---|---|---|---|---|
| Consumer Price Index | $\frac{\Sigma p_t q_0}{\Sigma p_0 q_0}$ | Retail | Consumption goods and services; Includes imports | Fixed quantity weights | One month |
| Wholesale Price Index | $\frac{\Sigma p_t q_0}{\Sigma p_0 q_0}$ | Wholesale | Larger basket of goods, including intermediate goods. But no services | Fixed quantity weights | Two weeks |
| GDP Deflator | $\frac{\Sigma p_t q_t}{\Sigma p_0 q_t}$ | Retail | All domestically produced final goods and services | Quantity weights not fixed | One year |

## *Getting a Feel for the Data*

How do the three measures of price discussed above fare in actually explaining annual movement in general price levels in India? Table 2.9

[15] There are reports that the government is working on a price sensitivity index for five service sectors, namely, banking, insurance, telecommunications, road transport and railways. The index will be merged into the wholesale price index.

summarizes the data and the chart shows the trends in prices. CPI data are reported for three different groups: (a) industrial workers (IW), (b) urban non-manual (UNM) and agricultural labourers (AL). WPI is a single series expressed as annual average. GDP deflators are calculated from Table 2.3.

***Table 2.9 India: CPI, WPI and GDP deflator, 1998/99 to 2008/09 (Indices)***

| Year (1) | CPI–IW[a] (2) | CPI-UNMW[b] (3) | CPI-AL[c] (4) | WPI[d] (5) | GDP deflator[e] (6) |
|---|---|---|---|---|---|
| 1998/99 | 414 | 337 | 293 | 140.7 | 96.34 |
| 1999/00 | 428 | 352 | 306 | 145.3 | 100.00 |
| 2000/01 | 444 | 371 | 305 | 155.7 | 103.53 |
| 2001/02 | 463 | 390 | 309 | 161.3 | 106.66 |
| 2002/03 | 482 | 405 | 319 | 166.8 | 110.71 |
| 2003/04 | 500 | 420 | 331 | 175.9 | 114.64 |
| 2004/05 | 520 | 436 | 340 | 187.3 | 121.05 |
| 2005/06 | 542 | 456 | 353 | 195.5 | 125.98 |
| 2006/07 | 579 | 486 | 380 | 206.1 | 132.99 |
| 2007/08 | 616 | 515 | 409 | 215.9 | 138.67 |
| 2008/09 | 671 | 561 | 450 | 233.9 | 147.44 |

*Source:* Reserve Bank of India, *Handbook of Statistics on Indian Economy*, http://www.rbi.org.in/

[a] 1982 = 100
[b] 1984–85 = 100
[c] 1986–87 = 100
[d] 1993–94 = 100
[e] 1999–2000 = 100

Abbreviations: IW, industrial workers; UNMW, urban non-manual workers; AL, agricultural labourers.

Figure 2.1 shows the movement in prices between 1998/99 and 2007/08, based on different measures of price change.

It is interesting to note from Figure 2.1 that, though the annual per centage change varies across different indices, the direction of change is similar. In respect of WPI and GDP deflator, the movements are strikingly similar.

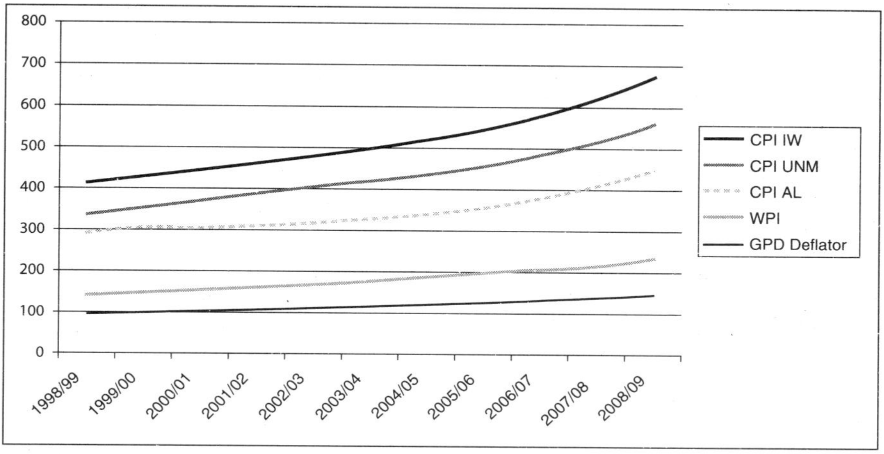


**FIGURE 2.1** *Price Movements based on Different Measures of Inflation*

## *Box 2.1 Changes in Prices based on CPI and WPI*

It is important to note that because of differences in coverage of commodities in WPI and CPI (the former being wider), the weight of a particular commodity, or a group of commodities, will differ

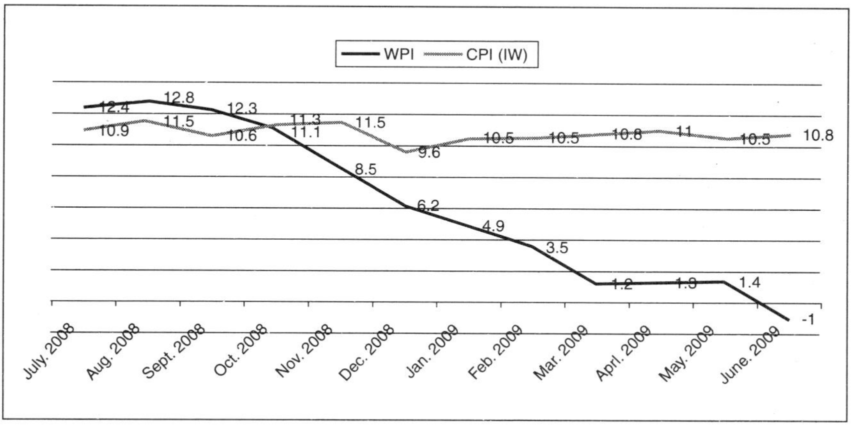


between these two indices. For example, as the chart shows, at present, in India, while the per centage rise in prices measured through WPI is moderate, that measured through CPI is very steep.

The difference can be ascribed to the differences in the weights assigned to different commodity groups in these two price indices. These are shown below:

| CPI (IW) | | WPI | |
|---|---|---|---|
| Commodity Groups | Weights | Commodity Groups | Weights |
| Food Group | 46.2 | Primary Food | 15.4 |
| Pan, Supari, Tobacco, etc. | 2.3 | Manufactured Food | 11.54 |
| Fuel & Light | 6.4 | Other Primary Goods | 6.63 |
| Housing | 15.3 | Other Manufactured Goods | 52.2 |
| Clothing | 6.6 | Fuel | 14.24 |
| Miscellaneous Group | 23.3 | | |
| Total | 100 | All | 100 |

From the above it can be seen that in CPI, the weight assigned to food group is much higher than in WPI. In WPI the predominant commodity group is manufactured products. Now, if food prices rise faster than others those will show up much more prominently in CPI than in WPI. The price of the same food items will be rising almost equally sharply in WPI as well, but their weights being low in the overall basket, the overall impact on WPI may still be moderate.

The reverse is also true. If manufactured goods prices rise faster than others that will show up much more prominently in WPI than in CPI.

The rapid rise in inflation based on CPI in India today can thus be explained by a very sharp rise in the prices of food products which have a much larger weight in CPI compared to WPI. Not very far back, however, it was the opposite. Inflation rate based on WPI was higher than CPI inflation. This was because of a sharp rise in raw material prices which impacted the prices of manufactured products more than others.

## 2.6 Inflation: The Basics

Inflation refers to a *continuous* rise in general price level.[16] In India, we estimate inflation based on the movement in WPI, which is reported every

[16] There is also a term called 'core inflation', defined as year-to-year change in prices, excluding the price of food and energy and, perhaps, administered prices. The exclusion of these prices is done because they are subject to fluctuations beyond the control of the monetary

week with a two-week lag.[17] CPI is used to arrive at cost of living changes and for the calculation of dearness allowance or cost of living allowance. In many other countries, inflation is derived from movements in CPI. In no country, GDP deflator is used as a measure of inflation because, the long lag of over one year and other measurement problems do not render it useful for the formulation of policy.

### 2.6.1 What Causes Inflation?

Inflation can be caused by demand factors, referred to as "demand-pull" inflation or by cost factors, referred to as "cost-push" inflation. *Demand-pull inflation* can be caused by an increase in any of the components of aggregate demand, i.e., consumer demand ($C$), investment demand ($I$), government demand ($G$) or net foreigners' demand ($X - M$) or some combination of the above. Usually, however, it is an increase in $G$, which is the primary cause of demand-pull inflation. When the demand increases, the extent of price increase depends on the supply situation. At one extreme, let us assume that there is massive excess capacity all around the economy and the suppliers in the economy can meet the excess demand for goods and services without resorting to increase in prices, then we may not see any rise in prices consequent to an increase in demand. At the other extreme, let us assume that the economy is operating at its full capacity and there is no scope for increasing production. In that case, the entire increase in demand will be dissipated by way of a rise in prices. In real life, however, we neither encounter economy-wide massive excess capacity nor do we come across a situation where output cannot be increased at all. In real life, as demand increases, prices and output both increase; when the economy is closer to capacity output, price rise is steeper and, vice versa, when there is some excess capacity in the economy.

*Cost-push inflation* is driven by an increase in costs, independently of demand. The logic underlying this phenomenon is as follows. Conceptually, the contribution that a factor of production, say, labour, makes to the revenue of a firm is the additional output that the firm gets by employing that labour times the price of the output. The wage that the labour gets, therefore, is supposed to reflect this. Now, if, because of union pressures wages are

---

policy, such as, random fluctuations in weather or, OPEC decisions. Core inflation, thus, focuses on the more persistent movements in inflation and, thereby, helps understand policy effectiveness better.

[17] Starting November 14, 2009, WPI is being released on a monthly basis. The government, however, continues to provide weekly data on prices of primary articles and fuels.

pushed up, without any increase in the worker's contribution to the output, per unit cost of production goes up at each level of output. If firms face a rise in costs, they will respond partly by raising prices and passing the cost on to their consumers and partly by cutting back on production. Note that unlike demand-pull inflation where both prices and output go up, cost-push inflation results in a rise in prices and a fall in output. We have taken the example of labour costs here, but costs could also go up because of an increase in material costs, import costs, due to increase in oil prices, strong bargaining power of producers. In short, any increase in costs or money gain, greater productivity will result in increase in prices.

Demand-pull and cost-push are, of course, convenient starting points for explaining what causes inflation. Beyond a stage the distinction between the two gets blurred. What may have started as a demand pull-inflation may turn into a cost-push inflation as workers demand higher wages, suppliers want higher prices for raw materials. Again, cost-push inflation may turn into a demand-pull inflation if the government ('*G*' is a component of aggregate demand) ends up spending more to give more dearness allowance to its staff, or bail out some units adversely affected by cost-push inflation. The rule of thumb is that if output and prices are both increasing, demand side factors predominate. On the other hand, if a rise in prices is accompanied by a fall in output, it is the cost factors which are more important.

Inflation can, also, be *expectation driven*. If people expect inflation to be say, $x\%$, then based on this expectation, people will revise prices and actually take the inflation to $x\%$. Expectations are formed based on past inflation rates. Policy challenge, under the circumstances, lies in finding ways to douse the expectations. The key is policy credibility. Otherwise, expected inflation may drive actual inflation.

## *Inflation and Money Supply*

Inflation, as we have defined, refers to a *continuous* rise in prices. A one shot increase in prices does not fit into our definition of inflation, though price *levels* may be higher than before. Let us say government spends more money as a result of increased demand for goods and services. In other words, there is a demand-pull. This will lead to an increase in prices and the extent of price rise, as we have discussed earlier, will depend on the supply capacity of the economy. Now, consider the GDP identity: $Y = C +$

$I + G + X - M$. The left hand side of the equation is the actual output and the right hand side of the equation is the total spending, or aggregate demand. Let us, for analytical convenience, assume that we have reached a stage where actual output ($Y$) is constant and cannot be increased any further. Then an ever growing government expenditure ($G$) must crowd out $I$, $C$ and $X - M$, eventually reaching a point where all production is purchased by the government. When this happens there is no further scope for increase in $G$ and no further rise in prices. But this is not inflation, which we have defined as continuous rise in prices. We will say that there was a rise in price level but that has fizzled out, as the government has no more money to spend.

Now consider cost push. Let us say there is an increase in the price of petrol. Petrol being such an important product, all other prices will most certainly go up in the economy. Unless our incomes increase or we chose to save less, we will probably cut down our expenditure somewhere else to meet the increased cost of petrol. So there will be increase in prices in some sectors along with a downward pressure in prices in sectors where demand for goods and services have fallen. And, the economy will, in course of time, settle at a new general price level, which, on balance, may settle roughly where it began. So, where is the continuous rise in prices?

The question we are asking is: what makes price rise continuous, which is the definition of inflation? The answer is that while the initial increase in prices, whether driven by demand-pull or cost-push factors may take some time to get fully absorbed by the economy, and therefore, one may observe rising prices for some time, such a rise in prices cannot be sustained for long, unless there is further spending of money. In other words, if money supply is held constant, then, beyond a stage, there is no scope for further spending of money and inflation will fizzle out. However, the central bank may have to increase the money supply to meet the growing demand for government spending to pay additional dearness allowance to its employees who have been hit by an increase in the price level or for meeting other commitments. This makes the price rise continuous. By implication, then, what we are saying is that a continuous rise in prices is possible only if it is accommodated by an increase in money supply. Indeed, inflation, in the long run, is a monetary phenomenon. It is sustained by an increase in money supply.[18]

[18] This relationship draws from our discussion on money in Section 2.2. You may like to refresh Section 2.2. Note that in arriving at this relationship between money supply and prices, we are assuming that the number of times money changes hands in an year is stable.

## *Inflation and Interest Rates*

Our focus in this section is on the relationship between inflation and nominal interest rate. The discussion is in broad terms; nevertheless, it will be useful to grasp the basics. Let us begin by drawing from our previous learning in Section 2.3 where we discussed the basics of interest rates. We said that real interest rate is equal to nominal interest rate minus expected inflation. We also said that because of difficulties in arriving at expected inflation, actual inflation is sometimes used as a proxy. Symbolically $r = i - \pi^e$ where $r$ is the real interest rate, $i$ is the nominal interest rate and $\pi^e$ is the expected inflation. Now, let us rewrite the equation as: $i = r + \pi^e$. This says that nominal interest rate is equal to real interest rate plus inflationary expectations. And, as before, actual inflation can be used as a proxy for inflationary expectations.

Let us now give an economic interpretation to the concept of real interest rate. Real interest rate is nothing but the return on the stock of capital or, roughly, investment. For the economy as a whole the return on the stock of capital over time is given by the real GDP growth. Therefore, GDP growth sets the limit for real interest rate. Or $r$ can be roughly used as a proxy for real GDP growth. Now, consider the equation: $i = r + \pi^e$. In a period of slowdown as GDP growth slows down, we have seen, expected inflation will be low and so will be nominal interest rate $i$. In a booming economy, as GDP growth accelerates, expected inflation will be higher and so will be the nominal interest rate. Finally, if we say that real interest rate, which is capturing the real GDP growth, is constant, there exists a relationship between expected inflation and nominal interest rates.

Intuitively, what we are saying is that one reason why interest rate (nominal) exists is inflation. People who lend money would like to be compensated for the loss of purchasing power of what they lend. Interest rates, therefore, will be low if inflationary expectations are low. Since inflationary expectations are formed based on current inflation rates, interest rates are low when inflation rate is low and interest rates are high when inflation rate is high.

## *Costs of Inflation*

If we all knew with certainty what the annual price rise would be, we would all make adjustments accordingly such that the costs of inflation would be minimum. However, inflation tends to be unanticipated. And, unanticipated inflation can be costly.

The first set of costs is what is known as distribution costs. Inflation penalizes people with fixed income. With inflation, the value of the money these people earn, goes down. Thus inflation redistributes incomes away from this group in favour of those, whose incomes keep pace with inflation. Similarly, inflation also redistributes income between the lender and the borrower. Lender loses because of a fall in the real value of financial assets, he gets back while the borrower gains because the real value of the monetary assets, he returns has, come down.

Also, while inflation means, generally, rising prices, all prices do not rise at the same rate. Some prices rise more and some by less than the overall. This creates changes in relative prices and can be a source of uncertainty to business.

Aside from the above, unanticipated inflation can also affect growth. A high inflation rate diverts financial savings, which support investment demand and thereby growth to non-investible resources like gold, land, and commodities that usually have a tendency to keep pace with inflation but do not contribute towards growth. Inflation can also lead to a flight of capital from the country, thus, further reducing economy's access to investible resources. Last but not least, inflation can also slow down external sector demand for domestically produced goods and services. As we discussed in Section 2.4, if the domestic inflation rate is higher than other trading partners' inflation rate, our goods and services become less competitive compared to that of our trading partners.

## *Management of Inflation*

What is a manageable rate of inflation? There is a general agreement among economists that inflation should be relatively low and stable but there is no consensus on the rate. An acceptable rate will depend on a host of factors, including economic growth and social justice objectives and also political considerations. In India, an acceptable rate of inflation can be considered as between 5% and 6%[19] per annum. In other countries, it may be less. The important thing is that the inflation rate should be stable.

If the inflation is triggered by demand-pull, at least theoretically, the problem is amenable to macro policy management. Assume that inflation

---

[19] Rangarajan, C., "The Changing Context of Monetary Policy" in *Indian Economy, Essays on Money and Finance*, UBS Publishers' Distributors Ltd, 1998. -

has overshot the desirable level as a result of demand-pull factors. Recall that when there is a demand-pull inflation, with prices, output also rises. A contractionary fiscal or monetary policy (lower *G*, higher taxes, higher interest rates) can be used to slow down the economy till both output and inflation are brought back to the original level. However, if the overshooting of inflation is due to cost-push factors, policy makers have a more difficult job at hand. This is because, in case of cost-push inflation, with inflation, output also falls. Now, if you follow a contractionary fiscal or monetary policy and slow down the economy, prices will fall because of lesser demand for goods and services, but also the output would fall. If on the other hand, you want to target output, by following expansionary fiscal and monetary policies, you cannot bring down prices. In other words, in case of cost-push inflation, it is very difficult to get back to the original output and price combination by use of conventional macroeconomic policy tools. In this situation, therefore, the solution has to be found not from the demand but from the supply side that has caused the cost-push inflation. Conventional macroeconomic policies do not offer a readymade solution to cost-push inflation (Box 2.2).

To the extent, real life inflation is a combination of both demand-pull and a cost-push factor, in addition to being driven by expectations, actual management of inflation is not an easy task. The problem is one of identification. If the rise in prices is due to one-time factors like increase in oil prices or upward revision of administered prices, the central bank may not like to slowdown the economy to tame prices. On the other hand, if the inflation is due to a sustained rise in demand, the central bank may need to take a more decisive step in terms of containing demand. But then does the central bank know for sure what is causing the price rise? If not, can it dampen expectations? These are some of the dilemmas the central banker is faced with in the conduct of monetary policy.

### *Box 2.2 More on Why is Supply Side Inflation More Difficult to Manage?*

The difficulty the policy makers face in controlling supply side inflation can be explained with a set of demand and supply curves. In the following diagrams, AD refers to aggregate demand for goods and services in an economy in a given period of time and AS refers to aggregate supply of goods and services produced in an economy in a given period of time. *P* refers to general price level. The aggregate demand curve (AD) is downward sloping because as the general price level (*P*) increases, the value of money that we have to spend on goods and services comes down and with that reduced value of money we buy less goods and services. The aggregate supply curve (AS) is upward sloping because the producer needs to be given an incentive to produce more, in response to rising demand, because increasing production at the margin costs more. The *y*-axis measures the general price level (*P*), which is a weighted average price of all goods and services produced in the economy. And the *x*-axis measures GDP (*Y*). The point of intersection between AD and AS gives us the equilibrium level of GDP (e.g., $Y_0$, $Y_1$) and equilibrium level of price (e.g., $P_0$, $P_1$)

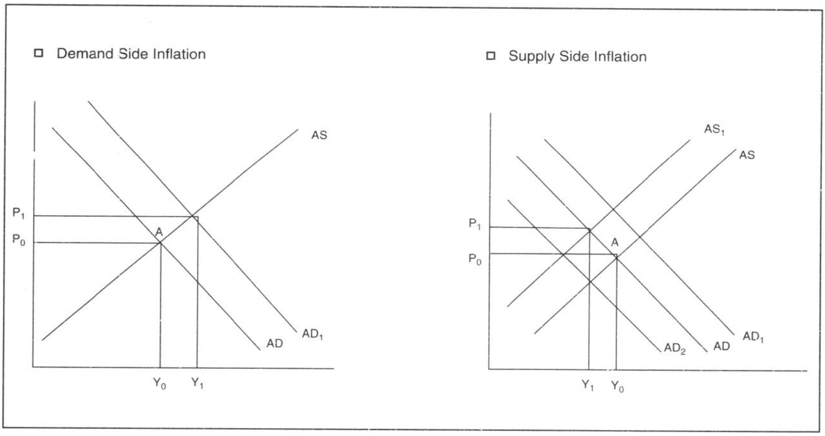


Let us consider demand side inflation first. Assume $Y_0$ represents 9% GDP growth and $P_0$ 5% inflation. Since these numbers are consistent with India's growth and price stability objectives (Chapter 1), the policy maker would like to stay at point A. Now, for some reason, AD goes up and the AD curve moves to the right to AD1. As a result, GDP growth increases from $Y_0$ to $Y_1$ (> 9%) but so does inflation from $P_0$ to $P_1$ (> 5%). Since inflation is out of line with price stability objective, the policy maker would like to revert back to A. A contractionary macroeconomic policy will be followed (e.g. signaling a rise in the interest rates by RBI), and in normal times, AD1 will move back to point A. The time it takes to move back to point A is the policy lag.

*(contd.)*

The point is that if the disturbance originates from the demand side, which usually is the case, macroeconomic policies, which are geared towards handling demand side disturbances, can take the economy back to the desirable point with a predictable lag.

However, this is not so if the inflation originates from the supply side. In a supply side inflation, as can be seen from the second diagram, the inflation is caused not by a rightward shift in the AD curve but by a leftward shift in the AS curve. And, when that happens, we end up in a situation where a higher inflation exists simultaneously with a slower growth of GDP.

A leftward shift in the AS can be caused by an increase in commodity prices (oil, steel, cement, aluminum), which are important ingredients in the production process. As a result, the cost of production goes up; producers reflect this increase by charging a higher output price; higher output price lowers demand and at the end of the day the economy ends up with higher prices and slower growth of output. A leftward shift in the AS can also be caused by a crop failure consequent to an inclement weather. Here, supply falls short of demand and prices rise to bring the market to equilibrium.

If the problem originates from the supply side how does one get back to point A? A little reflection will show that policies like fiscal and monetary policies, which are geared towards addressing disturbances arising from demand side, cannot bring the economy back to point A, at least, not in a short period of time. If an expansionary set of macroeconomic policies are followed, the AD will shift to $AD_1$. The point where $AD_1$ touches $AS_1$ will be the new point of equilibrium. And it can be seen that at that point the economy will be able to reach the desired level of GDP growth Y, but at a rate of inflation which is even higher than $P_1$. Similarly, if a contractionary set of policies are followed, AD shifts to $AD_2$, the point where it intersects $AS_1$ is the new point of equilibrium. At this point, the economy can have the desired level of inflation ($P_0$) but at slower growth of output compared to $Y_0$. Either way, point A will not be reached.

The solution to a supply side disturbance is to shift $AS_1$ back to AS. One way to do it is to augment domestic production, but that can be time-consuming; the other way is to increase imports, but the feasibility of that will depend on global prices vis-à-vis domestic prices; finally, one can think of institutional mechanism to manage available supplies through controls; but that may interfere with market signals and may not be sustainable. Usually, therefore, a supply side disturbance is less amenable to policy correction.

In the event of a supply side disturbance, the policy maker is in a dilemma. Should it target growth ($Y_0$) or Inflation ($P_0$) since it cannot target both simultaneously? If it targets growth, price stability objective will have to be compromised with[20]; if it targets inflation, growth may suffer. A practicing manager is worried about this situation because, given this choice; the policy maker usually goes for price stability.

## 2.7 Summing Up

In this chapter, we have attempted to familiarize the readers with certain key concepts in macroeconomics, which affect business bottom lines. A set of demand variables, captured by GDP and related measures, which are crucial to revenue growth have been introduced first. Then, the discussion shifted to cost variables like interest rates, exchange rates and prices. So far, the familiarization has been mostly at a conceptual level. Now, we will apply these concepts to see how they affect the business environment and how macroeconomic policies address business concerns.

Chapter 2 is an important chapter. The reader should carefully grasp the concepts introduced in this chapter. The rest of the book will build on the foundation laid out in this chapter. Many of the basic concepts covered in this chapter will be assumed as known, or at best, a quick refresher will be provided, in subsequent discussions. The reader will be well advised to go through this chapter each time he/she moves to a new chapter.

# REVIEW QUESTIONS

1. Why should a manager monitor GDP growth? Explain clearly what GDP growth does and does not signal to the manager.
2. Why do we consider /z«a/ goods and services while estimating GDP? Suppose the reference period is the calendar year and on December 31,

[20] Supply side inflation may further spillover to the demand side because of growth and it may be difficult to contain inflationary expectations.

thousand tons of cement is produced. Will this be treated as a final or intermediate product? Give reasons for your answer.

3. From the text Table 2.3, estimate real GDP using 2000-01 as the base year. What is the average annual rise in prices between 1993-94 and 2002-03? How does it differ from when you use 1993-94 as the base year and why?
4. Assume last year's real GDP was Rs. 5000 crores, this year's nominal GDP is Rs. 6150 crores and the GDP deflator for this year is 120. What was the growth rate of real GDP?
5. Why do we have two measures of economic activity, namely GDP and GNP? Suppose an American company outsources production of a good to its subsidiary in India how does it affect India's GDP and GNP? How does it affect America's GDP and GNP?
6. What is the difference between GDP/GNP at factor cost and GDP/GNP at market prices? Why is this difference important?
7. For a manager which is more relevant: GDP or NDP. Why? Can gross investment be negative? How?
8. Given GNP at factor cost = 114601; Depreciation = 8062; Subsidies = 2822; NFIA = +330 and indirect taxes = 16745, find (a) GNP at market price, (b) NNP at market price, (c) NDP at market price and (d) NDP at factor cost.
9. If GDP says nothing about the quality of life of the average population, why do we worry so much about GDP growth? Discuss.
10. Show that a country, which absorbs more than its income must have a current account deficit. Use Indian example (1990-91) to elucidate your point.
11. What are the similarities and differences between WPI, CPI and GDP deflator? Which one of these we use in India to measure inflation and why?
12. What do we mean by the following terms: (a) price stability; (b) an acceptable rate of inflation; and, (c) core inflation. Why are these important to the manager?
13. What is the difference between demand-pull and cost-push inflation? Give examples of both. Why cost-push inflation is considered less amenable to macroeconomic policy changes?

CHAPTER

3

# Determinants of Aggregate Demand

In Chapter 1, we had mentioned that short-run fluctuations in output and prices were caused by fluctuations in aggregate demand. In this chapter we focus on aggregate demand. We will address three questions: (a) What are the components of aggregate demand? (b) What does each component depend on; and (c) How macroeconomic policies address the concerns arising out of fluctuations in aggregate demand?

## 3.1 Components of Aggregate Demand (AD)

You have already been introduced to different components of aggregate demand while discussing expenditure method of estimating GDP in Section 2.1.4 (in Chapter 2). Aggregate demand has four essential components, which includes on total spending on:

1. Consumption goods and services (*C*) by the private sector
2. Investment goods and services (*I*) by the private sector
3. C and I by the government sector (*G*), and
4. C and I by the external sector (*X*) *minus* all imports (*M*)

Aggregate demand, thus, is broken down into private sector spending, government sector spending, and net external sector spending on final consumption and investment goods and services in the economy.

Symbolically, the relationship between aggregate demand and GDP can be stated as: $Y = C + I + G + X - M$. This is an identity where the left-hand side of the equation ($Y$) stands for actual GDP and the right-hand side of the equation stands for aggregate demand. This identity implies that aggregate demand is equal to actual GDP. In other words, as aggregate demand increases, so will actual GDP up to the point of full capacity; beyond that, any increase in aggregate demand will be fully dissipated by a rise in prices.[1]

Now assume that we are investigating a slowdown. In order to find out what is happening in the economy and which indicator to focus on, it is important to know which component of demand has triggered the slowdown. While in every economy the components of demand are the same as outlined above, the trigger for a slowdown need not be so. For example, in large parts of East Asia, aggregate demand is driven by the external demand, i.e., demand for goods and services originating from foreigners ($X$). The foreigners' demand for goods and services in the East Asian economies has, traditionally, originated from Japan, United States, and the European region. In the recent past all the three regions have experienced a major economic slowdown, which, to varying degree, is still continuing. Since the buyers of East Asian countries' goods and services have experienced a slower growth of income (GDP) aggregate demand growth and actual GDP growth in East Asian countries have also slowed down. Suppose you want to know, when the economies of East Asia would revive, you will find that $C$, $I$, $G$, and $X$, all would be showing a slower growth. But the trigger is external demand.The chain reaction will be as follows: because there is a slowdown in $X$, there will not be a need to produce so much for $X$ and $I$ will also be slowing down; because $I$ is slowing down fewer number of people will be employed as $C$ will be slowing down and because $C$, $I$ and $X$ are all slowing down, government will collect less tax revenues and hence $G$ will also be slowing down. So which component do you monitor? Clearly, the external sector demand, because that is not only an important component of aggregate demand for the Asian economies but is also the component, which triggered the slowdown. You may have noticed that the recent revival of some of the East Asian economies is primarily due to higher external demand from China, which has somewhat made up for the loss of market in the traditional export destinations of United States, Japan and the European region. As a result, $C$, $G$, and $I$ have all gone up.

[1] In Chapter 4, we will deal with this topic in detail.

If external sector demand growth is the key to revival of the East Asian economies, it is the growth of consumption demand (*C*), which is being closely monitored in the United States to find out how quickly the U.S. economy might revive. Similarly, in the Indian economy, the key component of aggregate demand, which is considered essential for the sustained growth of the economy, is investment demand (*I*)[2], both in the government and the private sector. Therefore, what is to be learnt from these examples is that the components of demand are not to be looked at just as a part of GDP identity. They throw up a lot in terms of where the problem lies and the problems are not same across countries, though the components of aggregate demand are the same.

## 3.2 What Does Each Component of AD Depend On?

### 3.2.1 Consumption Demand

#### *What is Consumption Demand?*

Consumption demand is the aggregate expenditure on *current* consumption of final goods and services, that is, goods and services that are used up for consumption purposes during a given period. Expenditure on food items, travel and entertainment, paying rent on our houses, paying electricity bills, paying for haircuts, taking different lessons are some examples among thousands of other activities on which we spend our income for current consumption purposes.

A consumption function is usually expressed to show the relationship between aggregate consumption and disposable income. As we will see later current disposable income, indeed, is an important determinant of aggregate consumption expenditure. The relationship is positive. As the disposable income goes up, the consumption expenditure also goes up. The change in consumption expenditure in response to a change in disposable income is called the marginal propensity to consume (MPC). This is an important variable in macroeconomics as it tells us by how much we can expect consumption demand and, thereby, aggregate demand to go up, if

[2] We will go deeper into the Indian case in the latter part of the chapter.

there is an increase in the disposable income. Since disposable income is divided between consumption and saving, what is left out of disposable income after consumption is saving. Thus, if disposable income increases by Rs. 100 and Rs. 75 of this increase is spent on current consumption of goods and services, then MPC is given as 0.75. The balance is saved. Therefore, Rs. 25, out of an increase in disposable income of Rs. 100, is the marginal propensity to save (MPS). Then, MPS = 1 – MPC. We can see that, since the balance of disposable income not consumed goes towards saving, an analysis of aggregate consumption expenditure also throws light on the level of savings in the economy, which, as we know, plays a crucial role in determining the size of investment and future growth of the economy.

Consumption demand is the most important component of aggregate demand in India. Private sector consumption expenditure in recent years has accounted for about 55 per cent of GDP. To that, if we add government consumption expenditure on goods and services, then total consumption expenditure comes to two-thirds of aggregate demand or actual GDP in the country. Figure 3.1 shows the trends in private consumption expenditure as a per centage of GDP in the last nine years.

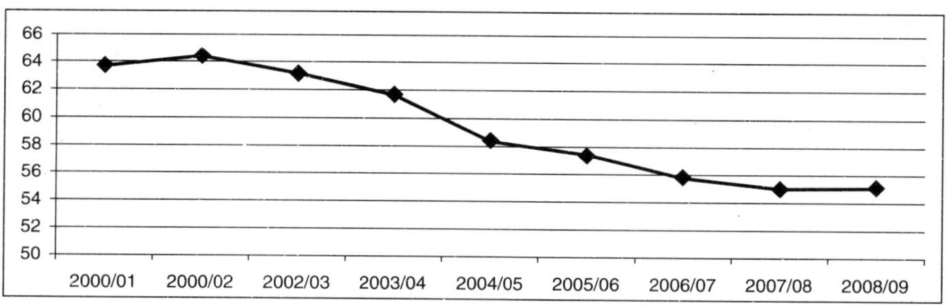


**FIGURE 3.1** *India: Private final consumption expenditure 2000/01–2008/09 (% of GDP)*

Though the ratio has gone down steadily over the years, consumption expenditure remains the largest component of aggregate demand.

## *What Determines Aggregate Consumption Expenditure?*

Here we need to pose a question: How does an individual decide how much of his/her income to consume and how much to save? Once we are able to identify the factors, which govern a person's decision between consumption and savings, we will be in a better position to understand what causes fluctuations in consumption demand and how macroeconomic policies can influence this important component of aggregate demand in an economy. We will first provide a framework for analyzing consumer behaviour based on the existing research work (see Box 3.1) and then use the framework to understand macroeconomic demand management in an economy.

The framework can be developed based on the following premises:

1. We all want to have a smooth consumption throughout our lifetime. We do not want to consume whatever we have during our working life and be left with little or nothing after retirement. A smooth consumption pattern maximizes our welfare.
2. The lifetime consumption path that we choose depends on our lifetime income. Lifetime income has two components: (a) the income that we expect to get out of work, and (b) the income (the rate of return) that we expect to receive from our wealth, held in the form of various assets.
3. While arriving at lifetime income, we also make a distinction between permanent and transitory income. Permanent income is more persistent (an average lifetime expected income) and transitory income is a random deviation from average income. For example, if a tax cut is perceived to be temporary, it will not be viewed as a permanent increase in income from work, and will therefore, not affect consumption path to any significant extent and vice versa. On an average, consumption is proportional to permanent income. By the same analogy, lifetime consumption is also proportional to lifetime permanent income.
4. Finally, we save/accumulate assets during our working life in order to support the desired level of consumption, we want to have when we have no work.[3]

But how do we know what will be our lifetime income from work and lifetime income from wealth? Obviously, no one knows the future with certainty. Therefore, these are based on what people *expect* to earn over a

[3] The actual amount will vary given the uncertainty of when death will occur, existence of social security, interest rates, saving for bequests for heirs and various types of lifetime earnings. But all these considerations can be accommodated into the framework without losing the essence of the main argument.

considerable period of time. But how are these expectations formed? Let us look at it this way:

1. While individuals, indeed, plan to consume a proportion of their permanent income, they cannot actually ascertain what their permanent income will be. Future is unknown and probabilistic. The individuals, however, know their current and past actual incomes at any given point of time with certainty. If someone asks them, what will be their income 15 or 20 years hence, clearly, they can extrapolate their future incomes on the basis of their current and past incomes. Therefore, while the focus, all the time, is on lifetime permanent income, current and past incomes, with varying weights, form an important basis for arriving at potential future income.
2. In other words, permanent income is based on long-run expected income and, expectations are continually revised in the light of current and past actual experience.

Let us now integrate the above points and draw some implications. We said that (a) people try to maintain the highest smooth consumption path they can get, (b) this is derived from people's expectations about permanent lifetime income both from work and wealth and, (c) in forming expectations, current and past income from wealth and work play an important role. The implication of this is that any setback to current income from wealth or work, if perceived as permanent, will change people's expectations about lifetime income and these expectations are also likely to influence current consumption and saving decisions. For example, if consumers, based on current experience, expect future income growth, either from work or wealth, to slow down, then, given the framework, they would cut down current consumption and instead, try to save more as a precaution against future shortfalls.

So what causes fluctuations in consumption demand? Let us, for the time being, assume that the wealth income remains constant. Then, change in consumption expenditure will depend on change in real disposable labour income. Real disposable labour income could decrease in an absolute sense if other components of aggregate demand decrease, that is, the actual growth of GDP slows down. It can also come down in a relative sense if personal taxes or consumer interest rates go up,[4] since both reduce the disposable

[4] We have seen in the previous chapter the relationship between disposable income and taxes. Since many of the purchases of consumer goods, particularly consumer durables, are financed through borrowings, an increase in the interest rates also, effectively, reduces the disposable income available for the purchase of various consumption goods.

income of the consumer even though absolute incomes have not changed. Note, however, that both personal tax rates and consumer interest rates and level of economic activity, in general, can be influenced by macroeconomic policies, namely fiscal and monetary policies. Therefore, we can say that one component of change in consumption expenditure, other things being equal, is due to change in policy-induced variables, and to that extent, amenable to macroeconomic policy changes.

"Other things," however, are not equal. While it is understood that wealth income, ordinarily, does not change very much,[5] it can, at times, get adversely affected if there is massive erosion of wealth due to a crash in the stock market or a crash in the real estate market, created, let us say, by a bubble burst. When this happens, people's expectations of life time income change. Their sentiments turn negative. And, if the negative sentiment is a prolonged one, it can not only slow down consumption expenditure out of wealth but also out of labour income, independently of what happens to policy-induced variables. Policy-induced changes in disposable work income may fail to generate the desired change in consumption spending. Instead, people may decide to save for the uncertain period ahead.

To summarize, consumption expenditure has two components: (a) induced component, whereby consumption can be induced by macroeconomic policy variables like tax rates and interest rates etc., and (b) an autonomous component driven by sentiment, which can affect consumption, independently of what happens to policy-induced variables. From this, it follows that when sentiments are stable, macroeconomic policies can play a very effective role in inducing changes in consumption and through those changes in aggregate demand. But if the autonomous component is very strong, then it may render macroeconomic policies ineffective because the challenge before the policy makers becomes not just coming out with a set of policies, which influence tax rates or interest rates but coming out with a set of policies, which additionally bring about a change in the sentiment of the people. Since sentiments are driven by perceptions and expectations of the people, policy credibility, on a sustained basis, becomes very important. Understandably, these things take a long time to become effective and the slowdown prolongs.

We mentioned earlier that the U.S. economic revival hinges heavily on revival of consumption expenditure, let us take two examples from the United States to gain a better insight into the issues related to consumption within our framework. In the United States, in the 1990s, there was a genuine

---

[5] Random fluctuations in actual rate of return will always happen and that is normal.

technological revolution in the form of an IT revolution, which considerably enhanced the prospects of increasing the production of goods and services in the economy. However, the share prices of IT companies were driven up by the financial market to levels that were disproportionate to the opportunity offered by the IT sector in terms of more production of goods and services. Stock prices were too high to be justified by their earnings prospects. As a result of the manifold rise in the share prices, two things happened. On the investment side, massive investments, both from within and outside United States, ensued in the IT sector in optical fibre cables, business to business, business to consumer, and other IT-related activities. On the consumption side, people found a phenomenal rise in their net worth consequent to an increase in share prices. They used their net worth to borrow and spend on all sorts of goods and services. This resulted in setting up of new capacity in non-IT sectors as well. There was an impressive rise in consumption expenditure because of positive sentiment and was largely driven by the autonomous component of consumption. Nothing worth mentioning had happened in the induced variables. And, this continued for a number of years. People started forming expectations that boom time was here to stay.

However, there was an excess capacity in the IT sector and the past rate of growth could not be sustained. The bubble burst. Share prices tumbled. Consumers found their wealth diminishing and they were in debt. Non-IT sectors also ended up with unsold inventories and unutilized capacity. The rate of unemployment went up. Sentiments turned negative. The policy-induced variables were activated. The Federal Reserve Chairman, Alan Greenspan resorted to several interest rate cuts in a row; President George Bush announced massive tax cuts. But the autonomous component of consumption (negative sentiment) was strong and it outweighed the positive signals emanating from the policy-induced changes. People decided to save more out of their increased disposable income from the tax cut and decided to retain high-cost debt from the interest rate cuts, rather than spend more. The problem got aggravated by the terrorist attack and Afghan war. It took longer than usual for policies to revive the economy.

In the more recent period, the crash in the property prices in the United States, as a result of the sub-prime crisis, has resulted in a massive erosion of wealth and also a financial meltdown.[6] The impact has been considerably more severe than the previous case cited so much so that no part of the world is spared from its spill over effects. The consumer

[6] We will discuss sub-prime crisis and financial meltdown in detail in Chapter 6.

sentiment has turned negative. Once again the effectiveness of fiscal and monetary policies to revive the economies has considerably weakened. It is taking lot more time to bring about the desired effect. In this context, we will say that it is more the autonomous than the induced component, which is driving consumer behaviour in the United States and many other parts of the world.

The mindset of an average American consumer can be conceptualized as follows: his wealth has been eroded; he is in debt; job security does not exist, and he has not saved much. His perception of lifetime income has changed and he wants to save more in order to redistribute his income more evenly over a period of time. The policy-induced changes, i.e., tax cuts and interest rate cuts are not bringing about the desired results due to two reasons. First, the autonomous component, in terms of negative sentiment, is very strong and, second, the American consumer does not believe that tax cuts and interest rate cuts are permanent to warrant a faster growth of current consumption. The United States economy is now looking for a more credible indicator for turning the negative sentiment around and that is, more employment. Somehow, this indicator is eluding the policy makers. Even though there are early signs of revival, it is turning out to be a jobless revival and, hence, its sustainability is in question.

Examples of similar happenings can also be cited from other countries.[7] The Japanese slowdown in the 1980s, for example, started with a manufacturing boom, which drove the share prices disproportionately up. The bubble burst. Subsequently, the weak financial institutions in Japan could not cope with the slowdown and it led to a full- fledged financial crisis. In India, though not supported by rigorous research, many people feel that the so called "dream" budget of the then finance minister P. Chidambaram (1997-98) failed to induce the desired increase in consumption because of a stock market scam and a real estate price crash, which just preceded it, which led to many people losing their wealth. Once again, the negative effect of the autonomous component outweighed the positive effect of the policy-induced changes in the budget.[8]

[7] The severity will vary from country to country depending on the consumers' exposure to capital and property markets. In the United States, such exposures are stronger than in other parts of the world.

[8] There is a view, particularly in the American context, that consumers do not base their consumption on "hopes and fears" but on cash flow, which can very well be induced by tax cuts and interest rate cuts. But, clearly, weak labour and financial markets, terrorist

The manager can learn much from this section. First, considering the sheer size of consumption in the aggregate demand, trends in consumption has to be carefully monitored.[9] Second, consumption expenditure is based on a profile of lifetime consumption, which in turn, depends on expected permanent lifetime income from wealth and work. Third, changes in consumption have an induced component and an autonomous component. If the autonomous component is stable, changes in consumption demand are amenable to macroeconomic policy changes. If the autonomous component is very strong, macroeconomic policies may take much longer to have the desired effect.

The implication of the above points on demand is that (a) fiscal and monetary policies, at times, may fail to effect the desired change in the consumption expenditure, if the overall consumer sentiment is negative, (b) even if sentiments are normal, consumption may not respond to changes in the real disposable labour income, if the change in income is not perceived to be permanent. This applies particularly to announced tax cuts and, (c) consumption may go up even if real disposable labour income does not, if expectations are positive.

## 3.2.2 Investment Demand

### *What is Investment Demand?*

Unlike aggregate consumption expenditure, which is for *current* consumption of final goods and services, aggregate investment expenditure is for purchase of new assets, which will help in the production of *future* goods and services. Examples of investment goods will be purchase of new machinery, expenditure on setting up a new power plant or a new automobile plant, among thousands of other capital goods, which are used in the production process. It is important to make a distinction between investment in stocks and shares and investment in newly produced capital equipment. The former is a portfolio reallocation and does not result in the creation of new assets; the latter does. In macroeconomics, investment refers to the latter only.

---

threat, highly unpredictable capital and property markets have dampened, for the average consumer, both his confidence and his expectations of the future.

[9] In the United States, the University of Michigan reports the consumer confidence index; in India, these are reported, from time to time, in business newspapers based on surveys and also by think tanks like National Council of Applied Economic Research (NCAER).

## Box 3.1: How the Theory of Consumption Evolved

The framework developed in this chapter on what determines consumption expenditure derives from the following seminal works. Every other consumption theory is based, to varying degrees, on at least one of these works.

### Absolute Income Hypothesis

Absolute income hypothesis (AIH) is ascribed to Keynes[1] and it specifies consumption as a stable (if not linear) function of disposable income. Marginal propensity to consume (MPC) is defined as the amount consumed out of an additional rupee of income. Average propensity to consume (APC) is the ratio of consumption to income.

Keynes believed that MPC was between zero and one which means that if disposable income increased by, say, Rs. 100, consumption expenditure in response to change in disposable income will rise by less than Rs. 100. Keynes also believed that APC decreased as income increased.

Keynes was proved right in the short-term. But this had a major implication. Economists were worried that, if this also held true in the long run, secular stagnation would occur as economies prospered. This was because APC was believed to fall as income increased.

In the long run, however, APC was found to be constant. Economists then wanted to know what explained the difference between short-term and long-term consumption behaviour.

### Life Cycle Theory

Life cycle theory of consumption (LCT) is ascribed to Modigliani.[2] According to LCT, people like to maintain the highest, smooth consumption path they can get. The principal determinants of consumption are income and wealth. It can be surmised from the above that existing wealth is consumed over a person's life time and thus, the proportion

[1] Keynes, J. M. (1936), *The General Theory of Employment, Interest and Money*. Macmillan, London.

[2] Modigliani, F. (1954), Life cycle, individual thrift, and the wealth of nations, *American Economic Review*, 76, 297–313.

*(contd.)*

of existing wealth that is consumed each year is 1 over the number of years that person still has to live. Similarly, consumption from income depends on the number of years a person receives income from work relative to the number of years that this person still has to live and finance consumption from that income.

Modigliani, therefore, solved the puzzle regarding long-term constancy of APC by showing that APC depended on income–wealth ratio and, income and wealth grow together over time. An individual has the largest amount of wealth at the time of retirement. LCT can be expanded to take into account uncertainties such as when death will occur, existence of social security (pension, for example), the interest rate, savings for bequests for heirs, and various types of lifetime earnings.

However, LCT does not deal well with what should happen if incomes fluctuate erratically over time. Nor is it very forthcoming on how to arrive at lifetime consumption. For this, another theory, the permanent income hypothesis provides the answer. The PIH and LCT are not contradictory, but theories that complement each other.

## Permanent Income Hypothesis

Permanent income hypothesis (PIH)[3] views current income as the sum of permanent income and transitory income. Permanent income is more persistent while transitory income is a random deviation from average income.

On an average, consumption is proportional to permanent income. Studies which show that high income households have lower APCs (and APC falls as income rises). This is because of positive transitory income; but, over long periods of time APC remains constant because over these long periods of time, the variation in income is dominated by the permanent income.

PIH also addresses the question: how do we get hold of lifetime income? The idea is that consumption depends on what people expect to earn over a considerable period of time.

[3] Friedman, M. (1957), *A Theory of the Consumption Function*. Princeton University Press, Princeton, NJ.

How are these expectations formed in general? Individuals plan to consume a proportion of their permanent income (average life time expected income), but cannot actually ascertain what their permanent income is. They know only their current and past actual income at any given point of time. They use these as basis. An individual whose income is highly variable will put less weight on current income than individuals who receive a steady income stream.

We can now combine the LCT and PIH by saying that consumption is determined by wealth and, the weights given to annual income at different periods of time. We can also bring in elements of AIH by saying that current income and how it has changed in the past does matter in arriving at lifetime income and, thus consumption.

In order to understand how we arrive at investment, let us first define capital stock. Capital stock is the rupee value of new plants, capital equipment, machinery etc. at a point of time. We may, therefore, say that a company has employed a capital stock of Rs. 10 crores in the business. But this is not investment. Investment is the change in capital stock over a period of time. Investment is a flow while capital is a stock. We can calculate the investment flow by looking at the difference between the capital stock at the end of the period and the capital stock at the beginning of the period. In our example, if the capital stock in the period '*t*' is Rs. 10 crores and it increases to Rs. 11 crores in period '*t*+1', investment is Rs. 1 crore. Investment is, thus, the addition to the stock of capital each year.

Investment[10] accounts for close to 40 per cent of GDP in the Indian economy. Figure 3.2 shows the trends in investment demand in India between 2000/01 and 2008/09. Though investment demand constitutes a smaller proportion of aggregate demand when compared to consumption demand, it is a very important component of aggregate demand for at least two reasons. First, it is generally subject to wider fluctuations compared to consumption. In some years, investment may even register a negative growth just as in other years it may show big spurts. Therefore, it is an important factor explaining fluctuations in aggregate demand. We will see later in the chapter that the recent impressive growth of India's GDP is largely propelled by a smart rise in gross investment. Second, it affects

[10] By investment, we here mean business fixed investment like new plants, capital equipment, machinery etc. In this discussion, we exclude inventory and residential investment demand.

not only aggregate demand but also a country's production capacity, and thereby, the long-term growth potential of the economy.

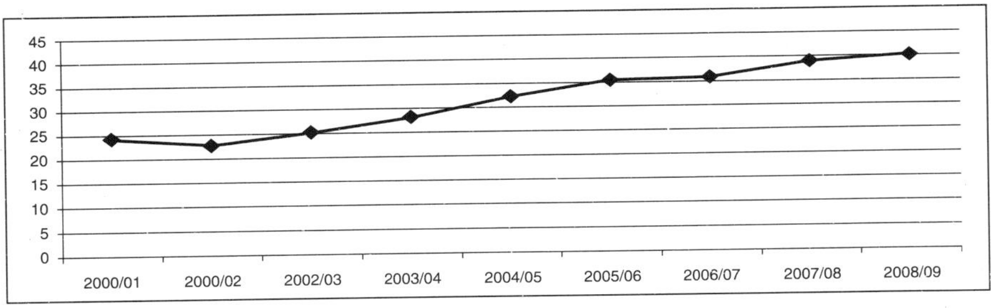


**FIGURE 3.2** *India: Trends in Gross Investment 2001/02-2008/09 (% of GDP)*

## *What Determines Aggregate Investment Spending?*

Let us consider addition to the stock of machinery. The question is how does an investor decide whether to purchase the new machinery or not? Obviously, there has to be a benefit from the purchase of new machinery and, there has to be a cost of the new machinery. If the benefits from the purchase of the new machinery outweigh the costs of the purchase of new machinery, it is worth investing in the new machinery. Otherwise, it is not.

Benefits depend on projected increase in the value of the output, as determined by the final demand, from the use of the new machinery. Since investment is undertaken for future production, it is the *expected* increase in output, which is the key. Similarly, in the case of investment also, it is the expected permanent increase in output that assumes particular relevance. In other words, from the point of view of assessing the benefits, investments are planned on the basis of expected permanent increase in output.

How are expectations formed? Once again, in arriving at expected permanent output, current output plays a role. If the current change in output is large and perceived to be permanent, people will form positive expectations about future output growth. Larger the current and expected output, larger will be the need to add to the existing stock of capital to produce that output. In simple words, other things being equal, if investors feel they can sell more at a later date, they will invest in new capital stock to produce more for that later date.

What about costs? Costs depend on the increase in the total costs arising from the acquisition of the machinery, usually given by the rental cost of capital. The idea behind the concept of rental cost of capital is as follows: if the machinery is rented, the user will have to pay a rate per hour of use of the machinery, equivalent to the rental cost of capital. But not everyone rents; in fact, most buy. Even then the idea is the same. If the machinery is owned, the concept of rental cost is still valid, except that the rental rate is now implicit. It is arrived at as if the firm is renting the machine from itself. Typically, this is given by the price of the machinery *multiplied* by the rate of depreciation *plus* market (nominal) rate of interest *minus* the expected rate of inflation.[11]

An example will clarify. Assume the person has purchased machinery. Suppose the price of the machinery is Rs. 50,000. Assuming that it will last for 10 years, and while fixing the depreciation rate at 10 per cent per annum, and the nominal interest rate at 15 per cent and inflationary expectations at 5 per cent per annum, giving a real interest rate of 10 per cent. Now, depreciation of 10 per cent per annum will cost the person Rs. 5,000 per annum. Market interest rate of 15 per cent per annum will cost another Rs. 7,500 per annum. So far the total cost is Rs. 12,500 per annum. Against this we must offset the impact of inflation of 5 per cent per annum, discussed in Chapter 2 in the section on inflation, as the inflation benefits the borrower by the amount of difference between the effective rate at which he borrowed (in this case 15 per cent) and the effective rate at which he will repay (in this case, 10 per cent). This comes to Rs. 2,500 per annum. The rental cost of capital per annum, then, is Rs. 5,000 + Rs. 7,500 – Rs. 2,500 = Rs. 10,000. Symbolically, $r_c = d + i - \pi^e$, where $r_c$ (10,000) is the rental cost of capital, $d$ (10 per cent or, Rs. 5,000) is the depreciation rate, $i$ (15 per cent or, Rs. 7,500) is the market rate of interest and $\pi^e$ (5 per cent or, Rs. 2,500) is the offsetting effect of inflation.

Finally, capital will be demanded up to the point where the addition to the value of output from the machinery is equal to its rental cost.

Let us now analyse the implications of what we have discussed so far from the point of view of managerial decision-making. We know that from the benefit side, the key determinant of investment is the expected growth in output. And from the cost side, the key determinants are depreciation rate ($d$) and ($i - \pi^e$), which, you will recall from Chapter 2, is nothing but the real interest rate. Further, if we assume depreciation to be a fixed proportion of capital stock, then the change in capital stock, from the cost side, is, indeed

[11] For a lucid treatment of the subject see Parkin, Michael. *Macroeconomics*, Prentice Hall, Englewood Cliffs, NJ, 1984, pp. 228–236.

a function of $(i - \pi^e)$ or, the real interest rate. Thus, assuming a given rental cost of capital, higher the expectations about future output growth; higher would be the demand for investment and vice versa. Similarly, for a given level of expectation about output growth, the lower the rental cost of capital the larger would be the demand for investment and vice versa. Of course various combinations are also possible.[12]

Now, real interest rate is a policy-induced variable and, as we will see later, monetary policy can influence the real interest rates through its influence on nominal interest rates and inflation. If we treat real interest rates slightly broadly as a proxy for all costs, then fiscal policy, by reducing corporate income tax, or increasing investment subsidy, can also induce changes in investment by reducing the rental cost of capital. However, businessmen's expectations about future growth of output can be subjective. Particularly, if new technology or economic liberalization is perceived to offer tremendous growth opportunities, business optimism will prevail, and investment in the economy can show a rapid rise, even if the cost of capital is not very conducive. Similarly, if the business sentiment is characterized as one of pessimism, investments may slow down, even if the cost of capital is cheap. Therefore, like consumption, investment also has two components: an induced component and an autonomous component. The induced component (change in real interest rates, taxes, subsidies etc.) is amenable to macroeconomic policy changes. The "gut" feeling of the businessman, on the other hand, drives the autonomous component. And if the autonomous component is very strong, macroeconomic policies may lose their effectiveness in bringing about the desired change in investment. Of course, extremes in business sentiments are not common occurrences, but today and for the last few years, it is the extremes in sentiments, characterized by business optimism or pessimism, which seem to be driving investment decisions globally.

In what follows, we will apply the framework developed above to understand how private sector investment decisions may have been taken in India in the post-liberalization period. We will frame a few questions to the Indian businessman and then study his answers to the questions to see how well they fit into our framework. The answers are based on the author's casual conversation with senior managers in the country.

[12] It is important to note here that the increase in investment demand, even in these conditions, may get arrested for two reasons: (a) if the gap between the existing stock of capital and the desired stock of capital is already very narrow; that is, if there is already an excess capacity and (b) if there is long time lag, for various reasons, between the decision to invest and actual investment.

*Question:* In 1993/94, both the nominal and real interest rates were very high. Why were you investing so much?

*Answer:* My investment was driven by the autonomous component, i.e., business optimism. Indian economy was opening up after being closed for 45 years and our expectations were that there would be a massive rise in demand across the board. Our investment was driven by expected future volume growth.

*Question*: Today the interest rates are ruling relatively soft. Why are you not investing?

*Answer*: Once again, the autonomous component is driving my investment decision. Except that now it is business pessimism. Interest rates may be ruling low, but I don't see any volume growth.

*Question:* We have specified the investment demand as depending on two sets of variables: expected output growth and real interest rates. But your investment decisions seem to be driven only by the expected output growth. Is there anything wrong with the specification of the investment demand? Don't real interest rates play a role?

*Answer:* No. Real interest rates and other policy-induced variables can certainly play an important role if the business sentiment is not going through extremes. Monetary policy, in this case, can play an enabling role and induce fresh investments. For example, now there are some early signs of revival of the economy. If RBI continues with its soft interest rate policy, this will speed up recovery and facilitate fresh investment.

*Question:* What lessons do I draw from this interview?

*Answer:* All sharp rises and sharp falls in investment are caused by the autonomous variables. These are mostly driven by expectations and are caused by certain shocks in the economy like fundamental changes in the economic policy, financial sector collapse and so on. Macroeconomic policies, in such situations, can become less effective. However, when business sentiment does not show extremes, macroeconomic policies can play an important role in stimulating investment.

*Question*: How does one tackle extremes in business sentiments?

*Answer:* In order to avoid erring on the side of excess, it is important to emphasize the role of correct demand forecasting. On the other hand, if the extreme is on the side of pessimism, policy credibility is important.

This stylized conversation sums up the main issues with regard to decision on investment in an economy. Like consumption, investment also has an autonomous component and an induced component. When the autonomous component is strong, macroeconomic policy induced changes may not be very effective. Again, as in consumption, investment is driven by expectations of permanent increase in output. An increase in demand during Deepawali festival, for example, does not lead to an increase in investment because this is not considered as permanent. However, unlike consumption, investment tends to be more volatile because, as our stylized conversation reveals, even if the increase in output/demand is considered permanent, investment may proceed very fast, initially, "to get there before someone else does", but this may be short-lived and vice versa. On the other hand, in case of consumption, if the income rise is considered permanent, consumption will rise at a smooth pace.

## 3.2.3 Government Expenditure

What determines government demand for goods and services in an economy? True, over a period of time government expenditure is induced by the level of income (GDP) in the country. Cross-country comparisons show that in countries where the level of GDP is high, the proportion of GDP accounted for by government expenditure is also high. But it must be admitted that at any point of time, change in government expenditure is an autonomous variable, given to political and economic considerations prevailing at that point of time and may not reveal a rational behaviour. Scattered evidence from other countries (mostly western countries), of course, seem to suggest the following[13]:

1. Government spending goes up just before the elections and comes down after that
2. Countries, which have coalition governments, have higher government deficits, and
3. Countries, which face frequent changes in the government, also leave a larger size of the deficit for the next government to cope with.

These are interesting findings and one can, perhaps, relate these to government expenditure in India in selected periods. But, by and large, government expenditure, indeed, is autonomous. It depends on a complex political bargaining process. And that has major implications, both positive

[13] Sachs, Jeffery D, and Felipe Larrain, *Macroeconomics in the Global Economy*, Prentice Hall, Englewood Cliffs, NJ, 1993, pp.206–208.

and negative, for the conduct of macroeconomic policies. We will defer discussion of such issues to the next chapter on fiscal policy.

### 3.2.4 Net Exports (*X* – *M*)

Finally, what does net export demand depend on? Let us answer this with the help of Table 3.1.

*Table 3.1 Determinants of net exports (X – M)*

| Items<br>(1) | Home country's GDP up<br>(2) | Other country's GDP up<br>(3) | Real exchange rate up<br>(4) |
|---|---|---|---|
| Net exports (X – M) | Down | Up | Up |

The essence of columns 2 and 3 of Table 3.1 is that if GDP increases, import demand increases. This implies that imports are a positive function of income. This happens because as GDP increases, we demand more of goods and services, which include both domestically produced and imported goods and services. Column 2, for example, says that if Indian GDP increases other things remaining the same, it will lead to an increase in India's import demand. Therefore, our net exports will come down or the current account will worsen. Column 3 similarly says that if foreign incomes go up, other things remaining the same, foreign demand for imports (which are our exports) will rise. Thus, our net exports will increase and the current account will improve. It follows, as we discussed earlier, that countries which depend heavily on export demand for a sustained growth in their GDP, have to rely heavily on growth of GDP in other countries which are buyers of their products. If incomes in the buyer countries slow down, it may have a repercussion effect on export-driven economies also.

While columns 2 and 3 capture the effect of changes in income on net exports, column 4 captures the price effect. Column 4 says that, holding incomes constant, if the real exchange rate of rupee rises or, a real depreciation takes place,[14] this means that prices of imported goods and services have increased relative to domestic prices of same goods and services. The competitiveness of our products increases as our products become relatively cheaper compared to imports. As a result, both we and foreigners buy more of our domestically produced goods and services. Our exports increase but

[14] Go back to the section on exchange rates in Chapter 2 to brush up on real exchange rates.

imports, correspondingly, do not and our net exports go up. The opposite will hold true, if real exchange rate of rupee falls or there is a real appreciation.

When net exports change in response to change in incomes (GDP), we call it the income effect and when net exports change in response to changes in real exchange rates, we call it the price effect. The final impact on net exports is the sum of income and price effects. For example, presently Indian rupee is depreciating, suggesting a positive price effect, which should improve our net exports. However, foreign (our buyers) income growth continues to be sluggish, suggesting a negative income effect, which should worsen our net exports position. Since Indian export growth has remained sluggish for past several quarters in a row, we will conclude that the negative income effect is stronger than the positive price effect.

## 3.3 Section Summary

We can learn several concepts from the above discussion on determinants of aggregate demand. It is important to understand that both investment and consumption have an autonomous component and an induced component. In normal times, when sentiments are stable, any fluctuation in consumption and investment demand can be addressed through fiscal and monetary policies. However, when sentiments show extreme behaviour in terms of either optimism or pessimism, macroeconomic policies may not be very effective in the short run. Extreme sentiments are, of course, not regular events and develop usually in response to certain shocks or rigidities in the economy. Today, in the global context, consumption and business sentiment is driven largely by the autonomous component. Economic recovery, therefore, is slow.

An off-shoot of this discussion is that, in extreme situations, if changes in private sector consumption and investment demand cannot be effected quickly through macroeconomic policies, government expenditure, at least theoretically, can play an important role in bringing about the desired change. But then the question arises as to why it is not able to stabilize the economies of the world? Clearly, as we will see in the next chapter, the quality of government expenditure holds the key. Moreover, when government expenditure is largely the result of political bargaining process, quality cannot always be assured.

Finally, we discussed the external sector demand. The discussion showed that imports were a positive function of GDP growth. In other words, in a globally integrated world, if GDP of a country goes up, the effect is felt not only on the domestic economy, but it also results in an increase in foreign incomes through higher net exports. On the other hand, real depreciation of the currency increases the country's competitiveness in the world markets. As a result, domestic income is increased but foreign income is reduced.

## 3.4 THE INDIAN CASE

In this section, we will attempt a macroeconomic assessment of the Indian economy. We will argue that macroeconomic policies work best when there are few inhibitions in the smooth transmission of a set of policy measures towards achieving their desired objectives. In the previous sections, we have highlighted the role of negative sentiments, usually ascribed to shocks, which may undermine policy effectiveness. In this section, we will additionally highlight the role of structural rigidities coming in the way of effective conduct of macroeconomic policies. Not just in India, but also in many transition and emerging economies, which are embarking on free market policies, structural rigidity is posing a stumbling block in the way of proper functioning of policies.

We begin by giving a brief account of how economic policies in India have evolved over the years.

### 3.4.1 Indian Economic Policy (1950–1990)

At the end of British rule in India, India's per-capita income had stagnated, standard of living was very poor, industrial development was lacklustre and a disproportionately large section of the population was dependent on agriculture, which itself was backward. The state of the economy at that time and the economic policies followed by the British, which resulted in the current state, had, thus, a decisive influence on the framing of economic policies in the post-independence period.

First, there was a great disillusionment with the idea of free enterprise in an economy where infrastructure facilities were poor, per-capita income and the levels of savings were extremely low and there was great inequality in the distribution of income. Second, the idea of free trade was ridiculed, and was considered tonot to reflect comparative advantage enjoyed by countries, as it could easily be manipulated to meet the individual needs of a country. Third, there was an export pessimism prevailing since exports were looked upon as drain of resources out of the country. Fourth, foreign investment was equated with foreign domination, but since one could not do without foreign capital, debt was preferred to equity and that too, under strict monitoring. Fifth, core of economic development was considered to lie in rapid industrialization. Sixth, within industrialization, capital goods or heavy industries were seen as requiring special emphasis. Seventh, rapid industrialization was desirable also for the growth of agriculture, employment, services etc. as industry had strong backward and forward linkages and finally, the state must play an active and central role in the development process through planning.

Out of this thinking process emerged India's post-independent economic policies, which developed essentially as an antithesis of British economic rule in India. And, interestingly, there was unanimity of opinion on the imperative of following this course of action.

India, thus, embarked on a course of planned economic development whereby the Government attempted to coordinate, influence and control some of the key economic variables like GDP, consumption, employment, investment, saving, exports, imports etc. to achieve the set development objectives. The broad objectives were the following:

1. Rapid growth in production with a view to achieving a higher level of national and per-capita income.
2. Full employment.
3. Reduction of inequalities in income and wealth.
4. Socialistic pattern of society, with a democratic framework, based on equality and justice and absence of exploitation.

The strategy of planned economic development emphasized rapid industrialization based on increasing production of coal, electricity, iron and steel, heavy machinery, heavy chemicals and other infrastructure industries to increase India's capital base and reduce dependence on imports. Particularly, small scale and cottage industries were also allowed to operate for the production of consumer goods since heavy industrialization had a long gestation period. The assumption underlying this strategy was that industrialization would help draw surplus labour away from agriculture into industry, thereby, reducing unemployment. It would also help the growth of agriculture through backward and forward linkages. Besides, special measures to improve productivity of agriculture were to be initiated. Foreign capital was to be obtained mainly through concessional loans. On paper, there was a mention of need for generating export surplus, but in reality, there existed no road map to achieve this. Finally, social development objectives, i.e. equality and justice, were to be achieved partly through growth trickling down to different sections of the population and partly through fiscal policy measures. Thus, a rapid and balanced economic development was ensured under this strategy.

The specific elements of policy can now be discussed first for industry, then agriculture and finally, social development. To foster industrial development, the main policy measures adopted were the following:

1. Trade and regulatory regimes designed to shield industrial producers from competition. This took the form of very high tariffs, industrial licensing of production and investment, Monopoly and Restrictive Trade Practices (MRTP) Act to put a restriction on scale, scope and location, Foreign Exchange Regulation Act (FERA), export restrictions and so on. The whole idea was to protect Indian industry from external competition, have restrictions on foreign investment, direct domestic investment and encourage more medium- and small-sized units (through reservations) rather than big ones to avoid concentration of economic power in the private sector.
2. Directed allocation of subsidized credit through the commercial and developmental banking system. Interest rates were administered and financial institutions were mandatorily required to lend for specific purposes at the administered interest rates. Exchange rates were also fixed. They were fixed at a level, which did not correctly reflect the economic value of the foreign exchange. In other words, the exchange rate was overvalued. Thus, financial sector and exchange rate controls were aimed towards ensuring an inexpensive source of credit and cheap imports for the government.
3. Price controls were imposed for many products. Additionally, a rigid labour law, whereby it was difficult to shed labour was in place.
4. Finally, direct public investment in industrial activities. Under this, core industry was in the Public Sector of which the government was 100 per cent equity holder. The private sector was expected to work in line with the overall objectives of economic planning but, as stated above, was under strict regulation.[15]

[15] It should be noted that there was some attempt at liberalization of the industrial sector in the 1980s, particularly, in respect of industrial licensing, MRTP, small-scale sector etc. But those were piece-meal attempts. Major thrust on liberalization came only in 1991, to which we devote a separate section in this chapter.

In respect of agricultural sector, government policies were directed primarily towards the crop sector and, within that, mainly food grains, followed by edible oils, sugar and cotton. The broad objective of the policy was to ensure reasonable supplies to domestic market. And this was achieved, initially, through larger investment in irrigation and agricultural extension but subsequently technological change played an important role.

In the crop sector, on the output side, a procurement price[16] was fixed, which in times of surplus worked as a minimum support price at which the government was ready to purchase any amount offered to it. At other times, the government mandatorily procured a part of the grain at the procurement price and distributed it to the vulnerable section of the population through the network of ration shops. On the input side, there was an explicit subsidy on fertilizer. Additionally, there were implicit subsidies on irrigation, power and credit.

A need to mop up surplus for domestic use resulted in trade restrictions. These included quantitative restrictions on exports and imports by way of import and export licensing, "canalization" in which only one specified parastatal was allowed to import or export the commodity, and, the use of minimum export prices. In the area of domestic trade, there were from time to time, restrictions on inter-state movement of agricultural products and other types of controls.

As regards, non-crop sector, government policies were formulated with the intention of regulation and control under the assumption that these were "elitist" products. Taxes were high and there was no co-ordinated effort to give a push to the agro-industries.

On the social front, government gave considerable emphasis on higher education. World-class institutes of higher learning were set up. They were highly subsidized. In the process, primary education was neglected to some extent. As far as poverty eradication was concerned, governmental policies shifted, as it gained more experience, with time. Initially it was assumed that rapid growth was the key. Once that set in, the benefits, through various linkages, would trickle down to different sections of the population and incomes and employment, as a whole would rise. However, sometime in the mid-1970s, it became clear that a growth-oriented strategy as a means of mitigating poverty and unemployment had its shortcomings. Given the

[16] Procurement price is the price fixed by the government for procuring grain from the farmers. Minimum support price covers cost of production plus some normal profits. Minimum support price is lower than the procurement price.

structural and institutional inequalities that existed in the agricultural sector (where majority of the poor live) with regard to ownership of land, availability of water, resource endowments, access to credit and modern inputs etc., the production increased rapidly only on irrigated areas and on relatively well-off farms. On small farms and rain fed areas, which dominated the agricultural scene, production either stagnated or advanced very slowly. Another aspect, which came to the fore, was that growth had to be very rapid in order for it to generate income and employment, and thus, purchasing power for the poor.

Thus, subsequently, it was recognized that a strategy with primary emphasis on increased production could not attain its objective on a sustained basis unless all groups took part in this activity. To ensure this policies and programmes had to address all groups and areas and had to be so designed. Secondly, a production oriented strategy, even it succeeded in raising output, could not be counted upon as a principal means of simultaneously eradicating poverty since its ability to generate additional employment and income on its own was rather limited and needed to be supplemented by other subsidiary enterprises both in agriculture and non-agricultural sectors.

A three-pronged strategy was thus formulated to achieve increased production and better standard for its people simultaneously. First, accelerated growth and improved pattern of production to ensure that all groups of farms on both irrigated and un-irrigated areas could participate in the process. Second, special programmes and policies for alleviation of poverty, in addition to increased production, were announced. Thus, asset creation programmes, employment generation programmes and minimum needs programmes were launched both in rural and urban areas and finally, various intervention programmes were developed to meet the more pressing problems of hunger and malnutrition.

## *Did the Policies Work?*

Once again let us consider each sector separately. As far as industry[17] is concerned, it registered a growth of 6 per cent per annum between 1951 and 1989. The annual increase was 7.7 per cent between 1951 and 1965; it came down to 4 per cent between 1966 and 1980 and rose again to 7.7 per cent between 1981 and 1989. Industry's share in GDP also rose from 15 per cent in 1950 to 27 per cent in 1990.

[17] See, for example, World Bank, *India: An Industrializing Economy in Transition*, Washington DC, 1989.

The industrial policies achieved their objectives in many ways. The importance given to heavy industries increased the share of basic and capital goods industries from less than 10 per cent of manufacturing value added in 1950 to 57 per cent two decades later. Public sector investment accounted for more than half of investment in manufacturing, and was pivotal in many basic and heavy goods, as was postulated in the policy. India's dependence on agro-industries dropped from 47 per cent in 1960 to 25 per cent in 1984. A diverse variety of goods were being produced and a high degree of self-sufficiency achieved. In the 1980s, for example, imports accounted for only 5 to 10 per cent of the total domestic consumption of manufactured goods in India. Industrial decentralization had been impressive. Industry was well spread and the initial dominance of Calcutta, Bombay and Madras was on the wane. Better infrastructure and availability of skilled labour helped considerably in the spread of industry. The role of foreign companies had dropped sharply. The state was in control. Managerial and technical capability had been built up over a period of time within the country. India was self-reliant in industry.

However, there were also negative points of the policy of industrialization adopted by India. And almost all of these resulted from the policy. To start with, there was no competition. Because there was no competition research and development (R&D) efforts were very low. Technological up gradation was not a high priority item. Again, emanating from the above, incremental capital–input ratio went up considerably up in the 1970s and fell only marginally in the 1980s. Total factor productivity also came down. Capacity utilization fell. The industrial strategy also failed to achieve the desired rise in employment. Nor did it substantially check concentration of economic power. A few large firms continued to reap high profits.

It is, therefore, clear that policies gave little consideration to comparative advantage and specialization. Much of the advantage gained was at a high cost. The policies also gave low importance to use of internal competition, import competition and export rivalry as devices to guide adaptation and stimulate innovation and cost cutting. There emerged deeply entrenched interest groups, which had benefited from the existing industrial set up and wanted it to continue. This resulted in favouritism, nepotism and widespread corruption. Public sector jobs came to be used as a means to distribute favours, pricing policy was sub-optimal, return to investment fell to pathetically low levels, and autonomy in decision making was missing. In short, India was industrialized but most inefficiently[18].

How did the agricultural sector perform? Agricultural sector performed well. Between 1950 and 1980 food grain production increased by 2.8 per cent per annum. A larger share of this increase, over a period of time, came from productivity gains and multiple cropping made possible by the development in the 1960s of new short-stemmed varieties of wheat and rice, which ushered in green revolution by taking advantage of improved and more regular supplies of water and fertilizer.

However, certain areas of concern remained in agricultural policy during this period. First, in the 1980s there was a drastic fall in the growth of investment in agriculture. As a result, R&D suffered, development of irrigation lagged behind plan targets and there was a perceptible slowdown in the growth of area under high-yielding varieties and fertilizer consumption. These factors adversely affected food grain productivity in the 1980s and the long-term trend in growth slowed down. Second, there was a substantial rise in subsidy both explicit (food and fertilizer) and implicit (credit, water, and electricity) causing a serious drain on the budget. Third, there was a continued neglect of the non-crop sector. In short, though India became self-reliant in agriculture, particularly food grains, question remained that at what cost and how long could this be sustained.

In respect of social sector development also, the story is the same. The achievements are not inconsequential. Over a period of 17 years from 1970–71 to 1987–88, for which comparable data are available, the proportion of population below poverty, both in rural and urban areas dropped significantly – from 46.17 per cent to 37.76 per cent in urban areas and from 58.75 per cent to 48.69 per cent in rural areas. Average life expectancy improved from 32.1 per cent in 1950–51 to 58.7 per cent in 1990-91. Death rate fell from 27.4 per cent to 12.5 per cent during the same period. Similarly, the literacy stood at 52.2 per cent in 1990–91 compared to 18.33 in 1950–51. Higher education made rapid strides in all areas during this period.

However, because of population growth, in an absolute sense, the problems of the social sector were still a matter of concern. The implementation of social sector programmes did not yield the desired results. The programmes

[18] Also see Bardhan Pranab, *The Political Economy of Development in India*, Oxford University Press, Delhi, 1984.

had not always reached the target group; leakages were high; the subsidy element had skyrocketed and above all, it was not clear at all if such massive expenditures in their present form should have continued.

## *Summing Up*

Indeed, after independence, we went in for a very rigid economic structure. Not only was production controlled but also the cost variables, like interest rates, prices and exchange rates were administratively set. The economic activity was, clearly, not driven by market forces but by government directive. There was little scope for macroeconomic policies to play their traditional role. Therefore, any discussion on macroeconomic policy climate for business would appear infructuous in such a regime.

Perhaps, a rigid structure was justified in India at the time of independence. Given the state of the economy at that time, market forces would have catered only to the well-off sections of the population who had means of access to the market.

Economic policies followed by India between 1950 and 1990 also made the country self-reliant both in industry and agriculture. A fair amount of success in social indicators was also discernible. But it also became clear that Indian economy was becoming a very high-cost economy. The lesson that we learnt was that controls, or a rigid structure, even if justified initially, could not be allowed to continue for an extended period of time. Controls bred inefficiency and corruption.

The above could be sustained for a period of time, particularly up to 1980–81, since on domestic account the government was, more or less, staying "within its means" (it was not borrowing to meet its day to day expenditure) and almost the entire deficit on the external account (current account) was financed through inflows of concessional loans, which kept the debt servicing burden low.

However, cracks started appearing in the strategy in the 1980s. Domestically, the government had started borrowing heavily to meet its day-to-day expenses (subsidies, interest payments etc.), which brought no return. Even in respect of such spending known to bring adequate return (i.e., capital expenditure), the actual returns came down perceptibly because of poor performance of public sector undertakings. On the external front, import costs were raising consequent to oil price hike, exchange rates had become unsustainable and India's access to concessional loans had drastically shrunk. Total government borrowings from all sources, domestic and external, had reached crisis levels by 1990–91. The external debt/GDP ratio went up from 17.7 per cent in 1984–85 to 24.5 per cent in 1989–90. Internally also, continued government borrowing raised the size of public debt to alarming levels and a large part of government revenue was going towards payment of interest on the debt. And, as we discussed in Chapter 2 (Section 2.1.12), government deficit fed into the current account deficit, which kept rising steadily until it reached 3.5 per cent of GDP and accounted for 43.4 per cent of exports in 1990–91.

There was nothing in the economic policy adopted during 1950–1990, which could make it responsive to these changing internal and external circumstances. India did not have a viable strategy for the management of the crisis. A change had become imperative.

## 3.4.2 Indian Economic Policy – Post-1991

The post-1990 economic policy, popularly known as the policy of economic liberalization, was launched in June 1991. It was in response to a crisis in the external sector where India was almost on the point of default. The reasons for this external crisis build-up were two-fold. First, a massive rise in the government deficit that spilled over to the current account deficit (Chapter 2, Section 2.1.12), and second, our inability to respond to external shocks (increase in oil prices, decreased access to concessionary loans etc.) by earning more foreign exchange because of structural rigidities, which made our products globally non-competitive.

The question before the Indian policy makers, in the wake of the crisis, was how to increase India's capability to earn more foreign exchange so that we could avoid getting into the type of a situation that India got into in 1990–91. The answer was to address the problems that caused the crisis. That is: (a) make the structure more competitive; and (b) contain government deficit, particularly wasteful expenditure, which not only increases the size of the debt but also spills over to the current account deficit.

The policy of economic liberalization, henceforth referred to as economic reforms, accordingly, has two components: (a) structural change; and (b) fiscal stabilization. Structural change aims towards removing structural hurdles, which come in the way of India becoming globally competitive.

This is in recognition of the fact that much of India's problem is of a structural origin and if structural rigidities are removed, then, given the technology, it is possible to achieve substantial increase in GDP. With technological breakthroughs the possibilities are immense. Thus, trade policy reforms have done away with most quantitative restrictions and have reduced the tariff levels; industrial policy has removed barriers to entry and limits on growth in the size of firms; regimes for foreign investment and foreign technology have been liberalized considerably; domestic tax structure has been rationalized; financial sector is deregulated to a degree and, so on. All these reforms were initiated as a part of "first generation reforms" and substantially completed. India is now grappling with "second generation reforms", which are politically more sensitive in nature and are, therefore, more difficult to implement. Examples of second-generation reforms will be privatization of public sector undertakings, an exit policy for labour, reforms of the agricultural sector, reforms of the state governments etc. These reforms, in view of their sensitive nature, are moving at a political pace, albeit in the right direction.

The Indian experience shows that there is no uncertainty about the direction of reforms. Irrespective of which government has come to power, the economic policy agenda has been the same. Coalition politics, where the government is represented by many parties (read, interest groups), thus, may slow down the pace of reforms but it is unlikely to change the direction of reforms.

Fiscal stabilization is emphasized for several reasons. We have already seen how government deficit can spill over to the current account deficit and cause a crisis. But what we have not discussed and will do so in Chapter 4 is that there also exists a very close relationship between government deficit and some of the key cost variables that affect the business sector, like interest rates, prices, tax rates and exchange rates. In summary, we can say that while structural changes, by removing structural barriers to entry, signal opportunities and challenges for business, fiscal stabilization focuses on the cost of doing business.

The relationship between stabilization measures and structural reforms has to be clearly understood. Without stabilization (i.e., stable prices, balance of payments, etc.) structural reforms cannot bring the desired results. On the other hand, even with the most successful stabilization, the economy cannot grow rapidly unless structural reforms are introduced. It is also important to understand that a balance has to be struck between these two policy measures. For example, a progressive reduction in the indirect tax rates as a part of structural reform, without broadening the tax base, will put additional strain on the stabilization objective. Similarly, financial deregulation will mean more by way of interest payments on the part of the Government and, hence, more pressure on the budget. Therefore, the pace and quality of the reforms is crucial to their success. Finally, it should be noted that while stabilization measures have a relatively quick impact, structural reforms take longer to bring results.

Studies[19] have shown that the impact of these policies is felt in phases. In the first phase, while the fiscal deficit correction (stabilization measures) helps in combating price rise and brings about a better balance in the external account, it adversely affects investment and growth because of demand contraction (remember '*G*' is a component of GDP). It can also, if prolonged, result in pessimistic expectations and dampen investment. In the second phase, structural reforms start bearing fruits. The rate of economic growth picks up. But in many areas the private sector goes through a "wait and watch" situation. It monitors factors like political stability, the government's commitment to reforms, and infrastructural support, which make structural reforms meaningful and pave the way from stabilization to growth. In the last phase, once the economy is stabilized, there is a sustained recovery.

How have we fared in India vis-à-vis structural reform and fiscal stabilization? On the structural reform side, as discussed earlier, we have covered a wide range of areas under these reforms. However, bottlenecks persist. These relate to rigid labour laws, infrastructural constraints, bureaucratic hassles, tardy pace of privatization, and higher tariffs relative to Asian neighbours and so on. In fact, in global comparisons, India does not look very good in either competitive indicators or institutional governance and transparency indicators. Nevertheless, it is worth repeating that even if the pace of structural reforms is slow, the direction has been right.

Coming to fiscal stabilization, the track record is mixed. Government deficit as a per centage of GDP, over a period of time, went up and down, but improved considerably in the recent years, up to 2007–08. In 2008–09 and 2009–10 government deficit took a turn for the worse. We will postpone discussion of the full implication of this to the next chapter. Right now, it is important to keep in mind that both structural features and the extent

---

[19] Serven Luis and Andres Solimano, "Private Investment and Macroeconomic Adjustment: A Survey" in *Research Observer*, 7(1), January 1992, The World Bank, Washington DC.

of fiscal stabilization are crucial to understanding the business climate in the country.

### 3.4.3 India's Economic Performance – Post-1990/91

There are several features of the post-1990–91 economic performance. First, India has reached a higher trajectory of growth. The highest growth achieved in the pre-liberalization period was 5.6 per cent per annum during 1981–91. As against that, during the 10-year period 1992–93 to 2001–2002 India's GDP growth was 6.1 per cent and it advanced further to around 8 per cent during the next decade. Correspondingly, average annual per-capita GDP growth accelerated from 3.2 per cent during 1981–91 to 6.2 per cent in the present decade.[20] Not only are the average growth of GDP and per capita GDP higher, deviations around trend are also smaller, thereby, suggesting a more stable overall growth pattern.

Second, the impressive growth in India's GDP in the recent years has been facilitated by a sharp rise in investment in the economy, financed largely by domestic savings (Figure 3.3). Of the four components of aggregate demand ($C + I + G + X - M$), $I$'s *contribution* to growth surpassed that of $C$ during 2002–07, though $C$ continued to be the largest component of GDP.

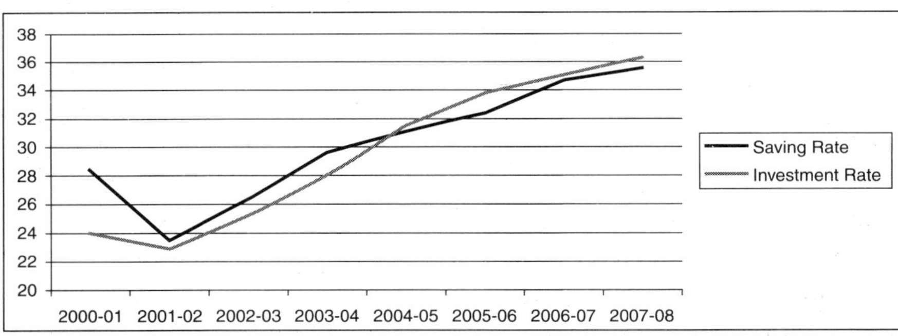


**Figure 3.3** *India: Saving and Investment Rates (% of GDP)*

Finally, the structure of the Indian economy is such that achieving 8 per cent or more growth of the economy on a sustained basis is no longer

[20] This based on a population growth of 2.2 per cent in the 1980s and 1.8 per cent in the present decade.

infeasible. For example, the share of services, industry and agriculture sectors in India's GDP today are estimated at 57, 28 and 15 per cent, respectively.[21] The average growth rate of services and industrial sectors between 2003–04 and 2007–08 was 10 and 9.5 per cent, respectively. The growth of agriculture sector was random, depending on weather. With this track record of services and industry sectors, even if agriculture growth is assumed to be zero, the weighted average growth will work out to 8.3 per cent.

However, there are areas for concern. First, as Table 3.2 reveals that while poverty levels, based on comparable data,[22] have come down over time, the absolute number of poor remains a formidable 300 million plus, almost one-third of India's population. Close to 75 per cent of those are in rural areas.

**Table 3.2:** ***Poverty ratio (% of population) and absolute number of poor in India***[a]

| Year | Rural % | Urban % | Total % |
|---|---|---|---|
| 1973/74 | 56.4 (261.3) | 49.0 (60.0) | 54.9 (321.3) |
| 1977/78 | 53.1 (264.3) | 45.2 (64.6) | 51.3 (328.9) |
| 1983 | 45.6 (252.0) | 40.8 (70.9) | 44.5 (322.9) |
| 1987/88 | 39.1 (231.9) | 38.2 (75.2) | 38.9 (307.0) |
| 1993/94 | 37.3 (244.0) | 32.4 (76.3) | 36.0 (320.4) |
| 2004/05 | 28.3 (220.9) | 25.7 (80.8) | 27.5 (301.7) |

[a] Figures in parenthesis are absolute numbers

*Source*: www.planningcommission.nic.in

[21] The services sector consists of trade, transport, storage, communication, finance, insurance, real estate, business services, public administration, defence and other services; the industrial sector consists of manufacturing, construction, electricity, gas and water supply; and the agricultural sector consists of agriculture, forestry and logging, fishing, mining and quarrying. http://www.finmin.nic.in Economic Survey, 2009–10, pp. 4–5.

[22] Recently an expert committee headed by Professor Tendulkar has suggested a broader definition and an improved methodology for estimation of poverty in India. However, even though the new methodology gives a higher estimate of poverty, the extent of poverty reduction in comparable per centage point decline between 1993–94 and 2004–05 is not very different from that inferred using old methodology.

Also, regional disparities have widened. Among major states, Orissa, Bihar, West Bengal and Tamilnadu had more than 50 per cent of their population below poverty line in 1983. By 1999–2000, while Tamilnadu and West Bengal had reduced their poverty ratios by nearly half, Orissa and Bihar continued to be the two poorest states with poverty ratios of 47 and 43 per cent respectively. In 2004–05, six states (including Orissa and Bihar) had close to or more than 40 per cent of population below poverty line. There is also some evidence to suggest that interpersonal inequality may have widened. What this means is that while the income of the poor have increased in certain regions leading to a fall in absolute poverty, the income of the non-poor have increased faster leading to a rise in relative poverty. Inequality in the distribution of income has, thus, grown.

The data on unemployment rates is also mixed (Table 3.3). In the post-liberalization period unemployment rate initially fell, but subsequently rose. Unemployment rate rose in the latter period despite a rising GDP growth, thus, casting aspersions on the nature of growth of overall GDP and its sustainability.

***Table 3.3: Unemployment rates in various NSS rounds—India***

| Year | Unemployment rate (% of labour force) |
|---|---|
| 1972/73 | 8.35 |
| 1977/78 | 8.18 |
| 1983 | 9.22 |
| 1993/94 | 6.06 |
| 1999/2000 | 7.31 |
| 2004/05 | 8.28 |

*Source*: www.planningcommission.nic.in

Finally, select health indicators (Table 3.4) show improvement over time but they still need to catch up with the progress made in GDP per-capita. These numbers also compare unfavourably with the progress made by other countries, including emerging economies. For example, life expectancy at birth in 2007 was 74 per cent in Sri Lanka and 73 per cent in China; similarly adult literacy rate during the same period was 93 per cent in China and 92 per cent in Indonesia. No wonder India's Human Development Index (HDI) ranking is 132 (Table 2.4) among 180-odd countries in the world.

*Table 3.4 India: Select health indicators*

| Parameter | 1991 | Current level |
|---|---|---|
| Crude birth rate per 1000 population | 29.5 | 22.8 (2008) |
| Crude death rate per 1000 population | 9.8 | 7.4 (2008) |
| Total fertility rate per women | 3.6 | 2.7 (2007) |
| Infant mortality rate | 80 | 53 (2008) |
| Adult literacy rate | 52 | 66 (2007) |
| Life expectancy at birth | 59.4 | 63.5 (2002-06) |

*Source*: www.finmin.nic.in Economic Survey – 2009–10

Who are the poor, unemployed and socially deprived people in India? Majority of them live in rural areas (even among urban poor a good part consists of rural migrants). They are either landless agricultural workers or small farmers with some land, but so small in size, that even with best cultivation practices they are unable to generate an income, which will sustain them through farming. The poor are also located in areas/regions, which are ill-served with infrastructure, both social and physical.

Why did we allow this kind of inequality to perpetrate? The answer is that we have not paid due attention to agriculture sector growth. A sector-wise growth of GDP growth, indeed, shows uneven trends (Figure 3.4).

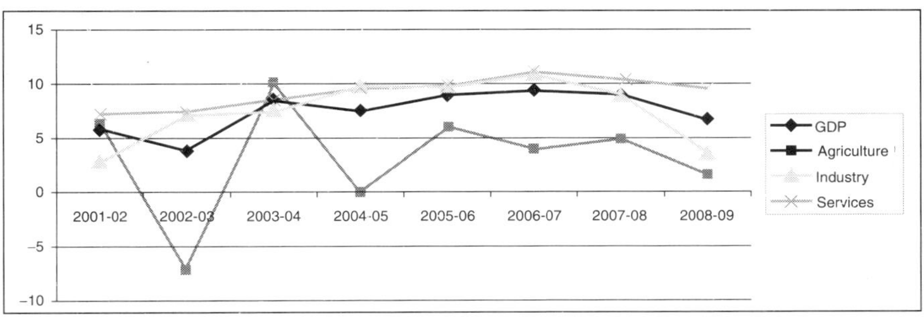


**FIGURE 3.4** *India: Sectoral Growth Rates*

Clearly, the growth of the agricultural sector has been random. In some years, it has been very high, in others negative. Agricultural sector growth has performed according to the rainfall pattern. Services and industrial sector growth, by contrast, are steadier. As mentioned earlier, given the share of agriculture in the GDP, it may not have impacted overall GDP growth too much, but considering the fact that this sector houses 75 per cent of the poor and supports almost 60 per cent of the labour force, its importance cannot be ignored in the interest of long-term sustainability of growth.

Figures 3.5 and 3.6 adequately capture the main reasons for the lacklustre performance of agricultural sector in India. The supply of cultivable land in India is inelastic. The future growth, thus, has to come from productivity gains. And, productivity growth in agriculture has failed to keep pace with the rate of growth of population, such that per-capita production of many crops has improved little over time. Figure 3.5 brings it out for cereals but the situation is no different in respect of edible oils, sugar and pulses.

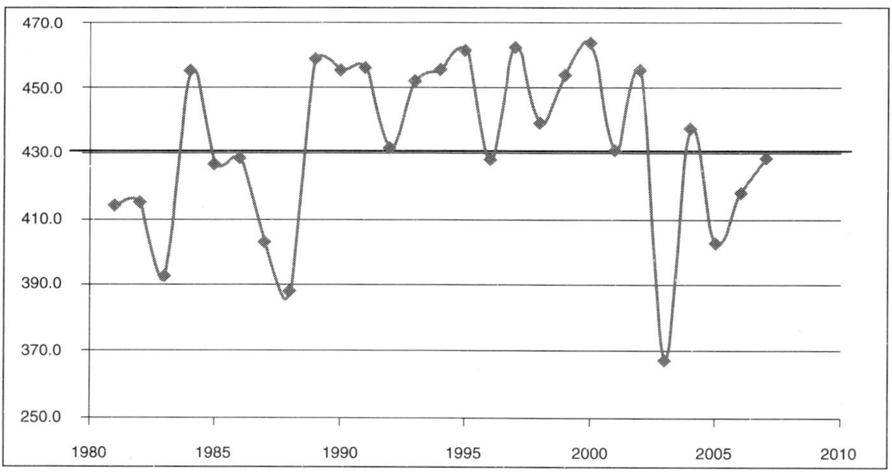


**FIGURE 3.5** *India: Per-capita Production of Cereals (grams per day)*

The reason for slow growth in productivity can be ascribed to lack of investment in the sector. As Figure 3.6 shows, the gross capital formation in agriculture is as a per centage of total gross capital formation, in real terms. It has been declining over time. This, combined with operational inefficiency and poor delivery system of existing infrastructure, has impacted research and development in high yielding varieties of seeds, investment in irrigation and other supporting infrastructure.

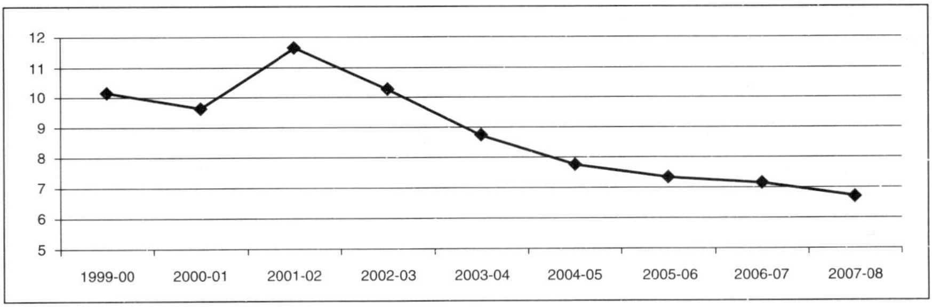


*Source:* www.planningcommission.nic.in

**FIGURE 3.6** *India: Gross Capital Formation (GCF) in Agriculture as % of Total GCF (1999–2000 prices)*

As the latest Economic Survey[23] succinctly puts it, "since farm productivity is not showing desirable growth there is urgent need to focus on research as well as better agricultural practices to ensure that productivity levels are increased in the shortest time possible. Special attention may be required for states with relatively low productivity. Production and productivity in pulses and oilseeds are of growing concern. A sizeable proportion of these items is met through imports. The scope of import of pulses is limited due to the limited number of countries producing it."

The survey goes on "to sum up, we need to address the challenges of agriculture sector through comprehensive and coordinated efforts. Renewed attention needs to be paid to improving farm production and productivity, better utilization of agricultural inputs, proper marketing infrastructure support, stepping up investment in agriculture with due emphasis on environmental concerns and efficient food management".

Where does the India story lead us? There are two parts to the story. In one part, growth is happening. In the other part, there is poverty and deprivation. The challenge confronting the policy makers is two-fold: (a) how to sustain growth over a longer period of time, and (b) how to use this growth to make it more inclusive.

Interestingly, the prescription for sustained growth along with poverty mitigation is common. That is, more investment in infrastructure, both social and physical. Services and industrial sector growth will face a roadblock, unless growth is supported by infrastructure by way of investment in

[23] www.finmin.nic.in, Economic Survey – 2009–10, pp. 207.

roads, airports, seaports, power and, so on. Mitigation of poverty similarly calls for investment in agriculture, education and health, rural roads and markets. Investment in infrastructure thus is a basic pre-requisite for long-term sustenance of India's growth story.

If we know that investment will trigger growth in India, what is coming in the way of stepping up investment? There are three ways through which we can give a boost to investment demand. First, remove the structural rigidities (e.g., stringent labour laws, reservations, high tariffs, administered prices, procedural delays, excessive presence of public sector etc.), which come in the way of undertaking investment. Second, change certain policy variables like interest rates and tax rates that can induce private sector investment demand. Finally, step up investment demand through direct government intervention by way of increased government spending. Of course, various combinations are also possible.

What are the implications of each? Any attempt to remove structural rigidities will have to be carefully weighed against the political costs of doing so. Such changes will, therefore, have to proceed at a political pace. In India where we have a coalition government and several parties are involved, it is safe to assume, that this process of change will be gradual. Now consider the second option. True, macroeconomic policy tools can be activated to induce changes in the aggregate demand, but, if the rigid structure acts as a barrier to entry, businessmen may not respond to policy changes enthusiastically. Finally, the option of government stepping in directly to boost investment will be constrained by the availability of funds. Of course, public-private participation offers promise, if the environment is right.

## 3.5 Chapter Summary and Conclusions

The lessons from this chapter for the manager are many. First, it is important to identify which component (s) of aggregate demand requires attention of the policy maker and focus on that. Second, it is important to appreciate that macroeconomic policies are one of the several ways through which changes in the aggregate demand can be impacted. Aggregate demand may not respond to changes in macroeconomic policies if there are structural rigidities in the economy or if sentiments are negative. Third, in emerging economies, including India, structural rigidities are still a bottleneck in the proper conduct of macroeconomic policies.

Specifically on India, while India has begun the process of liberalization and has also made considerable headway, structural rigidities play an important role in deciding the pace of change in demand for goods and services in the economy. Infrastructural constraints in power, transport, ports, roads etc. deter investment demand. Rigid labour laws, weak bankruptcy and exit laws, poor project delivery, problems with privatization process, red tapism and bureaucracy etc., have also hampered investments. In fact, as mentioned earlier, India fares rather poorly in global comparisons of competitiveness. It is also rated low in respect of institutional governance and transparency indicators. Clearly, in such circumstances, macroeconomic policies alone cannot stimulate demand.

The drivers of aggregate demand have to be analyzed in their totality. Figure 3.7 provides a schematic framework. It shows that ability to influence aggregate demand depends on three sets of factors. The first set consists of policy-induced factors, like changes in the interest rates, tax rates, exchange rates etc. A change in these variables could induce demand. A second set of factors, which govern aggregate demand, relates to people's perceptions about the future. Here, expectations that people form about the future becomes crucial to influencing demand. Finally, the economic structure also plays an important role in impacting demand. The more rigid the structure less will be the effect of any policy change on demand. For example, a soft interest rate or tax rate regime will unlikely to move demand, if prices are

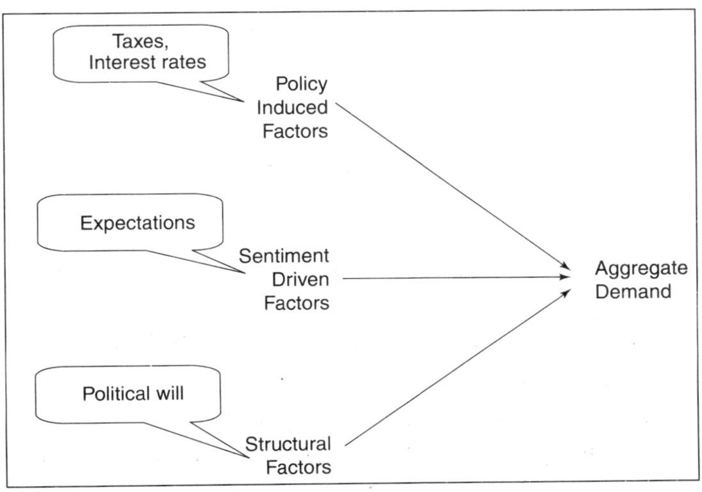


**FIGURE 3.7** *Determinants of Aggregate Demand*

controlled, labour laws are inflexible, there are problems in land acquisition, and bureaucratic delays are present, and so on. Structural considerations could, themselves, then, be the cause of negative sentiment.

Under these circumstances, what does the manager do? It is perhaps useful to proceed on the assumption that structural changes will be gradual in a country like India. But they are unlikely to change direction, given the stability in policy that has prevailed in India since economic liberalization. Economic activity must go on at the given pace. Therefore, instead of a knee-jerk reaction to any political change, the critical question the manager should be asking is: do we expect unexpected changes in rules, laws and policies that materially affect our business? The answer, usually, will be in the negative. Sentiments seldom take extreme behaviour, unless there are shocks of the type we discussed. When they do turn negative, however, conventional macroeconomic policy tools do not work. In those situations, there is usually pressure on government to kick-start the economy. The pros and cons of that have to be understood and that will be the focus of the next chapter. Finally, when sentiments are normal, and structural rigidities are not formidable, macroeconomic policies indeed play an important role in not only inducing demand but also setting the tone of cost variables like interest rates, prices, tax rates and exchange rates in an economy.

# REVIEW QUESTIONS

1. What are the various components of Aggregate Demand? Why is it important to break them down into C and I and further into private sector, government sector and net external sector demand?
2. What is meant by marginal propensity to consume? What is meant by marginal propensity to save? Why are these terms important to business?
3. If a country redistributes income from rich to poor what will happen to the overall demand for food? Why?
4. What determines consumption expenditure in an economy? What roles do current disposable income and wealth play in the determination of consumption expenditure?
5. What did we mean by autonomous and induced changes in consumption? Why are macroeconomic policies less effective if consumption is driven by the autonomous component?

6. Which will be greater? Marginal propensity to consume out of transitory income or permanent income? Why? If the government imposes a surcharge on income tax, what will be the impact on aggregate demand?
7. How is investment defined in economics? In what ways it is different from investment in fixed deposit of a bank or in shares?
8. What are the determinants of investment? Discuss the role that expectations play in investment decisions of a firm?
9. What is meant by rental cost of capital? How does it reduce to real interest rate?
10. In the Indian economy, both nominal and real interest rates had ruled low by historical standards in recent years. Yet private sector investment in the economy did not pick up. How do you explain this?
11. What is meant by structural rigidity? How does presence of structural rigidity in an economy impact growth of aggregate demand?
12. What are the determinants of net exports? Why do you think India's exports are doing well despite an appreciation of rupee against the US dollar?

CHAPTER

4

# FISCAL POLICY

Fiscal policy is all about government expenditure, its composition and its financing. There are several ways through which a government can raise money. It imposes various taxes. It also has access to non-tax revenues. It can also raise non-debt receipts through public sector disinvestments. Besides, the government also borrows. The total government expenditure reflects what it collects from these different sources.

Fiscal policy influences aggregate demand for goods and services in an economy in several ways. Government expenditure (*G*), we know, is a component of aggregate demand. Any change in government expenditure will, therefore, directly impact demand. However, when government expenditure is financed through borrowings, it adds to government debt. Debt-financed government expenditure has much wider implication for business, as it impacts not only government spending but also overall private sector spending on goods and services, both at present and in the future. This, in fact, is the most important component of fiscal policy that needs to be monitored by managers. Finally, a change in the tax rates can change the disposable income with individuals and companies. This can influence total spending on consumption and investment goods and services in the economy.

# 4.1 Government Expenditure, Taxes And Government Debt: An Overview

We begin with an overview of government expenditure.

## 4.1.1 Government Expenditure

Figure 4.1 is a good starting point to understand the various components of government expenditure.

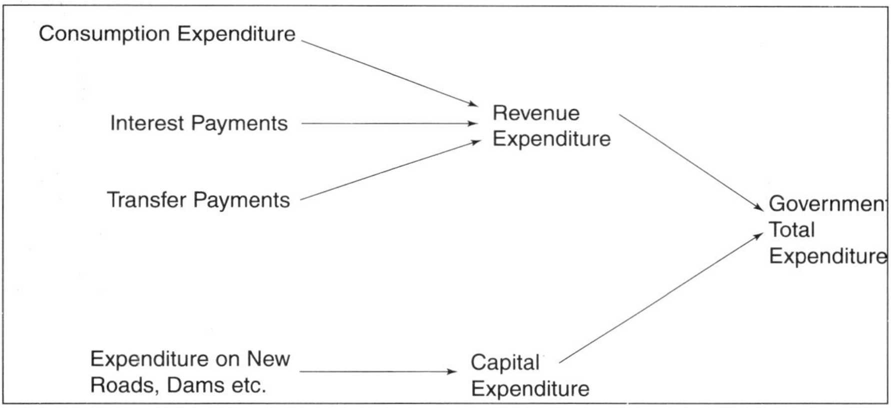


**Figure 4.1** *Government's Total Expenditure*

Government expenditure is divided into two parts: (a) revenue expenditure (current expenditure), and (b) capital expenditure. Let us understand them one by one.

Revenue expenditure can be classified under three broad categories:

The first category of revenue expenditure refers to government spending on consumption goods and services. This includes payments for the purchase of *goods* by the government, which are in the nature of consumables and are used up in the process of providing a good or service, for example, stationary, medicines for the hospitals run by the government, uniforms, furniture etc. Consumption expenditure, besides goods, also includes payments for consumption of *services* provided by the government servants belonging to police, defence, and other government ministries and so on. In other words, this category of revenue expenditure can be equated with Government 'C' in our GDP discussion in Chapter 2.

Another category of revenue expenditure consists of what are known as "transfer payments." These expenditures are so called because they are not payments in lieu of any current production of goods or service by the receiver (and, therefore, do not add to GDP). They are just transferred from one section of the society (tax-payers) to another section (which needs it) without adding to production of any goods and services in the economy. Examples will be payments towards food and fertilizer subsidy, unemployment benefit, pension etc. These are not paid against any exchange of goods and services.

A third category of revenue expenditure is interest on national debt. This is also a transfer payment but is treated as a separate category. Interest payments on national debt are transfer payments in the sense that they are payments for money borrowed over a period of time for various reasons, including war or slowdowns, and are not payments for any current goods or services produced. They deserve a special category as the size of the interest outgo reflects the size of the national debt.

In contrast to revenue expenditure, capital expenditure refers to government '*I*' as we discussed in Chapter 2. Capital expenditure is government's spending on new roads, new buildings and structures, new machines and equipments and other such durable assets, which result in further production of goods and services over an extended period of time. Capital expenditure adds to growth while revenue expenditure, once incurred, is gone and, at best, can have a short-term impact on the economy.

Government expenditure, as reported, is classified in different ways: (a) by departments; i.e., development and non-developmental expenditure under various departments of the government. Thus, components of revenue and capital expenditure will find a place in both development and non-development expenditure; (b) by plan and non-plan expenditure representing new and existing works under India's five-year plans. Here also, both plan and non-plan expenditure will have elements of revenue and capital expenditures; and, (c) by revenue and capital expenditure, irrespective of development/non-development or plan/non-plan. In the discussion of India's fiscal policy in this chapter, we will follow the classification given in (c) above, i.e., revenue and capital expenditure[1]. This

[1] It should be noted, however, that certain items of expenditure like spending on education, which is essentially spending on human capital, is treated as revenue expenditure, excluding the school building which is considered as capital expenditure. Similarly, expenditure on R&D is treated as revenue expenditure rather than capital expenditure. Revenue expenditure may, therefore, be somewhat overstated and capital expenditure understated.

is the most relevant classification to understand the growth implications of fiscal policy.

Figure 4.2 gives the trends in total government expenditure of central and state governments in India between 2001/02 and 2008/09.[2] The expenditures are expressed as per centages of GDP. Besides bringing out the trends, this will also help us to analyze the implications of such expenditures on the economy.

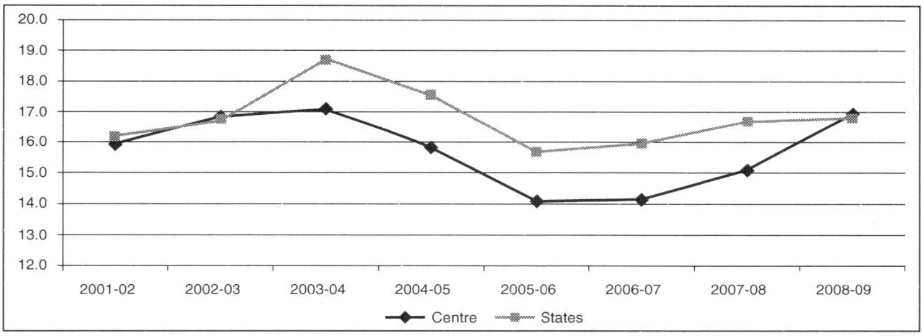


**FIGURE 4.2** *India: Trends in Total Government Expenditure (% of GDP)*

From the chart, two points emerge: (a) the share of total government expenditure in GDP, on average, till 2002/03 was about the same for both the central and state governments, roughly 16–17 per cent each. Together, they accounted for about one-third of India's GDP and, (b) since 2002/03 share of state government expenditure in GDP has outpaced central government share, though the trend is broadly the same.

Figure 4.3 similarly gives the trends in revenue expenditure of central and state governments between 2001/02 and 2008/09. The chart also reveals two other aspects. First, the revenue expenditure (12 to 13 per cent of GDP) accounts for about 80 per cent of total government expenditure in both central and state governments (15 to 16 per cent of GDP vide Figure 4.2 above), and second, the trend in more recent years is upward.

Within revenue expenditure (2007/08), about 30 per cent of central government's expenditure went towards payment of interest on government debt (category 3 of revenue expenditure classification), about 12 per cent on transfer payments (category 2 of revenue expenditure classification) and

[2] All the data in this chapter showing different trends are culled out of "*Statistical Outline of the Indian Economy*", www.rbi.org.in/

the rest of the revenue expenditure, 58 per cent, was due to the current consumption needs of the government (category 1 revenue expenditure classification). The corresponding figures for state governments were 17, 10, and 73 per cent, respectively.

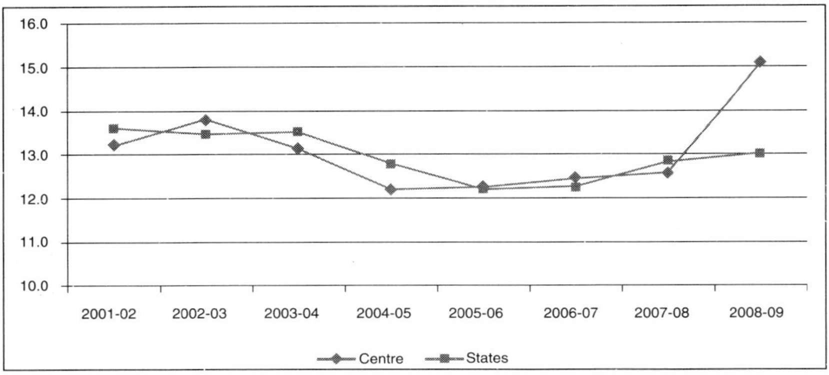


**FIGURE 4.3** *India: Trends in Revenue Expenditure (% of GDP)*

Trends in central and state government's capital expenditure as a per centage of GDP, over the years, are captured in Figure 4.4. The figure shows a gradual fall in capital expenditure, more so in the centre than in the states. This would suggest that a declining trend in total central government expenditure that we noticed in Figure 4.2 was achieved more by a cut in the capital expenditure than revenue expenditure. On the other hand, in states, the increase in both total expenditure and revenue expenditure was less than the cost of capital expenditure.

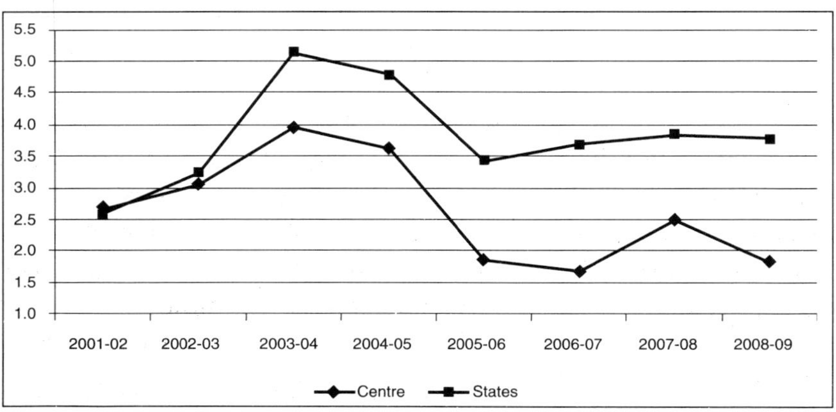


**FIGURE 4.4** *India: Trends in Capital Expenditure (% of GDP)*

## 4.1.2 Taxes

Once again, it will be useful to begin with a figure to see where taxes fit in total government receipts. This is shown in Figure 4.5.

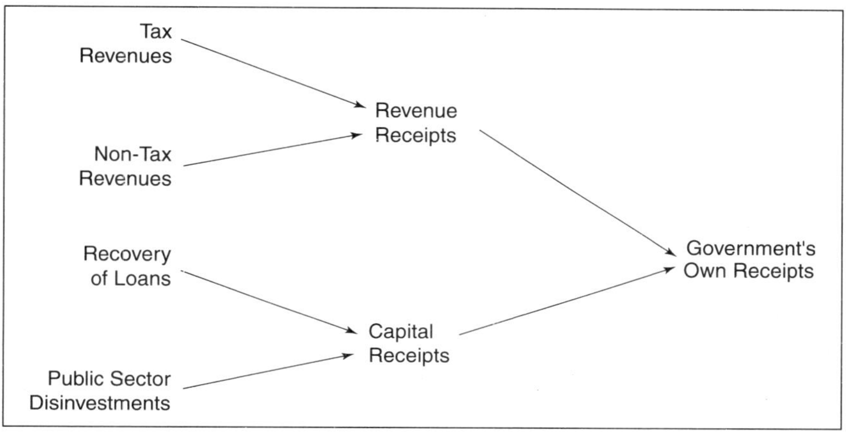


**FIGURE 4.5** *Government's Own Receipts*

Taxes are an important source of revenue for the government. In addition to taxes, government collects what are known as non-tax revenues. For the central government, these reflect interest and dividend received from its various investments, primarily, in public sector undertakings, fees etc. For the state governments, besides the above, a major part of non-tax revenue comes from lotteries and user charges. Tax revenue plus non-tax revenue constitute the revenue receipts or the current income of the government. In both central government and state government's own[3] total revenue receipts, non-tax revenue accounts for roughly one-fourth of the revenues. Additionally, governments receive money through recovery of loans and public sector disinvestments. These are part of capital receipts. Thus, tax revenue, non-tax revenue (revenue receipts) plus recovery of loans and receipts from public sector disinvestments (capital receipts), constitute the government's own money. The balance of receipts is what the government borrows, to which we will turn to later.

The focus of this section will, however, be on tax revenue. Figure 4.6 gives a break up of tax revenue.

[3] Here we are referring to state's own tax receipts. The states, however, also receive a share of central government's tax revenue.

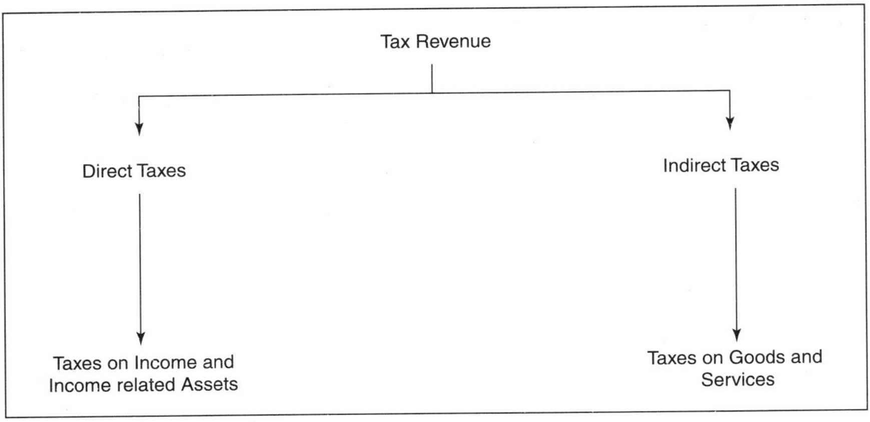


**FIGURE 4.6** *Government's Tax Revenues*

Taxes are of two types: direct and indirect. Direct taxes are levied on income or income-related assets. Thus, personal income tax, corporate income tax, wealth tax, capital gains tax etc., are all examples of direct tax. In India, most of the direct tax collection originates at the central government level. States have very little of their own direct tax revenues; however, they receive a share of centre's direct tax revenue. One characteristic of direct taxes is that they are progressive in nature, in the sense that as we move from one income bracket to the next, the incidence of tax on our income increases. For example, between Rs. 1,60,001 and Rs. 5,00,000, we pay 10% tax; between Rs. 5,00,001 and Rs. 8,00,000, we pay 20% tax; and, above Rs. 8,00,000, we pay 30% tax. In other words, as the marginal tax rate, i.e., the proportion of additional income, which must be paid in taxes, goes up from 10 to 20 to 30 per cent with each tax bracket, the average tax, i.e., the proportion of our total income, which has to be paid in the form of taxes also goes up. This implies that as GDP increases, direct taxes being progressive, their share should increase faster than the rate of growth of GDP.

Another characteristic of direct taxes is that they affect both aggregate demand and aggregate supply. A change in the tax rates will certainly affect aggregate demand, as we have stated earlier. But this will be the case only up to a point. If the tax rates are very high, this may lead not only to non-compliance but can also adversely affect incentive to produce and, thereby, stall aggregate supply growth. Most governments try to strike a balance between demand and supply sides of direct taxes.

Indirect taxes are levied on goods and services produced. Important items of indirect taxes for the central government are custom and excise duties. For the state governments, these are sales tax, state excise duties, motor vehicle tax, and stamp duty. Indirect taxes are regressive.[4] As the incomes rise, the incidence of tax on income goes down. Assume a person's monthly income to be Rs. 1000. Given this income, he will probably spend the entire amount in buying goods and services. The incidence of indirect tax will thus be on 100 per cent of his income. Now assume his monthly income is Rs. 1, 00,000, of which he needs Rs. 10,000 to meet his monthly purchases of goods and services. Thus the incidence of indirect tax, when his income rises to Rs. 1,00,000, comes down to only on 10 per cent of his income. This implies that as incomes (GDP) rise, the ratio of direct to indirect taxes should move in favour of direct taxes, since direct taxes are progressive and indirect taxes are regressive.

In Figure 4.7, we give the trends in total tax revenues as per centage of GDP of central and state governments between 2001/02 and 2008/09.

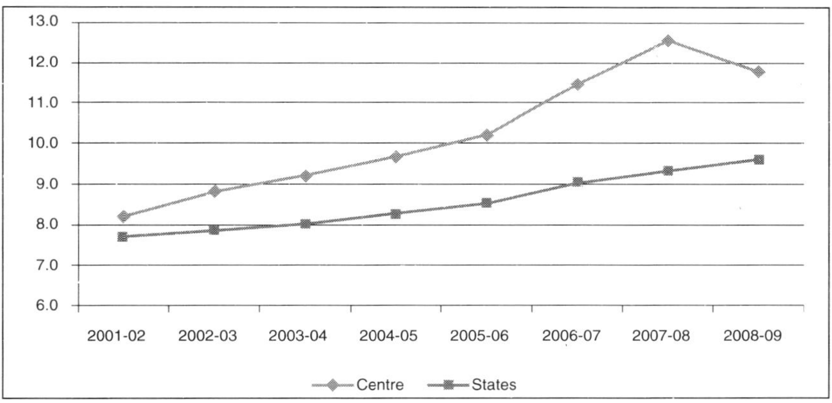


**FIGURE 4.7** *India: Trends in Total Tax Revenue (% of GDP)*

It is clear that both centre and state government's tax revenues, as a per centage of GDP, have been going up over a period of time. The buoyancy can be noticed more in centre's tax revenue than in states'.[5]

While the tax-GDP ratio is up, there is considerable scope for raising it further by widening the tax base through appropriate tax reforms. India's tax-GDP ratio continues to be one of the lowest among BRIC (Brazil, Russia, India, and China) countries with whom we usually compare.

[4] A certain amount of progressiveness can also be introduced in indirect taxes by taxing higher priced goods, say more expensive varieties of shoes or shirts, and also in a different way, by not taxing items of mass consumption. But indirect taxes are usually found to be regressive.

[5] The year 2008/09 was an exception to which we will turn to later in the chapter.

Figure 4.8 brings out the trends in direct tax revenues of central and state[6] governments. Central government's direct tax revenues have been rising and at the end of 2008/09, they constituted about 6.5 per cent of GDP and almost 60 per cent of the total tax revenue. State governments own direct tax revenues are very small and have only marginally increased over time.

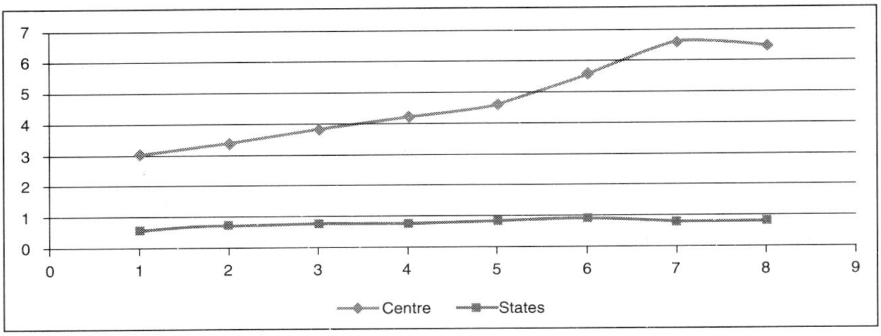


**FIGURE 4.8** *India: Trends in Direct Tax Revenue (% of GDP)*

We close this section by looking at the broad trends in indirect tax revenues of central and state governments. This is shown in Figure 4.9.

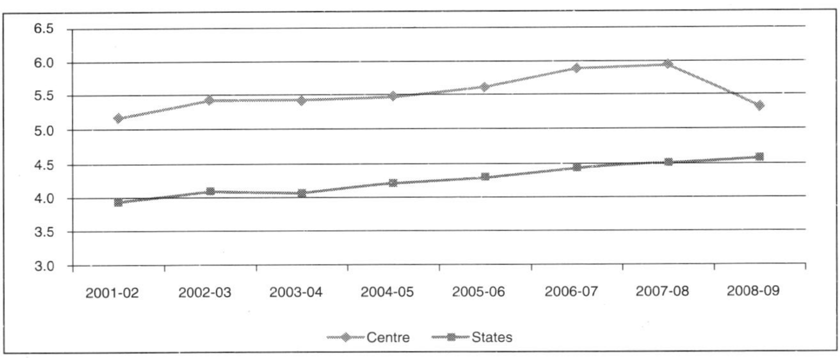


**FIGURE 4.9** *India: Trends in Indirect Tax Revenue (% of GDP)*

The central government's indirect tax revenues, as a per centage of GDP, have risen at a slower pace than direct tax revenues (Figure 4.8). Part of this is because of rationalization of indirect tax rates. But this is also consistent with our argument that direct taxes, being progressive and indirect taxes being regressive, over a period of time, the share of direct tax revenues both as per

[6] State government's direct and indirect tax revenues projected in Figures 4.8 and 4.9 exclude centre's contributions.

centage of total tax revenue and GDP should rise faster. State government's indirect tax revenues, on the other hand, show a steady to marginal rise.

### 4.1.3 Government Debt

We have been introduced to government total expenditure (Figure 4.1) and government's own total receipts (Figure 4.5). Government's total expenditure consists of revenue and capital expenditure. Similarly, government's own receipts consist of revenue (tax and non-tax) and non-debt capital receipts (recovery of loans and receipts from public sector disinvestments). In this section, we will provide an overview of government deficit and government debt.

Government deficit, henceforth called fiscal deficit, to be consistent with India's budgetary language, arises because total government expenditure exceeds government's own receipts (Figure 4.10). It is therefore the difference between what the government gets by way of tax and non-tax revenue, recovery of loans and receipts from the public sector disinvestments (total receipts) and what it spends annually (total expenditure). Fiscal deficit is an annual figure. This is financed through borrowing.

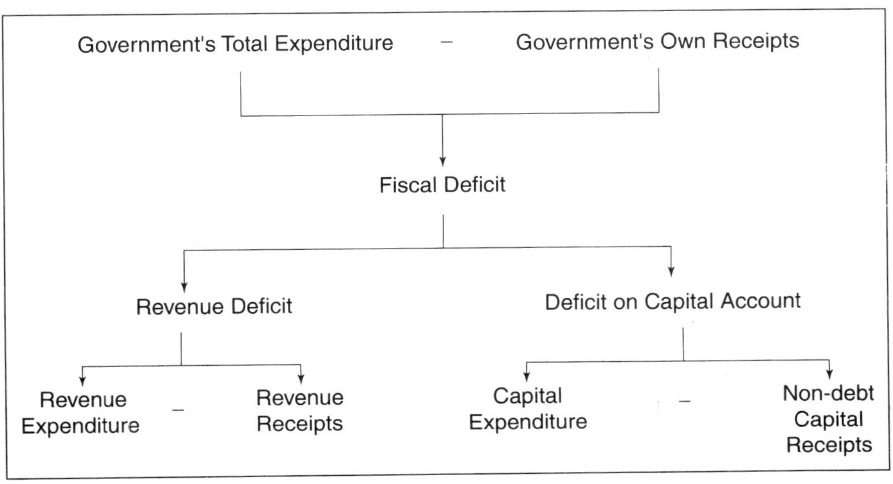


**FIGURE 4.10** *Government's Fiscal Deficit*

Fiscal deficit can be incurred either on revenue account, called the revenue deficit or on capital account. Revenue deficit arises when the revenue expenditure of the government exceeds the revenue receipts. In other words, the government is unable to meet its day-to-day expenditure (government's '*C*' + transfer payments + interest payments) out of its current income. The government is living beyond its means and is borrowing to finance the gap. Fiscal deficit on capital account, on the other hand, is due to government's '*I*'. In other words, the government borrows money to invest for creation of assets, which lead to further production of goods and services in the economy.

Fiscal deficit is financed through two sources: (a) domestic sources and, (b) external sources. central government's domestic sources include market borrowings (government floats a bond, for example) and other liabilities comprising of small savings, provident funds etc. State government's domestic sources include loans from the central government, market borrowings and state provident funds and small savings. External sources can be bilateral (from another country), multilateral (from international organizations like the World Bank or the Asian Development Bank) or foreign private banks. State governments access external sources of financing only through the central government.

Both central and state governments can borrow, also, from the central bank i.e., the Reserve Bank of India (RBI), though the mode of borrowing from the central bank has undergone a change through time. When the deficit is being financed from borrowing from RBI, it is called monetized deficit, so called because it results in an increase in money supply.[7] Monetized deficit is a part of fiscal deficit but is not reported separately because it is treated as a part of market borrowing where RBI, also, is a player.[8] Today, in India, government borrowings from either external sources or RBI are insignificant. Most of the borrowing is from the domestic market (80 per cent or more) and other liabilities.

When fiscal deficit, that is, the money borrowed to pay off the annual deficits, is accumulated over the years, we get a stock of debt that the government owes to the various entities from whom it has borrowed to finance each year's deficit. That accumulated debt is called government debt or, public debt or, national debt. Debt is a stock and deficit is a flow.

Before we look at the trends in government deficits and government debt, we will define another deficit concept, which is very important for

[7] More monetized deficit (and money supply) in Chapter 5.

[8] RBI credit to government is shown in RBI balance sheet (Chapter 5).

understanding how the government manages its finances. This is known as primary deficit. Primary deficit = fiscal deficit – interest payments. The idea is as follows: governments borrow money every year, which leads to an accumulation of debt on which interest has to be paid. If we want to find out to what extent the present government is living within its means we should not hold it responsible for the interest outgo, which is arising out of borrowings of previous governments for expenditures incurred in the past. It is not due to any current fiscal profligacy of the present government. So while fiscal deficit is the difference between government's *total* expenditure and its *total* receipts, primary deficit is the difference between the government's *current* expenditure (where current is defined as total expenditure minus interest payments), minus government's total receipts. Clearly, if there is still a deficit, i.e., primary deficit, and it is positive, this means that the present government is also resorting to borrowing to meet its current expenditure. This has implications for future debt build up in the economy, as we will see later in the chapter.

Figure 4.11 gives the trends in fiscal deficit as a per centage of GDP of the centre and state governments between 2001/02 and 2008/09. Compared to 2001/02, centre's fiscal deficit shows a declining trend, except for the year 2008/09; more or less the same trend emerges in respect of states' fiscal deficit as well. Today the combined fiscal deficit of centre and state governments amounts to more than 8 per cent of GDP.

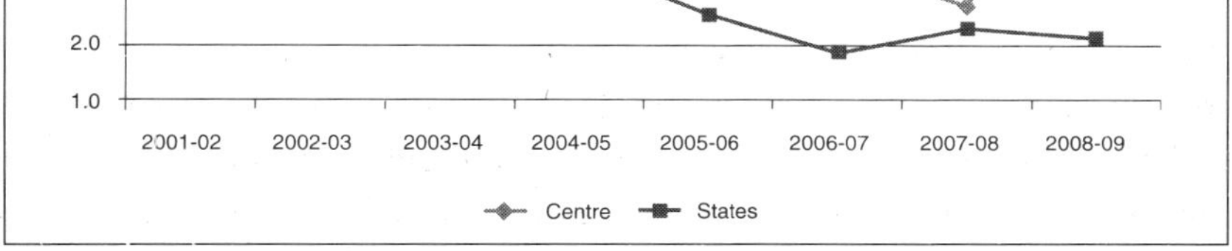


**FIGURE 4.11** *India: Trends in Gross Fiscal Deficit*

Figures 4.12 and 4.13 give a break-up of the total fiscal deficit into deficit on revenue account (revenue deficit) and deficit on capital account.

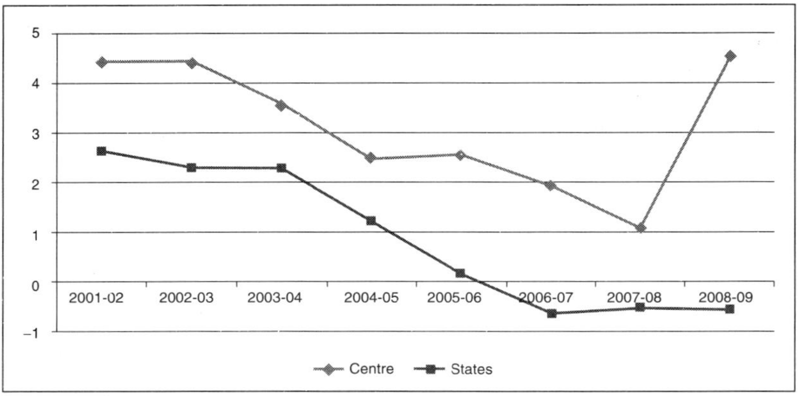


**FIGURE 4.12** *India: Trends in Revenue Deficit (% of GDP)*

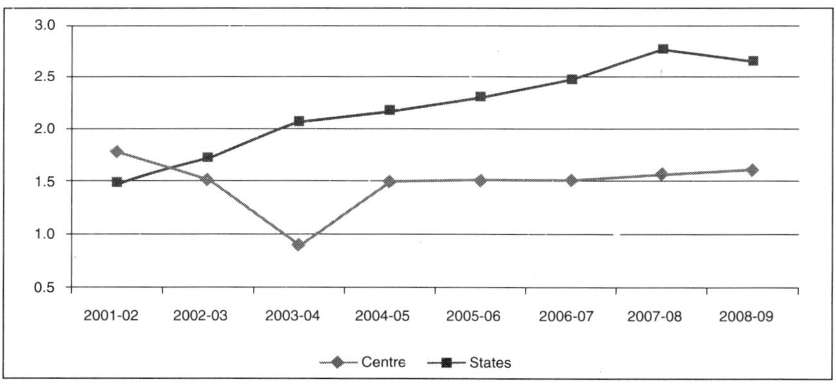


**FIGURE 4.13** *India: Trends in Deficit on Capital Account (% of GDP)*

In both centre and states, revenue deficit as a per centage of GDP have come down impressively. In fact, the states recorded revenue surplus in the last three years. When it comes to deficit on capital account (Figure 4.13) while central government's borrowings for capital expenditure as a per centage of GDP have levelled off, the states have maintained a rising trend. This suggests that both at the centre and states, the decline in fiscal deficit (Figure 4.11) was achieved more from revenue deficit than deficit on capital account. This is how it should be.

Finally we show the trends in primary deficit and, government or, national debt as a per centage of GDP with the help of Figures 4.14 and 4.15.

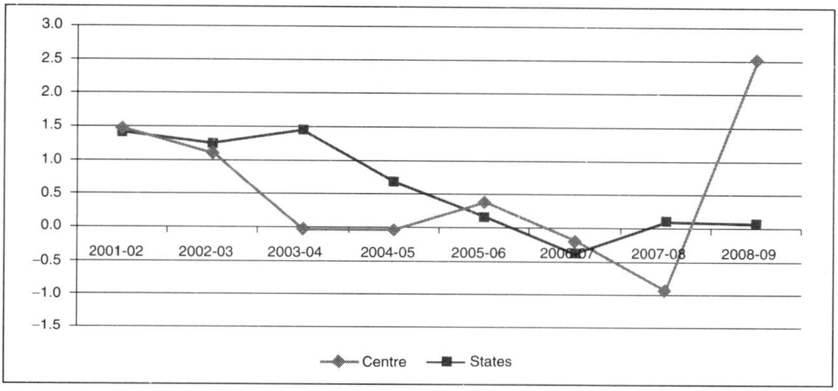


**FIGURE 4.14** *India: Trends in Primary Deficit (% of GDP)*

Generally, here too, the trend is towards decline. Except for 2008/09, in two out of the eight years considered, the centre recorded a primary surplus; in two other years (2003/04 and 2004/05), primary deficit was brought down to zero. This is the case with states as well: the decline in the primary deficit has been impressive and continued through 2008/09.

Figure 4.15 shows that total government debt (central and state combined) is more than seventy two per cent of GDP. The debt/GDP ratio rose till the year 2003/04 but has been falling since then.

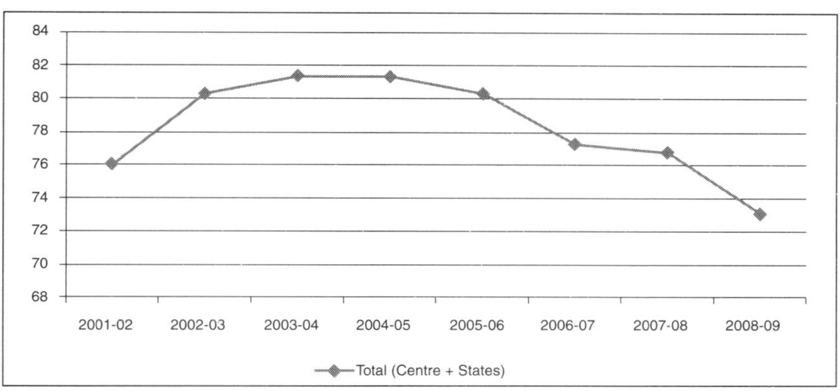


**FIGURE 4.15** *India: Trends in Total Government Debt (% of GDP)*

## 4.1.4 Government's Expenditure and Receipts at a Glance

Table 4.1, taken from the Ministry of Finance website, gives a sample of how the central government's expenditures and receipts are presented in the budget document. The actual figures, corresponding to each item in the budget, are also shown, for the year 2008/09. We will analyze the figures later, but make sure that you are able to relate each item to the discussion in the text. Very briefly, row 1 is revenue receipt after paying out the states' share and consists of tax and non-tax revenue. Out of the total capital receipts (row 4), rows 5 and 6 are government's own capital receipts; the balance (row 7) is borrowings.

Other receipts (row 6) are the same as receipts from disinvestments of public sector undertakings. The government just calls it "other receipts".

*Table 4.1 India: Union budget at a glance (Rupees in Crores)*

| Items | 2008–2009 ( Actual) |
|---|---|
| **1. Revenue Receipts (2 + 3)** | 540259 |
| 2. Tax Revenue (net to centre) | 443319 |
| 3. Non-tax Revenue | 96940 |
| **4. Capital Receipts (5 + 6 + 7)** | 343697 |
| 5. Recovery of loans | 6139 |
| 6. Other Receipts | 566 |
| 7. Borrowing and Other Liabilities | 336992 |
| **8. Total Receipts (1 + 4)** | 883956 |
| **9. Non-Plan Expenditure** | 608721 |
| 10. On Revenue Account of which | 559024 |
| 11. Interest Payments | 192204 |
| 12. On Capital Account | 49697 |
| **13. Plan Expenditure** | 275235 |
| 14. On Revenue Account | 234774 |
| 15. On Capital Account | 40461 |
| **16. Total Expenditure (9 + 13)** | 883956 |

*(Contd.)*

| | |
|---|---|
| 17. Revenue Expenditure (10 + 14) | 793798 |
| 18. Capital Expenditure (12 + 15) | 90158 |
| **19. Revenue Deficit (17 – 1)** | 253539 (4.5 % of GDP) |
| **20. Fiscal Deficit {16 – (1 + 5 + 6)}** | 336992 (6 % of GDP) |
| **21. Primary Deficit (20 – 11)** | 144788 (2.6 % of GDP) |

*Source*: www.finmin.nic.in

You have already been introduced to plan and non-plan expenditure (rows 9 and 13). Each expenditure has revenue and a capital component. But, as we said in the text, our focus will be on rows 17 and 18, that is, revenue expenditure and capital expenditure. Finally, the three deficit concepts (rows 19-21) namely, revenue, fiscal and primary deficits are presented both in crores of rupees and as per centages of GDP. You will notice that fiscal deficit is nothing but row 7.

You may also like to note, though not shown in Table 4.1, that the fiscal balance sheet or, budget at a glance, presented each year contains data for three years: the coming year, the year just completed and, the previous year. For the coming year we will have only the budget estimate (BE). For the year completed we will have two sets of estimates i.e., what was budgeted (BE) and the revised estimate (RE). Revised estimate is based on available data till that point and is subject to revision as more data comes in. Finally, for the previous year we will have the actual data (A).

Having familiarized ourselves with the broad fiscal parameters, let us now look at rudimentary fiscal policy at work. We begin by asking the question: how does fiscal policy affect aggregate demand? Then we gradually build on that.

## 4.2 How Does Fiscal Policy Work?

There are two elements to the working of fiscal policy. One is a non-discretionary (automatic) element and the other is a discretionary element. The non-discretionary element influences aggregate demand as follows: typically in a period of slowdown, the government spending increases in the form of benefits to the vulnerable sections of the population. This happens not because the government chooses to spend more, but because a slowdown increases the number of eligible beneficiaries. Government spending, we say, thus, automatically increases and, this has a moderating influence on the extent of slowdown. Similarly, in a period of a boom, since economic activity has picked up, the number of eligible beneficiaries shrinks and government spending comes down. This time, thus, government spending automatically tempers the growth of aggregate demand, which caused the boom. Again, income taxes being progressive, as an economy slows down, income growth slows down and people, progressively, pay less income tax. There is less leakage from the expenditure stream and they are able to spend, proportionately, more out of their income. This eases the slowdown. A booming economy does just the opposite. As income increases, so does the incidence of tax on the income. This lessens the impact of average disposable income and spending growth and, thereby, the boom. There is, therefore, one component of fiscal policy, which changes automatically to moderate fluctuations in aggregate demand. A side effect of this automatic change is, of course, a higher government deficit in a period of slowdown as government spending automatically rises and tax revenue automatically falls. However, as the growth picks up, government deficit falls.

In sharp contrast to the above, discretionary element refers to a situation where changes in fiscal policy do not happen automatically, but the government chooses to increase or decrease government expenditure or taxes to address the ups and downs in economic activity. For example, in India, the government may choose to invest in infrastructure to give a boost to demand; similarly, it may decide to offer tax concessions to specific groups of industries or sectors to achieve the same objective. The government, in the above examples, we say, is using its discretion to change the fiscal policy to meet certain macroeconomic objectives. Hence, we use the term discretionary fiscal policy.

In each case, an initial increase in government expenditure or a lowering of taxes results in a multiple change in aggregate demand. The change in aggregate demand is thus a multiple of change in government expenditure or taxes. This is how it works: suppose government expenditure ($G$) increases by one rupee. In the first round, aggregate demand has increased by one rupee because $G$ is a component of aggregate demand. Now, this one rupee will be paid out in the form of factor incomes to the different factors of production. Households and firms receiving this income will either spend it or save it.[9] Let us say, when the income changes by one rupee, people, on an average, spend 75 paise and save 25 paise. In other words,

[9] We are assuming here, for the purpose of illustration, that GDP, GNP, national income and disposable income are the same.

the change in consumption in response to a change in disposable income (called the marginal propensity to consume out of disposable income or, *MPC*) is 0.75 and, the change in saving in response to change in disposable income (called the marginal propensity to save out of disposable income or, *MPS*) is 0.25. Note also that when we consume, it is an injection into the expenditure stream, and therefore, adds to aggregate demand; on the other hand, when we save, it is a leakage from the expenditure stream and it does not add to the aggregate demand till it comes back into the expenditure stream in the form of investment demand.

Now, in the first round, as we said, spending increases by one rupee because government expenditure increases by the same amount. In round two, when this one rupee increase in spending is paid out in the form of factor incomes, then, based on *MPC* and *MPS* of 0.75 and 0.25 respectively, which we have assumed, they spend 75 paise and save 25 paise. Therefore, at the end of round two the increase in aggregate demand in response to a one rupee increase in government expenditure is not one rupee but one rupee and 75 paise. The process goes on. The increase in total spending by 75 paise in round two generates further increase in disposable income, leading to further increase in aggregate demand in round three by 75 paise times 0.75, the *MPC* or, by Rs. 0.56. In the fourth round, similarly, there is a further increase in aggregate demand by Rs. 0.56 x 0.75 = Rs. 0.42 and so on. However, since each round leads to a smaller and smaller increase in income, this cycle of higher spending leading to higher disposable income to further spending dampens over time. The overall effect is a geometric sum[10] and is given by: $\Delta AD/\Delta G = 1/1\text{-MPC}$, where $\Delta$ refers to 'change'. In this example, since we assumed $\Delta G$ to be one rupee and *MPC* to be 0.75, then a one-rupee rise in government expenditure, in our example, results in a 4-rupee rise in aggregate demand. Aggregate demand, thus, increases by a multiple of 4. This is called the multiplier and its size is directly related to the size of *MPC* i.e., how much of income gets passed on in each round.

When the government lowers taxes, the same process works but with a difference. When government expenditure increases by rupee one, this gets directly spent in the economy and, therefore, in round one, aggregate demand increases by rupee one. Then the multiplier process starts. In case of taxes, there is no injection of spending in the economy in round one. Only the taxes have been lowered by one rupee leading to an increase in disposable income by one rupee. Thus the spending cycle begins not as

[10] Those who are not familiar with geometric sum, just take this mathematical relationship as given, but do understand the logic behind how the multiplier works.

1 + 0.75 + 0.56 + 0.42 +...+, but as 0.75 + 0.56 + 0.42 and so on. The tax multiplier is, thus, smaller than the government expenditure multiplier by the initial amount of increase in government expenditure. It is given by: $\Delta AD/\Delta T$ = MPC/(1 – MPC). The difference between the tax multiplier and the government expenditure multiplier, as you can see, is one.

The choice of the fiscal stimulant, between increase in government expenditure and tax cut, is not clear-cut. While the expenditure multiplier is greater than tax multiplier, the choice is not obvious, for there may not be good projects on which to spend money to get quick results. Similarly, in considering tax cuts, it is important to decide whether the cut is aimed toward low-income or high-income groups. A tax cut for the low-income group will generate more spending than for higher income group, who already possess almost everything. But, other things being equal, the decision to use taxes or government expenditure, as an aggregate demand stabilization tool, is mainly ideological. In market-driven economies, policy makers give more importance to tax cuts in periods of slowdown and a cut in government expenditure in periods of boom. In state driven economies, it is the other way round.

The above model of tax multipliers is a useful starting point for an understanding of how fiscal policy works. However, in actual situations, the transmission mechanism between a fiscal policy change and its final impact on aggregate demand or actual output is not as smooth as depicted above. There are also other considerations, which need to be taken into account. Once we allow for those, the size of the multipliers and, thus, the impact of government spending and tax cuts on aggregate demand may be tempered. For example, prices may not remain constant; if so how will real demand change? Again, if government expenditure is financed through borrowing, what impact will it have on the rest of the economy's demand for goods and services, now and in future? In fact, fiscal policy influences a host of demand and cost variables in an economy and their impact on the economy will have to be carefully weighed before coming to any judgment on the final impact of a fiscal policy change on aggregate demand. In what follows, we will attempt that.

## 4.3 When is Government Expenditure Productive?

Government expenditure is, clearly, productive in the following areas: (a) government provides police services for the protection of self and personal property; (b) it provides legal services to ensure that contracts are honoured; and (c) it provides defence services to safeguard national property including lives of our citizens from foreign attacks. By providing these services, the government, thus, assumes a monopoly or coercive power to enforce law and order in the society. Without this, individuals and companies will have to divert a lot of resources that can be invested towards protection of self and property.

Another area where government expenditure is productive is in the provision of public and merit goods. Public goods are characterized as (a) non-excludable and (b) non-rival. The first characteristic means that it is not possible to exclude people from using these goods even if they do not pay for them. The second characteristic suggests that even if someone, who does not pay, uses the public good, it does not result in reduced access to others. Streetlights, street names, clean air and other types of public utilities are good examples of public good. It is not possible to exclude someone from walking under the streetlight even if he does not pay for it. On the other hand, if he does walk, it does not reduce access to others. For public goods, government makes provisions. The market is unable to provide these goods because of inability to charge adequately for them.

Merit goods are goods which the market can provide but not to the desired extent. For example, the market can certainly provide healthcare and education. We know of many hospitals, schools and institutes of higher learning being provided by the private sector in the market place. But market's participation will be limited by the ability to pay by the users for these facilities. These facilities will not be provided to those who cannot afford these. Therefore, the market will always under-provide merit goods. The government has to step in to set up schools, colleges, hospitals, primary health care etc. in the larger interest of the society. In the absence of these, people will be in a general state of belligerence and will not be very productive.

Finally, government expenditure in certain types of physical infrastructure, particularly, road systems, enhances the productivity of the economy. Strictly speaking, these activities can be undertaken by the private sector also. But given the high capital expenditure and the long gestation period involved in such infrastructure projects, private sector may be reluctant to take the lead. In fact, governments in many countries, in addition to investing in infrastructure of the type mentioned above, have invested in power, telecommunication etc. Even in developed market economies, the government, initially, actively supported these activities.[11]

[11] See for example, Joseph Stiglitz, "Do what we did, not what we say" in *Economic Times*, March 11, 2003.

In each of the cases cited above, the economy produces more output per unit of input, with government's presence than without. These are activities where the private sector is either unable or unwilling to participate to the desired extent, either completely or initially. Clearly, the benefit accrued to the economy and society through these spending is seen to outweigh the cost of financing these expenditures through taxes and, possibly, other means.

What happens beyond these activities? In other words, activities, which can be carried out both by the government and the private sector? Should the government be spending on these activities, particularly since the government may have to resort to deficit financing (borrowing) to finance these activities? How do the costs and benefits change under these situations? We will turn to these questions now.

## 4.4 Beyond That-How Do We Analyse Fiscal Policy?

The role of the government expenditure, in situations where a particular economic activity can be carried out by both public and private sectors depends on several factors.

### 4.4.1 State of the Economy

The state of the economy can be described in four different ways:

1. A state of the economy characterized by *massive excess capacity* across different sectors. In this situation, therefore, the actual demand, across sectors, is so much below the supply capacity and there is so much of slack in the economy that an increase in demand and, thus, in actual output, can be met without resorting to any increase in prices.
2. A state of the economy, where there is still *substantial excess capacity*, but not of the first type. An increase in actual output in response to an increase in demand will perhaps require payment of moderately higher wages or higher costs of materials such that an increase in demand is likely to be met with some moderate increase in prices. Nevertheless, in this state of the economy, the increase in actual output, consequent to a rise in demand, will be substantially greater than the increase in prices.

3. A state of the economy, where actual output is *close to capacity* output. In this state of the economy, as aggregate demand increases, in order to produce more to meet the increased demand, the producer may have to put up with a more rapid rise in wages and prices. Thus, an increase in demand will bring about some increase in output but a much larger increase in prices.
4. Finally, we can describe a state of an economy where the actual output is to its *full capacity*. Clearly, in this case, an increase in demand will be fully dissipated by a rise in prices.

In real life, a state of economy characterized by either (a) or (d) above is unlikely. Therefore, the choice, basically, narrows down to b. and c. and the entire range between the two. In situations closer to (b), essentially, what we are saying is that an increase in aggregate demand and thus in actual output can be brought about with very low inflation. And in situations closer to c. above, what we are saying is that the scope for increasing output is low and, therefore, if we still want to give a push to demand, we will have to put up with a higher rate of inflation. Given the fact that price stability is an important goal of macroeconomic policy, policy makers will probably not try to push demand too much under c. in the short run. That shifts the focus of attention of the policy maker to the range between (b). and (c). What is the role of policy in these situations?

Clearly, the range between (b) and (c) is a range of slowdown where the actual demand is below capacity output, except that the severity of slowdown is more when the economy is closer to (b) than (c). A sluggish growth in demand, we said in Chapter 3, could be due to policy-induced variables or due to autonomous variables. When autonomous variables (negative sentiment, structural rigidities etc.) prolong, these may blunt the economic impact of policy-induced variables like lower interest rates or lower tax rates. Under the circumstances, fiscal stimulus in the form of increased government expenditure can be a very effective tool for reviving the economy. In fact, given the nature of the current global economic slowdown, which, in many parts of the world (chapter 7), can be characterized more as negative sentiment (autonomous factors) driven, countries have combined tax cuts with increased government spending to rescue their economies from dipping further. Thus, government borrowing in the United States today (2009) is more than 11% of GDP; in United Kingdom it is more than 14 per cent; in Japan it is about 8 per cent; in Euro zone (Germany about 5 per cent;

France 8 per cent; Spain almost 11 per cent), despite constraints imposed by the "stability pact,"[12] government deficits are rising and almost throughout East Asia, government borrowings have gone up in the aftermath of global economic slowdown.

The message is clear. If the state of the economy is such that there is excess capacity and the cause of the slowdown can be related to a prolonged negative sentiment (autonomous variables), fiscal policy can be a very potent tool for stimulating the economy. Because here the choice, then, becomes not between public sector, (b) spending and private sector spending, but between public sector spending and a very muted overall spending. Moreover, experience suggests that a combination of excess capacity and prolonged negative sentiment is usually the characteristic of an economy closer to above.

However, it is important to keep in mind that not all slowdowns are driven by autonomous factors. In fact, the autonomous factor driven prolonged slowdown that we are witnessing in different parts of the world today is not a very common occurrence. On the other hand, there is an entire range between (b) and (c) where private sector spending, as is normal, is sensitive to changes in interest rates, tax rates and other policy-induced macroeconomic variables. In these situations, a rise in government deficit, consequent to a course of expansionary fiscal policy, can, not only slowdown the growth of the economy but also put a damper on fresh private sector investment in the economy.

Also, it will be incorrect to assume, even if the state of the economy demands a certain type of government action that the government will always be in a position, because of political economy reasons, to ensure that the money is being spent in the right sort of projects, or, the tax cuts are aimed correctly, which will spur growth. In other words, the government may fail to rise to the occasion. Such lags in decision-making, then, will only add to the size of the debt with little or no change in output.

In the following section, we will first analyze under what circumstances government deficits, resulting from increased government expenditure and/or lower taxes, can adversely affect private sector incentives. This we will attempt by considering how government deficit is financed and how that impacts private sector business environment. Then we will look at issues related to efficiency of government projects and tax schemes, even where fiscal policy intervention is called for. Finally, we will conclude on the role of fiscal policy as a demand stabilization tool.

[12] More on this in Chapter 7.

## 4.4.2 Mode of Financing

The government can finance a deficit through four sources: (a) borrowing from the central bank of the country, (b) borrowing from domestic market, (c) increasing taxes, and (d) borrowing from abroad. Let us analyze the impact of each on the economy, in turn.

### *Borrowing from the Central Bank*

In this case, the Central Bank of the country (RBI) picks up the government securities from the primary market.[13] This results in an increase in money supply. Every time RBI picks up government securities, we, therefore, say that the debt has been 'monetized', meaning thereby, that this component of government borrowing has been financed through creation of money in the economy.

The question, therefore, is if the money supply increases how does it impact the economy? It is instructive to revise Sections 2.2 and 2.6 in Chapter 2. What we said was that there was a relationship between increase in money supply and increase in prices. But the exact nature of this relationship depended on what happened to GDP, consequent to a change in money supply. Symbolically, we can state the relationship as follows:

$$p = m - g + v$$

where,

$p$ = per centage change in prices (inflation)

$m$ = per centage change in money supply

$g$ = per centage change in GDP and,

$v$ = velocity of circulation

What the above relationship says is that, if we assume '$v$' to be stable, then the impact of an increase in money supply ($m$) on inflation ($p$) is not given by '$m$' but by '$m - g$'. Only if '$g$' is zero, prices ($p$), over a period of time, will change in the same proportion as change in money supply ($m$). In other words, if an increase in money supply ($m$) is accompanied by a corresponding increase in the production of goods and services ($g$), there is no inflation. On the other hand, if an increase in money supply ($m$) does not result in any rise in the production of goods and services, this increase in money supply is fully dissipated by way of an increase in prices ($p$). In

[13] We will look at the money supply process more closely in Chapter 5.

between, the impact of a rise in money supply on prices will depend on the difference between money supply growth and GDP growth ($m$-$g$).

Certain caveats are, however, in order. First, '$v$' need not be stable. In a period of slowdown, money changes hands less frequently; hence '$v$' may come down. You will then find, from the above equation, that the economy is able to accommodate a larger growth in money supply, without a resultant rise in prices. During a period of boom, the situation may be the reverse. Besides, the impact of a change in money supply on GDP, even when '$v$' is stable, may not be instantaneous. There are usually long lags before a money supply change shows up when there is a change in prices. Also, there are differences of opinion on whether the relationship between money supply growth and inflation is direct, as suggested above, or it works through some other macro variables. These caveats apart, however, economists agree that the above causation between money supply growth and inflation holds.

We are, therefore, back to the state of the economy. If the state of the economy is characterized by the existence of massive excess capacity, money-financed government spending can be a good way of stimulating demand. However, if the excess capacity is not massive (the range between (b) and (c) in our discussion of state of the economy), one has to carefully look at the type of spending, the gestation period etc. before assessing the final impact on prices. Clearly, if the money-financed expenditure increases prices within an acceptable range, it may be worth pursuing it in the interest of higher output growth. On the other hand, if money-financed government spending results in inflation, which is higher than the acceptable level and, people expect this to worsen, it can cause inflation to build up and compound itself. A high rate of inflation is usually associated with high variability. And an unanticipated inflation can do considerable harm to the economy and to business environment. More specifically, a high inflation is not desirable for the economy and for business for the following reasons:

1. In a market economy, relative price changes provide a very important signal to the businessman in terms of most efficient allocation of goods and services in the economy. For example, if the price of '$x$' is rising relative to other prices, this signals an improved opportunity to invest in '$x$'. However, when inflation is high, a businessman may misinterpret the rise in price of a good as stemming from an increase in demand for that good relative to others and invest too much.

In other words, in a variable inflationary regime, it becomes difficult to make a distinction between relative and overall price changes. This results in misallocation of resources.

2. Inflation can also adversely affect long-term investment in the economy. This can happen because tax-deductible depreciation allowances for equipment and structures are not inflation adjusted. The businessman may be tempted to favour more investment in inventories and short-lived equipments than in long-lived plant and equipment.
3. Both individuals and businesses may expend resources, which could have been invested, in protecting themselves from the effects of high and variable inflation. Additionally, financial savings of individuals and households may get diverted to what are known, from the point of view of the economy, as non-investible resources like gold, land, and commodities. This can upset the saving investment balance in the economy.
4. Inflation can also make our products uncompetitive in the export market, thereby, increasing the gap between import and export of goods and services ($M-X$). For example, if inflation in India is higher than in the rest of the world, then, other things being equal, our exports become more expensive to the foreigner while our imports become relatively cheaper to the domestic buyer. Exports, as a result come down and imports go up. The $M-X$ gap widens.
5. There are high distributional costs attached to inflation. In a regime of high inflation, borrowers tend to benefit and savers (lenders) lose. The borrowers benefit because the money they return loses value and, therefore, effectively, they return less. The savers lose because, for the same reason, they effectively receive less. Since people who save usually are elderly and fixed income groups, who are not financially very sophisticated, this creates an unfair distortion in the distribution of income.
6. While higher deficit causes inflation, if it is financed through money creation, higher inflation, in turn, can also lead to further rise in deficit, thus, creating a deficit inflation spiral in the economy. This can happen because inflation on the one hand, reduces the real value of tax revenue collected; on the other hand, it increases the nominal interest outgo on borrowed money (revisit Section 2.17 to understand the relationship between inflation and nominal interest rate).

7. Last but not the least, perhaps the greatest adverse effect of a creeping inflation is that people lose faith in the credibility of government policy. Inflation management then becomes very difficult.

## *Borrowing from the Domestic Market*

The government borrows from the domestic market through the issue of bonds. In this case there is no increase in the money supply as the bonds are subscribed by individuals, corporate sector, commercial banks, and other financial institutions and, not by RBI. In other words, only demand for money increases, consequent to government borrowing; there is no increase in the supply of money. As the demand now is greater than before and there is no change in supply, the price of money goes up, which is the interest rate. This impacts the economy and business environment as follows:

1. In Chapter 3 we have seen that private sector investment is inversely related to interest rate. Accordingly, a rise in interest rate, as a result of government borrowing from the market, crowds out private investment. And, since private sector investment is more efficient than government investment, this amounts to replacing a more efficient investment by a less efficient investment. Growth suffers.
2. Also, as interest rates in the country rise, relative to the rest of the world, the country attracts more capital from abroad to take advantage of the interest rate differential. The supply of foreign currency increases relative to demand (see Section 2.4). Since supply is greater than demand, the price of the foreign currency falls. Or, the domestic currency appreciates vis-à-vis the foreign currency. Thus exports are crowded out. Growth, therefore, slows down, not only on account of crowding out of private investment but also because of crowding out of exports. Domestic manufacturing sector growth suffers.
3. If borrowing continues, then, over a period of time, debt builds up and becomes unsustainable. As we will see later in this chapter, this can have major inter-temporal implications.

These are, generally, the arguments against government borrowing from market to finance the deficit.

However, under certain situations, the above may not hold true. First, if the private sector has large unutilized capacity and/or, if the private sector is going through a period of prolonged business pessimism, then it may not be investing and, therefore, there may not be a competing demand for the money that the government is borrowing from the market. In that case, despite government borrowing, interest rates may not rise. The current level of soft interest rates prevailing globally, including in India until recently, in spite of rising government deficit financed through market borrowing, bears this out. Clearly, there is no crowding out.

Secondly, the sensitivity of private sector investment to changes in the interest rates may be very low. This will happen when investment decisions are largely driven by autonomous considerations. Private sector investment may be robust even if interest rates are rising, if the businessman's expectations about the future growth are very positive (and vice versa). This is what happened in the initial years of economic liberalization in India. Again, there is no crowding out.

In the case of exports also, as we have argued in Section 2.4, exchange rate is only one of the variables, which affect exports. If growth in importing countries is robust, there will be more demand for foreign goods and services and exports may still maintain a respectable growth. Again, export competitiveness may improve due to greater efficiency in production. For example, there have been times when despite appreciation of Indian rupee, exports did well. This was because Indian products had become more competitive as also, global demand was robust. Here is, thus, a situation where positive income effect outweighed the negative price effect and exports continued to grow.

Finally, increased government investment, in certain types of activities, can crowd in rather than crowd out private investment. If increase in government spending is for improvement in infrastructure, it can reduce costs of doing business and, therefore, increase private sector investment. Similarly, as mentioned above, if increased government spending causes increased expectation of economic growth private sector investment may increase even if interest rates go up. We have observed this phenomenon in India, in recent years, particularly, in respect of government investment in infrastructure. Joseph Stiglitz, in his article, cited earlier in the chapter, argues that, even in the United States, the first telegraph line was built by the government; the Internet was initially developed by the government and much of modern American technological progress is based on government-funded research.[14] All these expenditures had crowded in rather than crowding out private investment.

---

[14] Joseph Stiglitz, op cit.

Where does it leave us on the impact of government borrowing from market on growth and business environment? Clearly, the arguments against government borrowing do not hold when the state of the economy is closer to (b) and businessmen are not willing to borrow. Also, the argument becomes weak when investment is largely driven by expectations of future growth. And finally, government's role in funding investment in infrastructure, though, theoretically, may appear to be in conflict with private sector investment intentions, has to be put in proper perspective. They can, indeed, in given circumstances, play a very effective role in driving private sector investment in the economy. In the short run, therefore, one perhaps needs to have an open mind on the crowding out issue. But the arguments against government borrowing from the market will certainly hold, if government borrowing continues for an extended period of time, and as the state of the economy moves away from (b) and closer to (c).

## *Increasing Taxes to Finance the Deficit*

Raising taxes to finance the deficit in a period of slowdown can be disastrous. The Japanese government tried it in 1997 only to find that the economy was pushed back to recession. What is the argument?

Let us take direct taxes first. Assume a person gets an assignment which will fetch him/her Rs. 1,00,000. Now consider two scenarios: (a) the person was living in the regime of Mrs. Indira Gandhi when the marginal tax rate was more than 90 per cent and (b) the person is living in the present regime when the marginal tax rate is 30 per cent. Under the first scenario, it is quite possible that the person may not take up the assignment because he/she may feel that it is not worth the effort when all that he/she will get is Rs. 10,000 (Rs. 90,000 will be taxed away). Note that since the work has not been done there is no impact on either GDP or government's tax revenue.

Now consider the second scenario. Under this scenario, the person may take a decision that Rs. 70,000 is not all that bad and does take up the assignment. In this case, then GDP and government's tax revenue go up by Rs. 1,00,000 and Rs. 30,000 respectively. Note that the government's tax revenue goes up despite a lowering of the tax rate. How does it happen?

The answer to the above question is that taxes play a role of allocation in the economy. When tax rates are high, this acts as a disincentive to work and people choose leisure to work. When the tax rates are lowered, this ensures not only better compliance but also additional incentive to work.

The size of the GDP, thus, increases and from the enhanced size of the GDP the government collects more tax revenue even if tax rates are lower.

The argument can be extended to corporate income tax rates. Business spending heavily depends on post tax returns. If the tax rates are very high, the disincentive effect it generates may drive businesses to produce below their optimum level.

What about indirect taxes? Indirect taxes basically change the relative prices of goods and services and, thereby, the composition of aggregate demand in the economy. For example, if the government lowers the excise duty on tea with no change in the duty on coffee, the government is, essentially, changing the composition of demand in favour of tea away from coffee. Also, recall, as we said earlier, that indirect taxes are regressive. As incomes rise the incidence of indirect tax on the income comes down.

The arguments on indirect taxes, now, fall in place. They are twofold. First, in a market driven economy, the consumers should decide which goods and services to accept and which ones to reject. That maximizes consumer welfare. The government, by changing relative prices, should not influence consumer choice. There should probably be just one tax rate for most of the goods and services produced in the economy.[15] Second, the tax rate should be moderate; else, being regressive in nature, it will penalize the non-rich more than the rich.

The conclusion, then, is that raising tax rates may not be the best way to finance deficit. In respect of taxes, the most meaningful alternative is to ensure that the tax base is wide enough to have covered all who should be paying taxes and there is proper compliance. Beyond that, automatic stabilizers should be allowed to work so that a deficit in tax revenue in a period of slowdown is made up by a surplus in a period of boom.

## *Borrowing from Abroad*

Government incurs a deficit when it demands more goods and services than it can pay for. We have seen that when the government borrows from the central bank, it finances the purchase of goods and services through money creation; when the government finances this expenditure from the domestic market borrowing, it draws on the existing money supply; and, finally, when the government wants to finance the increased expenditure from taxes, it raises the tax rates. We have discussed the pros and cons of each

[15] The government may tax differentially products which are harmful to health or which cause environmental damage.

mode of financing the deficit on the economy and business environment in the preceding sections. We will now consider another mode of financing the deficit i.e., borrowing from abroad.

Under this scenario, the government meets the increased demand for goods and services through imports; as a result, the gap between imports and exports (*M*–*X*) widens and the government borrows from abroad to finance this gap. The borrowing can be from bilateral sources (another country), multilateral sources (World Bank, IMF, ADB etc.), or through private sources.

Clearly, if the borrowed money is put to productive use, i.e., if imports generate commensurate returns, there need not be a problem in servicing the debt. If not, debt servicing can become a problem. And, it will ultimately, show up in the form of an unstable currency. In this regard, it may be useful to keep the following causation in mind:

1. When we export (*X*), the demand is for rupees and the foreigner who buys our products supplies dollars to purchase the rupees.
2. When we import (*M*), the demand is for dollars and we supply rupees to get dollars.

If *M* persistently outpaces *X*, i.e., situation 2 above is prevailing over situation 1 above, *M*–*X* gap widens. Then, from the above, two things are happening: (a) the supply of rupees is persistently outpacing the demand for rupees, and (b) put differently, the demand for dollars is persistently outpacing the supply of dollars. In the first case, you will see that since supply of rupees is greater than demand for rupees, the price of rupees (in relation to dollar) falls. In the second case, since the demand for dollars is greater than the supply of dollars, the price of dollars (in relation to rupees) rises. Either way, the rupee is under pressure of depreciation against the dollar.

Businessmen may not like to invest in a currency, which is unstable. Particularly, if the volatility of the currency is because of unproductive debt, they may take a dim view of the ability of the government to honour its external commitments.

## 4.4.3 Fiscal Policy—Implementation Issues

In the previous sections, we examined the effectiveness of fiscal policy in relation to the state of the economy. We did not address the question of quality of fiscal policy. In other words, we did not consider whether fiscal policy, even if the state of the economy demands its intervention, could always be counted upon to deliver what it is set out to deliver. This is a very important question, particularly, in emerging economies where, for a combination of reasons, government's product or service delivery issues have assumed as much importance, if not more, as finding money to finance such activities. In fact, poor delivery of fiscal policy can neutralize all the positive effects of fiscal policy that we discussed earlier.

Typically, when it comes to a discussion of fiscal policy implementation problems, macroeconomic textbooks talk about fiscal lags, which may come in the way of effective functioning of a fiscal policy move. These are called inside lags and outside lags. *Inside lag* is divided into: (a) recognition lag, i.e., the time it takes for policy makers to realize that a disturbance has occurred and that a policy response is warranted. This happens because it is not always clear whether a slowdown is transitory in nature or an emerging trend, (b) decision lag, i.e., the time it takes to decide on the most desirable policy response. This decision, usually, is the result of a complex political bargaining process, (c) legislative lag, i.e., the lag in the legislative process to give a go ahead to the proposed fiscal policy measures, and (d) the action lag, i.e., the time it takes to implement the policy measure in terms of obtaining clearances from related ministries, meetings with different stakeholders, floating tenders and lining up contractors etc. *Outside lag* refers to the time, it takes for a policy measure, once implemented, to have an effect on the economy. This may be due to leakages, delays and so on. Clearly, if lags are very long, the whole purpose of a fiscal correction may be defeated, even if the state of the economy demands fiscal intervention.

It is generally said that, in case of fiscal policy, the inside lags are very long but the outside lags are relatively short. In other words, it takes long time to get a fiscal policy action initiated but once it is implemented, the impact on the economy can be felt within a short period of time. However, sometimes, outside lags can also be long, if the government expenditure is not of the right type or if the tax changes do not address the right concerns. For example, as in India, government borrowing may be going more towards financing revenue expenditure when the need is to increase capital spending. Again, even if it is the right type of spending, one has to worry about whether it is a quick yielding project or a project, which has a long gestation period. Similarly, as in the United States, the tax cuts meant to stimulate the economy, some believe, failed to bring the desired results because they were aimed more towards the rich who did not spend more because they already had everything.

In emerging economies like India, the outside lags can be long, also because of poor delivery system. The problem can be conceptualized as follows:

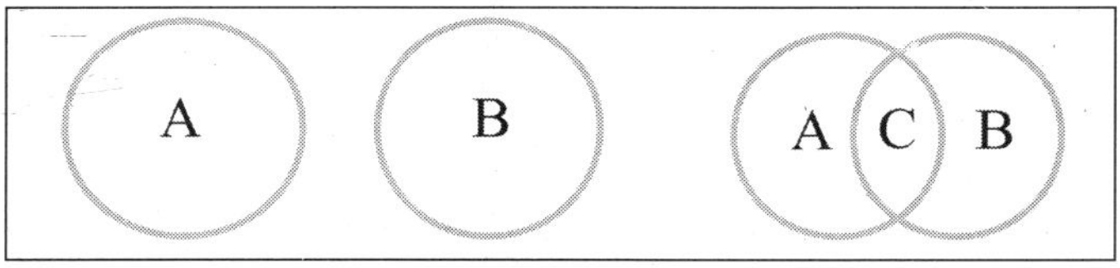


A = Fiscal Action, B = Mind Set, and C = A intersection B

**FIGURE 4.16** *Fiscal Policy: Understanding Implementation Problems*

In Figure 4.16, we have drawn three sets, A, B, and C. Set A represents the launching of a fiscal action (project) after the inside lags are accounted for, and set B represents the mindset of the people who are responsible for implementing the project. If the two do not intersect, the fiscal action will not take off. The extent of implementation and, therefore, the impact on the economy will depend on the size of set C, that is, where the mindset jells with the policy action launched; or, where set A intersects with set B. Larger the size of set C, better is the implementation and greater is the economic impact of a fiscal action. The size of set C, in turn, will depend on the attitude of bureaucracy, cooperation of state governments, political will and a host of factors, which we are trying to capture in set B under Mindset. In emerging economies the size of set C is still small, albeit, growing. Therefore, besides worrying about the mode of financing of the debt, governments also have to worry about delivery issues. If money is spent and it does not deliver, the problems of the economy may multiply manifold.

## 4.4.4 From Deficits to Debt

Government deficit incurred over the years accumulates into government debt. How does government debt build-up affect the economy? Let us trace the arguments from our discussion of deficits so far. We said, against government deficit, the following:

1. Increased borrowing by the government raises interest rates, potentially crowding out private investment and net exports. Since the government may not spend the borrowed money for investment,

or, even if it does, it may not be efficient, a large build-up of debt slows down the rate of capital accumulation. Domestic jobs and manufacturing base suffer. Future economic growth slows down. The standard of living for future generations deteriorates.

2. The debt may become so large that the central bank may be forced to finance the debt by increasing money supply. To the extent the debt is money-financed may stoke the flames of inflation in the economy.[16] The government may face a credibility problem, leading to a build-up of inflationary expectations. This may result in further inflation. Once this happens, inflationary expectations may become difficult to adjust downwards quickly.
3. If taxes have to be raised to pay back part of the debt, disincentives to work, save, and invest may result, reducing the level of output.
4. Finally, to the extent foreigners also hold a part of the debt, if they demand back their principal plus interest, there will be an outgo of real resources from the country. This is in sharp contrast to a situation where the debt is domestically held. In this situation, servicing the debt does not result in a drain of resources out of the country. It only has a redistributive effect away from tax-payers (mostly lower and middle income) to bondholders (mostly high income).

In favour of deficits, on the other hand, we argued that budget deficits are not necessarily bad and are often needed to stimulate the economy out of a recession. Similarly, deficit reduction often can cause the economy to slow down as aggregate spending is reduced. So how do we assess the impact of debt on the economy?

Clearly it is not the size of the deficit or national debt that matters, but its proportion to GDP. The importance of the debt-GDP ratio (the national debt divided by GDP) has to be understood. If GDP grows faster than the debt, the debt-income ratio will decline and budget deficits may not be much of a problem. But if the debt-income ratio rises, the debt problem will eventually become unsustainable and all the negative effects of deficit cited above will surface.

The factors, which cause debt-GDP ratio to rise or fall, are three-fold:

- Primary deficit/surplus
- Interest rate, and
- GDP growth

[16] Creation of money in excess of what is needed to meet the demands of a growing economy and the resultant inflation is called the inflation tax. When the government creates this money, it is able to spend on goods and services or on transfer payments in exactly the same way that it does through regular tax revenue collection. Thus money creation is like a tax.

The relationship between debt–GDP ratio and primary deficit, interest rate, and GDP growth can be expressed as follows[17]:

$\Delta b = b\,(r - y) - z$
where,
$\Delta$ = change
$b$ = debt–GDP ratio
$r$ = real interest rate
$y$ = real GDP growth, and
$z$ = primary surplus as a per centage of GDP

Let us try to understand the above relationship. We start with the primary surplus ($z$). You will recall, we had earlier defined primary deficit as fiscal deficit *minus* interest payments. The reason for introducing the concept of primary deficit was to find out to what extent the government was able to meet its expenditure, without including the interest that it pays on its debt, out of its own receipts. If, even after excluding interest payments, the government was unable to meet its expenditure from its own revenue, then we have a primary deficit. In this case, the government will need to borrow more; debt will accumulate further and the interest outgo will rise, further resulting in worsening of the deficit and debt. If, on the other hand, the government is able to meet its non-interest expenditure exactly out of its own revenue, the primary deficit will be zero and there will not be any further debt build-up and the government's interest outgo will be contained at the present levels. Finally, if the government, after meeting its non-interest expenditure out of its own revenue, ends up with a surplus, we have a primary surplus. A primary surplus ($z$) in the above relationship, other things being equal, can be used to retire the debt and thereby help to bring down the debt–GDP ratio.

The debt–GDP relationship, $\Delta b = b\,(r - y) - z$, says that, with primary deficit either in balance or in deficit, the higher the difference between the interest rate and the growth rate ($r - y$), larger will be the debt-GDP ratio. What this means is that if the real interest outgo (the cost of borrowed money) is greater than the real output growth (the return from the use of the borrowed money), then the government will have to borrow more to pay the interest and debt–GDP ratio will rise. Thus, in order to reduce the ratio of debt to GDP, there must be either a primary surplus ($z$ should be positive) or the economy ($y$) must grow faster than the rate of interest ($r$) or both. If only one of those conditions holds, it must be large enough to outweigh the adverse effect of the other.

[17] For derivation of this relationship, see Chapter 19 of Dornbusch and Fischer, *Macroeconomics*, McGraw Hill, New York, 1994._

The combined effect of interest rate, GDP growth, and primary surplus on debt–GDP ratio can be seen as follows: (a) if $b\ (r - y) - z > 0$, debt–GDP ratio will rise; (b) if $b\ (r - y) - z = 0$, debt–GDP ratio will be constant; and (c) debt–GDP ratio will fall, if $b\ (r - y) - z < 0$.

Instability will arise only if debt–GDP ratio is rising because under the circumstances one or all of the following three aspects will happen:

1. The government will have to increase taxes to raise additional revenue to finance the debt.
2. The government will have to cut down on its expenditure to contain the deficit and
3. The government will have to resort to money creation and, thus, inflation, to bring the real interest rates down.

## 4.4.5 Summary

The state of the economy is the key determinant of fiscal policy effectiveness in influencing aggregate demand. The farther the economy is from the full-capacity level of output (i.e., the closer it is to the state of the economy characterized by '*b*'), the stronger is the case for money-financed fiscal deficit. For, at a time when excess capacity is high, inflationary pressures are likely to be low. So increasing money supply will not cause rapid price increases. A moderate inflation may be preferable to a continued slowdown in output since the latter, over a period of time, may turn out to be more costly for the economy. Also, a small increase in prices in one country need not tilt the balance of relative prices too much against that country to make its products uncompetitive globally. Further, in a globally integrated world, economic events and policies tend to synchronize; hence, relative price changes may be small. However, when the economy is close to full capacity, (the state of the economy gets closer to '*c*'), bottlenecks develop more easily. In this situation, monetizing the deficit will cause inflation to increase sharply with all its accompanying problems, discussed earlier.

Government expenditure financed through borrowing from the domestic market will be desirable if, due to negative sentiments, either out of heavy loss in the past or because of structural rigidities in the economy, the private sector is not willing to invest. Or, if the private sector's expectations of future growth are highly optimistic such that a rise in the interest rate, consequent to increased government borrowing, does not come in the way of undertaking new investment. But it is important to realize that prolonged borrowing from the market will eventually crowd out more efficient private investment and slowdown growth. This will happen faster, if the government fails to invest the borrowed money in productive activities and, instead, uses it up towards consumption and transfer payments. The role of fiscal policy, thus, should be seen as one of kickstarting the economy, when the economy is not willing to start on its own, and not as the main driver of investment in the economy. Surely, the role of fiscal policy must not be seen as using borrowed money to finance government's consumption expenditure and transfer payments.

The alternative of financing the deficit by raising taxes, particularly, in period of slowdown, does not work. Even otherwise, higher taxes dampen incentives to work and invest and, thereby, slowdown growth. Tax policy should ensure that while the tax rates are moderate, the tax base is wide enough to include everyone who should be paying taxes.

The need to borrow from abroad arises because of a widening of the gap between imports and exports ($M-X$). As long as the higher imports are utilized to increase the capability of the country to earn more foreign exchange, servicing the foreign debt need not be a problem. Else, real resources will have to be drained out of the country to service the debt. Exchange rate may become highly unstable.

Even if the state of the economy demands certain type of fiscal intervention, the government may not be able to always rise to the occasion. Fiscal policy is the result of a complex political bargaining process. The objectives of fiscal policy may be multiple and not just demand stabilization. The choice of policy may not be best suited to the needs of the economy, but may be driven more by ideological considerations. All these may result in large inside and outside lags. In emerging economies, the role of outside lags assume particular importance.

The end result of fiscal intervention, both in quantitative and qualitative terms, shows up in debt—GDP ratio. Deficits every year accumulate into debt. If deficits do not result in increase in output either because of the state of the economy or because of failure of governance, debt–GDP ratio will rise. A persistent rise in debt–GDP ratio is unsustainable and will cause considerable instability in the economy. On the other hand, if debt–GDP ratio is falling, fiscal deficit need not be a matter of immediate concern. And the strategy to achieve this is to ensure that high fiscal deficit in a period of slowdown is accompanied by a fiscal surplus in period of boom.

A manager should know that there is a close relationship between fiscal deficit and stability in prices, interest rates, tax rates, and exchange rates in an economy. The manager should also understand that fiscal deficit need not always be non-conducive to business. In certain situations, it can stimulate the economy. The manager should also be aware of the vulnerability of fiscal policy to political twists and turns, that the quality of fiscal deficit is a function of governance. Finally, a key indicator of the extent to which fiscal deficit can create instability in the economy is the trend in debt–GDP ratio.

## 4.5 The Indian Case

At the end of Chapter 3, we concluded that investment in infrastructure held the key to both sustained growth of GDP and social sector development in India. We also said that the options for stepping up investment in infrastructure were three-fold:

1. Ease the rigidities in the structure of the economy, which come in the way of private sector investment in the economy.
2. Provide more fiscal and monetary incentives to induce private sector to invest more in infrastructure.
3. Step up public (government) investment in infrastructure, and
4. Encourage more public–private partnership in infrastructure investment.

While analyzing the options, we said that (a) option 1 is not an immediate possibility because it had to move at a political pace; (b) option 2 may not always work in the presence of structural rigidities in the economy; (c) option 3 is, thus, seen as offering promise not as a way of taking over investment activities in the economy but as a way of kick-starting the economy, which will eventually attract more private sector investment, and (d) option 4 follows from option 3 above.

It is against this background, we will look at India's fiscal policy. That is, the state of the economy demands massive investment in infrastructure and the fiscal policy must, therefore, ensure that (a) the available savings in the economy are directed towards investment and (b) a more conducive environment is provided for private sector, both domestic and foreign, to invest in the Indian economy.

The analysis will be carried out for central government finances but a similar analysis of state finances will throw up same results. Therefore, the implications are similar. We begin by asking several questions.

## *Has government expenditure addressed the investment needs of the economy?*

We have already looked at the broad trends in central government expenditures in Figures 4.2 to 4.4. We provide the relevant data for selected years in Table 4.2 for a more in depth analysis.

An analysis of the data suggests the following:

1. The trend in total government expenditure as a per centage of GDP, barring 2008/09, is by and large downward.
2. However, revenue expenditure constitutes the largest chunk of the government expenditure. It has ranged between 78 per cent and 88 per cent of the total and the trend is generally upward.
3. There has been some deceleration in government's transfer payments and interest outgo as per centage of GDP. The increase in revenue expenditure is, therefore, largely on account of government's consumption expenditure, including defence consumption expenditure.
4. Government's capital expenditure, as a proportion of GDP, has come down over the years. The fall is more glaring if we exclude, from the total capital expenditure, the capital expenditure on account of defence.

***Table 4.2 India: Central government expenditures, 2002/03 to 2008/09***

(% of GDP)

| Item (1) | 2002/03 (2) | 2003/04 (3) | 2004/05 (4) | 2005/06 (5) | 2006/07 (6) | 2007/08 (7) | 2008/09 (8) |
|---|---|---|---|---|---|---|---|
| 1. Total Expenditure | 16.84 | 17.11 | 15.82 | 14.10 | 14.13 | 15.09 | 16.93 |
| 2. Revenue Expenditure (2a+2b+2c) | 13.80 | 13.14 | 12.20 | 12.25 | 12.46 | 12.58 | 15.10 |
| 2a. Cons. Expenditure | 7.23 | 7.03 | 6.71 | 7.23 | 7.44 | 7.46 | 9.05 |
| 2b. Transfer Payments | 1.77 | 1.61 | 1.46 | 1.32 | 1.38 | 1.50 | 2.43 |
| 2c. Interest Payments | 4.80 | 4.50 | 4.03 | 3.70 | 3.64 | 3.62 | 3.62 |
| 3. Capital Expenditure (3a+3b) | 3.04 | 3.96 | 3.62 | 1.85 | 1.67 | 2.50 | 1.83 |
| 3a. Defence capital expenditure | 0.61 | 0.59 | 1.01 | 0.89 | 0.82 | 0.78 | 0.77 |
| 3b. Non-Defence capital expenditure | 2.43 | 3.37 | 2.61 | 0.96 | 0.85 | 1.73 | 1.06 |

*Source*: Compiled from budget data provided by the Ministry of Finance in their website www.finmin.nic.in/

It is clear from the above, that government's non-defence capital expenditure, which primarily finances government investment in infrastructure, has come down and, at best, been highly erratic. This lacklustre growth in government's capital expenditure could not be made up by a corresponding increase in private sector investment in infrastructure. Overall growth in investment in infrastructure, therefore, slowed down during this period. Poor implementation of the projects further widened the gap between expenditure and outcome.

## *Could the Government not have borrowed more to finance investment in infrastructure?*

Table 4.3 provides data on central government borrowing in selected years. Once again, the broad trends are shown in Figures 4.7 to 4.9. We will now discuss the implications.

Fiscal deficit (row 1), which is the total borrowing of the government is on two accounts: (a) revenue account (row 2) and (b) capital account (row 3). When the government borrows on revenue account, it means that the government is unable to meet its revenue expenditure, consisting of government consumption, transfers, and interest payments from its tax and non-tax revenues. It is borrowing to finance the gap. When the government borrows on capital account, it means that it is doing so to finance its capital investment, which is usually earmarked for infrastructure growth. The fundamental difference between the two is that while government borrowing on revenue account does not generate assets, which can be used to increase production of goods and services in the economy, government borrowing on capital account does and therefore results in further production of goods and services. In the context of what we discussed earlier, if the state of the economy demands government intervention to kick-start infrastructure investment and the government, instead, uses a large portion of its borrowing to finance revenue expenditure, it is only going to add to debt and not to GDP. Every time the government borrows to finance revenue deficit, an equivalent amount of savings in the economy will get diverted away from investment and growth to consumption and transfers. Thus, the larger the size of the revenue deficit, the slower will be the growth of the economy.

To illustrate, today investment in the Indian economy is roughly 36 per cent of GDP. Our GDP growth in the last five years, barring 2008/09, has been, on an average, about 9 per cent. Therefore, the incremental capital-output ratio is of the order of 4:1. Now consider row 2 in Table 4.3. If we exclude the abnormal year 2008/09 and consider the two years prior to that, revenue deficit was around 1.5 per cent of GDP. This means that by diverting 1.5 per cent worth of savings away from capital to revenue expenditure, India has lost 0.37 per cent growth (applying the incremental capital-output ratio of 4:1) in its GDP. In other words, India's GDP growth would have been 9.37 per cent per annum if we were able to use all our savings for investment. The loss will be more if we also take into consideration the revenue deficits of the state governments.

***Table 4.3 India: Central government's deficits, 2002/03 to 2008/09***

(% of GDP)

| Item (1) | 2002/03 (2) | 2003/04 (3) | 2004/05 (4) | 2005/06 (5) | 2006/07 (6) | 2007/08 (7) | 2008/09 (8) |
|---|---|---|---|---|---|---|---|
| 1. Fiscal Deficit | 5.91 | 4.48 | 3.99 | 4.08 | 3.45 | 2.69 | 6.14 |
| 2. Revenue Deficit | 4.40 | 3.57 | 2.49 | 2.57 | 1.94 | 1.11 | 4.53 |
| 3. Deficit on Capital Account | 1.51 | 0.91 | 1.50 | 1.51 | 1.51 | 1.58 | 1.61 |
| 4. Row2÷1x100 | 74.45 | 79.69 | 62.41 | 62.99 | 56.23 | 41.26 | 74.59 |
| 5. Row3÷1x100 | 25.55 | 20.31 | 37.59 | 37.01 | 43.77 | 58.74 | 25.41 |
| 6. Primary Deficit | 1.11 | -0.03 | -0.04 | 0.38 | -0.19 | -0.93 | 2.51 |

*Source*: Compiled from budget data provided by the Ministry of Finance in their website www.finmin.nic.in/

This is the crux of the problem. On the positive side, as a per centage of GDP, government's fiscal deficit appeared to have moderated, particularly, between 2005/06 and 2007/08 (Table 4.3, row 1).[18] A similar trend could be discerned with respect to revenue deficit. But what is worrisome is that despite this fiscal restraint, the revenue deficit (row 4) remained, on an average, more than 50 per cent of the fiscal deficit during this period and the 2008/09 data on which we will have a separate discussion in Section 4.6 does not auger well for the future. Obviously, borrowed money available for capital expenditure had to be measured. Any manager, trying to assess

[18] The year 2008/09, as we have seen, has been an unusual year on all fiscal parameters. The special case of 2008/09 is discussed separately in section 4.6.

the policy climate for business in India, must closely monitor the trends in revenue deficit, as this is an important determinant of future growth of demand for goods and services in the economy. Larger the size of the revenue deficit larger will be the diversion of savings from the economy away from investment and growth to current consumption and slower will be the future growth of demand for goods and services in the economy.

## *Is there any way of reducing the government's revenue expenditure to reduce the size of the revenue deficit?*

Let us look at the breakdown of central government's revenue expenditure as per centage of GDP and how each has changed over the years. This is shown in Table 4.4. Row 1 shows the trends in total revenue expenditure as a per centage of GDP. Rows 2–5 provide a breakdown of the total. Row 2 provides data on non-defence consumption expenditure. Row 3 furnishes information on defence consumption expenditure. Similarly, rows 4 and 5 bring out revenue outgo on account of interest and transfer payments.

*Table 4.4 India: Central government's revenue expenditure*
(% of GDP)

| **Item (1)** | **2002/03 (2)** | **2003/04 (3)** | **2004/05 (4)** | **2005/06 (5)** | **2006/07 (6)** | **2007/08 (7)** | **2008/09 (8)** |
|---|---|---|---|---|---|---|---|
| 1. Revenue Expenditure (row 2+3+4+5) | 13.80 | 13.14 | 12.20 | 12.25 | 12.46 | 12.58 | 15.10 |
| 2. Non-defence Consumption | 5.57 | 5.46 | 5.32 | 5.89 | 6.19 | 6.31 | 7.67 |
| 3. Defense Consumption | 1.66 | 1.57 | 1.39 | 1.34 | 1.25 | 1.15 | 1.38 |
| 4. Interest | 4.80 | 4.50 | 4.03 | 3.70 | 3.64 | 3.62 | 3.62 |
| 5. Transfers | 1.77 | 1.61 | 1.46 | 1.32 | 1.38 | 1.50 | 2.43 |

*Source*: www.finmin.nic.in/

The data shows that both defence consumption expenditure (row 3) and transfer payments (row 5) have been somewhat contained. The interest outgo (row 4) also seems to be going down, though that could be partly due to the soft interest rate regime that prevailed for most of the period.

However, despite moderation, interest and transfers together still constitute an alarming 40 per cent of the total revenue expenditure. Unless this is brought down, it will be difficult to make a dent on the total.

Government's non-defence consumption expenditure, of course, has been growing persistently over the years. A priori there would appear to be a case for reduction in expenditure under all the heads. But in coalition politics, these expenditures are not easy to bring down drastically. Many of these are also committed. In fact, expenditure reduction on revenue account, though can be effected over a period of time, cannot be counted upon as an immediate measure for limiting the central government's fiscal imbalance.

## *What are the chances that tax revenues can be substantially stepped up to ease the revenue deficit?*

Let us look at the key tax indicators in India. These are summarized in Table 4.5. Row 1 shows direct tax revenue of the central government as a per centage of GDP. Row 2 shows similar trend in indirect tax revenues. Row 3 provides information on gross tax revenue as a per centage of GDP or, the gross tax/GDP ratio and row 4 brings out the direction of net (after paying the states' share) tax revenue as a per centage of GDP, or the net tax/GDP ratio.

***Table 4.5 India: Central government's taxes 2002/03 to 2008/09***

(% of GDP)

| Item (1) | 2002/03 (2) | 2003/04 (3) | 2004/05 (4) | 2005/06 (5) | 2006/07 (6) | 2007/08 (7) | 2008/09 (8) |
|---|---|---|---|---|---|---|---|
| 1. Direct Tax Revenue | 3.38 | 3.82 | 4.22 | 4.61 | 5.57 | 6.61 | 6.48 |
| 2. Indirect Tax Revenue | 5.43 | 5.42 | 5.47 | 5.60 | 5.89 | 5.94 | 5.32 |
| 3. Gross Tax Revenue | 8.81 | 9.23 | 9.68 | 10.21 | 11.47 | 12.56 | 11.80 |
| 4. Net Tax Revenue | 6.46 | 6.79 | 7.14 | 7.54 | 8.50 | 9.31 | 8.76 |

On the positive side, the ratio of direct tax revenue to indirect tax revenue has been rightly moving in favour of direct taxes. The share of direct taxes has risen from 38.36 per cent of total tax revenue in 2002/03 to 54.91 per cent in 2008/09 (Row 1 ÷ Row 3 x 100). Both gross and net tax–GDP ratios have also been marching on, though there is considerable scope for improvement. India has one of the lowest levels of the tax–GDP ratio in the world. This low tax–GDP ratio has been a central feature of India's fiscal problem.

There are two tax proposals in the pipeline, one in respect of direct taxes (Direct Tax Code) and the other in respect of indirect taxes (Goods and Service Tax). These tax proposals are likely to be implemented starting fiscal year 2011–12.

The philosophy underlying direct tax code (DTC) is threefold: (a) keep the rates moderate; (b) do away with exemptions; and (c) make the tax collection simple. DTC seeks to consolidate and amend the existing laws relating to all direct taxes, that is, income tax, dividend distribution tax, fringe benefit tax, and wealth tax so as to establish an economically efficient, effective and equitable direct tax system which will facilitate voluntary compliance and help increase the tax-GDP ratio. Another objective is to reduce the scope for disputes and minimize litigation.

The goods and service tax (GST) is a comprehensive indirect tax levy on manufacture, sale and consumption of goods as well as services at a national level. The idea is to do away with distortions created by different treatments of manufacturing and service sector. Also, by abolishing multiple layers of taxation such as octroi, central sales tax, state level sales tax, entry tax, stamp duty, telecom licence fees, turnover tax, tax on consumption or sale of electricity, taxes on transportation of goods and services etc., it will eliminate the cascading effects of taxation. GST will facilitate seamless credit across the entire supply chain and across all states under a common tax base. Experts believe that GST is likely to improve tax collections and boost India's economic development by breaking tax barriers between states and integrating India through a uniform tax rate.

## *Can the government not give a boost to infrastructure by allowing the fiscal deficit to go up while making sure that the incremental deficit is for capital expenditure?*

There is a case for this if the economy shows presence of considerable excess capacity; private sector is reluctant to invest and demand for credit is slack and finally, there is enough cushion in the form of buffer stock of grains and foreign exchange reserves, which can be used to meet any supply constraint, in case the capacity does not last very long. So irrespective of whether the deficit is money financed or financed through market borrowing, it should not exert too much of a pressure on either prices or interest rates.

However, the answer is not cut and dry. First, in case of infrastructure projects, being long duration projects, it is not clear how long the excess capacity or the cushion will last. Second, and more important, one cannot ignore the lags. In case of road construction project, for example, the inside lag was more than 5 years. Again, while we keep complaining about the sharp fall in government's capital expenditure as a proportion of GDP over the years, a closer look at the fiscal data reveals that even this smaller amount in some years did not get spent because of failure to identify productive investment avenues. Here is another example of inside lag. Finally, the outside lags are well known. There is a wide gap between what a project sets out to do and what it actually does because of leakages, diversions, time and cost overruns, poor service delivery and so on. Somehow the entire emphasis in government programmes is on spending rather than on outcomes.

The point merits consideration. If the borrowed money spent, even on capital expenditure, does not generate the expected increase in output, then the expenditure is neither desirable nor sustainable. This is not to suggest that government investment in infrastructure has had no role to play in the Indian economy. On the contrary, it cannot be denied that when it came to infrastructure investment in India, for a combination of reasons, the choice was not between public sector investment and private sector investment but between public sector investment and no investment. Outside lags, therefore, came to be accepted as normal. Efficiency considerations were relegated to the background. However, with the burgeoning fiscal deficit, it is becoming increasingly important that government's capital expenditure brings adequate returns and the outside lags are kept at a minimum. Otherwise the borderline between revenue deficit and deficit on capital account becomes very thin[19].

---

[19] Roy Shyamal, "*India's Rising Fiscal Deficit: Should we worry*"? *WSJ*, October 5, 2009.

## *If government investment is known to have long outside lags, how come the road construction project (Golden Quadrilateral and Corridors) is, more or less, on course?*

Clearly, there is something to learn from and further build on the road construction experience. A major source of financing the road construction work is cess collected on fuel consumption. The Central Road Fund (CRF) stipulates that every year this amount collected will be voted on by the Parliament for transfer to CRF. Though the transfer is not automatic, but once transferred to CRF, it cannot lapse and can be used only for specified road related purposes. CRF then transfers it to the National Highway Authority of India (NHAI), which is the implementing agency.[20] Here is a case where outside lags can be considerably reduced if the funds earmarked for capital expenditure are held in a committed account where, once in that account, there is little scope for leakage or diversion. This way, government's policy credibility goes up, thereby creating a more conducive environment for business. The idea of a dedicated or committed fund offers a real possibility of ensuring a steady return on government investment in infrastructure. In course of time, the committed funds, instead of being used for direct financing of projects, could be used as leverage for attracting more private sector investment in infrastructure.

## *What has been the trend in debt–GDP ratio in India?*

Figure 4.15 gives the trends in debt–GDP ratio in India. Debt–GDP ratio initially rose and then fell. At the end of 2008/09, it stood at about 73 per cent of GDP. This is high compared to other BRIC countries (Brazil 46.8 per cent, China 18.2 per cent, and Russia 6.9 per cent). Fortunately, our external debt–GDP ratio is small; so there is no serious concern about real resources getting out of the country to finance the debt. Nevertheless, domestic debt also has to be financed. And, unless checked, a rising domestic debt may lead to rise in taxes, interest rates, and prices. To arrest this situation, therefore, either we have to bring the primary deficit down (hopefully to a surplus) or step up our real growth of GDP. We have to carefully monitor which way the economy goes in the years ahead.

[20] I have benefited from e-mail exchanges with Partha Mukhopadhyay and, my student, K P Krishnan in understanding how CRF works.

## 4.6 The Special Case of 2008-09 and What it Holds for Future Fiscal Correction

The year 2008/09 offers a unique opportunity to apply some of the fiscal policy concepts developed in this chapter as also to understand the issues they give rise to.

If we take the five-year period preceding 2008/09, it can be seen (Table 4.6) that Central Government finances showed a steady improvement between 2003/04 and 2007/08. At the end of 2007/08, fiscal deficit was brought down to 2.69% of GDP and revenue deficit to 1.11 per cent. There was also a primary surplus, albeit low, at 0.93 per cent of GDP.

This improvement was facilitated by a very impressive rise in GDP growth at close to 9 per cent per annum, which in turn, gave a boost to tax revenue collections (Table 4.5). There was some moderation in expenditures as well, but nothing significant (Table 4.2). Receipts from public sector disinvestments were also inconsequential.

In the year 2008/09, Indian economic growth suffered a setback. The growth rate slowed down to 6.7 per cent when compared to 8.9 per cent average in the previous five year period. This was mainly the result of a global economic and financial meltdown (more on this in Chapter 6) which manifested itself in:

1. Sharp deceleration in export growth.
2. Liquidity crisis arising out of drying up of funds from: (a) external sources, (b) domestic capital markets, and (c) non-banking financial institutions.
3. A more cautious attitude towards lending by the commercial banks.
4. A generally negative consumer and business sentiment.

Clearly, as we discussed in Chapter 3 and beginning of Chapter 4, if private sector consumption and investment spending is characterized by a sense of pessimism (being driven by autonomous variables) and export growth is constrained by the growth of GDP of the buyer countries, fiscal policy has a major role to play in providing a boost to aggregate demand and, thereby, reviving private sector confidence in the economy.

Accordingly, the government lowered excise duty across the board by 6 per cent and service tax by 2 per cent. Also, there was a sharp increase in government expenditure to make up for the lacklustre growth in private demand and to provide income support in rural areas. Government expenditure as a per centage of GDP, which was 15.01 per cent in 2007/08 rose to 16.93 per cent in 2008/09.[21]

Fiscal stimulation had its effects, as conventional wisdom would suggest. Fiscal stimulation not only arrested GDP slowdown to 6.7 per cent in 2008/09 but also led a smart recovery to 7.5 per cent in 2009/10. Data on contribution of different components of aggregate demand to GDP growth in these years[22] amply bear this out.

However, the entire fiscal stimulation came from borrowed money, mainly market borrowings. And, this caused a marked change in the state of public finances of the Central Government as shown in the table below.

*Table 4.6 India: Central government's deficit as % of GDP*

| Item | 2007/08 | 2008/09 | 2009/10 (Revised Estimate) |
|---|---|---|---|
| Fiscal Deficit | 2.69 | 6.14 | 6.7 |
| Revenue Deficit | 1.11 | 4.53 | 5.3 |
| Deficit on Capital a/c | 1.58 | 1.61 | 1.4 |
| Primary deficit | –0.93 | 2.51 | 3.2 |

Between 2007/08 and 2008/09, the central government's fiscal deficit, as a per centage of GDP, more than doubled. The upward trend continued in 2009/10 as well. But, more important, the revenue deficit, which was 41 per cent of fiscal deficit in 2007/08 rose to 77 and 79 per cent in 2008/09 and 2009/10, respectively. Similarly, the primary deficit, which was a modest surplus in 2007/08, jumped to a whopping 2.51 per cent of GDP in 2008/09 and further to 3.2 per cent in 2009/10.

The policy makers are now in a dilemma. While a sharp rise in fiscal deficit, largely propelled by revenue deficit, has helped the Indian economy to revive, neither the size nor the quality of this fiscal deficit is sustainable over a longer period of time. Each year's deficit will add to the size of the debt. This will increase the interest burden of the government. The government will have to resort to further borrowing and further rise in

[21] Fiscal stimulation was ably supported by monetary policy stimulation through concessional credit to crisis hit sectors, cut in interest rates for home and car loans and by lowering the mandatory requirement of lending to the government by banks from 25 to 24 per cent of their deposits.

[22] Economic Survey, 2009–10, Table 1.4, pp.6.

revenue deficit. Interest rates in the economy will rise. Private sector revival will get scuttled.

On the other hand, if the government pulls out of the fiscal stimulation package by reverting to pre-stimulation period tax rates and/or by moderating government expenditure, it will have to be certain that the private sector revival is robust enough to maintain the tempo of growth. If not, the economy may slide back to modest growth rates and sentiments may again turn negative.

In the Union budget 2010/11, the finance minister (FM) has treaded a very cautious path. The FM announced a partial reversal in tax rates but no cutback in government expenditure. He also provided a road map (Table 4.7) for bringing fiscal and revenue deficits down over the next several years.

*Table 4.7 India: Road map for fiscal correction (% of GDP)*

| Item/Year | 2009/10 (Revised Estimate) | 2010/11 (Budget Estimate) | 2011/12 (Target) | 2012/13 (Target) |
|---|---|---|---|---|
| Fiscal Deficit | 6.7 | 5.5 | 4.8 | 4.1 |
| Revenue Deficit | 5.3 | 4.0 | 3.4 | 2.7 |

The conceptual basis for FM's announcements has to be understood. First, when spending decisions in the economy are driven by autonomous variables, policy-induced changes by way of changes in tax rates may not matter much. To an extent that was the case; it was safe to partially reverse the tax rates rather than government expenditure. Second, a roadmap gives a signal to the private sector that government is serious about containing fiscal and revenue deficits. Thus, the cost of doing business in India need not be prohibitive. Expectations turn positive.

However, the immediate question that arises is: how is the FM going to bring down the fiscal deficit to 5.5 per cent of GDP in 2010/11 from 6.7 per cent in 2009/10 when he has not announced any reversal of stimulation package other than a token reversal in the indirect tax rates? The answer is that many items of expenditure like payment of pay commission arrears, loan waiver payments, petroleum subsidies which were incurred in 2009/10 will not be there in 2010/11. Also, the government is counting on one time receipt from 3G spectrum auction (non-tax revenue) and other receipts due to disinvestment in PSU. Some analysts have estimated that the saving on account of these items will amount to between 1.2 and 1.4 per cent of GDP, thus enabling a lower fiscal deficit in 2010/11 compared to 2009/10.

But will it be possible to sustain this fiscal correction in the coming years as set out in the road map? Before we answer this question, it may be useful to introduce the concepts of *cyclical* and *structural* deficits. Cyclical deficit is the borrowing that is resorted to at the low point of the business cycle. A good part of the fiscal stimulation in India is, for example, cyclical in nature. By definition, the cyclical deficit should be repaid by a cyclical surplus at the peak of the business cycle. The structural deficit, on the other hand, is the deficit that remains through the business cycle, because the general level of government spending is too high for prevailing tax levels. In the Indian context, this will reflect structural rigidities which show up in the form of petroleum subsidy, fertilizer subsidy and food subsidy as also an outmoded tax structure.

Let us now come back to the question posed earlier about the sustainability of fiscal correction in the coming years. The arguments are as follows:

1. To the extent part of this deficit is cyclical, that part will be subject to automatic correction as the GDP growth gathers momentum.
2. Primary deficit, accordingly, will come down.
3. India, unlike many other countries, enjoys the option of raising a substantial amount of money through public sector disinvestment.
4. Since part of revenue expenditure (e.g., expenditure incurred for human capital development) adds to long-term growth and can be equated with capital expenditure, all the deficit may not be of poor quality.

However, while the above arguments are well taken, the final test of sustainability of public finances will depend on government's ability to rein in the structural deficit. On the cost side, it will depend on how quickly we can bring down the subsidies (petroleum, fertilizer, and food); and, on the revenue side, it will depend on restructuring of taxes through speedier implementation of GST and DTC.

Globally also, there is a growing concern about the sustainability of fiscal deficit. Fiscal stimulation, globally, is of the order of $3 trillion. It was necessary to bail the economies out of deep recession. However, the entire amount was raised out of borrowings. On the one hand, therefore, whatever revival we see in the global economies is ascribed to fiscal stimulation; on the other hand, there is a lingering fear that if the government expenditure remains over extended, that may slow down the process of private sector revival.

There are two differences between Indian and the developed world situations. Private sector revival is slower in the developed world compared to India. Those countries can thus, perhaps, put up with high fiscal deficit a little longer without the fear of domestic interest rates rising. Second, much of the fiscal deficit in the developing world is seen as cyclical in nature and therefore amenable to automatic correction, once the revival gathers steam. On the other hand, in India, the revival is faster and the deficit is also structural. On top of that inflationary pressures are building up. Hence, the role of fiscal policy in these two situations has to be seen in perspective.

If the fiscal deficit, both in quantitative and qualitative terms, continues as at present, how will the business scenario look? We have already discussed the impact of a high fiscal deficit on the growth of demand for goods and services in the economy. In Figure 4.17, we summarize the implication for cost. What Figure 4.17 says is that if the government has a fiscal deficit, it has to be financed. There are four ways of financing it: (a) borrow from the RBI (money-financed), (b) borrow from the domestic market (bond-financed), (c) increase taxes (tax-financed) and, (d) borrow from abroad (externally financed).

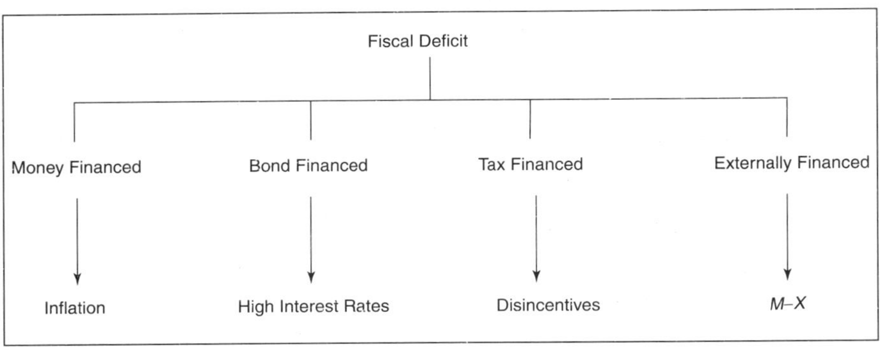


**FIGURE 4.17** *India: Cost Worries from High Fiscal Deficit*

The arrows show that, irrespective of which mode the country chooses to finance the deficit, it will be inimical to the growth of private sector. In the first case, it will be inflationary; in the second case it will put pressure on domestic interest rates; in the third case it will act as a dampener on incentives to produce; and, in the last case, it will widen the gap between imports and exports and, thereby, destabilize the currency.

## 4.7 Concluding Comments

Fiscal policy still, to a large extent, drives the business environment in India. The issues are as follows: When there is substantial excess capacity in the economy, and changes in interest rates and tax rates are not bringing the desired results, a fiscal stimulant can turn the economy around. However, it is not the quantity but the quality of government intervention that ultimately matters. Government deficit used to finance unproductive expenditure can affect revenue growth by adversely impacting the growth of overall demand for goods and services in the economy. It can also impact the cost variables through its destabilizing effect on taxes, interest rates, prices and exchange rates. The debt/GDP ratio will steadily rise. The manager should, therefore, not only focus on the state of the economy, but also the quality of government expenditure.

In India we have two problems. First, there is a need to reduce government deficit that goes towards financing unproductive expenditure (revenue deficit). On the other hand, there is, perhaps, a case for increasing government spending (deficit) in infrastructure. Infrastructure growth, we have seen, holds the key to a sustained growth of GDP in the country. And, private sector, partly due to structural rigidities in the economy and partly because of the nature of investment, has shied away from investing in the country's infrastructure. But the issue here is one of outside lags. If the lags are too long, even the so called "investment" expenditure may turn out to be unproductive.

There is, therefore, a twin need. First, the government must find innovative ways of financing investments such that yields result in the shortest possible time. The financing of road infrastructure project has thrown up certain possibilities in this regard. Second, the government must aim towards bringing the size of revenue deficit close to zero so that borrowed money is not used up for activities that bring no return.

In recognition of the above problem, the government had passed the Fiscal Responsibility and Budget Management Act (FRBMA) in 2004. FRBMA stipulated elimination of revenue deficit by 2008/09, with a minimum annual reduction by 0.5 per cent of GDP. In the case of fiscal deficit FRMBA set a target of 3 per cent of GDP by 2008/09. India made a good beginning towards achieving the FRBMA targets. However, the final achievement got derailed because of the global economic slowdown. There is a need to return to the FRBMA mandate at the earliest. The concerns are:

(a) to what extent the government will be able to target the revenue deficit, given the complex coalition political structure at the centre; (b) the speed with which it will be able to eliminate structural rigidities both on the side of cost and revenue; (c) what will be the pace of disinvestment in PSUs; (d) steps the government will be able to take in reducing the outside lags[23], and (e) how quickly state governments also fall in line vis-à-vis their own fiscal management.

An astute manager should understand that it is not the level but the stability of macroeconomic variables, which is the key determinant of business environment. The manager should be able to understand the relationship between fiscal deficit and stability/instability of GDP growth, interest rates, tax rates, prices, and exchange rates. The fiscal variables that the manager should monitor are as follows: (a) size of the revenue deficit as a per centage of GDP and the factors driving it; (b) quality of deficit spending on capital account in terms of cost and time overruns; and (c) the trends in the debt/GDP ratio.

[23] The Right to Information Act (RTIA) has already made some difference. Additionally, a new major initiative to set up the Unique Identification Authority of India (UIAI) with a mandate to create an online database with identity and biometric details of Indian residents, which is likely to be completed by 2010/11, will enable enrolment and verification of services across the country.

ANNEXURE

# STATE OF THE ECONOMY

State of the Economy, so very important to assess the effectiveness of various macroeconomic policies, can be understood with the help of some simple diagrams as shown below.

An aggregate demand (AD) curve shows the relationship between the general price level (*P*) and quantity of goods and services demanded in the economy (*Q*). The AD curve slopes downwards. This is because, other things being equal, as general price level (*P*) rises, real value of money (*M*/*P*) falls, resulting in reduced spending on goods and services, and vice versa.

An aggregate supply (AS) curve shows the relationship between general price level (*P*) and the quantity of goods and services produced in the economy (*Q*). The AS curve generally slopes upwards, though in extreme cases, can be horizontal or vertical. A horizontal AS curve signals presence of massive excess capacity across the economy so that production of goods and services can be stepped up without affecting a rise in prices. A vertical AS curve means that the economy is operating at full capacity and there is no scope for further increase in output. An upward sloping AS curve, on the other hand, provides possibilities of raising output but at higher price levels.

We are now able to put our discussion of the state of the economy in a diagrammatic form. This is shown in the following Box. Charts 1 and 2 correspond to states of the economy (a) and (d) described in section 4.4.1. Chart 1 shows that the slack in the economy is so much that the AS curve is a horizontal straight line. Under the circumstances, if AD increases from $AD_1$ to $AD_2$, let us say, because of a rise.

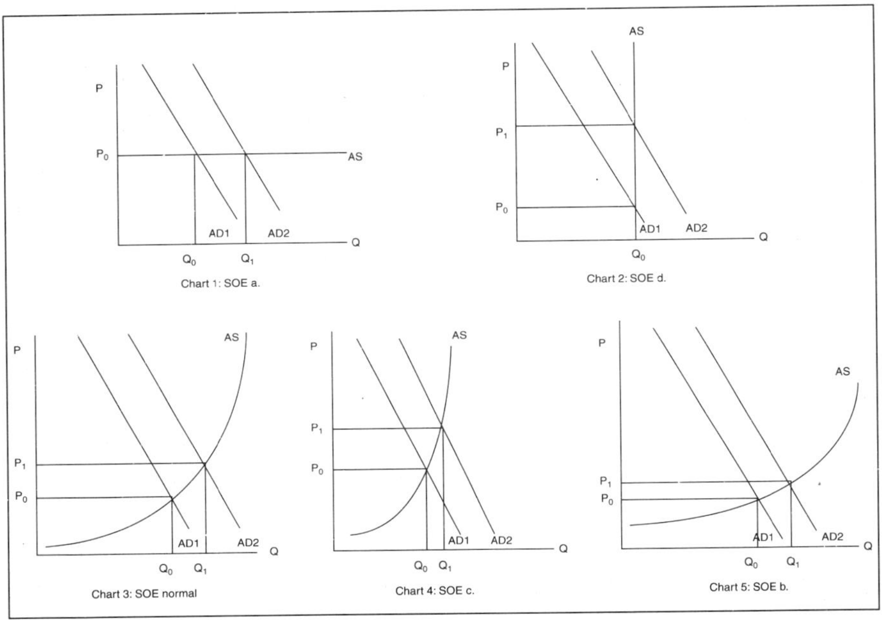


**FIGURE A4.1** *Understanding Different Status of Economy (SOE) Diagrammatically*

In government expenditure, output increases from $Q_0$ to $Q_1$, but there is no change in the general price level. Chart 2 depicts the other extreme where economy wide full capacity is already reached such that AS curve is vertical and if the AD increases from $AD_1$ to $AD_2$, the increase in demand will be fully dissipated by a rise in prices from $P_0$ to $P_1$ and there will be no increase in output.

Of course, both the cases presented above are extreme cases and do not usually picture the real life situations. In real life, the AS curve is upward sloping as shown in Chart 3 above, which says that as AD increases, there is a rise both in output and prices. But within an upward sloping AS curve, we can have a steep AS curve (Chart 4) or, a flat AS curve (Chart 5). Chart

4 and Chart 5 correspond to our discussion of the state of the economy (c). and (b). respectively, in Section 4.4.1. We can see that when the state of the economy is characterized by (b). in Section 4.4.1 (Chart 5 in the box), the AS curve is flat, thereby, implying presence of substantial excess capacity but not quite like in Chart 1 to make it a horizontal straight line. Here, the producer will probably have to pay a moderately higher price for inputs to realize the increased output, consequent to an increase in demand. But the important point to note is that in situations as shown in Chart 5, the increase in real output ($Q_1$ to $Q_0$) will be greater than the increase in prices ($P_1$ to $P_0$).

But this will not be so if the state of the economy is characterized as (c). in our discussion in Section 4.4.1 (Chart 4 in the box). You can see from Chart 4 that if the AS curve is steep, then consequent to a rise in demand from $AD_1$ to $AD_2$, the increase in prices ($P_1$ to $P_0$) will be sharper than the increase in real output ($Q_1$ to $Q_0$). This happens because the economy is closer to full capacity and, therefore, any attempt to increase output will require a much sharper rise in input prices. Between Charts 5 and 4, of course, there will be an entire range, captured by Chart 3, where depending on at what point the economy is on the AS curve, output and prices will change accordingly.

The manager has to be clear about two points. First, the flatter the AS curve or closer the state of the economy is to (b). larger, in general, will be the role of fiscal policy in stimulating the economy. It is also important to reiterate that the objective of macroeconomic policy is twofold in nature: sustained growth in output along with stability in prices. You will notice from Charts 3–5 in the box that with an upward sloping AS curve, it will always be possible to increase output. But the issue is at what price level? An increase in output, if it is not consistent with price stability, will not be favoured by the policy maker.

# REVIEW QUESTIONS

**1.** Four economists are debating the impact of fiscal deficit on the economy. This is what each has to say:

(a) Economist 1: Fiscal deficit is an excellent way of stimulating the economy

(b) Economist 2: No, fiscal deficit crowds out private investment

(c) Economist 3: No, fiscal deficit crowds in private investment and,

(d) Economist 4: Whatever you say, fiscal deficit is matter of concern in India

Assume each economist is correct in what he/she is saying. Just spell out the conditions that must hold true in the economy for each argument to be correct.

**2.** Suppose the government has the option of stimulating the economy through (a) an increase in government expenditure and (b) a reduction in taxes. Other things being equal, which will have a larger impact on GDP and why?

**3.** Based on your answer to question 2 above, state how the government decides between the above two methods of stimulating the economy?

**4.** Given

Revenue receipts 91083
Recovery of loans 11952
Market borrowings 56743
Non-plan revenue expenditure 93847
Interest payments 44049
Non-plan capital expenditure 19514
Plan revenue expenditure28265
Plan capital expenditure 19514

Compute: (a) revenue deficit, (b) monetized deficit, (c) fiscal deficit, and (d) primary deficit.

**5.** Discuss what each of the deficit figures above signal for business.

**6.** Trace the relationship between fiscal deficit and (a) prices (b) interest rates (c) tax rates and (d) exchange rates. In India, for several years between' 1997-98 and 2001-02, the above cost variables have ruled steady, despite a high fiscal deficit. How do you explain that?

**7.** From your answer to question 6 above, should we be worrying about fiscal deficit? Give reasons for your answer.

**8.** What is the difference between deficit and debt? When is debt sustainable and when it is not? State clearly what roles real interest rates, real GDP growth and primary deficit play in arriving at your answer and why?

**9.** Based on your answer to question 8, do you think the size of India's debt is a cause of concern? If so, how will you address the problem? What macroeconomic variables will you monitor?

**10.** What is the allocative role that taxes play in an economy? Why are direct taxes progressive and indirect taxes regressive? What do they mean for tax policy?

**11.** "In the long run debt financing of increased government spending may be more inflationary than money financing". Do you agree with this statement? Why or why not?

CHAPTER

5

# Monetary Policy

In Section 2.2[1] in Chapter 2, the basics of money were briefly introduced. We said that the primary role of money was to serve as a medium of exchange. Money is what we use to make payments. However, money also acts as a measure of value and store of wealth. We defined money supply as currency with public and chequeable deposits with banks because that is what we use to make payments. We also discussed the determinants of money demand and how money affects aggregate demand or actual GDP. In this chapter, we will build further on these concepts plus have an in-depth discussion of money supply process and issues related to the conduct of monetary policy. We will begin with a formal definition of money supply.

## 5.1 Money Supply – How is it Defined

We use the following definitions of money:

M1 = currency with public + demand deposits with banks + "other deposits" with RBI[2]

[1] Review the entire Section 2.13 before you begin this chapter.

[2] Demand deposits held with the RBI by international agencies, financial institutions, state governments etc. This is a very small amount. We will ignore this component of money supply in later discussions.

M3 = M1 + time deposits with banks[3] (i.e., currency with public + all bank deposits).

M1 is a narrow measure of the function of money as a medium of exchange; M3 is a broader measure of money that also reflects the function of money as a store of value, which can be converted to make payments. When we talk about money supply, we usually refer to broad money supply or, M3.

At the end of 2008/09, currency with public was Rs. 6,66,364 crores; demand deposits were Rs. 5,81,247 crores; "other deposits" were Rs. 5,573 crores; and time deposits were Rs. 35,10,835 crores. M1 was Rs. 12,53,184 crores and M3 was Rs. 47,64,019 crores. In other words, in M1, currency with public was the biggest component (53 per cent), followed by demand deposits (46 per cent). Other deposits were inconsequential at 1 per cent. In M3, however, deposits form a much larger proportion (86 per cent) compared to currency with public (14 per cent).

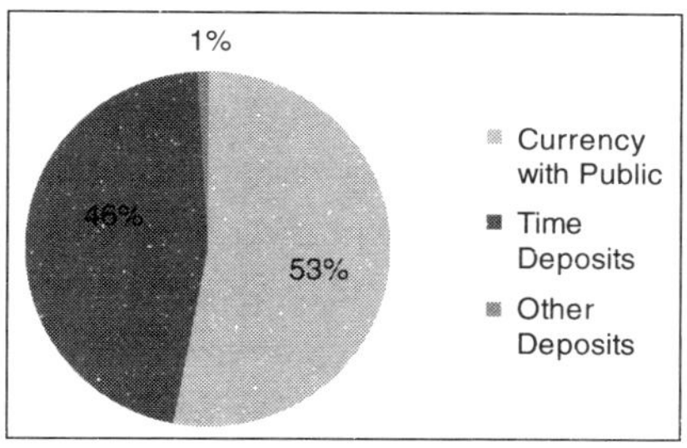


**FIGURE 5.1** *Components of M1, 2008/09*

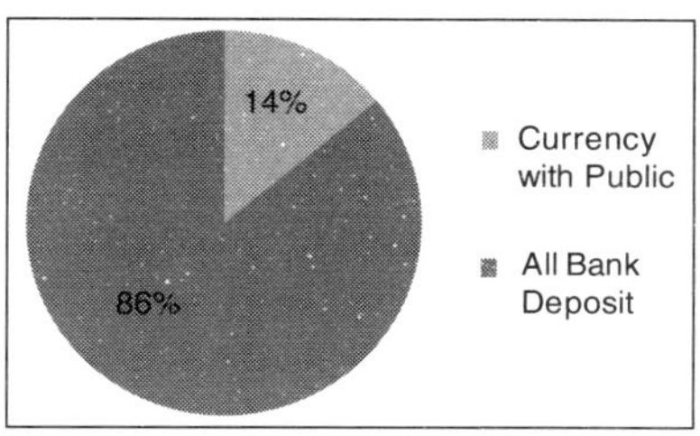


**FIGURE 5.2** *Components of M3, 2008/09*

In the olden days commodities, notably silver and gold, were used as money. Subsequently, when paper money and chequeable deposits were introduced, they were convertible into commodity money. Presently,

[3] There is also M2 = M1 + post office saving deposits and M4= M3 + all post office deposits. But post office deposits are not treated as part of money supply in the discussion on money supply. We will, therefore, stick to M3.

however, everywhere in the world, money that is circulating is in the nature of a fiat money, money that is issued and guaranteed by monetary authorities, without legal constraints.

## 5.2 Demand For Money

It may be useful to recall a few points from our earlier discussion on demand for money in Section 2.13 in Chapter 2. First, when we talk about demand for money we are talking about desire to hold money in idle form, which carries no (currency) or very little (demand deposits) interest. Second, when we talk of money, demand we are referring to real money demand, after adjusting for inflation.

Having clarified the above points, it is to be noted that the demand for money is driven by three motives: (a) transaction motive, (b) precautionary motive, and (c) speculative motive. Transaction motive for holding money arises out of need to transact in goods and services; precautionary motive for holding money is to provide a cushion for unexpected events; and speculative demand for money arises out of a desire to speculate in the bond market and reap capital gains or avoid capital loss. We also specified a demand function of money as an increasing function of income (GDP) and a decreasing function of interest rate, which means that, other things being equal, demand for holding money on all three counts will grow with income but will come down as interest rate goes up and the cost of holding money in idle form increases.

Let us now elaborate on the above. Transaction demand for money depends mostly on income. Individuals are assumed to hold money because it is a medium of exchange that can be used to carry out every day transactions. The level of people's transactions primarily determines this demand. Since transactions are proportional to income, the transactions demand for money is also proportional to income. It depends less on interest rates.

However, demand for money for transaction purposes will depend on frequency of payment. Demand for money will be less if a person is paid weekly than if he is paid monthly. If a person is paid Rs. 100 every week and he distributes this amount equally over the week, his average (middle of the week) holding of money will be Rs. 50. On the other hand, if the person is paid every month and receives Rs. 400, assuming, again, that he will distribute this amount equally over the month, his average (middle of the month) holding of money will be Rs. 200. Another way to look at it is that when the demand for money is less (in case of weekly payment), the number of times money changes hands (income velocity of money) is more and when the demand for money is more (in case of monthly payment), the income velocity of money is less. This is because larger the amount of money held in idle form, less will be its circulation. By definition, idle money cannot circulate. It can then be seen that if someone was paid daily, demand for holding money for this person in idle form would be very low and the number of times the given money would change hands would be very high.

Transaction demand for money also depends on financial sophistication. As people switch to credit cards or ATMs, the demand for money comes down. Typically, financial liberalization is accompanied by a fall in the demand for money.

On both the above counts, however, demand for money may be predicted with a certain degree of accuracy. Payment habits do not change frequently. Demand for money can also be assumed to be a steady function of financial sophistication.

Precautionary demand, of course, is also a function of income but it is likely to be more sensitive to interest rates. If the interest rate rises, the cost of holding money for precautionary reasons will go up and the demand will come down.

Speculative demand depends on expected change in interest rates, exchange rates, and so on. If people expect interest rate to go up (bond prices to fall), speculative demand for money will rise, as people would like to hold on to their money rather than bonds, to avoid a capital loss when the interest rates go up (bond prices fall), and vice versa, if people expect interest rates to fall (bond prices to go up)[4]. Similarly, if I am an importer and I expect the rupee to appreciate, I will hold on to my money rather than dollars, to avoid a capital loss when rupee appreciates, or value of dollar falls. The demand for money will, therefore, go up and vice versa, if I expect rupee to depreciate.

Stability of demand for money is important for proper conduct of monetary policy. While it is almost universally true that demand for money is an increasing function of income and a decreasing function of interest rate, what is not clear is how stable this relationship is. The source of instability arises primarily from the fact that a good part of demand for money is expectation driven. For example, we have seen the following scenarios:

1. Expectations about interest rates and exchange rates play a key role in the determination of demand for money. In an era of uncertainty

[4] See Chapter 2, Section 2.12.

about inflation, exchange rates and interest rates expectations will be hard to predict. Expectations will be susceptible to rumours and political events.

2. Demand for money is inversely related to expected interest rates and expected exchange rates
3. Income velocity of money is inversely related to demand for money and,
4. If expectations are hard to predict, so is velocity.

Clearly, the relationship between money demand, income and interest rates is not the issue. The real issue is whether this relationship can be predicted with a certain degree of accuracy.

## 5.3 Monetary Policy Transmission Mechanism

Monetary transmission mechanism describes the routes through which a monetary policy change affects output and prices. We explained this in general terms in Section 2.12 in Chapter 2. Now we will take a closer look.

A monetary policy change first impacts the financial variables. Changes in financial variables, in turn, affect consumer and business spending, and thereby, aggregate demand for goods and services. Finally, a change in the aggregate demand impacts output and prices in the economy. Schematically, the monetary policy transmission mechanism is shown in Figure 5.3.

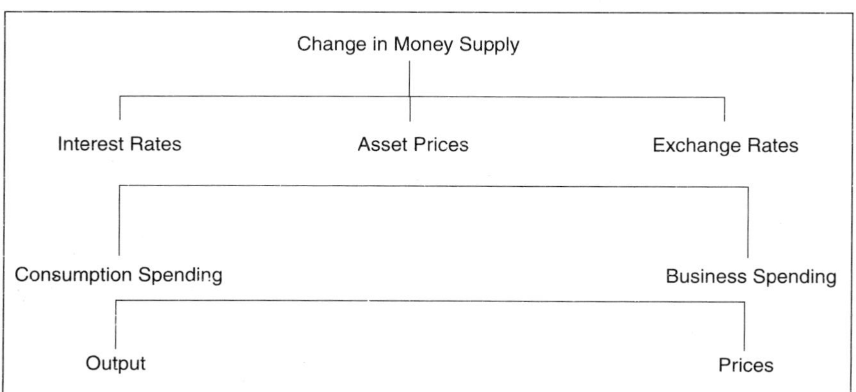


**Figure 5.3** *Monetary Policy Transmission Mechanism*

## 5.3.1 Impact on Financial Variables

We begin with a discussion of monetary policy impact on financial variables.

### *Interest Rates*

Assume an initial position of equilibrium, where demand for money in the economy is equal to supply of money in the economy. Corresponding to this position, there is an interest rate, capturing the price of money. Now, suppose the monetary authorities decide to increase the money supply (let us not bother till next section as to how the money supply goes up). At the prevailing interest rate and level of income, people are holding more money than they want. The supply of money is greater than the demand for money.

People will, thus, go for portfolio adjustment and try to reduce their money holdings by buying interest-bearing assets, what we call bonds. Bond prices will go up; bond yields will come down. Interest rates will come down. Similarly, if the monetary authorities decide to contract the money supply, compared to the initial position, we will have a situation where supply of money will fall short of demand for money. People will sell their bonds to obtain more money to meet their current demand for money. The price of bonds will fall; yields on bonds will rise and the interest rates in the economy will rise. Therefore, the first impact of a change in monetary policy (a change in money supply) is felt on the interest rates in the economy. If the monetary policy stance is perceived to be temporary, the pressure, initially, is on short-term interest rates. If it is sustained, the pressure may extend to long-term rates as well.

Changes in interest rates, caused by monetary policy changes, in turn, affect several financial variables in the market place, though the relative importance of these variables varies from time to time. Let us take the case of an expansionary monetary policy where an increase in money supply has resulted in a fall in the interest rates. This will generate the following effects on other financial variables.

### *Asset Prices*

We have already seen the existence of an inverse relationship between interest rates and bond prices. A policy-induced decrease in the interest rates raises the value of long-lived assets like stocks, bonds, and real estate. This increases the net worth of households and businesses (positive wealth effect). The value of the collateral they offer for obtaining loans, correspondingly, goes up.

### *Exchange Rates*

Depending on how free the movement of capital is between countries, a fall in the interest rate in one country relative to another country will make investment in the other country's markets more attractive. Capital will flow out of the country. People will sell local currency to buy more foreign currency to invest in that country's markets because interest rates in that market are now relatively more attractive. The demand for foreign currency will go up compared to the supply of foreign currency. The price of foreign currency will rise in relation to the local currency. The local currency will depreciate in value vis-à-vis the foreign currency.

## 5.3.2 From Financial Markets to Consumer and Business Spending

### *Consumer Spending (C)*

Here we are asking the question: how do changes in financial variables, discussed above, affect consumer spending? Let us consider each financial variable, in turn. A fall in the interest rates, consequent to an expansionary monetary policy, affects consumer spending in two ways. For those who have debt, the interest outgo is less than before. The remaining disposable income, thus, goes up. This enables them to spend more on goods and services. For those who are not in debt, a fall in the interest rates (returns on savings) makes current consumption more attractive than future consumption. They are tempted to spend more and save less.

An increase in the asset prices, similarly, impacts consumption spending in the economy in two ways. Since an asset price rise increases the net worth of the individual, consumer spending goes up because the consumer 'feels' wealthier (positive consumer sentiment) and because he now 'actually' finds it easier to borrow (value of the collateral has gone up) and spend more on goods and services.

Finally, depreciation of the local currency affects consumption spending in the economy in the following way. Currency depreciation makes imports relatively more expensive than before. The competitiveness of domestic producers of goods and services, therefore, goes up. This encourages spending away from imports to domestically produced goods and services. Overall domestic spending goes up.

### *Business Spending (I)*

Changes in market interest rates, asset prices and exchange rates that follow a monetary policy change, affect business spending in the economy in a similar manner. Let us look at the impact on each of these once again. We already know that investment is inversely related to interest rates. A fall in the interest rate enhances new investment in plants and equipments and in expansion of labour force. This is because now the return that companies will require from new investment projects (captured by the cost of money) will be less. More investment projects will get cleared. Also, companies who rely on loans will see their profits going up resulting from a lower interest outgo and, will, therefore, have more money to invest.[5]

An increase in the asset prices also facilitates investment spending in the economy. Bank loans and other loans are usually secured on assets. If the asset prices rise, the net worth of the company increases and it becomes easier for the company to borrow and invest.

Finally, the effect of currency depreciation affects investment spending through two routes. As already discussed, currency depreciation will shift the demand of domestic consumers towards domestically produced goods and services, away from imports. The total demand for domestically produced goods and services will, thus, go up, thereby necessitating further investment in the production of those goods and services. A depreciation of the currency will also generate more demand for our goods and services by the foreigners (exports) since now the price of our products to the foreigner has come down relative to their own. This will also put additional pressure to produce more for meeting the increased demand.

## 5.3.3 From Aggregate Demand to Actual GDP and Prices

The changes in the behaviour of consumers and businesses, in response to a monetary policy change, as discussed above, result in an increase in the aggregate spending in the economy. This increase in aggregate spending (demand) will result in some increase in actual GDP and some increase in general price level. The extent of increase in each will depend on the

[5] With regard to consumption and investment spending, in both cases, those who have borrowed at fixed rates will not face lower interest rates till their fixed term expires. But new borrowers will benefit.

extent of excess capacity in the economy (Chapter 4; Section 4.4.1). In the actual conduct of the monetary policy, the monetary authorities will have to consider the state of the economy, so that in its attempt to stimulate growth, prices do not go overboard.

In this context, it is important to understand that central banks are not providers of saving but are providers of liquidity (money) in the economy. For example, when savings go up, interest rates fall because the supply of loanable funds goes up in relation to demand. At lower interest rates, more demand is generated. The economy produces more goods and services. Both actual GDP and the economy's productive capacity increase. On the other hand, when the central bank is following an expansionary monetary policy, it is increasing money supply in excess of savings in the economy. The savings remains the same. This is being done either because there is a misalignment between liquidity and saving and/or the available saving is not getting translated into investment. The objective of central bank is to provide the banking system with the correct amount of liquidity, given the level of savings. Obviously, if the economy is operating at full capacity (there is no misalignment between saving and investment), an expansionary monetary policy does not make sense, as it will only result in higher prices.

## 5.3.4 Certain Caveats in the Monetary Transmission Mechanism

Certain important aspects of monetary policy transmission mechanism have been glossed over in the above simplistic presentation. However, it is important to highlight those as necessary caveats to the above presentation. For example:

1. When the monetary authorities resort to lowering of interest rates to spur economic activity, they, clearly, target nominal interest rates. However, as discussed in Chapter 2, saving and investment decisions depend not on nominai but on real interest rates. Real interest rate, as was defined, is nominal interest rate *minus* expected inflation. And, since expectations about future inflation are formed based on current inflation, we said, that current inflation can be used as a proxy for future inflation. Thus, when monetary authorities increase the money supply to effect a fall in the interest rates, they assume inflationary

expectations to be constant. Given that, a fall in the nominal interest rate also results in a fall in the real interest rates. And, the rest of the monetary transmission mechanism follows. However, if inflationary expectations are changing, the difference between nominal and real interest rates becomes important. After all, a tight or soft monetary policy is assessed in terms of its impact on real and not just nominal interest rates.

2. Expectations play a very important role in determining the efficacy of a monetary policy move. As we discussed in Chapter 3, a fall in the interest rate may fail to generate the desired change in aggregate demand, if consumer sentiment is negative or, if business sentiment is characterized as one of pessimism[6]. Similarly, if the changes in interest rates are already anticipated, the impact of a rate change on demand will be blunted. Again, whether the interest rate cut is perceived as a means to arrest falling prices vs. as a means to arrest a slowing economy will affect future expectations differently. In other words, the transmission mechanism from financial variables to consumer and business spending may not always be smooth.
3. Finally, the impact of monetary policy moves on financial variables, on consumption and business spending and, ultimately, on GDP and the general price levels is not instantaneous. By the time, a monetary policy announcement is made and its final impact on output and prices, there are long and variable lags. These long lags have important implications for the strategy of monetary policy. Clearly, in the presence of these lags, monetary policy authorities need to take pre-emptive moves. But for a pre-emptive move to be effective, monetary authorities should be able to arrive at an intelligent judgment on how a monetary policy move today will affect output and prices at a later period and by how much. These are not easy questions to answer. And it is these hazards in policy formulation that makes monetary policy exercise both challenging and, at times, frustrating.

## 5.4 THE MONEY SUPPLY PROCESS

The question we are addressing in this section is: What causes change in money supply? To simplify our description of money supply process, we

[6] In this case, people may just like to hold on to their money and not spend it. Thus, income velocity of money falls.

will ignore "other deposits" from the definition of money supply. We will define money supply as follows:

$$M = C + D$$

where, $M$ stands for money supply; $C$ for currency (notes and coins) held by the public; and $D$ stands for bank deposits. This says that people allocate their money holdings between currency and deposits. If '$x$' is the fraction of $M$ held in the form of $C$, then $1 - x$ is the fraction that constitutes bank deposits.

There are three groups which affect the supply of money in the economy:

1. First is the central bank of the country. Central bank's policy is the most important determinant of money supply. To start with, the central bank is the sole issuer of notes. But more important, through its policies, it affects the most important component of money supply, e.g., bank deposits.
2. Second are the commercial banks. We have already seen that bank deposits constitute the largest component of money supply. Banks can themselves expand the amount of bank deposits, and hence, the money supply, by a process called "credit creation".
3. Third is the public that holds money either in the form of currency or bank deposits. Public's choice between currency and deposits can influence money supply growth.

## 5.4.1 Balance Sheet of the Commercial Banks

The key to understanding the money supply process is to realize that the central bank requires commercial banks to hold, as reserves, a fraction of the deposit they accept. The amount kept as reserves is the money the banks cannot lend out. In other words, if the total deposit of the banking system is Rs. 100 and the reserve requirement is 10 per cent, the banks can lend up to Rs. 90 and the balance must be kept as reserves. Banks hold these reserves partly as cash in their vaults and partly as deposits with the central bank. The central bank in turn keeps changing these reserves in order to influence the money supply.

Table 5.1 shows, in a simplified form, the balance sheet of commercial banks. On the financial asset side, the first item is banks' lending to the government. Item number two is banks' loans to other than government and their own investments. The last two items are reserves, held partly as vault cash and partly in the form of deposits with the central bank. This reserve is a proportion of the total deposits. Some of it is mandatory; some may be non-mandatory, what are known as "excess reserves". On the monetary liability side we have bank deposits and banks' borrowings from the central bank. "Other assets" are, for example, physical assets and "non-monetary liability" will constitute the net worth of the bank.

***Table 5.1 Balance sheet of commercial banks***

| Assets | Liabilities |
|---|---|
| Financial Assets | Monetary Liabilities |
| a. Credit to Government<br>b. Loans and Advances and Other Investments<br>c. Vault Cash (part of reserves)<br>d. Deposits with RBI (part of reserves) | a. Demand Deposits<br>b. Saving Deposits<br>c. Fixed Deposits<br>d. Borrowing from RBI |
| Other Assets | Non-Monetary Liabilities |

Why do banks hold currency as vault cash or deposits with the central bank? Clearly, banks need to hold notes and coins to meet the demand for currency from the bank's customers. For example, when you and I go to the bank to withdraw money, the bank pays us from its vault cash. Banks also need to keep a deposit with the central bank so that it can make payments to other banks. This happens when the total value of cheques made out by a bank's customers exceed the value of the cheques received by its customers in a given trading period. For example, let us consider two banks, State Bank of India (SBI) and Indian Overseas Bank (IOB). On a given day, cheques written by SBI customers to IOB customers represent money that SBI owes to IOB. Similarly, cheques written by IOB customers to SBI customers represent money owed by IOB to SBI. At the end of the trading day, these two sets of debt are compared. If IOB owes some money to SBI, the RBI acts as a clearing agency. It debits IOB's account with it and credits it to the account of SBI. The debt is settled.

Clearly, it is important for banks to maintain adequate liquidity (reserves) in order to meet the demands of its customers. This lends credibility to the two components of money supply e.g., currency and bank deposits.

Customers know that if they want to withdraw currency or if they want to make a payment through cheque those will be honoured. Many banks even find it prudent to keep some excess reserves.

What determines demand for reserves in idle form by the banks? Like we did in the case of demand for money by the public, we can specify a demand function for reserves (money) by the banks. We will say the demand for reserves depends on:

1. The size of the deposit a bank has accepted. Larger it is, bigger will be the size of currency reserves in its vault cash and deposits with the central bank that it will be required to maintain. Particularly, larger the proportion of demand deposits to time deposits, larger the holding of excess reserves.
2. The market interest rate. When interest rates rise banks may be tempted to reduce their excess reserves, knowing that they can always borrow additional funds from other banks (that have extra reserves) or, from the central bank. The cost of borrowing from other banks is the call money market rate and the cost of borrowing from the central bank is the bank rate. Final decision to reduce excess reserves will be inversely related to the difference between interest rate they could have earned by not having excess reserves and the rate they would have to pay, if running short of reserves, and,
3. Uncertainty regarding a bank's cash flow, since banks face a constant trade-off between profitability and safety (need for reserves).

## 5.4.2 Balance Sheet of the Reserve Bank of India

We now turn to the balance sheet of Reserve Bank of India (RBI), the central bank of the country. A simplified version is presented in Table 5.2. In comparison, foreign exchange assets of RBI are the largest component of financial assets of the RBI (item d), followed by RBI credit to the government and RBI lending to banks and the commercial sector (financial institutions).

Largest liability of RBI is the currency outstanding. This is currency in circulation by the public and that held in the vaults of the banks. According to the demand for notes from the public, the amount of bank notes are issued by RBI. The other major liability of RBI is the banks' deposits with RBI about which we discussed in the previous section. "Other assets" of

RBI include physical assets like premises and equipments. "Non-monetary liabilities" include reserves and other accounts.

*Table 5.2 Balance sheet of Reserve Bank of India (RBI)*

| Assets | Liabilities |
|---|---|
| Financial Assets<br>a. Net RBI credit to the government<br>b. RBI credit to banks<br>c. RBI credit to commercial sector<br>d. Net foreign Exchange Assets of RBI | Monetary Liabilities<br>a. Currency<br>- In circulation with public<br>- Vault cash<br>b. Reserves (Banks' deposits with RBI)<br>- Statutory reserves<br>- Excess reserves |
| Other Assets | Non-Monetary Liabilities |

Let us now introduce a term called monetary base (also called 'high-powered money' or, 'reserve money'). Monetary base (MB) consists of currency in circulation with the public + reserves. We already know that reserves are equal to vault cash + banks' deposits with RBI. We can, therefore, see that monetary base is nothing but "monetary liability of RBI" in the RBI balance sheet.

RBI can increase or decrease MB by increasing or decreasing its financial assets. An increase in MB leads to a further increase in money supply through the banking system such that the final increase in the money supply ($M_3$) is a multiple of MB. Let us see how the money supply process works.

## 5.4.3 How Does the Money Supply Process Work?

Let us say that RBI lending to the government has increased by Rs. 100 crores. The government needs this money to construct roads and, therefore, writes a cheque drawn on its account with the RBI to the contractor to start the work. The contractor deposits this money in his bank (say, bank A) and the bank returns this cheque to RBI increasing its balance with RBI by Rs. 100 crores[7]. The monetary base of RBI, therefore, has increased by Rs. 100 crores.

[7] The bank could have also redeemed it as currency. In either case, the monetary base would have risen by Rs. 100 crores.

As discussed earlier, banks want to make profits while maintaining adequate liquidity. Let us assume that 10 per cent of total deposits is considered safe for the purpose of ensuring liquidity. (Or, the reserve-deposit ratio is 0.10). The bank then finds that it has excess reserves with RBI to the extent of Rs. 90 crores because all it needs to keep is 10 per cent of this deposit of Rs. 100 crores, e.g., Rs. 10 crores, in the form of reserves. The bank, therefore, lends out Rs. 90 crores. The recipient of Rs. 90 crores deposits the amount in his bank (say, bank B). At the end of the trading period, RBI credits Bank B's balances with RBI with Rs. 90 crores and debits Bank A's balances with RBI by the same amount. Bank B now finds that it has excess reserves with the RBI to the extent of Rs. 81 crores, because, as 10 per cent of the new deposit it needs to keep only Rs. 9 crores by way of reserves. Bank B lends out Rs. 81 crores. The recipient of this cheque deposits it in his bank (say, bank C). At the end of the trading period Bank C's balances with RBI are credited with Rs. 81 crores and the same amount is debited from Bank B's balances with RBI. Bank C now finds that it has a reserve of Rs. 81 crores when all it needs to keep is Rs. 8.1 crores. Bank C, therefore, lends out Rs. 72.9 crores. And the process goes on.[8] You will notice that this is another geometric series of the type we discussed under multiplier analysis in Chapter 4 and as long as the value of the reserve—deposit ratio is less than one (in our example, it is 0.1), it will have a finite solution. This final solution is given by 1÷reserve-deposit ratio. 1÷reserve—deposit ratio is called the money multiplier, which in our example is 1÷0.10, equal to 10. And, the reserve–deposit ratio is called cash reserve ratio (CRR). The final impact of an increase of Rs. 100 crores in the monetary base on money supply is MB x 10 or, Rs. 1,000 crores. In other words, money supply ($M_3$) is a multiple of MB.

However, in the above example, we have ignored the fact that all money does not get deposited. Public holds part of the money as cash outside the banks, the extent depending on public's preference for currency over deposit. In the money supply process, then, in each round, some of the extra money will leak out of the banking system and the overall money multiplier will come down. To take an extreme example, if the entire increase in the monetary base of Rs. 10 crores is held in the form of currency and nothing is deposited, there is no money for banks to lend out and $M_3$ = MB.

[8] We have categorized the banks for ease of explanation into bank A, B and C. But you should be able to see that the process will hold even if it is the same bank. In this case its balance with RBI will be debited and credited at the same time. So the excess reserve will remain.

The currency-deposit ratio or the amount held in the form of currency as a proportion of deposits will depend on:

1. Spread of banking habits, expansion of bank branch network, financial intermediation, and so on. Currency–deposit ratio will be inversely related to these developments.
2. Payments by cheques or credit cards and other financial sophistication. Again, currency–deposit ratio will fall as these developments take place.
3. Illegal and black money transactions. Currency–deposit ratio will move positively with these transactions.
4. Interest rates. The cost of holding currency will be greater Higher the interest rates, greater the cost of holding currency. Currency–deposit ratio will, therefore, vary inversely with interest rates.

By and large currency–deposit ratio is a behavioural parameter. In general, in a developing country like India, one would expect currency–deposit ratio to come down as financial sector developments advance.

We have discussed how each group, i.e., the central bank, the commercial banks, and the public play a role in the money supply process. Let us now formally bring together each group's role in the form of an algebraic relationship.

We know:

$M = C + D$ ..........................................................(1)

where $M$ is broad money (M3); $C$ is currency in circulation; and $D$ is bank deposits.

We also know that:

$MB = C + R$ .......................................................(2)

where $MB$ is monetary base; $C$ is currency in circulation; and $R$ is reserves (vault cash plus banks' deposits with the RBI).

Dividing and multiplying $(C + D)/(C + R)$ by $D$ we have:

$M = (C/D+1)\ D$ and

$MB = (C/D+R/D)\ D$

We also know that the multiplier (call it '$m$') is $M/MB$. Or

'$m$' $= (C/D) + 1 \div (C/D) + (R/D)$ ...................(3)

where $C/D$ stands for currency reserve ratio; $R/D$ stands for reserve deposit ratio and '$m$' stands for money multiplier.

Equation (3) says that variables that matter in determining '$m$' are, $C/D$ and $R/D$. An increase in $C/D$ reduces '$m$'. Also an increase in $R/D$ lowers '$m$'.

Finally we have:

$M = MB \times 'm'$ ......................................................(4)

Equation (4) says that $M$ is a multiple of $'m'$ of $MB$. A one-rupee change in $MB$ causes a multiple change in $M$. Given $'m'$, a decrease in $MB$ slows down the growth of M. Given $MB$, a decrease in $'m'$ can slow down $M$.

For example, assume, as we did in the beginning of Section 5.4.3, that the change in monetary base (MB) is Rs. 100 crores and the reserve—deposit ratio ($R/D$) is 0.10. But now the additional variable that we introduce is the currency–deposit ratio ($C/D$), which is assumed to be 0.20. The contractor will then withdraw Rs. 16.66 crores, maintaining a $C/D$ of 0.20 and Rs. 83.34 crores will be the increase in the deposits. Since $R/D$ is assumed to be 0.10, the bank will keep Rs. 8.33 crores in the form of reserves and lend out Rs. 75.00 crores. In the second round, out of this, Rs. 12.50 crores will be withdrawn in the form of cash, again maintaining a $C/D$ of 0.20. Rs. 62.51 will be the deposit and, after keeping Rs. 6.25 crores towards $R/D$, Rs. 56.26 will be lent out. And, the process will go on.

Total increase in Deposits will be given by:

$83.34 + 62.51 + 46.88 + \ldots = 83.34[1 + 0.75 + (0.75)^2 + (0.75)^3 \ldots]$

$= 83.34/1 - 0.75 = 333.36$ crores

Total increase in currency will be:

$16.66 + 12.50 + 9.37 + \ldots = 16.66[1 + 0.75 + (0.75)^2 + (0.75)^3 \ldots]$

$= 16.66/1 - 0.75 = 66.64$ crores

The total increase in money supply will be Rs. 400 crores. This is precisely the value we would get from the equation $M = MB \times 'm'$. With $C/D = 0.2$ and $R/D = 0.1$, $'m' = (C/D) + 1 \div (C/D) + (R/D) = 1.2/0.3 = 4$

The increase in $MB$ was Rs. 100 crores. Thus the increase in $M$ is $MB \times 'm'$ $= 4 \times 100 =$ Rs. 400 crores.

To summarize:

1. $M = MB\ (1 + C/D)/(R/D + C/D)$. This shows that $'M'$ is a multiple $'m'$ of $'MB'$. A one-rupee change in $'MB'$ causes a multiple change in $'M'$.
2. Variables that matter in determining $'M'$ are $'MB'$, $'C/D'$, and $'R/D'$. An increase in $'C/D'$ reduces $'m'$. Also an increase in $'R/D'$ lowers $'m'$. Given $'m'$, a decrease in $'MB'$ slows down the growth of $'M'$. Given $'MB'$, a decrease in $'m'$ can slow down $'M'$.
3. $'R/D'$ and $'C/D'$ both are not fixed but change in response to economic variables such as income and interest rates and institutional changes.

Hence, mechanical relationship need not hold. Can '*m*' be predicted with some accuracy is the issue.

Before we end this section, let us clarify a few points which sometimes create doubts about the money supply process. First, where did RBI find Rs. 100 crores to credit to the account of government of India? The answer is that RBI created (printed) this money. It created it against government securities. This Rs. 100 crores, when spent by the government, it is being circulated in the economy for the first time. RBI, therefore, has widened the monetary base (*MB*) by Rs. 100 crores.

Second, how did Rs. 100 crores of money creation by RBI turned into Rs. 400 crores increase in money supply? This is the multiplier effect. And the key to understanding the multiplier process is to realize that at any point of time only a fraction of the deposits gets withdrawn. The banks can, therefore, by following a fractional reserve system, create more deposits by lending. So the final increase in money supply is a multiple of *MB*.

Finally, if the money, thus created, is put to work in actual productive investment, it will enhance the size of GDP. Alternately, if there are not enough productive avenues for deploying this money, some of it may find its way into real estate or stock markets which, in turn, may create an asset price boom with little real increase in the production of goods and services in the economy. The central banks closely monitor these developments.

### 5.4.4 Funds Flow Approach to Money Supply Change

In Section 5.4.3, we have looked at the money supply process by linking broad money supply to the reserve money through a multiplier process. The principle of money supply targeting is based on the multiplier model of money supply determination. The money multiplier approach to money supply determination helps us to understand the difficulties monetary authorities face in monetary targeting.

However, RBI also provides an accounting framework by which one can read the variation in money supply by source. Conceptually, this method combines the balance sheets of commercial banks and RBI and breaks down its financial assets sector-wise. If we consider consolidated balance sheet of RBI and the banks, RBI credit to bank cancels out as an internal transaction. What we are left with is total banking system credit to the government, commercial sector and the foreign sector.

The source of change in M3 is thus, given by:
Net Bank credit to the government (RBI + Other Bank's)
+ Bank credit to commercial sector (RBI + Other Bank's)
+ Net foreign exchange assets of the banks (RBI + Other Bank's)
+ Government's currency liabilities to public
- Net non-monetary liabilities of banks (RBI + Other Bank's)

The last two items need some introduction. Government's currency liability refers to liability of government of India as against that of RBI. The government of India mints coins (it also used to print one rupee notes) and the RBI prints notes of rupees 2 and above denomination. The government's money (coins) is also a part of money supply. But since it is a very small component of money supply (0.21 per cent of $M_3$ in 2008/09), we ignored it in Section 5.4.3.

Net non-monetary liabilities of the banking sector refer to non-monetary liabilities *minus* other assets. Any change in net non-monetary liability does not lead to a change in money supply. One crude way to understand this is that, to the extent part of the banking system credit is met from retained profits of the banks; it neither changes the monetary liability of commercial banks nor, of RBI.

## 5.5 Control of Money Supply

The central bank can control money supply in several ways: (a) through open market operations, (b) by changing the bank rates, (c) by changing reserve requirements of the banks (CRR), and (d) through direct credit controls. These are shown in Figure 5.4, followed by a brief discussion on each of them.

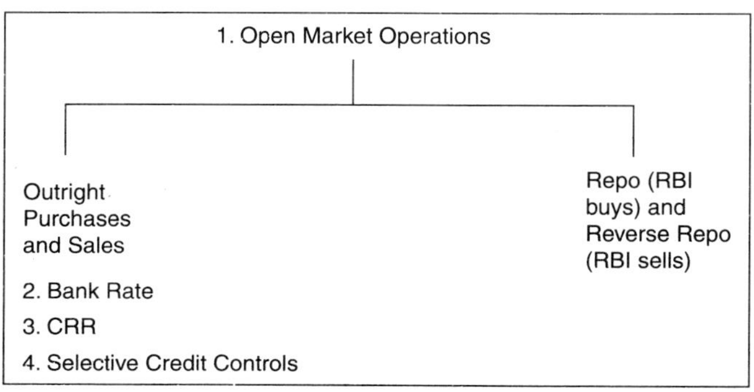


**Figure 5.4** *Conduct of Monetary Policy*

## 5.5.1 Open Market Operations (OMO)

Open Market Operations (OMO) are of two types:

- Outright buying/selling of government securities to either inject or absorb liquidity on a long term basis and,
- Repo transactions, i.e., buying/selling of government securities to either inject or absorb liquidity for a short-term with a repurchase obligation.

The term 'repo' refers to purchase of securities by RBI (injection of liquidity) with an agreement to sell them back at an agreed price on an agreed date. The interest rate at which RBI offers repurchase facilities is the repo rate. The repo rate is, therefore, the rate that RBI charges for lending money to the banks and other participating institutions through purchase of securities. Similarly 'reverse repo' refers to sale of securities by RBI (absorption of liquidity) with an agreement to buy those back at an agreed price on an agreed date. The interest rate at which this reverse repurchase facility is made available is the reverse repo rate. The reverse repo rate, thus, is the rate that RBI pays to the commercial banks and participating institutions for borrowing money from them against sale of securities.

How does OMO work? Every time RBI makes an open market purchase of government securities either through outright purchases or through repo transactions, on the asset side of the central bank's balance sheet (refer to Table 5.2), the financial assets of the central bank go up by the amount of the purchase. The central bank writes a cheque to the bank or participating institution from whom it has purchased the securities. They deposit the cheque in their accounts with their banks (commercial banks). The commercial banks submit these cheques to the central bank for clearance. The central bank credits their account with it. On the liability side of RBI's balance sheet, Banks' deposits with the central bank (part of reserves) go up equivalently. Monetary base (or, monetary liability) goes up; M3 goes up by a multiple of *MB* based on the relationship $M = MB \times `m'$. The opposite happens if RBI resorts to open market sale of government securities either by way of outright sales or through reverse repo transactions. On the asset side of central bank's balance sheet, the holdings of government securities come down by the amount of the sale. The buyer of the security gives a cheque to the central bank on his/her bank. RBI debits that bank's account with it by the amount of the cheque. On the liability side, banks' reserves with the central bank come down by an equivalent amount. *MB* comes down and M3 comes down by a multiple $MB \times `m'$.

How does OMO impact interest rates in the economy? In general, we know that if the money supply goes up (i.e., $M/P$ increases) interest rates come down. And if the money supply comes down, interest rates go up.[9] Repo rates have a special significance for short-term interest rates in the economy. Repo rates have the role of stabilizing the call money market rate within a range. The call money market rate is the rate at which one bank lends to the other and is considered as a prime indicator of availability of liquidity in the system. For example, if the reverse repo rate (the rate at which RBI borrows) is, say, 3.5 per cent (the prevailing rate in India) that puts a floor on call money market rate.[10] If it were not so, it would make sense to borrow in the call market at less than 3.5 per cent and lend to the central bank at 3.5 per cent. Similarly, if repo rate (the rate at which RBI lends money) is 5 per cent (the prevailing rate in India), this puts a ceiling on the call money market rate. Else, banks will borrow from the central bank and lend in call market.

However, more important, a rise in repo rate (called the policy rate) is taken as a signal by RBI that market interest rates in general in the economy will now move upwards. Hence, the extent of rise in repo rates is not as significant as the rise itself.

In an open market transaction, a central bank can exercise the option of fixing the amount of sale or purchase of government securities and let the market decide the price or the interest rate. In this case, after setting the quantity target, the central bank invites bid/auction price. The central bank, before the bidding/auction starts, usually, sets a minimum price (interest rate) if it is purchasing government securities and a maximum price (interest rate) if it is selling government securities. The central bank, alternatively, can fix the price (interest rate) on sale and purchase of securities and let the market decide on the quantity, given the price. In this case, the central bank may announce a quantitative limit on the sale and purchase of government securities. Between the two, the first practice is more common.

Thus, RBI's open market operations affect the banking system in two ways. First, through effecting a change of reserves and second, through

---

[9] Recently, using the same principle of OMO, the Federal Reserve System of the United States resorted to quantitative easing whereby it bought long-term bonds and some mortgage-backed securities. It was a desperate move to make interest rates on mortgages extremely low so that homeowners are able to refinance their loans at lower rates and save on their monthly payments. The assumption was that this would free up money that will be used to buy goods and services and, thereby, help revive business spending.

[10] In the United States, the call money market rate is called the federal funds rate.

signalling of interest rates based on the minimum and maximum interest rate set for the purchase and sale of government securities.

## 5.5.2 Changing the Bank Rate

RBI lends to the commercial banks through its discount window. The commercial banks may need to borrow against securities from RBI for meeting the depositors' demands and reserve requirements. The interest rate that RBI charges the commercial banks for this purpose is called the bank rate. Every time the RBI lends money to the commercial banks, it increases the monetary base. For example, if the banks borrow Rs. 100 crores from RBI and deposit the amount in their reserve account with the central bank, on the asset side of the central bank's balance sheet, central bank's lending to the commercial banks goes up by Rs. 100 crores and on the liability side of the balance sheet, reserves go up by the same amount.

RBI can influence the money supply growth by changing the bank rate from time to time. If RBI wants to inject more liquidity into the banking system, it will lower the bank rate. At the lower rate, banks will borrow more. This will increase the monetary base. Money supply will grow by change in monetary base ($MB$) × the money multiplier ('$m$'). Exactly the opposite will happen, if the central bank wants to siphon off liquidity from the system. Bank rate will be raised. Commercial banks will find it more costly to borrow. They will borrow less. The monetary base will fall. Money supply growth will come down.

Thus, a rise in the bank rate signals monetary tightening and a rise in the interest rates in the economy. And, a fall in the bank rate signals monetary softening and a fall in the interest rates in the economy.

The discount window, however, is not always open to the commercial banks. The central bank may deny access to the commercial banks to borrow from the central bank. The commercial banks can then borrow from other banks that have extra reserves at the call money market rate.

## 5.5.3 Changing Reserve Requirements

Recall the discussion we had in Section 5.2 on money supply process. We said that banks hold a per centage of their deposits ($R/D$) in the form of reserves with the central bank (and as vault cash) partly as a statutory requirement and partly for prudential reasons (excess reserves). The balance of deposits they lend out. For a given monetary base, this leads to a multiple change in money supply through the multiplier ('$m$') process. You can also see from equation 3 that, other things being equal, the larger the reserve requirement ($R/D$), smaller is the value of the money multiplier ('$m$') and vice versa.

One way, therefore, for the central bank to control money supply is to increase (decrease) the reserve requirement depending on whether it wants to bring about a decrease (increase) the money supply. An increase in the reserve requirement will make it mandatory on the part of the banks to hold a larger proportion of their deposits in the form of reserves with the central bank. This will reduce the size of their deposits. They will lend less. Money will multiply less, given the monetary base. This will have a moderating effect on money supply growth. This is how it works. Assume banks have a deposit (liability) of Rs. 50 crores and the reserve ratio is 10 per cent. Then on the asset side banks will have Rs. 5. crores as reserves and Rs. 45 crores as advances. (refer to Table 5.1). Now suppose the reserve requirement goes up to 15 per cent. Then Rs. 5 crores that is held in the form of reserves must now constitute 15 per cent of deposits and not 10 per cent. The deposits must fall to Rs. 33.33 crores and the advances to Rs. 28.3 crores. The process through which the deposit falls is that when the increased reserve ratio is announced, the banks find that they are out of reserves. They call back loans or sell their bonds. The buyers of the bonds or the borrowers of the money drain their checking deposits. The process ends only when the banks have brought down their deposits to 6.66 times and not 10 times their reserves.

## 5.5.4 Direct Credit Controls

Direct credit controls prevail in highly regulated banking systems. These controls can take various forms. The central bank can administer the interest rates directly. The central bank can also fix the quantity of bank deposits or can direct the allocation of credit. With the liberalization of the financial sector, many of the direct controls do not exist anymore. However, in India and some other parts of the developing world, allocations of credit to selected sectors are still directed by the state.

While direct controls can be effective, particularly in a crisis situation, they breed inefficiency and scuttle competition. Allocation of credit to select sectors, additionally, distorts market signals.

### 5.5.5 The Pros and Cons of Each Method

What we have discussed in this section are various ways through which money supply growth can be controlled. Open market operations and change in bank rates keep the money multiplier unchanged and work through change in monetary base. Change in the reserve ratios keeps the monetary base unchanged and works through the money multiplier process. Direct controls directly influence the financial variables. In the actual conduct of monetary policy, the monetary authorities use a combination of the above measures.

What are the pros and cons? OMOs are used most often by the central bank since those can be undertaken every business day, can be undertaken to a large and small degree, and can be easily reversed. Banks' reserves are immediately affected to a desired degree with the initiative lying solely with the central bank.

Bank rate can be used as a signal for a change in monetary policy, but often a change in the bank rate simply reflects an adjustment to existing money market conditions.

While changing the reserve ratio is a quick way of reducing the growth of money supply, it has three problems. First, since the statutory reserves do not carry interest, an increase in the reserve ratio imposes a tax on the banking system, which is not good for efficiency. Second, if the banks have excess reserves, which they usually do, they can circumvent the effect of a rise in the reserve ratio. Third, the impact of a rise in the reserve ratio on output may be too harsh.

Repo rate, reverse repo rate, and bank rate are called policy rates which RBI uses to signal a change in the market rates. A rise in these rates in general, raises funding costs for businesses across the board. Increasing the reserve ratio, on the other hand, impacts excess liquidity in the banking system.

Selective credit controls are out of fashion but some central banks, including RBI, do use those to address specific conditions.

### 5.5.6 A Wrap Up

It is important to be able to relate what we have discussed in this section to what we discussed earlier on monetary policy transmission mechanism.

Every time money supply or liquidity goes up, banks find that they have more reserves than what they need. They buy bonds or lend money. In case of bonds, the bond prices increase and the yields drop, bringing the interest rates down. In case of lending, banks, to lure customers, lower the price at which they can lend. Once again, the interest rates come down. The rest of the transmission mechanism follows. The opposite happens when the reserves come down.

At the lower interest rate demand for money increases (recall that demand for money is a decreasing function of interest rates). A new point of equilibrium is reached where the demand for money is equal to supply of money, and the process begins all over again.

## 5.6 Issues in Monetary Policy

In this section, we will discuss some of the dilemmas the central banker faces in the conduct of monetary policy, given conflicting goals.

There are certain general issues. For example, how smooth is the transmission mechanism between a change in MB and M3? The imponderables are the stability of $C/D$ and $R/D$. Even if the desired change in M3 is achieved, there may be uncertainties about how it will impact interest rates in the economy. And, even if interest rates change in the desired direction, its impact on GDP and prices may not be on expected lines if consumption and investment demand are not very responsive to changes in the interest rates. Similarly, raising CRR may not achieve the purpose if banks already have excess reserves; bringing the CRR down may also not ease credit availability to the commercial sector if banks decide to invest in government securities instead. These are uncertainties that the central banker has to constantly grapple with.

But there are also specific issues as discussed below.

### 5.6.1 Target Broad Money Growth or Interest Rates?

One option is to focus on the growth of money supply. That is, the central bank targets the money supply. It changes the monetary base (MB) and takes the view that this will have a predictable influence on broad money growth (M3), consistent with the expected growth in GDP and an acceptable rate of inflation. In other words, if the expected growth in GDP is 9 per cent and an acceptable rate of inflation is 5 per cent, the central bank will set a target for monetary base such that, through the multiplier process, the total broad money growth is around 14 per cent. The manner in which RBI will change MB has already been discussed in the previous section. Briefly, it will resort to open market purchase of government bonds which will result in an increase in bank reserves and, through the multiplier process, to an increase in M3. Note that when RBI buys bonds, bond prices rise; bond yields fall and interest rate comes down. A change in the money supply and an opposite change in the interest rates are thus two sides of the same coin. One cannot happen without the other.

Now, if RBI targets money supply and, it has to work smoothly, the following conditions must hold true: (a) the demand for money, particularly the velocity of circulation of money, is stable; (b) the money multiplier, both $R/D$ and $C/D$ are predictable; (c) the expected growth in GDP will materialize, and (d) M3 is easily measurable and not subject to frequent revisions. If any of these do not hold, the actual money supply growth will differ from the targeted growth. The central bank will then take corrective action by intervening in the bond market to get back to its money supply target. This will change interest rates. Thus, to the extent (a), (b), (c) and (d) above may not be very stable, the central bank may have to resort to frequent changes in the interest rates to achieve the money supply target. Some central bankers may view uncertainty caused by frequent changes in the interest rates to be more harmful to the economy than changes in the quantity of reserve money, or, monetary base.

A second option open to the central banks, therefore, is to target the interest rates (could be the call money market rate or yield on government securities) and allow broad money supply to change to achieve the interest rate target. In this case the central banker, therefore, views a stable interest rate regime as desirable for achieving sustained growth in output and, through it, stability in prices. Now suppose, due to supply side disturbance, inflation goes up. This will lead to a rise in the nominal interest rate (Section 2.6). The central bank, in order to target interest rate will have to increase money supply. If the money supply growth turns out to be long- lived and there is no corresponding decline in the velocity of circulation, this may build inflationary expectations and the central bank may then have to resort to an increase in interest rates to curb inflation fears. Countries that target interest rates, also, therefore, set a target for inflation.

The points to note from the above discussion are three-fold:

1. The central bank cannot target broad money growth and interest rates at the same time. If it targets the broad money growth, interest rates will need to be frequently changed to achieve the targeted growth in broad money. On the other hand, if it targets the interest rate, broad money growth will have to be accommodative.
2. While frequent changes in the interest rates are not conducive to sustained growth of output, an accommodative money supply growth may militate against the objective of price stability.
3. The central banker, therefore, constantly faces a dilemma as to whether to stabilize prices by targeting the broad money growth or go for growth by targeting interest rates. To the extent both cannot be achieved simultaneously, the central banker has to draw a fine line to best accommodate both the objectives.

## 5.6.2 Bringing in Exchange Rate Stabilization as a Target

The problem of the central banker does not end with the above choices. So far we have assumed that stabilization of the exchange rate is not one of the objectives of monetary policy. This will be the case under a flexible exchange rate regime. Under a flexible exchange rate system, as we discussed in Chapter 2, the exchange rate is determined by the interplay of demand and supply. If the supply (inflow) of foreign exchange, say dollar, is greater than the demand (outflow) for dollar the price of dollar will fall vis-à-vis the local currency. Or, rupee will appreciate. Similarly, if the demand for dollar is greater than the supply of dollar, the price of dollar will rise vis-à-vis the local currency. Or, the rupee will depreciate. If the central bank allows the exchange rate of the rupee to be determined in the market place, then, clearly, stabilization of the exchange rate is not one of the objectives of the central bank.

But rarely this is so. Every central bank, to some extent, attempts to achieve a certain amount of stability in the exchange rate. For example, an increase in the price of imported goods and services, consequent to a depreciation of the currency, can be inflationary, particularly if it is an import driven economy. Similarly, an increase in the price of exports, consequent to an appreciation of the currency, can slow down the growth of the GDP, particularly if it is an export driven economy. Central banks may also like to pursue a stable exchange rate policy to build confidence in the currency by stemming any speculative attacks and create a more conducive environment for business. Exchange rate stability, therefore, indeed, is one of the goals of monetary policy.

Central banks stabilize currencies by intervening in the foreign exchange markets. They, typically, buy foreign exchange when the domestic currency is under upward pressure (rupee appreciates) and they sell foreign exchange when the local currency faces a downward pressure (rupee depreciates). When the central bank buys foreign exchange, it goes towards the building of reserves; when it sells, reserves get depleted. Size of foreign exchange reserves, thus, becomes a key variable in the central bank's management of the exchange rate.

What are the additional issues that crop up if the central bank also wants to stabilize the exchange rate? First, assume the value of rupee is appreciating against the dollar. This will happen if the supply of dollars is greater than the demand for dollars. Now, let us say that the central bank, for a variety of reasons, including possible detrimental effect of an appreciating currency on exports, decides to stabilize the exchange rate at its previous level. In order to do so, it must remove the excess supply of dollars. The central bank will thus purchase dollars from the market till the supply of dollars is equal to the demand for dollars and the old exchange rate is restored. What is the implication of this for monetary policy?

Go back to the balance sheet of RBI in Table 5.2. Operationally, the central bank's purchase of foreign exchange from the open market is no different from open market operations that RBI resorts to for changing the money supply. In the latter case, the focus is on open market operations in government securities and the objective is to change the money supply; in the former case, it is open market operations in foreign exchange with the objective of stabilizing the exchange rate. However the impact on MB and M3 are the same.

For example, when RBI buys foreign exchange from the market, RBI's financial assets under "net foreign exchange assets" go up by the amount of the purchase. So do the monetary liabilities. Those who sell dollars to the central bank receive cheques drawn on the central bank. They deposit the cheques in their respective commercial banks. The commercial banks present those cheques to the central bank. The commercial banks' reserves with the central bank go up by an equivalent amount. The monetary base increases by the amount of the purchase. This results in an increase in broad money through the multiplier process.

Similarly, assume now that the rupee is depreciating against the dollar. This will happen when the demand for dollars is greater than the supply of dollars. Again, let us say that the central bank wants to stem the fall of the rupee against dollar. Since the fall is due to an excess of demand for dollar over supply, the central bank will have to increase the supply and will, therefore, sell dollars in the open market. The financial assets of the central bank due to "net foreign exchange assets" will come down. Those who have bought dollars will write cheques to the central bank drawn on their commercial banks. The central bank will debit commercial bank's account with it by the amount of the cheques. Their reserves with the central bank will come down equivalently. The monetary base will come down. So will broad money supply.

When stabilization of the exchange rate becomes a target of the central bank, this raises some additional issues:

1. When the rupee is appreciating against the dollar and the central bank wants to stabilize the exchange rate, the monetary base and broad money supply growth also goes up. The central bank, therefore, cannot stabilize the exchange rate and the broad money supply growth simultaneously. In other words, if it wants to stabilize the exchange rate, it should be willing to put up with a higher rate of inflation, consequent to an increase in broad money supply. If it does not want a higher rate of inflation, it should stop buying dollars from the market and, thereby, be willing to put up with an appreciation of the rupee.
2. When the rupee is depreciating against the dollar and if the central bank wants to stabilize the rupee, the monetary base and the broad money supply have to come down. This will put upward pressure on the interest rate. The central bank, therefore, cannot stabilize the interest rate and exchange rate at the same time. In other words, if it wants to stabilize the exchange rate, it must settle for a rise in the interest rate. On the other hand, if the central bank wants to stabilize the interest rate, it must allow the rupee to depreciate.
3. There is no way, in the above scenario, that exchange rate, interest rate and money supply growth can all be simultaneously targeted.

Another way of looking at it is that if the central bank focuses on the external sector (exchange rate stabilization), domestic interests (interest rate or price stabilization) may suffer. On the other hand, if the central bank focuses on the domestic sector (domestic interest rates or price stabilization), external concerns (exchange rate stabilization) will have to be given a go by.

4. It is important to closely follow the central bank's policy thrust to arrive at a judgment on how monetary policy may affect different cost variables in the economy.

## 5.6.3 Target General Price Level and/ or Asset Prices

This issue first came to limelight in the wake of Japanese asset price bubble in the eighties and the United States asset price bubble in the nineties. The issue has gained alarming proportions recently (2008/10) after the property market crash in the United States, which brought in its wake the global economic and financial meltdown and from which countries have not recovered even now.

An asset price bubble may become intractable because it can exist simultaneously with low and stable inflation. Monetary policy would appear to be doing its job of achieving price stability perfectly. And yet stability in prices may not ensure financial stability. However, when the bubble bursts, it can lead to a prolonged slowdown in affected economies. Clearly, inflation targeting is not enough to ensure a smooth functioning of the asset markets. Particularly, because the rise in the asset prices does not get captured by the movements in the general consumer price index which is used to measure inflation in these countries.

The issue, therefore, is: should central banks also take into consideration movements in asset prices while framing monetary policy? More specifically, should the central bank follow a monetary policy of contraction (raise interest rates) to tame an asset price rise? There are differences of opinion. Americans seem to believe against it. Their argument is: how do we know that the rise in the asset prices is irrational? They could very well be genuine. In that case, why interfere with a blunt weapon like interest rates? The British and the Australians, on the other hand, seem to be of the view that some pre-emptive action by way of a rise in the interest rates, even if inflation is stable, may be justified if there are reasons to believe that credit growth is too rapid.

If a general rise in the interest rate appears to be too harsh to prick an asset price bubble, better bank regulation can perhaps do the trick. For example, central banks can use certain tools to discourage formation of bubbles. This can be done by insisting on higher capital ratio norms. These norms will ensure that capital is adequate to absorb unexpected losses or risks involved. If there is higher risk, then it would be needed to be backed up by capital and vice versa.

Even if a consensus view on how to address an asset price boom does not exist, this is an emerging issue and is likely to receive the attention of central bankers globally, as financial liberalization continues and economies get more and more exposed to financial risk.

## 5.7 Monetary Policy in India

The goals of monetary policy in India have been growth with stability in prices. Depending on the evolving situation, RBI has tried to strike a balance between the two goals, with a broad accent on keeping inflation within a reasonable bound. Towards the pursuit of these goals, RBI has been, in recent years, also trying to maintain orderly conditions in the foreign exchange market by intervening in the market as and when necessary.

### 5.7.1 Monetary Policy Targets

RBI has been framing its monetary policy, for some years now, largely by targeting broad money supply. Thus, RBI sets a target of M3, consistent with the expected growth in GDP and an acceptable rate of inflation. Based on the M3 target, it provides for the desired expansion in monetary base or, reserve money. The final increase in money supply (M3) is a multiple of '*m*' of base money, where '*m*' is the money multiplier. Clearly, to hit the targeted broad money supply growth several conditions must hold.

First relates to RBI's ability to provide the desired expansion in reserve money. From the RBI balance sheet (Table 5.2), we know that RBI's ability to control the reserve money depends on RBI's ability to control its financial assets. The two important items on the financial asset side, which matter in this regard, are net RBI lending to the government and net foreign exchange assets of RBI. On neither of these, strictly speaking, RBI has any control. Government's borrowing needs drives the former and the latter is governed by the need to stabilize the exchange rates. In the past, the pressure on monetary targeting emanated largely from uncontrollable net RBI credit to the government. In more recent years, government borrowing is under control. Ad-hoc borrowing of the government from RBI has been replaced by the practice of Ways and Means advances. As a result, the government can directly borrow from the RBI only in case of temporary mismatch between receipts and payments and, that too, up to a limit of Rs. 10,000 crores in the first half of the year and another Rs. 6,000 crores during the second half, with no carry forward. However, management of exchange rate is posing a formidable challenge for RBI (Figure 5.5). We will discuss these issues in some detail later in the chapter.

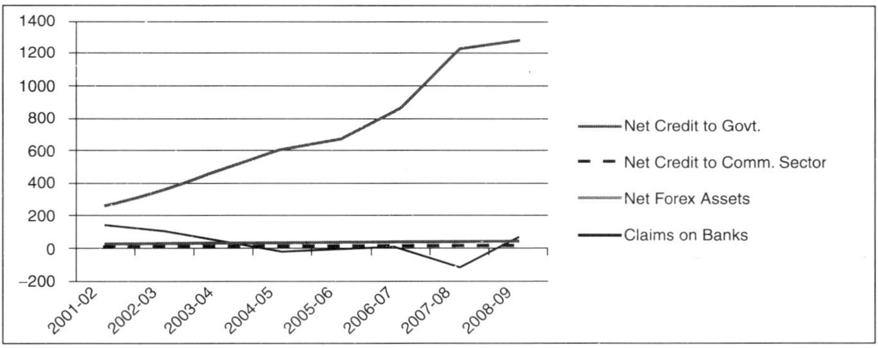


**FIGURE 5.5** *Components of Reserve Money RBI, 2001/02 to 2008/09*

Second, targeting the broad money growth requires that the ratio of broad money to reserves, or, the money multiplier '$m$' is predictable. Looking at the Indian data (Chart 5.6), both currency-deposit ratio ($C/D$) and reserve-deposit ratio ($R/D$) are not always stable. That makes the money multiplier unpredictable. A fall in currency–deposit ratio is to be expected as financial liberalization and financial sophistication gathers momentum. Reduction in reserve—deposit ratio is policy-induced. If the central government lowers the mandatory part of the bank's reserve requirement, then unless excess reserves increase, $R/D$ will come down. Theoretically, the changes in $R/D$ can be adjusted for reserve money, but ultimately it will depend on how banks adjust their excess reserves.

Finally, a condition that must hold true for monetary targeting to work effectively is a stable demand function for money. If the demand for money in response to change in GDP and in interest rates is not stable, targeting the money supply growth can become a problem. One way to capture the stability of the demand function for money is to look at the income velocity of money over the years (Chart 5.7). The income velocity of money has been falling, perhaps because of low inflation (and, nominal interest rates) and financial liberalization, both of which usually result in an increase in demand for money and, thereby, a decline in the velocity. If there are frequent unexpected changes in income velocity of money, pursuit of monetary growth targets can have the disadvantage of causing frequent short-run swings in interest rates and real output.

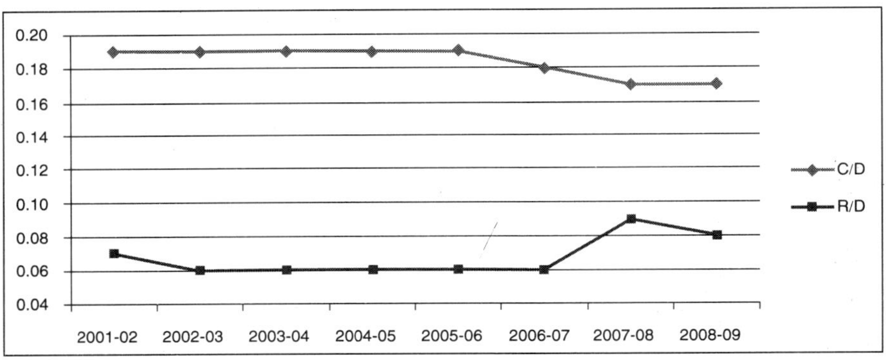


**Figure 5.6** *Select Monetary Ratios, 2001/02 to 2008/09*

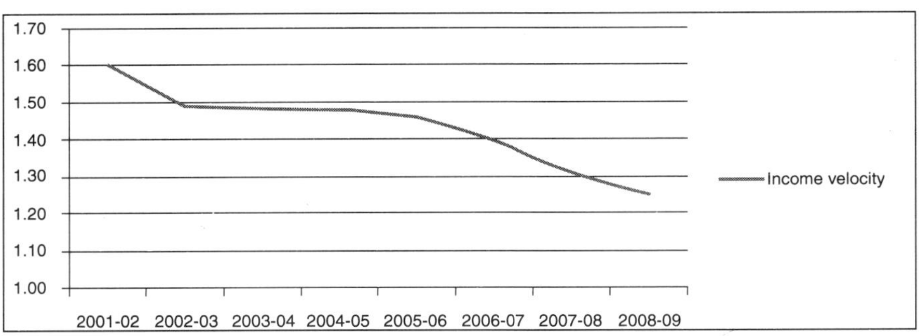


**Figure 5.7** *Income Velocity, 2001/02 to 2008/09*

It is because of these uncertainties about the behaviour of monetary aggregates, both on demand and supply sides, that monetary policy in India is increasingly supplementing interest rate, also, as an anchor of monetary policy.

In a regime, where cross border capital flows are getting liberalized, maintaining orderly conditions in the foreign exchange market has also become important for the sustainability of the external sector. In the initial phase, given that foreign exchange markets are not perfect, the exchange rate stabilization objective of RBI has assumed pre-eminence, and, to that extent, short-term monetary policy adjustments have been driven by this objective.

## 5.7.2 Monetary Policy Instruments

### *Change in the Reserve Requirements of Banks (R/D)*

In India, the reserve–deposit ratio is called the cash reserve ratio (CRR). Changing the CRR from time to time has been a very important instrument of monetary control in India. Recall that money supply equals *MB* x '*m*'. Change in CRR impacts '*m*' and not *MB*. RBI uses the instrument of CRR to perform its usual function of siphoning off or injecting liquidity into the banking system. Besides, at times, when, because of conflicting goals, RBI finds it difficult to control *MB*, RBI changes '*m*' by changing CRR to gain a control on overall money supply growth. Recently (2009) RBI increased CRR to 5.75 per cent to suck out excess liquidity from the banking system.

### *Open Market Operations*

An open market operation in government securities is perhaps the most important monetary policy tool currently being used by RBI. This is facilitated by secondary market reforms in government securities, whereby government securities are traded at market related rates of interest. Open market operations, as stated earlier, are in the nature of both outright purchase and sales and repo transactions. Repo and reverse—repo transactions are for short-term liquidity management, usually, for a maturity of up to 14 days. This is a part of RBI's liquidity adjustment facility (LAF).

As discussed in Section 5.3, the repo rate has a direct relationship to the call money market rate, the rate at which banks and primary dealers (PD) borrow money from each other for one day to typically 14 days. The repo rate provides a floor for the call money market rate and the reverse repo rate the ceiling. By announcing these policy rates, RBI thus provides a corridor within which it likes to see the call money market rate move.

## *Change in Bank Rates*

RBI reactivated bank rate, as an instrument of monetary policy in 1997. The bank rate, as of April 2010 is 6 per cent. A change in the bank rate signals a change in the lending rate. The impact of bank rate changes has been most pronounced on the prime lending rate (PLR), the rate at which banks lend to their most favoured customers. Besides, the rate at which RBI refinances the banks for export credit as also for general refinance are linked to the bank rate. In fact, the LAF of the RBI which involves injecting liquidity into the system through export refinance credit, collateralized lending and liquidity support to primary dealers are linked to the bank rate.

Needless to say that none of the instruments of monetary policy discussed above works in isolation. They are mutually reinforcing. RBI regularly supports CRR changes or, bank rate changes with open market operations. RBI's periodic auctioning of government securities, by itself, can signal the overall stance on the appropriateness of interest rate and liquidity.

## *Direct Credit Controls*

Direct credit controls in India are of three types. First, a part of the interest rate structure, on small savings and provident funds are administratively set. Second, banks are to keep 25 per cent of their deposits in the form of government securities as a mandatory requirement. This is called Statutory Liquidity Requirement (SLR). Though, of late, the interest on these securities has become competitive, nevertheless, SLR imposes a control on bank lending. Finally, banks are required to lend to the priority sectors to the extent of 40 per cent of their advances. This requirement continues, despite recommendation of various committees to the contrary.

Direct controls may perform a social function. But they do come in the way of smooth functioning of monetary policy transmission mechanism. They, thereby, undermine the role of monetary policy.

# 5.7.3 Issues in Monetary Policy

Section 5.4 of this chapter described the dilemmas faced by central bankers all over the world in the conduct of monetary policy. The nature of the dilemma will depend on the evolving situation. In what follows, we will highlight certain emerging issues facing the RBI in its monetary management.

We will specifically discuss three issues: (a) the issue of exchange rate management in the wake of large capital inflows into the country, in the more recent period; (b) the issue of interest rate management arising out of heavy government borrowing from the market; and (c) the issue of administered interest rates and their impact on the monetary policy transmission mechanism.

## *Exchange Rate Management*

In the last few years, in India, foreign exchange inflows, particularly dollar inflows, have increased substantially. We have seen that, when inflows (supply) exceed outflows (demand), the price of foreign currency falls, vis-à-vis the domestic currency. The rupee, therefore, has been under pressure of appreciation against the dollar.[11]

Under these circumstances RBI has three options:

First, RBI, in order to stem the rise of the rupee, can choose to intervene in the foreign exchange market. Since an excess of supply of dollars over demand has caused the rupee appreciation, RBI will start buying dollars from the market to remove the excess supply and stabilize the value of the rupee. However, it will not come without a cost. As discussed in Section 5.4, RBI's purchase of foreign exchange, from the market, increases its financial assets (net foreign exchange assets of RBI) and monetary liabilities (reserves) by the same amount. The monetary base goes up. Broad money increases by multiple of '$m$' of base money ($MB$). An increase in the net foreign exchange assets or reserves of RBI can, thus, be inflationary. And, we have seen that inflation, beyond an acceptable level, can add substantial cost to the economy.

Besides cost to the economy, there are also costs to RBI. This happens because the interest that RBI earns by deploying the foreign exchange reserves (usually in foreign government securities), is considerably lower than what its rupee equivalent would have fetched if deployed in the domestic market.

Under this option, therefore, RBI, faces a dilemma whether to stabilize exchange rates or prices and if, former, how long to bear the cost of interest loss.

Second, RBI may try to address the dilemma of exchange rate vs. price stability through sterilized intervention. Here is how it works: RBI chooses

[11] We will look into the causes of inflow in greater detail in Chapter 6.

to intervene in the foreign exchange market, as in the first option, to stabilize the exchange rate, but, this time, it sterilizes the impact of foreign exchange purchases on the monetary base (*MB*) by simultaneously selling government securities into the open market. In terms of RBI balance sheet thus, an increase in *MB* consequent to an increase in net foreign exchange assets of RBI will be offset by a decrease in *MB* consequent to a fall in net RBI lending to government and there will be no change in *MB* , and, thereby, in broad money supply growth.

RBI can also, at times, sterilize the impact of foreign exchange purchase on broad money supply growth, not through control of *MB* by simultaneously selling government securities in the market, but by reducing the size of money multiplier '*m*' through a rise in CRR. Thus, given the relationship $M = MB \times 'm'$, RBI may allow MB to rise but sterilize the impact on *M* by lowering '*m*'.

On the face of it, the second option, outlined above would seem to stabilize both exchange rates and prices. But it can be costly. While sterilization may keep the inflation in check, it does not solve the original problem of excess supply of foreign exchange over demand. For example, a country attracts foreign exchange inflow because of better returns the economy offers. This better return, among other things, is captured by the interest rate differential between countries. The reason for the massive inflow of foreign exchange in India is no different. If this trend needs to be reversed in the interest of stabilization of the exchange rate, broad money supply should be allowed to rise, such that a fall in the interest rate that will result from a rise in the money supply, will make it unattractive for foreign money to take refuge in India and, in course of time, the original equilibrium between inflow and outflow will be restored. Under sterilized intervention, this is not possible because money supply growth is not allowed to rise. Therefore, through sterilized intervention, RBI is perhaps able to address the issue of price stabilization but is not able to address the issue of foreign exchange inflows (supply) exceeding foreign exchange outflows (demand). On the other hand, by continuously selling government securities in the market and/or reducing '*m*' by raising CRR, RBI siphons off liquidity from the system. RBI thus leaves enough room for a rise in the domestic interest rates which further aggravates the problem of capital inflows.

There is also cost to the RBI from sterilization. The cost is the difference between the return on foreign assets (i.e., U.S. Government T-bills return) and the interest paid on servicing the domestic debt from the sale of government securities. If interest paid on Indian debt is taken to be 7 per cent and similar interest earned on U.S. assets is 2 per cent, the spread comes to 5 per cent. This will be the cost of sterilization to RBI.

Finally, RBI may choose the option of not to intervening in the foreign exchange market and allow the value of the rupee to be determined in the market place. Given the current scenario, this will result in an appreciation of rupee against dollar. There is a risk that Indian exports may become less competitive against our competitors' if the rupee value appreciates. Also, rupee appreciation may lead to a rise in imports since imports are now relatively cheaper at the going exchange rate. A rise in import demand coupled with a fall in export demand will widen the current account deficit (*M-X*). RBI, therefore, has to carefully weigh the cost of non-intervention.

In short, if RBI chooses the first option, it cannot stabilize the prices at the same time. If RBI chooses the second option, it cannot stabilize interest rates at the same time. If RBI chooses the third option, it cannot stabilize the exchange rate at the same time.

RBI appears to have tried all the three options from time to time. During periods when domestic inflation rate was less than the acceptable rate, RBI, used that cushion to intervene in the foreign exchange market. In periods, when rupee appreciated against the dollar but not by as much as our competing countries' currencies, RBI appears to have allowed the rupee to appreciate as long as there was no relative appreciation. And finally, in those periods when inflation posed a worry, RBI resorted to sterilized intervention either by selling government securities or by lowering '*m*' or both. The option of selling government securities in the market to sterilize the impact of foreign exchange purchases may have been very popular. Because we are told that, as a result of extended sterilized intervention in the foreign exchange market, RBI's stock of marketable government securities came down drastically. The RBI and the government, therefore, signed an MOU to launch, as of April 2004, a Market Stabilization Scheme (MSS). Under the scheme, the government issued treasury bills in the open market in excess of its normal borrowing requirements to draw in cash and suck out liquidity from the system. The amounts raised by the government under the MSS are held with the RBI in a cash account. This cash cannot be used by the government for its expenditure and thus helps reduce liquidity in the system.

How has the RBI assigned priorities against the conflicting goals? Obviously, RBI cannot state it explicitly. Also, it will depend on the evolving situation. However, there is a suggestion that when the rupee was under downward pressure, RBI assigned highest priority to exchange rate stabilization. Only when the rupee remained stable over a period of time, RBI attempted to bring the interest rate down.[12] For example, at the time of Asian crisis (October to December, 1997), when the rupee depreciated sharply, RBI promptly raised the CRR, repo and bank rates. Again, at the time of Pokhran blasts (May–June 1998) when the rupee came under downward pressure, repo rate, and CRR went up. Subsequently, when imports went up and the rupee again was under pressure of depreciation, RBI raised the repo, CRR and Bank rates. In between when rupee was stable, RBI reduced the interest rate.

Similarly, when the rupee underwent an upward pressure, RBI's priority appeared to be exchange rate and price stabilization rather than interest rate stabilization. The soft interest rate regime witnessed recently was more a result of decline in demand for rather than supply of liquidity. Though RBI pumped in lots of liquidity into the system, there were not many takers.

## *Interest Rate Management and Fiscal Deficit*[13]

Any government that is unwilling to show fiscal restraint will ultimately be faced with excessive money growth and an increase in the inflation rate. Though restrictions have been imposed on the government of India in respect of direct borrowing from RBI to finance its deficit, continued large government fiscal deficits, even if financed through market borrowings, can create a policy dilemma for RBI. RBI has to decide whether to allow the interest rate to go up or monetize the debt. If RBI decides not to finance the debt, the increased borrowing needs of the government will drive interest rates up, leading to the crowding out of private spending and exports (Chapter 4). The RBI may then be blamed for slowing down economic growth. But if the RBI is worried about high interest rates and, in order to keep interest rates low, monetizes the debt through open market purchases, inflation will rise and the RBI will be blamed for the higher inflation rate. In fact, debt financing may actually be more inflationary than money financing in the long run, since higher interest rates lead to higher interest payments on the national debt. This adds to the fiscal deficit, and, eventually, a higher national debt will need to be money financed, thereby, fuelling inflation.

---

12 Mukhopadhya Hiranya, " Exchange Rate Management & Monetary Measures, RBI Policy Dilemma in the context of Currency Crisis ", *Money & Finance*, ICRA, July—Sept, 1999.

13 The discussion in this section draws from Chapter 4. Make sure you are able to relate.

If the economy is farther from the full-employment level of output, RBI may be willing to monetize the deficit. Because when excess capacity is high, inflationary pressures are low, so increasing money supply may not cause rapid price increases. Also, a small increase in inflation may be tolerable since a high unutilized capacity is costly in terms of lost output. However, when the economy is close to full employment, bottlenecks develop more easily. In this situation, monetizing the deficit will ultimately fail to keep interest rates down or stimulate the economy further. Instead, a higher rate of monetary growth will cause inflation to increase sharply.

Monetary and Fiscal policies are, therefore, closely linked. Successful conduct of monetary policy depends also on fiscal policy. In India, today, the government is financing almost the entire deficit through market borrowings. This has not yet resulted in an upward pressure on interest rates for a number of reasons, essentially transient in nature, which we discussed in Chapter 4. As industry revival forges ahead, sooner than later, industry demand for funds for new investment will rise. This is likely to put pressure on interest rates. RBI then will be faced with a real dilemma whether to stabilize interest rates, prices or, exchange rates. Government of India's adherence to the provisions of Fiscal Responsibility and Management Act, therefore, becomes crucial for creating a more conducive environment for some of the critical cost variables in the economy.

## *Administered Interest Rates and Monetary Policy Transmission Mechanism*[14]

In India, we have a number of small savings schemes like the Public Provident Fund (PPF), various postal savings schemes[15]etc., which were launched with the objective of providing a safe avenue for savings for small savers, both in urban and rural areas. Interest rates on these small saving instruments are administered. Monetary policy changes do not impact these. The interest rates have been revised from time to time, but purely as administrative decisions. In addition to interest rate being fixed, small saving schemes enjoy certain tax benefits.

In order to get an idea of the magnitude, total small-scale savings outstanding at the end of 2008/09 constituted about 10 per cent of GDP. Aggregate bank deposits outstanding during the same period were 72 per

[14] For a more incisive study on this issue see Kausick Saha, "Issues in Monetary Policy Transmission in India", FPM dissertation, Indian Institute of Management, Bangalore, 2004.

[15] These will include, in addition to different post office savings, Indira Vikas Patra, Kisan Vikas Patra, National Saving Certificates etc.

cent of GDP. Small savings, therefore, are almost 14 per cent of aggregate bank deposits. Interest rates on small savings have ruled higher than security yields of different tenures and commercial bank deposits. And, in the wake of a soft interest rate regime, while yields, across financial instruments, came down substantially, small saving rates did not fall *pari passu*. Additionally, as stated above, these schemes have enjoyed tax benefits under various Sections 88, 80L, and 10 of Income Tax Act of the government of India.

While small saving schemes were launched with a social objective and they do, perhaps, fulfill those objectives, they seriously distort the monetary policy transmission mechanism. The distortion arises because we have a dual market in interest rate structure. In one market, interest rates are market determined. In the other market, interest rates are administratively set. Interest rates in the controlled market are not only higher than comparable rates in the open market, but they are also inflexible to changes in monetary policy. And here, the size of the controlled market is not inconsequential.

Now assume that RBI follows an expansionary monetary policy. Under normal circumstances, as we have discussed in Section 5.1, this will result in an increase in bank reserves. Banks will buy bonds. Bond prices will go up. Bond yields will come down. Interest rates will fall. However, if there is a controlled market, however restrictive it may be, where interest rates are higher, people may switch, at least partially, from their existing bond holdings or, even time deposits, to small savings. The increase in bank reserves will, therefore, to some extent, get offset by a decline in bank reserves and the fall in the interest rate will be, correspondingly, smaller. In other words, in a dual market of the type we have in India, the interest rate prevailing in the open market will always be higher than what it would have been if there was a single market. This reduces the effectiveness of monetary policy transmission mechanism.

Aside from monetary policy impact of small saving schemes, there is a cost to the government. It costs the government more to borrow out of small savings than through marketable instruments of the government like dated securities and 364-day treasury bills, because of interest rate differential. To this, if we also add tax revenue foregone on small savings, the effective cost of government borrowing increases considerably. Obviously, this will have an impact on the size of fiscal deficit and, through fiscal-monetary interface, on the conduct of monetary policy.

Though various committees have suggested measures to get out of the above problem by way of doing away with some tax concessions or, benchmarking small scale rates to secondary rates of government securities of comparable maturities or, to some measure of inflation, the topic is politically sensitive and involves tough political bargaining process which may not be easy in the current coalition political equation.

## 5.8 Banking Sector Efficiency

This section has a specific focus. We have seen that monetary policy influences interest rates through changes in bank reserves. An increase in reserves leads to an increase in broad money supply and that results in a fall in the interest rates. We have also seen that there are constraints to which monetary policy can influence interest rates. These constraints emanate from the state of the economy, conflicting targets facing RBI, fiscal policy and, structural rigidities imposed by a system of dual interest rate structure. The question we are addressing here is: are there ways, other than through change in money supply, by which we can influence interest rates in the economy? Can the banking sector efficiency be improved so that the spread between deposit and lending rates can be narrowed and part of the benefit of this efficiency gain can be passed on to the borrowers in the form of lower interest rates?

The above questions assume particular importance in economies (India being one of them), where the banking system had been highly repressed. Important manifestations of banking sector repression were statutory lending to the government (SLR), high CRR, mandatory requirement to lend to priority sectors, regulated interest rates, overstaffing, lack of computerization, and, a host of restrictions on the commercialization of the banks. The various mandates imposed on the banks almost forced them to support activities that were not competitive, without any consideration of repayment, and severely restricted them from exploring alternative commercially profitable ventures. The number of bad loans (non-performing assets) went up. And, the banks could neither expand into alternative profitable activities, nor, could they charge market determined interest rates on a good portion of their loans. Therefore, the only way to cross subsidize was to charge a very high interest rate for commercial component of the lending. Market interest rates, therefore, ruled very high under banking system repression.

With economic liberalization, a number of measures have been initiated to do away with banking system repression by enabling banks to operate freely in a commercially justifiable manner in a competitive environment. Measures include "reduction of statutory pre-emption, deregulation of interest rates and giving banks greater autonomy and flexibility in day-to-day operations *while introducing strict discipline in terms of capital adequacy* (author's emphasis). Other measures in this direction include greater streamlining of the operations of development in financial institutions and deregulation of the capital market. Competition has been infused into the financial system by licensing new private banks since 1993. Foreign banks have also been given more liberal entry. The Union Budget 2002–03 announced the intention to permit private banks, depending on their size, strategies and objectives, to operate either as branches of their overseas parents, or, as subsidiaries in India. The latter would impart greater flexibility to their operations and provide them with a level playing field vis-à-vis their domestic counterparts. Progress has also been made through demonstration and spread effects of advanced technology and risk management practices among the new private banks and foreign banks. Given the fiscal constraint being faced by the government and in keeping with the evolving principles of corporate governance, the government permitted public sector banks to raise fresh equity from markets to meet their capital shortfalls or to expand their lending. Several private and public sector banks have accessed the domestic equity market. Public sector banks have also raised capital through GDR/ADRs. while many banks have raised subordinated debt through private placement route.[16]

The measures initiated towards improving banking sector efficiency, as outlined above, is a process, which has begun in right earnest but must go on. It has already brought some dividends. Gross non-performing assets of the banking system have come down considerably. In future monetary policy announcements, one can look forward to more measures to carry the banking reforms further. These measures will also, other things being same, have a decisive influence on interest rates.

## 5.9 Chapter Summary

Monetary policy works through change in money supply and its impact on financial variables, aggregate demand and, finally, on GDP and prices. The broad objectives of monetary policy are price stability and sustained growth

[16] Reserve Bank of India, *Report on Currency and Finance*, 2002–03, p. 65, RBI, Mumbai, 2004.

in output. However, price stability, over all, appears to be the primary goal of monetary policy. Monetary authorities can target money supply, interest rates or, exchange rates to achieve their goals. But, it is not possible to target all the three together. There is, therefore, a trade-off.

The efficacy of monetary policy depends on the stability of both money–demand function and money–supply function. The key variable to monitor in the demand function is trend in income velocity of money; the key variables to monitor in the supply function are RBI's ability to control the monetary base and the coefficients of money multiplier. None of the variables is stable; the real challenge before the monetary authorities, therefore, is to assess if they can be predicted with some degree of certainty. Monetary policy, partly because of uncertainty about the above variables and partly because of the adjustment time that financial and real sectors take to respond to a monetary policy change in normal course, is subject to long and variable lags. Monetary authorities, therefore, have to take pre-emptive action based on past experience and forecasts.

Monetary policy can also lose its effectiveness if there are rigidities in the transmission mechanism of monetary policy. One example of rigidity discussed in the chapter related to presence of a dual interest rate structure in the economy, one determined by market forces and the other, administered. Such rigidities distort market interest rates.

Fiscal and monetary policy interface is also crucial for proper conduct of monetary policy. If the government resorts to excessive borrowing from the market to finance its deficit, the RBI, in the interest of the real economy, may be forced to increase the money supply to arrest a possible rise in interest rate consequent to government borrowing. But, then, it may stoke the flames of inflation. RBI, therefore, is in a constant dilemma whether to let prices or interest rates loose.

A manager's interest in monetary policy stems from a desire to know what the policy signals about stability of prices, interest rates and exchange rates. As all three cannot be stabilized simultaneously, the manager has to come to an intelligent judgment on the thrust of the monetary policy vis-à-vis the three variables. The Indian experience seems to suggest that exchange rate and price stabilization have been the principal objectives of monetary policy (and, to the credit of RBI, it has achieved both with a reasonable degree of success). In between, when both have been stable, RBI has not hesitated to bring the interest rates down. It is perhaps safe to assume, not only in India, but also elsewhere in the world that price stability will continue to be the most important goal of monetary policy. In emerging economies, which are just opening up, exchange rate stabilization will also assume considerable importance.

What to expect from interest rates? As we discussed in Chapter 2, in a period of slowdown interest rates rule low. However, to expect interest rates to remain low, when the economy is on a revival path is being unrealistic, particularly, if the RBI wants to contain inflation within an acceptable level. In India any softening of the interest rate, in the present context, will have to come from fiscal policy rather than monetary policy. And this will be achieved, if the government tames its fiscal deficit, particularly revenue deficit, so that it does not have to resort to excessive market borrowing.

Another source of some relief on interest rate front may come from improved efficiency of the banking system. If the spread between the deposit and lending rates of the banks can be reduced, this efficiency gain can be passed on to the borrowers in the form of lower interest rates.

Monetary policy, henceforth, is likely to focus more on improving system efficiency rather than injecting more liquidity in to the system as a means of softening the interest rates.

ANNEXURE

# IS-LM Model

The IS-LM model provides a conceptual framework to understand how fiscal and monetary policies interact to impact the economy. This framework has become the main vehicle through which basic macroeconomic model is introduced to students in business schools. Some of the discussions in Chapters 4 and 5 derive their conceptual basis from the IS-LM model.

We start from a point of equilibrium. This is a point where the economy is willing to spend exactly the amount that is necessary to take the output off the market. There is neither overproduction, leading to piling up of unintended stocks, nor underproduction, leading to drawing down of inventories. Thus, in the market, where goods and services are produced in an economy (also called the real sector), a point of equilibrium is reached when Aggregate Supply (GDP) = Aggregate Demand (AD) and unintended inventories (UI) are zero.

Notice that the equilibrium condition in the goods and services market in an economy, i.e. GDP = AD can also be looked at as a point where Saving ($S$) = Investment ($I$). This is how we reason it: AD or the total spending in the economy can be broken down into spending on consumption goods and services ($C$) and investment goods and services ($I$). Suppose the economy has a disposal income of Rs. 100 and it typically saves 20% of this. Then, this saving or withdrawal of Rs. 20 from the spending stream comes back into the economy by way of investment spending ($I$). Thus every time consumption fails to take the total output off the market, '$I$' comes in as an injection of spending, which supplements consumption. And the engine of the economy rolls on.

However, while saving = investment, at times, it is possible for savings to exceed injection of investment or households may spend less than firms thought they would. As a result, unintended inventories may pile up. This can happen for the following reason. Actual '$I$' consists of intended and unintended (change in inventories) '$I$'. Actual '$I$' is always equal to $S$. When we say $S > I$, we mean that savings ($S$) is greater than intended '$I$'. As a result, unintended inventories (UI) are positive.

Therefore, in equilibrium two things happen, i.e., $Y$ = AD and $S$ = I (withdrawals = injections). And, UI = zero.

## *IS Curve*

The IS component of the IS-LM model starts from a point of equilibrium in the goods and services market in the economy where $S = I$. It then goes on to explain how the equilibrium level of output changes in response to a change in the interest rate in the economy. The relationship is captured by the IS curve as shown Figure A5.1.

On the vertical axis, we measure interest rate in the economy ($r$) and on the horizontal axis, we measure GDP ($Y$). The IS curve (so called) is a locus of points where $I = S$ and, at each point on the IS curve, the goods and services sector is in equilibrium. The IS curve, thus, shows the relationship between equilibrium level of GDP and interest rate in the economy. The relationship is negative. When the interest rate is $r_0$, the equilibrium level of GDP is $Y_0$. When the interest rate in the economy falls to $r_1$, the equilibrium level of GDP rises to $Y_1$. This happens because a decrease in $r$ increases investment demand ($I$) and, therefore AD, thus increasing the equilibrium level of GDP. The opposite will be the case if interest rates rise.

The slope of the IS curve is crucial to understanding the relevance of various macroeconomic policy initiatives. Take an extreme example where IS curve is vertical. This means that investment spending is independent of the interest rate. Deriving from this, we can generalize that steeper the IS curve (in the extreme example above, we made the IS curve steep to the extent of being vertical), less responsive is investment spending to changes in the interest rates. That is, a given change in the interest rate brings about

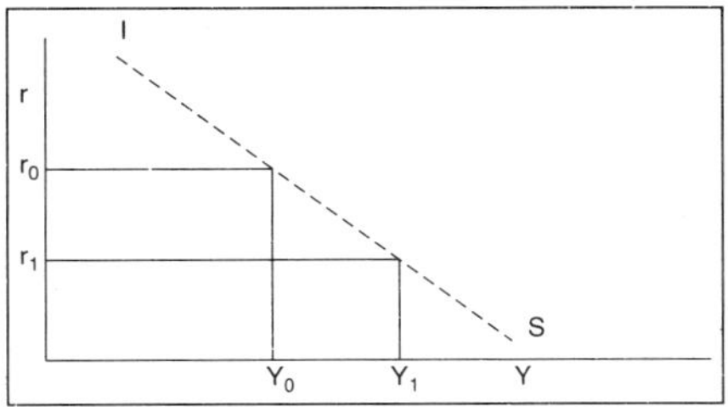


**FIGURE A5.1** *IS curve*

a very small change in equilibrium GDP. On the other hand, when IS curve is very flat investment is highly responsive to changes in the interest rate. A given change in interest rate brings about a much larger change in GDP.

Given the slope, a shift in the IS curve can w be caused by a change in any component of aggregate demand, i.e., a change in government expenditure or taxes (examples of fiscal policy initiatives), change in exports, or change in consumer or business sentiments. Usually, however, IS analysis focuses on the impact of a change in fiscal policy.

## *LM Curve*

The IS curve gives various combinations of GDP and interest rates at which the market for goods and services is in equilibrium. But which interest rate do we consider? That will be given by the equilibrium in the money market. Money market equilibrium is the point of intersection between demand for real money balances and supply of real money balances. In the IS-LM model, the supply of real money balances is initially assumed to be fixed and the equilibrium in the money market is arrived at when the demand for real money balances (which as we know, is an increasing function of GDP and a decreasing function of interest rate) is equal to the fixed money supply. From this relationship, it is now possible to derive the LM curve (Figure A5.2). The LM curve (L stands for liquidity preference or money demand and M for money supply) shows the combinations of income and the rate of interest that clears the money market. This curve slopes upward because at higher levels of GDP more money balances are required for sustaining larger scales of transactions. The attempt on the part of the asset holders to acquire more money at the expense of bonds results in lower prices of bonds or, a higher *r*[1]. In other words, when GDP increases, demand for money increases and with money supply fixed, *r* must rise to bring the money market into equilibrium.

[1] It will be helpful to read Sections 2.2 and 5.2 again.

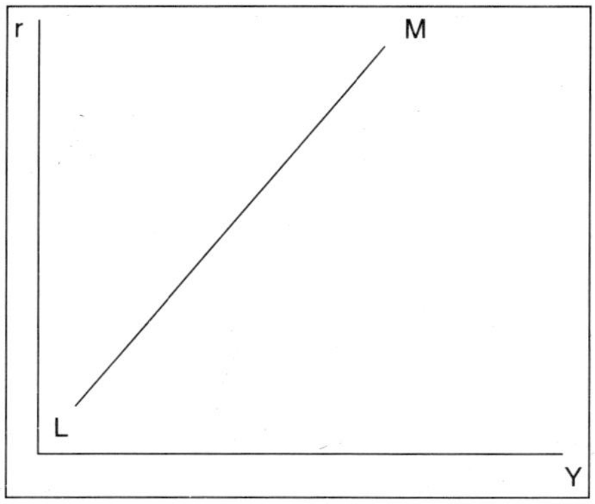


**FIGURE A5.2** *LM Curve*

The slope of the LM curve, as in the case of IS curve, assumes considerable policy significance. A flat LM curve means that demand for money is highly sensitive to changes in interest rate. In other words, if the demand for money, in response to a higher level of GDP increases, only a small rise in the interest rate will be required to bring the money market into equilibrium. On the other hand, in the case of a steep LM curve, which signifies a weak relationship between demand for money and interest rate, the change in interest rate, in response to a change in demand for money, will have to be large to bring the money market back to equilibrium.

LM curve, given the slope, will shift if the money supply changes. LM curve will shift to the right if money supply increases and, to the left if money supply slows down.

## *IS–LM Interaction*

The point of intersection between IS and LM curve (Figure A5.3) is the point at which the goods and services sector and the money sector are both in equilibrium. GDP = AD (and $I = S$) and the demand for real money balances equals the fixed money supply. There is no tendency for GDP or interest rate to change.

The IS–LM analysis helps us to understand the relationship between the market for goods and services and the money market. We now have a more comprehensive analysis of how macro economy works and how the composition of AD responds to a range of policy initiatives.

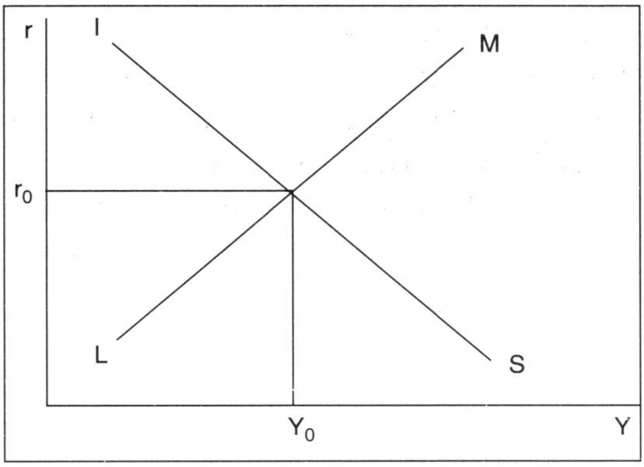


**FIGURE A5.3** *IS–LM Interaction*

When IS curve shifts to the right, income is affected first and the resulting increase in the interest rate offsets some of the increase in income by crowding out investment. When the LM curve shifts to the right, interest rates are affected first and the resulting increase in income affects some of the decrease in the interest rate by increasing money demand.

## *Policy Effectiveness under IS-LM model*

IS-LM model assumes constant prices and a closed economy. We will relax both these assumptions once we grasp the basic concepts behind the model.

# FISCAL POLICY

Assume an expansionary fiscal policy, in the form of an increase in government expenditure, G. IS curve shifts to the right. The manner it will impact the economy in the IS-LM model can be seen from the following transmission mechanism:

$$G \Uparrow \Rightarrow AD \,\&\, Y \Uparrow \Rightarrow M^d \,\&\, r \Uparrow \Rightarrow I \text{ and } Y \Downarrow \quad \text{.......................................(1)}$$

What the above means is that as government expenditure (*G*) increases, this leads to an increase in aggregate demand (AD)[2] and in the equilibrium level of GDP (*Y*). However, as the *Y* increases, this leads to an increase in

[2] Note that in the GDP identity: $Y = C + I + G + X - M$, $G$ is a component of AD.

demand for real money balances[3] ($M^d$). However, the supply of real money balances is fixed (no change in LM curve). Therefore, the interest rate ($r$) in the economy must rise to bring the money market into equilibrium. The change in $r$ negatively impacts $I$, which affects $Y$, thus modifying the initial changes in $Y$. This is how an increase in government expenditure ($G$), through a change in the interest rate ($r$) crowds out private investment ($I$).

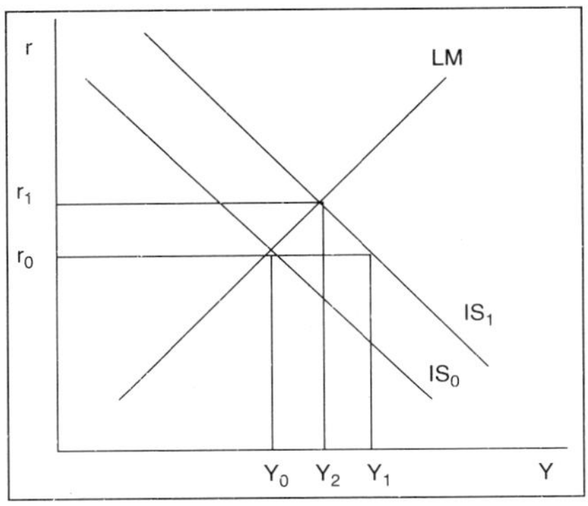


**FIGURE A5.4** *Expansionary Fiscal Policy in IS-LM Model*

This can be seen from Figure A5.4. Consequent to a rightward shift in IS curve output increases to $Y_1$. As a result, demand for money goes up. However since money supply is fixed, interest rate rises to $r_1$. This causes a fall in the private sector investment. $Y_1 - Y_2$ gets crowded out. The increase in output is $Y_2 - Y_0$ and not $Y_1 - Y_0$.

When is fiscal policy effective? In order to answer this, we break down the transmission mechanism (1) into four parts:

1. From an increase in $G$ to an increase in AD and $Y$
2. From an increase in $Y$ to an increase in demand for real money balances
3. From an increase in demand for real money balances to increase in interest rates
4. From an increase in interest rate to a fall in $I$ and $Y$

The effectiveness of fiscal policy will depend on how strong/weak is the link between each of the four parts of the fiscal policy transmission

[3] Real money balance is given by $M^d/P$. In IS-LM model, since prices are constant, there is no difference between $M^d$ and $M^d/P$. But the reference is always to changes in real money balances.

mechanism. In point 1 above, for example, we need to know by how much does AD and $Y$ increase in response to an increase in $G$? This will depend on the size of the government expenditure multiplier (Section 4.2). Fiscal policy will be more effective if multiplier is large and vice versa. Converting the concept of multiplier to a real-life situation, we can say that government expenditure will have a larger influence on AD and $Y$ if it is productive and the other way round if it is unproductive.

Similarly, in point 2, we ask by how much will the demand for real money balances increase in response to a change in $Y$? This will depend on the level of financial sophistication the economy has achieved. For example, if most of the transactions are through e-money, demand for real money balances in an idle form will be less. The implication of this for fiscal policy effectiveness is that if less money is demanded in response to an increase in $Y$, the subsequent rise in the interest rate, which is needed to bring the money market into equilibrium will be less; the crowding out of private investment will also be less.

Next, let us look at point 3 above. Even if demand for real money balances increases in response to change in $Y$, we need to know how much increase in the interest rate is needed to bring the money market into equilibrium. If the demand for money is highly responsive to changes in the interest rate, only a small increase in interest rate will be necessary to bring the money market into equilibrium. Again, the crowding out will be less.

Finally, we consider point 4. Even if the interest rate increases by how much will private sector investment fall? It will depend on how responsive is private sector investment to change in interest rate. If the private sector investment is largely driven by the autonomous component of investment (Section 3.2.2), a rise in the interest rate may not result in too much of crowding out of private investment.

We can thus generalize that fiscal policy will have greater effect on output to the extent multiplier is large, money demand is not very sensitive to income, money demand is very sensitive to interest rate, and private sector investment is not very sensitive to interest rate. In the aftermath of global economic slowdown (2007–09), fiscal policy has gained importance precisely because private sector investment was not responding to changes in the interest rate. While this is true, there are also concerns about the size of the fiscal multiplier, i.e., whether the global economic revival is sustainable or not.

# Monetary Policy

Assume now an expansionary monetary policy. The monetary authorities increase the money supply in the economy (LM shifts to the right). The transmission mechanism through which a monetary stimulation impacts output (Y) can be seen as follows:

$$Ms \Uparrow \Rightarrow r \Downarrow \Rightarrow I \ \&\ AD \ \&\ Y \Uparrow \Rightarrow M^d \ \&\ r \Uparrow \Rightarrow Y \Downarrow \ldots\ldots(2)$$

What this transmission mechanism (2) means is that as the real money balances (*Ms*) increase, people now hold more money than they used to and want to. They will seek to turn some of this money into bonds. This additional demand for bonds will drive up the price of bonds. Bond yields will fall. Interest rate (*r*) will fall. As interest rate (*r*) falls private sector investment (*I*) rises. Since private sector investment (*I*) is a component of aggregate demand (AD), both AD and *Y* rise. But the change in *Y* will affect $M^d$, modifying initial effects on *r*. There will be a subsequent fall in *Y*.

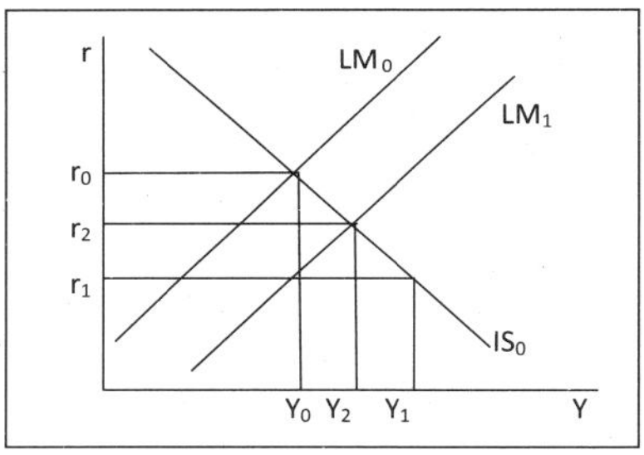


**Figure A5.5** *Expansionary Monetary Policy in IS-LM Model*

Diagrammatically (Figure A5.5), a rise in the money supply causes the LM curve to shift to the right. Interest rate falls to $r_1$. Output increases to $Y_1$. But an increase in money demand consequent to a rise in output to $Y_1$ raises the interest rate to $r_2$. $Y_1 - Y_2$ gets crowded out. Final effect on output is $Y_2$ and not $Y_1$.

When will monetary policy be effective? In order to answer this question we will again break down transmission mechanism (2) into four parts:

1. From an increase in money supply to a fall in the interest rate
2. From a fall in the interest rate to an increase in private investment and thereon on to aggregate demand and output

3. From an increase in output to an increase in demand for money
4. From an increase in demand for money to a rise in the interest rate and subsequent fall in output

What will Part 1 depend on? It will depend on the interest sensitivity of money demand. If money demand is not very sensitive to interest rate, it means that people regard non-money assets as imperfect substitutes for money. Regardless of the opportunity cost of holding money, there would be a certain amount of money that they may feel absolutely necessary to hold. In that situation, if the money supply increases, the fall in the interest rate will have to be sufficiently large to bring the money market back to equilibrium. Since monetary policy works through a change in interest rate the larger the fall in the interest rate, other things being equal, stronger will be its impact on GDP.

Part 2 of the transmission mechanism captures the relationship between a fall in the interest rate and private sector investment. The stronger the relationship, greater will be the impact of monetary policy on GDP.

In part 3, we are asking by how much the demand for real money balances increase in response to a change in $Y$? As we argued earlier, this will depend on the level of financial sophistication the economy has achieved. The implication of this for monetary policy effectiveness is that if less money is demanded in response to an increase in $Y$, the subsequent rise in the interest rate, which is needed to bring the money market into equilibrium will be less.

Part 4 says that if the increase in money demand in response to a change in GDP is less, crowding out of private investment will also be less.

Thus, monetary policy will have a greater effect on output to the extent that money demand is not very sensitive to interest rates, investment is very sensitive to interest rate, the multiplier is large and money demand is not very sensitive to income. In the current global economic meltdown, despite sharp fall in interest rates, neither investment spending nor consumption spending is rising. People are just holding on to their money. Monetary policy effect on GDP is weak.

## Combined Policy

IS-LM model also allows seeing the impact of both fiscal and monetary policy changes simultaneously. The crucial assumption here is that prices are fixed. That being the case, the transmission mechanism will be: when $G$ increases, this results in an increase in $M^d$ but $M^s$ also increases (in the earlier case we assumed that when $G$ increased, money supply was fixed), thus keeping the interest rate constant. There is no crowding out.

Thus, if $G$ is financed through borrowing from the market through issue of bonds there is crowding out. But if $G$ is financed through an increase in money supply, there is no crowding out. Mode of financing has an impact on GDP in the IS-LM model where prices are assumed to be fixed.

The reader should be able to see these changes with the help of Figure A5.6. We assume that the relationships between all the parts captured in the fiscal policy (1) and monetary policy (2) transmission mechanism are stable. In other words, we assume a normal looking IS and LM curve.

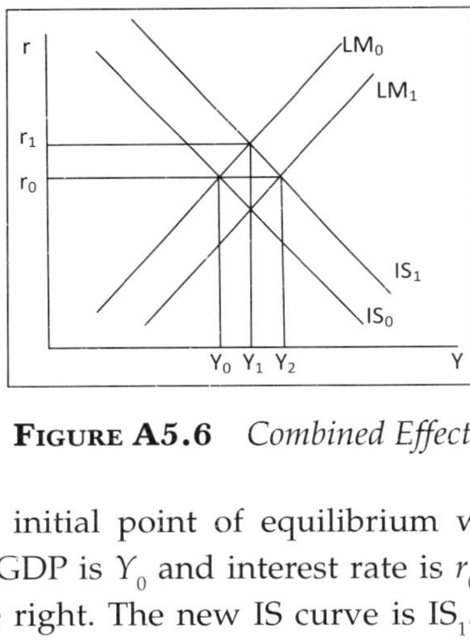


**FIGURE A5.6** *Combined Effect*

We start from an initial point of equilibrium where $IS_0 = LM_0$. The equilibrium level of GDP is $Y_0$ and interest rate is $r_0$. Now, $G$ increases or IS curve shifts to the right. The new IS curve is $IS_1$. If there is no change in money supply and LM curve remains at $LM_0$, increase in output to $Y_2$ will not be sustainable. At $Y_2$, demand for money will go up. With money supply fixed, this will result in a rise in the interest rate to $r_1$. Output will fall and the final increase in output will be $Y_1$ and not $Y_2$. $Y_2 - Y_1$ is what has been crowded out. However, to accommodate an increase in $G$, if the money supply also increases, resulting in a new LM curve, $LM_1$, interest rate will remain the same and there will be no crowding out.

## *Learning from IS-LM Model*

- IS-LM is a static short-term model where prices are assumed to be fixed.

- Nevertheless, the model enables us to understand the dynamics of adjustment following any fiscal or monetary policy change? How the goods and money markets interact to bring the final effect.
- IS-LM model introduces us to the concept of crowding out.
- It also shows that crowding out is a matter of degree
- IS-LM model also helps us to understand how different ways of financing an increase in government spending affect the economy.
- Finally that budget deficits are not always bad.

## *Further on IS-LM model: Allowing Prices to Vary – Derivation of Aggregate Demand Curve (AD)*

In the IS curve, the goods and services are expressed in real terms, i.e. after adjusting for any changes in prices. In the LM curve, however, money supply is expressed in nominal terms though our focus is on real money balances or, $Ms/P$. Since $P$ was assumed to be constant in IS-LM model, any nominal change in money supply also amounted to a real change in money supply and we shifted the LM curve by the amount of nominal money supply change to see its impact on interest rate and output. But this will not be the case, as we will see with Figure A5.7, if prices are allowed to change.

In the figure, the initial point of equilibrium is given by output $Y_0$ and interest rate $r_0$. The $LM_0$ was derived when the price was $P_0$. Now let us say the price increases to $P_2$ and there is no change in nominal money supply. Since we are expressing money supply in real terms, this amounts to a fall in real money balances and LM curve shifts to the left to $LM_2$. Similarly, if prices fall to $P_1$ and there is no change in nominal money supply, this would amount to an increase in real money balances and the LM curve would shift to $LM_2$. This shift in the LM curve will impact interest rate and output exactly in the same manner as we discussed earlier in the IS-LM model. Except that, in the IS-LM model the change in the real money balances and thereby LM curve was in response to a change in nominal money supply with prices fixed while in this case the change in the real money balances and thus LM curve is because of a change in prices with nominal money supply fixed.

In the lower quadrant of Figure A5.7 we now derive the aggregate demand (AD) curve. When price is $P_2$, AD is $Y_2$; when the price falls to $P_1$, AD increases to $AD_2$. When we join all these points, we get the aggregate demand curve. It slopes downward because a lower price index ($P$) raises the real money supply and stimulates expenditure and thus AD.

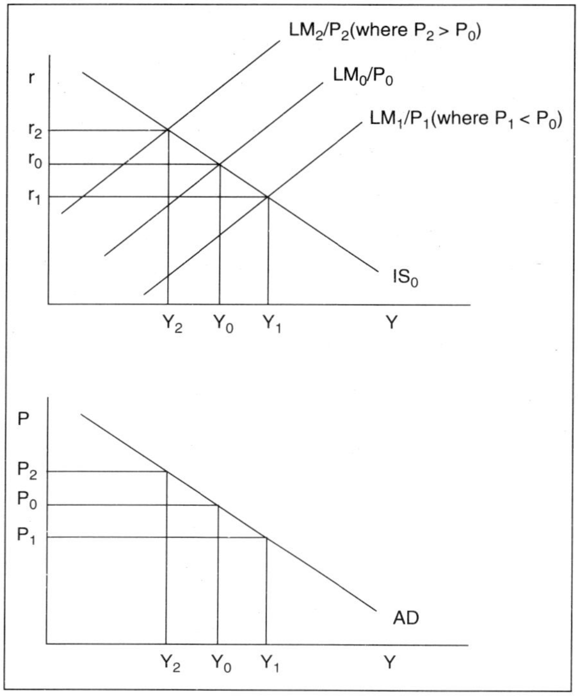


**FIGURE A5.7** *Allowing Prices to Change*

The AD curve shows all possible cross points of a single IS curve with different LM curves for each possible price level. Unlike the IS curve, along which only the goods market is in equilibrium, and a single LM curve, along which only money market is in equilibrium, everywhere along the AD curve both the goods and money markets are in equilibrium.

It should also be possible to see the following:

- Expansionary fiscal policy shifts the IS curve and also the AD curve to the right. However, the shift in the AD curve is less than the shift in the IS curve because of subsequent crowding out.
- Expansionary monetary policy shifts the LM curve and also the AD curve to the right. However, the shift in the AD curve is less than the shift in the LM curve also because of subsequent crowding out.
- A policy change like expansionary fiscal policy or expansionary monetary policy will shift either the IS or LM curve.

Once we have derived the aggregate demand curve, we can do an aggregate demand (AD)–aggregate supply (AS) analysis as we did in Chapter 4. If the AS curve is a horizontal straight line, thereby meaning a massive excess capacity, a rightward shift in AD will have no impact on prices. At the other extreme, if the AS is vertical, thereby meaning full capacity utilization, a rightward shift in AD will only result in increase in prices and there will not be any change in output. This increase in prices will keep shifting the LM curve to the left and interest rates will keep rising till there is total crowding out. In between these extremes, of course, there are numerous possibilities as discussed in Section 4.4.1 and in annexure to Chapter 4.

## *IS-LM in an Open Economy*

IS-LM model can also throw light on the efficacy of fiscal and monetary policies in an open economy (i.e. when capital is moving in or out freely) under alternate exchange regimes.

First consider fixed exchange rate regime with free capital mobility. Initially assume prices are constant.

Impact of an expansionary fiscal policy will be as follows:

- IS curve shifts to the right
- Interest rate goes up
- Inflow of capital
- Currency appreciates
- *Ms* goes up (LM shifts to the right) because central bank buys dollars to keep the exchange rate fixed
- Maximum increase in output
- Fiscal policy very effective.

Impact of an expansionary monetary policy will be as follows:

- LM curve shifts to the right
- Interest rate falls
- Outflow of capital
- *Ms* falls (LM shifts to the left) because central bank sells dollars to keep the exchange rate fixed
- Foreign exchange reserves fall
- Monetary policy is ineffective.

Now consider flexible exchange regime with free capital mobility. Again, prices are assumed to be constant.

The impact of an expansionary fiscal policy will be as follows:

- IS shifts to the right
- Interest rate rises
- Inflow of capital
- Currency appreciates
- Net exports go down/crowded out
- IS curve shifts to the left
- Fiscal policy is ineffective.

Similarly, the impact of an expansionary monetary policy is as follows:

- Ms increases
- Interest rate goes down
- Capital outflow
- Currency depreciates
- NX rises
- IS curve shifts to the right
- Maximum rise in output

What will happen if prices are not fixed? As we discussed earlier, any change in the price level will impact the LM curve. It will either move to the left or right depending on whether the change in price is more or less than the initial equilibrium price. The impact on interest rate and final output will also change accordingly. Some of these impacts are discussed in a story mode in Section 6.5, but largely derived from open economy IS-LM model.

# REVIEW QUESTIONS

1. Define money. What role does money play in an economy? What is money supply?
2. "Demand for money is an increasing function of income and a decreasing function of interest rates". What do we mean by this statement? Explain.
3. What problems does the central banker face in accurately measuring demand for money and why?
4. Assume the central bank reduces the money supply. How will it

affect the financial markets and, thereby, consumer and investment spending in the economy?

**5.** Why does the central bank resort to preemptive rise in interest rates when the economy is reviving? Why cannot it wait for prices to actually rise beyond the accepted level, before slowing down the economy?

**6.** "Money supply process involves three players: a) central bank, b) commercial banks, and c) public". Discuss the role of each.

**7.** If people use more credit cards and ATMs what will be the impact on the money multiplier and the money supply?

**8.** If the central bank brings the reserve ratio (CRR) requirement to zero, how will it affect the conduct of monetary policy? Similarly, if the central bank brings the reserves ratio to 1, how will it affect the money supply? How will the banks survive?

**9.** Assume money supply is Rs. 1000 crores, all bank deposits are Rs. 750 crores, the reserve-deposit ratio is 10% and the RBI purchases 20 crores of government securities from the market. What will be the increase in money supply?

**10.** In the above problem, is there any reason to believe that the actual increase in money supply may be lower than what you have estimated? If so why?

**11.** Why do we say that the central bank cannot simultaneously target exchange rate, interest rate and price? Where and how does the conflict arise?

**12.** "A rise in the asset prices can undermine the role of monetary policy" How? Will you then advocate that monetary policy also target asset prices?

**13.** How does small saving interest rates, which are administered, affect the overall interest rates in the economy?

**14.** "Interest rate is a monetary variable but the future level of interest rates in India will depend not so much on monetary policy as on fiscal policy". Explain.

CHAPTER

6

# THE EXTERNAL SECTOR

An understanding of how external sector impacts macroeconomic policy, and thus business environment, assumes importance because of the increasing pace of globalization among economies all over the world. Global economic integration takes place through the following:

1. Opening up international trade in goods and services
2. Opening up international production
3. Opening up international movement of capital and
4. Opening up international movement of labour.

When we consider the impact of global economic integration on macroeconomic policy, the focus is on points 1 and 3 above, i.e., integration through international trade and integration through movement of capital.

Table 6.1 shows the trends in trade as a per centage of GDP in selected regions of the world between 2000 and 2008. The table reveals three important points. First, trade accounts for more than 50 per cent of GDP globally. Second, in all regions, trade as a per centage of GDP is rising. Third, the rise is more pronounced in South Asia and the Caribbean.

Similarly, there has been a phenomenal rise in capital flows both by way of foreign direct investment and private capital flows. Foreign direct investment alone, as a per centage of GDP, in the three-year period 2006–

2008, increased from 2.2 to 3.3 per cent in India; from 2.9 to 3.4 per cent in China; from 1.7 to 2.8 per cent in Brazil; and, from 3 to 4.3 per cent in Russia. The newly emerging economies have forged ahead along with others who have already had substantial integration.

***Table 6.1 Integration with the Global Economy (% of GDP)***

| Region | Trade in goods | |
|---|---|---|
| | 2000 | 2008 |
| World | 41.1 | 53.5 |
| Northern Africa | 38.6 | 65.2 |
| Caribbean | 54.8 | 95.7 |
| Eastern Asia | 68.6 | 80.4 |
| Southern Asia | 26.2 | 40.4 |
| Europe | 58.8 | 66.0 |
| Sub-Sahara Africa | 55.1 | 66.2 |

*Source*: World Development Indicators, 2009.

The essence of external sector discussion is that macroeconomic policies followed by one country, in a globally integrated world, do not affect the economy of that country alone, but also have repercussions on the economies of other countries. The extent of this inter-relationship depends on (a) size of international trade in a country's GDP, (b) how mobile is capital between countries, and (c) the exchange rate regime. In what follows, we will first analyse the external balance of payment accounts to see where trade and capital movements fit in and what they mean for the macro economy. Then we will understand the different exchange rate regimes and macroeconomic policy responses under each regime. Finally, we will talk about open economy macroeconomic policy issues.

But before that, let us briefly describe why countries trade with each other and why they go in for mobility of capital.

## 6.1 Integration Through Trade and Movement of Capital: An Introduction

Why do countries trade with each other? The answer is simple: because they gain from trade. Assume two countries, country A and country B. Let us say that they constitute the globe. Also, assume that the two countries produce only two commodities, *x* and *y*. Now, if A can produce *x* cheaper than B and B can produce *y* cheaper than *x*, clearly A has an absolute advantage in the production of *x* and B in the production of *y*. Thus A will be better off concentrating on the production of *x* and B on the production of *y*. A will export *x* to B and B will export *y* to A. Both countries will gain from trade. But what happens if A has an absolute advantage in the production of both *x* and *y*? That is, A can produce *x* cheaper than B and it can produce *y* much cheaper than B. Will the globe be better off if A produces both *x* and *y* and B produces nothing? The answer is in the negative. The globe will be better off if A concentrates on the production of *y*, which it can produce much cheaper than B and B concentrates on the production of *x*, which it can produce less expensively than A. In other words, even if countries do not have an absolute advantage, they can gain from trade if they allocate their resources based on comparative advantage and trade with each other. The gain from trade, therefore, is twofold: (a) it brings in efficiency in production and consumption and, (b) it provides a market for goods and services.

The above conceptualization is based on the premise that there are no restrictions on trade between countries by way of tariff and non-tariff barriers, quantitative restrictions, etc. In real life, however, restrictions do exist, despite the existence of World Trade Organization (WTO), which is supposed to oversee free and fair trade among countries. To that extent, there is a deviation between expected and actual gain from trade. Nevertheless, countries maintain extensive trade links with each other to derive whatever benefits they can from it.

What is the relationship between trade and macroeconomics? We have already analyzed in Section 3.2 (in Chapter 3) how actions of one country can affect GDP of another country through trade. Very briefly, in a global economy, if a government implements expansionary macroeconomic policies, the effect is not only on higher domestic GDP, but also on increased foreign GDP. This is because in an open economy, part of the increase in domestic GDP will be spent on imports rather than domestic products. Imports are an increasing function of GDP.

But this may not happen if the increase in GDP in that country is due to a real depreciation in the exchange rates. A real depreciation increases the competitiveness of that country in world markets. As a result, it is able to export more and the country's GDP increases. But GDP of other countries may come down because of loss of competitiveness.

Why do countries go in for cross-border movements of capital? There are several reasons. In many economies, particularly emerging economies, the investment requirements for a sustained growth of GDP are massive. Domestic savings alone cannot meet such large investment needs. Access to foreign capital, thus, helps in mitigating the shortage of funds from domestic sources. The lenders also benefit if they see a higher return on their investment if their funds are invested abroad.

More specifically, countries go in for international capital because it:

1. supplements domestic savings and investment,
2. allows a choice between domestic and foreign assets for the investors,
3. increases financial sector efficiency by opening it up to global competition, and
4. helps in aligning global interest rates and prices, thereby enhancing the welfare of the residents.

However, unless properly managed, unrestricted movement of capital can cause major disruption in the economy. We shall discuss these issues later in the chapter.

## 6.2 Balance of Payments

### 6.2.1 Understanding the Balance of Payment Statements

Balance of payments (BOP) is the difference between receipts of residents of a country from foreigners and payments by residents to foreigners. A transaction, which increases the supply of foreign exchange, is recorded as a credit entry while any transaction that uses up foreign exchange is recorded as debit. BOP is a double book entry, that is, every transaction is entered twice. Hence, overall balance of payment is always in balance. It is the different parts of BOP accounts, which provide insights into the external balance of payments situation. Let us understand the structure of BOP accounts with the help of Indian balance of payment data for the year 2007–08. This is shown in Table 6.2.

*Table 6.2 India: Balance of payment accounts, 2007–08*

(million US dollars)

| Item | Credit | Debit | Net |
|---|---|---|---|
| I. Trade Account | **166162** | **257629** | **–91467** |
| II. Invisibles Account | **148875** | **73144** | **75731** |
| a. Services | 90342 | 51489 | 38853 |
| b. Investment Income | 14272 | 19339 | –5067 |
| c. Transfer Payments | 44261 | 2316 | 41945 |
| III. Current Account (I + II) | **315037** | **330733** | **–15736** |
| IV. Capital Account | **438357** | **331773** | **106584** |
| a. Foreign Investments | 271122 | 227796 | 43326 |
| b. Loans | 82192 | 41539 | 40653 |
| c. Banking Capital | 55814 | 44055 | 11759 |
| d. Rupee Debt Service | – | 122 | –122 |
| e. Other Capital | 29229 | 18261 | 10968 |
| V. Errors and Omissions | – | **1316** | **–1316** |
| VI. Overall Balance (III + IV)[a] | **753394** | **663862** | **89532** |
| VII. Monetary Movements | – | – | – |
| a. IMF Transactions | – | – | – |
| b. Increase in Reserves | – | 92164 | –92164 |

[a] After adjusting for errors and omissions.
*Source*: Compiled from Government of India, Ministry of Finance, *Economic Survey, 2009–10*, Tables 62–63.

Item I shows the *trade account*. Trade account shows the balance from export and import of merchandise only. These include physical movement of goods, i.e., manufactured products, semi-finished goods, capital goods, raw materials, agricultural products and so on. In 2007–08, India had a deficit on trade account to the extent of US$ 91.47 billion. This, thus, represents the excess of dollar value of merchandise imports (debit) over dollar value of merchandise exports (credit).

Item II is called the *invisible account*. Non-merchandise items are known as invisibles. They are broken down into three components: (a) services; (b) investment income and (c) transfer payments.

1. Services includes: (a) travel and tourism; when a foreigner, for example, travels to India he sells dollars to buy rupees to spend in India. This is entered as a credit item in the invisible account and vice versa when an Indian travels abroad; (b) transportation; for example,

a foreigner flying Air India is a credit item; an Indian flying British Airways is a debit item; (c) financial and other services including insurance; when foreigners use our financial services, it is a credit entry in the invisible account and when we use foreign financial services, it is a debit entry; (d) government; for example, when Government of India sets up embassies and High Commissions abroad, it is a debit item and vice versa when foreign governments set up embassies and High Commissions in India and; (e) miscellaneous include, among other items, India's software service exports. India had a surplus of about US$ 38.85 billion on services account in 2007–08.

2. Investment income refers to receipts (credit) and payments (debit) of dividends, interests, and profits arising out of Indian investments abroad and foreign investments in India. In 2007–08, the net foreign investment income in India was negative by US$ 5.06 billion, thereby suggesting that foreigners owned more assets in India than Indians did in foreign countries.
3. Transfer payments do not represent payment for any direct service rendered or any physical transfer of goods. They are in the nature of foreign aid, gifts, foreign workers' remittances to their home countries, etc. The latter is a very important component of transfer payment account in India. Mainly on account of inward remittances, net transfer payments showed a massive surplus of US$ 41.94 billion in India in 2007–08.
4. The invisible account in Table 6.2 can now be seen in its totality. It showed a surplus of US$ 41.94 billion on transfer payments account; a surplus of US$ 38.85 billion on services account; and, a deficit of US$ 5.06 billion on investment income account. That left the invisible account with a net surplus of US$ 75.73 billion in 2007–08.

Item III in Table 6.2 is the *current account* balance and is obtained as sum of items I and II. The current account balance, thus, refers to balance in flows of goods (merchandise) and services and other current receipts and payments (investment income and transfer payments) between countries. From Table 6.1, we note that in 2007–08 India had a deficit on trade account (Item I) and a surplus on invisible account (Item II) but the surplus on invisible account was not adequate to make up for the deficit on trade account and therefore India had a deficit on current account (Item III) of US$ 15.73 billion. A country can, of course, have a surplus/deficit in both trade and invisible accounts; surplus/deficit in one and not on the other. But a current account deficit is sustainable only to the extent a country can finance it. This brings us to a discussion of capital and monetary movement accounts in Table 6.2.

Under *capital account* (item IV), there is no export or import of goods and/or invisible items between countries. There is only inflow and outflow of capital and the difference between the two, represents a country's capital account balance. Capital inflows or outflows take place on account of (i) foreign investment; (ii) loans; (iii) banking capital; (iv) rupee-debt service, and (v) other capital. The first three are major items in our capital account while the last two are relatively minor. Let us briefly discuss each of them one by one:

1. Foreign investments are of two types – foreign direct investment and portfolio investment. In the former case, movement of capital in and out of country takes place with the intention of buying physical assets to start a business. These are, thus, called long-term capital movements. In the latter case, capital flows in or out to purchase financial assets in, say, securities market. These, along with NRI investments (reported under banking capital), are called short-term capital movements. An inflow of capital is a credit item and an outflow of capital is a debit item in the capital account.
2. Loans can be on government or private sector accounts. These can be from bilateral, multi-lateral or private sources. Loans can also be short-term or long-term. A loan received from foreign entities is a credit item, while repayments and loans made to foreign entities is a debit item in the capital account.
3. Banking capital refers to changes in foreign assets and liabilities of our banks that are authorized to deal in foreign exchange. NRI investments also come under banking capital. When capital flows in on this account (liability increases), it is a credit item and, when capital flows out (an increase in assets), it is a debit item.
4. The capital account also consists of two other minor items shown under "rupee-debt service" by way of obligation to repay foreign loan in rupees and "other capital", mostly accounted for by delayed receipts on account of exports.
5. On all the three major accounts, that is, foreign investment, loans and banking capital, India had a surplus in 2007–08. After adjusting for the negative item, capital account surplus in 2007–08 came to US$ 106.58 billion (item IV).

Though BoP transactions are recorded, based on double entry method, discrepancies may crop up between debits and credits because of data lags and other estimation problems. These discrepancies are captured by item V under "errors and omissions." A negative value indicates that receipts are overstated or payments are understated, or both, and vice versa. We, thus, get the overall balance (item VI) after adjusting for errors and omissions. The overall balance is obtained as a sum of current account (item III) and capital account (item IV) after adjusting for errors and omissions (item V). In 2007–08, India had an overall positive balance of US$ 89.53 billion.

Finally, we come to *monetary movements* (item VII). These movements keep a record of India's transactions with the International Monetary Fund (IMF) and India's foreign exchange reserves that mainly consist of RBI holdings of gold and foreign currency assets. Drawings (treated as a kind of borrowing) from IMF is a credit item, whereas repayments made to IMF are debit items. Drawing down of reserves, which is an inflow into the balance of payments from the reserve account, is a credit item. Like any other inflow, these reserves can be used to support a deficit elsewhere in the balance of payments. Similarly, additions to reserve account are an outflow from the balance of payments to the reserve account and are, therefore, a debit item.

When all the components of balance of payments are taken together, the balance of payment should be in balance. Credits should equal debits. In Table 6.2, both credits and debits come to US$ 92.16 billion. If RBI did not want to add to its reserves, then this equality in credits and debits would be brought about through exchange rate adjustments. Note that a surplus overall balance (item VI) represents excess of inflows of foreign exchange over outflows. If RBI did not intervene, this would lead to an appreciation of the rupee. This will discourage inflows since the foreigner will get less of Indian goods, invisibles and financial assets for the same dollar. At the same time, an appreciating rupee will encourage outflows as foreign goods and assets are now relatively cheaper. This will go on till inflows are equal to outflows, or, credits are equal to debits and item VI in Table 6.2 equals zero.

## 6.2.2 Analyses of Balance of Payment Statements

What does the manager make out of the balance of payment statements? The following points may be noted:

1. Balance of payment statements, which show the difference between receipts of residents of a country from foreigners and payments by residents to foreigners, is nothing but a statement of the difference between the supply of foreign exchange and demand for foreign exchange. Foreigners demand rupees to pay for our goods/services and financial assets and they supply foreign exchange to get the rupees. We demand foreign exchange to buy foreign goods/services and foreign financial assets and we supply rupees to obtain foreign exchange. The former is entered as receipts on the credit side of balance of payments and the latter enters as payments on the debit side. The credit side, thus, represents supply of foreign exchange (demand for rupees) and debit side represents demand for foreign exchange (supply of rupees). If the supply of foreign exchange (demand for rupees) is greater than the demand for foreign exchange (supply of rupees), the exchange rate of rupee will tend to appreciate and vice versa. Balance of payment statements are, therefore, key to understanding the determination of exchange rates.
2. A current account deficit is not sustainable unless it is matched by a surplus on the capital account and/or change in monetary movements.
3. Even if a country has current account deficit, its currency could be appreciating if the overall balance is positive, i.e., the capital account surplus is more than the current account deficit.
4. Capital account is important because movements in capital, to a great extent, decide; (a) the sustainability of current account deficit; and (b) exchange rate. Changes in monetary movements have similar implications.
5. Typically, there are four sets of "balances", which analysts closely monitor. They are: (a) trade balance (item I); (b) balance on goods and services (item III *minus* investment income and transfer); (c) current account balance (item III) and; (d) what is known as basic balance and defined as balance on current account *plus* long-term capital. By eliminating the volatile short-term capital from its estimation, the basic balance, thus, tries to capture the robustness of balance of payments.

   Further, based on what we have learnt so far, we can add the following:
6. Higher the share of exports in a country's GDP, faster will be the growth of the economy in response to an increase in overseas demand.

And, vice versa. Similarly, higher the dependence on imports, greater will be the vulnerability of the economy of the country to changes in import prices.

7. A current account deficit, if persistent, is not sustainable because, on the one hand, foreign capital may take a dim view of the country's ability to meet its foreign obligations and, therefore, cut down the flows, and on the other hand, monetary movements, particularly domestic reserve account, may also find the deficit unmanageable and get drained. Since a deficit represents an imbalance between demand for and supply of foreign exchange, a persistent presence of this imbalance can destabilize the currency.
8. A persistent surplus in the current account is also not desirable because it means that either the country invests the surplus abroad for the development of other countries or it allows its currency to appreciate. The former does not add to GDP; the latter slows down GDP growth by crowding out exports.

What is desirable is a period of current account deficit such that, in course of time, it turns to a current account surplus, as it enhances the capacity of the country to generate an excess of exports over imports, sufficient to pay for charges on account of interest or dividend on foreign capital.

## 6.2.3 Currency Convertibility

We close this section with a brief introduction to the concept of convertibility. It is easy to grasp this concept from the balance of payment accounts.

1. Current account convertibility means that the rupee is fully convertible into another currency and vice versa for all transactions on the current account. Thus, if a foreigner wants to buy our goods and invisibles (exports), the foreigner's currency is fully convertible into rupees at the going exchange rate. Similarly, rupee is fully convertible into another currency at the going rate for all purchases of goods and invisibles from abroad (imports). Of course, all transactions, even on current account, must fall within legal restrictions imposed on these transactions. In India we have, by and large, full current account convertibility.
2. Capital account convertibility means that rupee is fully convertible into another currency and vice versa for all transactions on capital

account. Thus, a resident wanting to buy foreign assets can, to do so, convert his rupee into another currency at the market rate. Similarly, a foreigner who wants to purchase Indian assets can freely convert his currency into rupees to buy our assets. In India, we do not have full convertibility on capital account, though capital account is getting increasingly liberalized.

3. Current account convertibility is universally considered desirable and, indeed, is in place in most countries. This gives the right signals to exporters and importers to gain from trade. However, there are differences of opinion on the desirability of full capital account convertibility, particularly, as we will see later in the chapter, unless right environment is created, they can be quite disruptive.

## 6.3 Exchange Rates[1]

### 6.3.1 Exchange Rate Definitions

*Exchange rate* is the price of domestic currency in relation to foreign currency. It tells us the amount of rupee that is needed to buy, say, a US dollar. If Rs. 46 is needed to buy US$ 1, we will say that the exchange rate between rupee and dollar is Rs. 46. When the value of rupee rises (appreciates) in relation to the dollar and, now, let us say, only Rs. 45 is needed to buy US$ 1, we say that exchange rate has fallen. Similarly, when the value of the rupee falls (depreciates) to, say, Rs. 47 to a dollar, we say that the exchange rate has gone up. It is, thus, important to be precise about how the exchange rate is being defined.[2]

*Nominal exchange rate* is simply the price of domestic currency in relation to another currency. The discussion in the preceding paragraph, for example, referred to nominal exchange rates between rupee and dollar. However, there is no one single foreign currency. There are as many foreign currencies as there are foreign countries. A more meaningful way to define exchange rate, therefore, is not in terms of value of domestic currency in relation to *another* currency but to a basket of currencies. This is called *nominal effective*

[1] Review Section 2.15 of Chapter 2 before starting this section.

[2] For example, the concepts will reverse, if exchange rate is defined as the price of foreign currency in relation to domestic currency.

*exchange rate* (NEER) and is arrived at as the weighted average of the price of rupee in relation to all other currencies, where the weights reflect the importance of each currency in India's foreign trade. Figure 6.1 compares the trends in nominal exchange rate between rupee and key global currencies as also NEER between 2000–01 and 2008–09. Clearly, they do not move in the same direction. There are years when rupee appreciated (depreciated) against some currencies but not against others. The value of NEER, which gives the price of rupee in relation to the basket of currencies, also moved differently than individual currencies in select years.

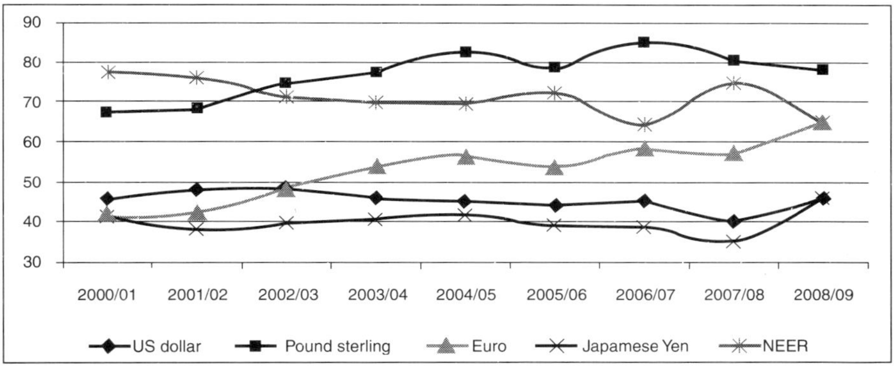


*Source*: Data culled out of www.rbi.org.in *Handbook of Statistics on Indian Economy*.

[a] In case of NEER, a rise is an appreciation against a basket of currencies and a fall is depreciation.

**FIGURE 6.1** *India: Trends in Nominal Exchange Rates* [a]

*Real exchange rate*, as explained in Section 2.15 (Chapter 2) is defined as the nominal exchange rate times the foreign price level divided by the domestic price level. Real exchange rate captures the competitiveness of a country's trade by additionally considering the relative price changes between the countries. It measures the net effect of exchange rate and price pressures. Real exchange rate can be defined as follows: Real = Nominal × $P_f/P_h$ where $P_f$ is the price in the foreign country and $P_h$ is the price in the home country. Other things being equal, if $P_f$ increases at a faster rate than $P_h$, $P_f/P_h$ will rise and the value of the real exchange rate will go up. We will then say that the rupee, in real terms, has depreciated though there is no change in the nominal exchange rate. Clearly, this is because of relative price changes that have made Indian products more competitive. The opposite will happen if $P_h$ rises at a faster rate than $P_f$.

Once again, using the same logic as NEER, it will be unrealistic to calculate real exchange rate in relation to just another currency. It has to be against a basket of currencies to be meaningful. *Real effective exchange rate* (REER) captures this. The principle involved in estimating REER is the same as for NEER. REER is arrived at as the weighted average of the real exchange rate of rupee in relation to all other currencies where the weights reflect the importance of each currency in India's foreign trade.

Figure 6.2 shows the movements in NEER and REER in India in 2000–01 and 2008–09. They, more or less, seem to have moved in the same direction during this period.

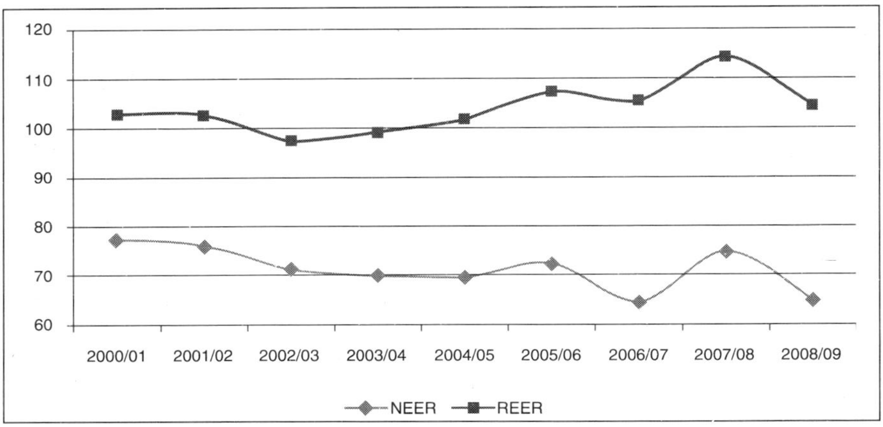


[a] Six currency trade based weights – Base 1993-94 (April-March) = 100. As they are calculated, a rise in NEER or REER denotes an appreciation and a fall denotes depreciation of rupee against the basket of currencies. *Source*: www.finmin.nic.in Economic Survey–2009–10, Page A7.

**FIGURE 6.2** *India: Trends in Nominal and Real Effective Exchange Rates* [a]

Except for the period 2002/03 to 2004/05, when there was a deviation between movements in REER and NEER, the trends in these two indices in other years were broadly same.

## 6.3.2 Exchange Rate Determination

What determines exchange rates? There are two theories: (a) purchasing power parity theory; and (b) interest rate parity theory. According to the former, in the long run, exchange rates adjust in order to reflect differences in inflation rates of the country. If, initially, a basket of tradable goods costs Rs. 40 in India and the same basket costs \$1 in the USA, then purchasing power exchange rate would be Rs. 40 = \$1. However, if price of the basket of goods in India doubles, then, to buy the same basket of goods in India as in the US, the purchasing power exchange rate now becomes Rs. 80 = \$1. The purchasing power parity theory says that, other things being equal, in the long run, exchange rates will be determined by the inflation differential between countries. And, the exchange rate between one country and another will be in equilibrium when their domestic purchasing powers at that rate of exchange are equivalent.

The interest rate parity theory is conceptually similar to purchasing power parity theory, except that it relates to trade in assets. The interest parity theory states that, other things being equal, interest rate differentials between countries will determine the exchange rates between countries. For example, if in country A interest rates are higher than in country B, investors will shift money into country A's securities. Two things will happen. First, country A's security prices will go up and interest rates will come down, while country B's security prices will come down and interest rates will go up. Second, as capital flows into A, its currency will be bid up relative to its expected future value. On both counts, country A's currency will be expected to depreciate. According to this theory, exchange rates will be in equilibrium, when the interest rate available in one country will be equal to the rate of interest available in another country.

Purchasing power parity theory is perhaps a long-term possibility. But it ignores transport costs and trade restrictions; nor does it recognize the fact that large volumes of goods and services are not, in practice, tradable internationally and even those which are tradable have to go through long adjustment lags. Interest rate parity theory overrides purchasing power theory in the short and medium term. But certain considerations like political risk perceptions and capital market rigidities between countries are left out. These theories are certainly instructive as useful benchmarks for comparative analysis, but rather simplistic in the modern complicated world. In today's world, it is perhaps safe to view exchange rate determination as a result of a combination of factors, which encompass not only changes in relative prices and relative interest rates but also changes in relative income growth, investment prospects, expected price differentials, expected interest rate differentials and speculation about exchange rate movements. These certainly make forecasting exchange rates an unenviable task.

### 6.3.3 Exchange Rate Regimes

Three main exchange rate regimes exist: (a) fixed, (b) managed float and (c) flexible (also called floating). Under fixed exchange rate system, the central bank of the country fixes the price of the domestic currency in relation to the foreign currency and agrees to maintain the value at that level. The central bank, as we will see in the next section, ensures the fixity of the rate through intervention in the foreign exchange market. Under flexible exchange rate system, the value of the domestic currency in relation to the foreign currency is determined in the market place based on demand for and supply of currencies. The managed float system is a combination of fixed and flexible exchange rate systems. Under this system, the central bank first allows the exchange rate to be determined in the market place but it has a view on an orderly behaviour of the rate and sets in to influence the rate from time to time to achieve what it desires. Fixed exchange regime, further, has many variants. These are captured in Figure 6.3.

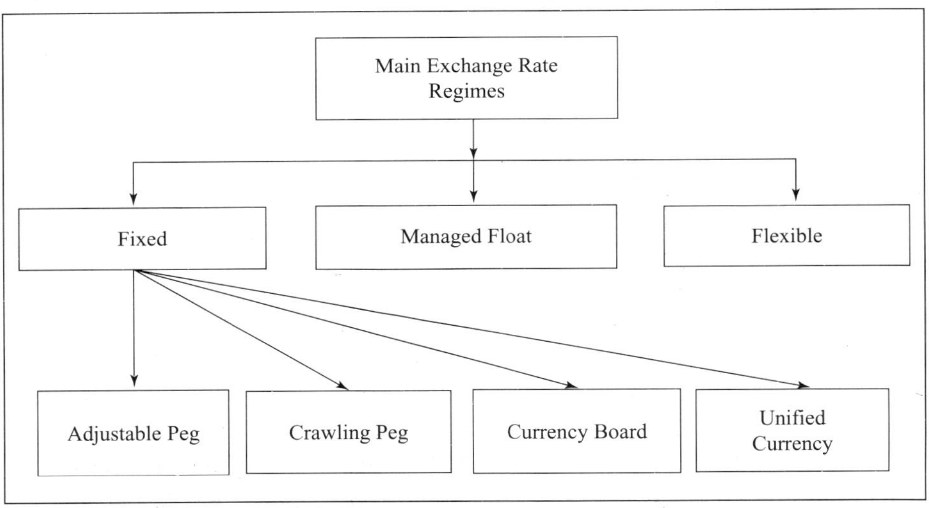


**FIGURE 6.3** *Exchange Rate Region*

Under adjustable peg, the exchange rate is fixed for extended periods, usually within narrow margins, but adjusted if the pressure is not withstandable. In crawling peg, the central bank allows a gradual adjustment of the exchange rate by intervening in the currency market in small measure but on a continuous basis to achieve the desired objective. Under a currency board, the exchange rate is irrevocably fixed by the board (or the central bank). The monetary base, i.e., currency + reserves, is fully backed by foreign currency and the central bank is ready to exchange the base money into foreign currency at the fixed exchange rate. Thus, unlike a conventional central bank, which can influence the monetary base at will, a currency board can influence the monetary base only when there are foreign exchange reserves to back it. Every time there is an inflow of foreign exchange, base money automatically goes up by the same amount; every time there is an outflow of foreign exchange, base money automatically comes down. Even if everyone wants to convert domestic currency into foreign exchange, there is no question of demand for foreign exchange (supply of domestic currency) exceeding the supply of foreign exchange (demand for domestic currency), as both are always the same. The exchange rate is automatically fixed and there is no intervention called for. Finally, under the unified currency system, independent currency is abandoned and some other currency is adopted. For example, Argentina went for dollar as the currency and discarded its own currency, peso. The member countries of European Union chose to adopt a full European monetary union with a single currency, Euro. In such cases, the price of the domestic currency is permanently set against dollar (Argentina) or Euro (for example, 13.7603 Austrian Schilling against Euro; 6.55957 French Francs against Euro and so on). Members are expected to adhere to strict macroeconomic discipline to ensure fixity of the currency.

# 6.4 Macroeconomic Adjustment To External Sector Imbalance Under Different Exchange Rate Regimes

## 6.4.1 Fixed Exchange Regime

Under fixed exchange rate system, as stated earlier, the central bank fixes the price of the domestic currency in relation to the foreign currency perhaps within a margin. Now, assume that the overall balance (current + capital account) is negative. This will happen when the outflow (demand for foreign exchange) is greater than inflow (supply of foreign exchange).

As the demand for foreign exchange is greater than the supply of foreign exchange, the price of foreign exchange will rise relative to the domestic currency. There will be pressure on the domestic currency to depreciate. Since the exchange rate is fixed, the central bank will not allow the currency to depreciate and will sell foreign exchange in the market from its reserves to increase the supply to maintain the fixed exchange rate.

The macroeconomic adjustment[3] takes place, in this case, as follows: when the central bank sells foreign exchange in the market, this reduces the monetary base and, the broad money supply, by a multiple '*m*' of the monetary base (Chapter 5, Section 5.4.2). As the money supply growth decreases, the macroeconomic adjustment takes place through two routes. First, works through the current account. In response to a slower growth of money supply, domestic GDP growth slows down. Imports, being a positive function of GDP growth, slows down the growth of imports. As a result, $X - M$ improves. The demand for foreign exchange comes down in relation to supply of foreign exchange and the pressure on the rupee to depreciate comes down. Also, a slowing economy puts a downward pressure on prices. This increases the competitiveness of goods and services in the external market. Again, $X - M$ goes up and the downward pressure on currency eases. The second adjustment takes place through the capital account. As money supply growth falls, interest rate goes up. Domestic interest rate in relation to interest rate in the rest of the world rises. This attracts more capital into the country. The supply of foreign exchange goes up. The combination of these two factors restores the exchange rate balance.

Now assume the opposite situation. The overall balance in the balance of payments account of the country, i.e., current account + capital account, is positive. This will be the case when total inflow of foreign exchange on current account *plus* capital account is greater than the total outflow on the same accounts. In other words, the supply of foreign exchange is greater than the demand for foreign exchange. The price of foreign exchange will fall in relation to domestic currency. There will be pressure on domestic currency to appreciate vis-à-vis the foreign currency. However, since the central bank is committed to keeping the exchange rate fixed, it will not allow the domestic currency to appreciate. It will mop up the extra supply of foreign exchange to support the fixed rate, which, in turn, will go towards the building of foreign exchange reserves.

---

[3] Note that this adjustment is immediate under currency board or unified currency regimes as the domestic currency has the full backing of foreign exchange.

The macroeconomic adjustment takes place as follows: The central bank buys foreign exchange from the open market. This leads to an increase in the monetary base. The broad money supply increases by a multiple '*m*' of base money (Chapter 5, Section 5.4.2). Increase in money supply reduces the interest rate. This has two effects. First, works through the current account. As GDP growth accelerates consequent to an increase in money supply growth, demand for imports goes up. As a result, $X - M$ deteriorates. An increase in imports, translated into currency terms, implies a higher demand for foreign exchange compared to supply. This puts downward pressure on the domestic currency and the exchange rate balance is restored. Again, a booming economy puts upward pressure on prices. Domestic products become uncompetitive in the external market at those prices. Net exports ($X - M$) deteriorate. This stems the rise in the value of the currency. Similarly, through the capital account, a fall in the interest rate consequent to a rise in money supply makes domestic interest rates unattractive relative to interest rates in the rest of the world. This reduces the supply (inflow) of foreign exchange. The exchange rate balance is restored.

The macroeconomic adjustment processes described above are summarized in Figures 6.4 and 6.5.

Note from the above two cases and also from Figures 6.4 and 6.5 that, under a fixed exchange rate regime, the macroeconomic adjustment takes place through a change in money supply. If the domestic currency is under pressure of depreciation (overall balance is negative), money supply has to fall to restore the fixity of the exchange rate. If, on the other hand, the domestic currency is under pressure of appreciation (overall balance is positive), money supply has to increase to restore the balance. The central bank, under a fixed exchange rate regime, therefore, ceases to have any control on money supply. Money supply growth is given by the imperative to keep the exchange rate fixed. Not only that, even if exchange rates are stable, the central bank is constrained to change domestic interest rates, in response to domestic economic needs, to keep any potential exchange rate disturbance at bay. If the central bank follows a contractionary monetary policy, it can be seen from Figure 6.4 that the domestic currency will have a tendency to depreciate in relation to the foreign currency. If, on the other hand, the central bank follows an expansionary monetary policy, it can be seen from Figure 6.5 that the domestic currency will be under pressure of appreciation against the foreign currency. Under a fixed exchange rate system, therefore, the central bank, simply, cannot follow an independent monetary policy.

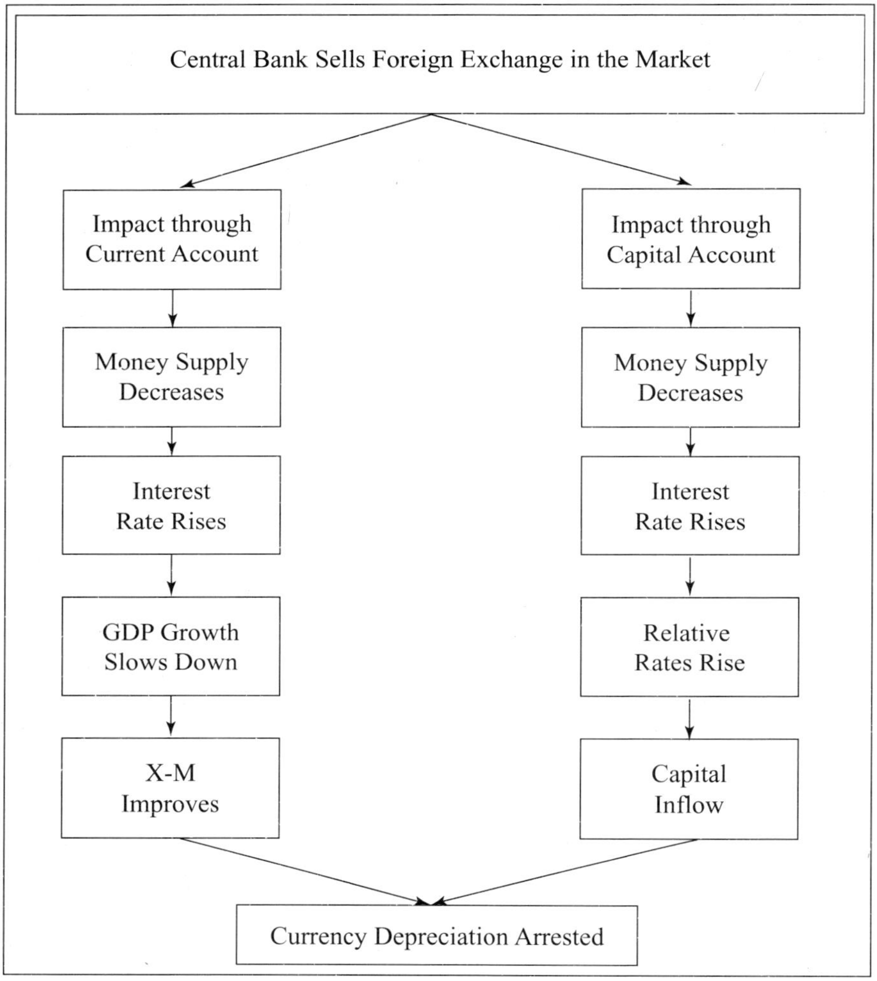


**FIGURE 6.4** *Macroeconomic Adjustment under Fixed Exchange Rate Regime: Case 2 - Overall Balance Negative*

Let us now sum up. What are the advantages of a fixed exchange rate system? There are two important advantages:

1. Provides businesses with sure basis for planning and pricing. In a fixed exchange rate system, there is no uncertainty about the rates. Businessmen prefer it because they know exactly how much of foreign exchange they will receive through export of goods and services and how much of foreign exchange they will have to pay

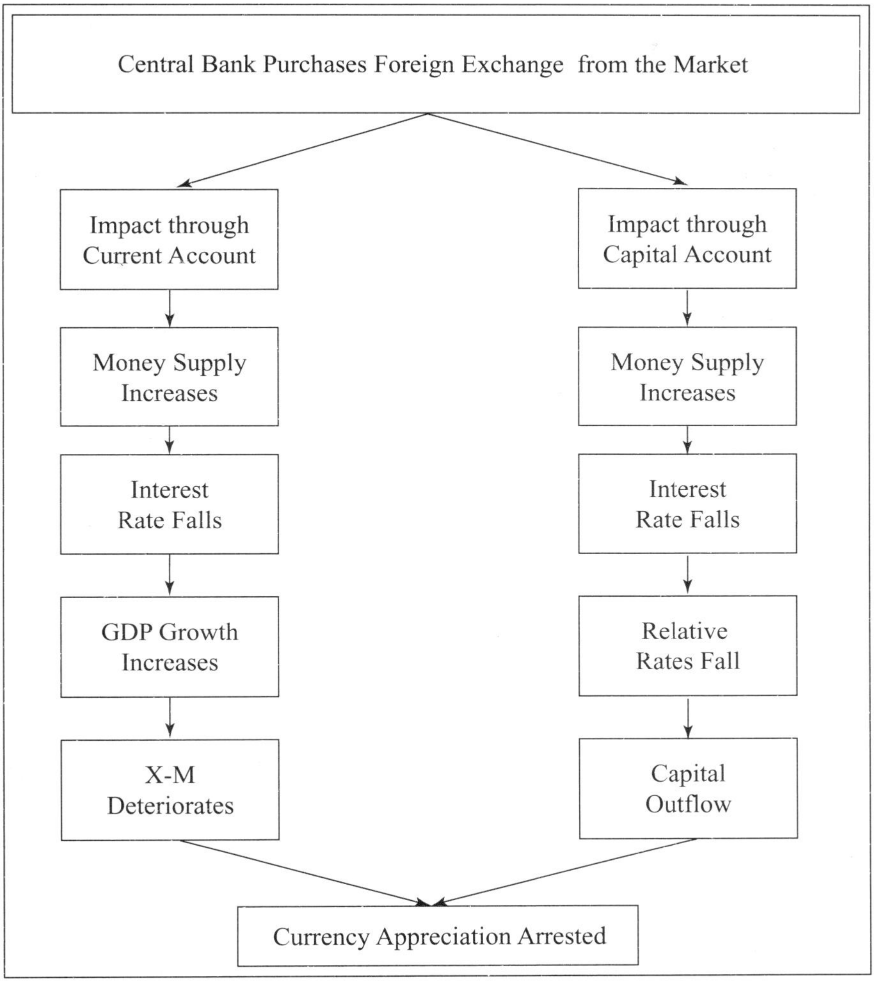


**FIGURE 6.5** *Macroeconomic Adjustment under Fixed Exchange Rate Regime: Case 2 - Overall Balance Positive*

for import of goods and services. They also know with certainty the price of foreign assets in domestic currency and the cost of domestic assets in foreign currency.

2. Imposes a constraint, as we have seen, on domestic monetary policy. This constraint on monetary policy imposes a monetary discipline. In the absence of this discipline, governments may resort to excessive borrowing from the central bank, thus fuelling inflation and creating instability in other macroeconomic variables (Chapter 4).

What are the disadvantages of fixed exchange rate system? There are three main disadvantages:

1. The macroeconomic adjustment under fixed exchange rate system described above may be protracted because of various rigidities in the economy. When the exchange rate is under pressure of depreciation and the central bank resorts to money supply cut to restore the balance, unless the adjustment process is quick, the slowdown may be prolonged and may result in considerable hardship to the people. Again, if the exchange rate is under pressure of appreciation and the central bank has to increase the money supply to correct the imbalance, unless the adjustment is fast, this may fuel inflation and cause considerable hardship. Both the outcomes may create economic and political difficulties for the government.
2. To support a fixed exchange rate system, the central bank must have adequate foreign exchange reserves or access to foreign capital. Particularly, if there is a persistent current account deficit, people may take a dim view of the central bank's ability to support the currency either out of its own reserves or through borrowings. Foreign capital may move out of the country in anticipation that the fixed rate may not be maintained. Speculators may convert their domestic currency into foreign currency with the expectation of reaping gains later when the fixed exchange rate becomes unsustainable. Either way, this increases the demand for foreign exchange, thus adding further pressure on the domestic currency. Ultimately, the central bank may be forced to abandon the fixed rate. And, the domestic currency may crash. Usually, the starting point of the problem is a persistent current account deficit, which means that the demand for foreign exchange is persistently outpacing the supply of foreign exchange and there is a pressure on the domestic currency to depreciate. Under the circumstances, trying to maintain the exchange rate fixed amounts to maintaining an overvalued exchange rate. And when a currency is overvalued or, perceived to be overvalued, investor's confidence on the government's ability to support the currency wanes and the currency becomes a target of attack by the speculators. This happened in Thailand in 1997 and earlier in Mexico in 1994.
3. Under a fixed exchange rate regime, as we have seen, the country also loses control on the conduct of monetary policy. Monetary

policy is dictated by exchange rate concerns. While it may impose monetary discipline, it may also adversely affect domestic economic growth. If domestic compulsions demand a soft monetary policy, it cannot be achieved because a fall in the interest rate will put a downward pressure on the exchange rate. The subjugation of the monetary policy will be total under currency board or under a unified currency system.

## *Devaluation and Revaluation of Currencies*

How do countries address the above concerns? There are two ways to address the problem; neither is foolproof. In the first place, if the currency is under pressure to deviate from the announced fixed rate either because demand for foreign exchange is outpacing supply or, vice versa, and, when the central bank finds it difficult to support it at the fixed rate, it can reset the price of the local currency in relation to the foreign currency. In other words, it can devalue or, revalue its currency.

How does it work? Assume that rupee dollar exchange rate was fixed at Rs. 10 to a dollar. Also assume that, at that rate, the demand for foreign exchange (outflows on current + capital account) is persistently outpacing the supply of foreign exchange (inflows on current account + capital account). And, the central bank is finding it difficult to continue to support the currency either because it is running out of foreign exchange reserves or because the macroeconomic adjustment is taking too long to effect or, both. It can then reset the price of the rupee to, let us say, Rs. 11 to a dollar or, devalue the rupee by 10 per cent. The logic is that devaluation will make outflows costlier (as people will now have to pay 10 per cent more rupees to buy one dollar worth of foreign goods/services or assets) and inflows cheaper (as foreigners will find that they are able to get Rs. 11 worth of Indian goods/services and assets for the same dollar). This will narrow the gap between outflow (demand) and inflows (supply) of foreign exchange. And, future management of the exchange rate, other things being equal, may become more manageable as the size of intervention and its consequent impact on money supply will be less. Similarly, if the currency is under pressure of appreciation and the central bank does not want to face the consequences of a continuous rise in money supply, it can revalue its currency, to say, Rs. 9 to a dollar. Using the same logic as above, revaluation will make inflows (supply) costlier and outflows (demand) cheaper. This will narrow the gap between inflows and outflows. The need for central bank to intervene in the currency market will come down. The consequent impact of money supply increase on the economy may be more amenable to control.

Where is the problem? From the preceding discussion, devaluation of currency results in decrease in price of domestic goods/services and assets to the foreigner and an increase in the prices of foreign goods/services and assets to the domestic buyers. As a result of the former, devaluation increases the inflows and as a result of the latter, devaluation decreases the outflows. Thus, in case of devaluation, a rise in inflows (supply of foreign exchange) and a fall in outflows (demand for foreign exchange) stem the downward pressure on the domestic currency and restores equilibrium. The opposite happens in case of revaluation of currency. In case of revaluation, price of foreign goods and services and assets to the domestic buyer falls and price of domestic goods and services and assets to the foreign buyer rises. Consequently, inflows (supply of foreign exchange) fall and outflows (demand for foreign exchange) rise. This arrests the upward pressure on the domestic currency and restores equilibrium. And, both happen in response to a change in price of domestic currency vis-à-vis the foreign currency. It, therefore, follows that the final effect of devaluation or revaluation would depend on how sensitive inflows and outflows are to change in relative price of currencies. For example, if foreigners' demand for our goods and services is not very sensitive to changes in the price of our currency relative to theirs, devaluation (revaluation) will not result in the desired increase (decrease) in inflows. Similarly, if our demand for foreign goods and services is not very sensitive to changes in relative prices, devaluation (revaluation) may not reduce (increase) outflows to the desired extent. The combined effect of the two will be self-defeating. Sensitivity of demand to changes in prices is, therefore, a very important consideration for devaluation and revaluation of currency.

Even if sensitivity conditions are met, for devaluation/revaluation to work, there must be real and not just nominal devaluation/revaluation of the currency. As we discussed in Section 2.15 of Chapter 2, if a currency is devalued in nominal terms by 5% but the inflation rate in that country is 5 per cent higher than in the rest of the world, the gain in competitiveness as a result of 5 per cent nominal devaluation is neutralized by a loss in competitiveness by the amount of the inflation differential with other countries and there is no real devaluation.

Also, the impact of, for example, devaluation on net exports ($X - M$) may not be instantaneous. This is for two reasons: (a) in response to devaluation while the prices of imports go up immediately, the volume of imports comes down with a lag. Thus, initially the value of imports may go up than down. Similarly, while the prices of exports come down immediately after devaluation, it takes some time, for various structural reasons, for export volumes to go up. In either case, devaluation can worsen net exports rather than improve it initially and (b) in times when a currency is highly overvalued, to start with, foreign market shares may have been permanently lost and a devaluation of the currency may not be enough to improve the trade pattern. For long periods, $X - M$ may, therefore, not show an improvement.

But the most important risk, of particularly devaluation, is that it may trigger speculation of further devaluation, thereby creating instability in the currency markets. For example, in 1994, when the Mexican government devalued the peso by 14 per cent against the US dollar, this weakened the confidence of domestic and international investors in government's ability to maintain the peso/dollar parity. They converted their pesos into dollars. As the demand for dollars increased rapidly compared to supply, the Mexican government was forced to abandon the fixed exchange regime and had to allow the peso to be determined in the market place. The Mexican peso fell against the US dollar by more than 40 per cent, resulting in a major slowdown of the economy, which continued until mid-1996. In Thailand in 1997, when the Bank of Thailand had to abandon the pegged exchange rate to dollar, consequent to a speculative attack on the currency, the Thai currency fell from baht 25 to a dollar to baht 54 to a dollar in a very short period of time. The economic crisis that ensued lasted almost four years. In 1999, when the Brazilian real was devalued by 8 per cent, confidence of investors in the government's ability to maintain the fixed exchange rate system got badly eroded. They converted their real denominated assets to dollar denominated assets, leading to a massive rise in the demand for dollars. The Brazilian central bank had to abandon the fixed rate regime. The real fell from 1.20 to a dollar to 2 per dollar.

The extent of disruption caused by devaluation, however, depends on the extent of mobility of capital from one country to the other. When India devalued the rupee in 1991, it did not lead to a speculative attack on the currency, as movement of capital was still restricted. Subsequently, India, on its own, went in for a more market determined exchange rate system.

Revaluation may cause other types of problems. China is a good example. China, for many years, pegged its currency at 8.2 Yuan to a dollar. The overall balance in China has been persistently positive. China, therefore, vigorously intervened in the currency market to keep the Yuan/dollar rate to 8.2. This resulted in a massive foreign exchange reserve build up, variously estimated at between US$ 2.5 and 3.0 trillion, which is potentially inflationary, besides being costly. Should China revalue its currency? There are strong arguments in its favour, particularly when Chinese Yuan is believed to be undervalued by between 40 and 50 per cent. But the answer is not cut and dry. China's economic growth today is triggered by its export growth. China's exports are also highly import driven. It imports a lot of goods, adds value to them and exports them. If China revalues its currency, it will not only slowdown China's economic growth but also stall the growth of other Asian regions, including Japan and South Korea, who export heavily to China. Therefore, the cost of holding huge foreign exchange reserves will have to be carefully weighed against the loss of economic growth to the region.

China, of course, has subsequently allowed its currency to revalue to approximately 7 Yuan to a dollar. Under pressure from the United States and G8 countries, China has also expressed a desire to further revalue its currency and follow a managed float system. However, uncertainty prevails and the initial euphoria at this announcement has given way to caution.

## *Sterilized Intervention*

Under a fixed exchange rate regime, central banks can counteract the effects of purchase and sale of foreign exchange on domestic money supply through sterilized intervention. This is how it works: when the central bank buys foreign exchange from the market, we know that it increases the monetary base and the broad money supply. Suppose the central bank does not want the money supply to increase, it can sterilize the effect of foreign exchange purchase on the monetary base by selling an equivalent amount of government securities in the market (Chapter 5, Section 5.5.3). Exactly the opposite will hold when the central bank sells foreign exchange into the market. We know that this will reduce the monetary base and the broad money supply. Once again, the central bank can sterilize the effect by purchasing equivalent amount of government securities from the market. In either case, the change in the foreign exchange assets of the central bank will be offset by a simultaneous change, in the opposite direction, in the change in government securities. This will keep the monetary base unchanged.

However, the problem here is that by restoring the monetary base to its original position, the central bank is not addressing the root cause of upward or downward pressure on the domestic currency. In the absence of this consideration, such pressures may remain. For example, if the currency is under pressure of appreciation, from Figure 6.5, we know that the macroeconomic adjustment has to take place through a rise in money supply and a consequent fall in interest rates. But through sterilized intervention if the central bank does not allow the money supply to change, the pressure on the exchange rate remains. How long can the central bank go on selling government securities to sterilize the impact of foreign exchange build up? Even if it manages to sustain it for some time, it can be prohibitively costly as the central bank ends up acquiring low yielding foreign currency assets in exchange for higher yielding domestic government securities.

## 6.4.2 Flexible Exchange Rate Regime

Under a flexible exchange rate regime, the exchange rate is determined purely on the basis of demand for and supply of foreign exchange in the market place. The central bank does not intervene at all. Thus, if a country has an overall positive balance, i.e., inflows (supply of foreign exchange) is greater than outflows (demand for foreign exchange), the price of foreign exchange in relation to the domestic currency will fall and the domestic currency will appreciate. That will equate demand with supply. The opposite will hold true if the overall balance is negative.

The important aspect to note from a macroeconomic point of view is that under a flexible exchange rate regime, the adjustment in the external sector takes place not through a change in money supply, as in the case of fixed exchange rate system, but through a change in exchange rate. Thus under fixed exchange rate system while the monetary policy is dictated by exchange rate considerations, under flexible exchange rate system it is not. The central bank, under flexible exchange rate system, allows the exchange rate to adjust to equate the supply of and demand for foreign exchange. Under flexible exchange rate system, therefore, the central bank can follow an independent monetary policy.

So what are the advantages of having a flexible exchange regime? There are three main advantages:

1. If markets are assumed to be perfect, then the exchange rate determined at the market place will reflect the true value of the exchange rate. There is no overvaluation or undervaluation of the currency.
2. Because of the above, there is no scope for speculation. Speculative attacks on a currency do not make sense in a flexible exchange rate system, and
3. The central bank can follow an independent monetary policy, as there is no need to intervene in the foreign exchange market to stabilize the exchange rate at the fixed rate. The central bank can, thus, increase or decrease interest rates depending on the requirements of the domestic sector of the economy.

What are the disadvantages of a flexible exchange rate system? Again, there are three of them.

1. Since markets are not perfect, a truly market determined exchange rate is a myth. Observed exchange rates in the market place may overshoot the 'true' market determined exchange rates.
2. Arising from the above, exchange rates may show high volatility, thereby, causing difficulty in business planning. In certain circumstances, the businessman can hedge against currency fluctuations but that has to come with a cost, and
3. While it is true that, under flexible exchange rate system, movement in exchange rates do not impact monetary policy, the reverse is not true. Monetary policy does, indeed, impact exchange rates. For example, an expansionary monetary policy, which results in a fall in the interest rates, also causes the exchange rate to come down, as, at reduced interest rates capital flows out (demand for foreign exchange increases) of the country. An expansionary monetary policy also affects the exchange rate through the price route. As prices, in response to an increase in money supply, go up, imports become relatively cheaper and exports relatively expensive. This puts downward pressure on the currency. In general, an expansionary monetary policy can be assumed to cause the domestic currency to depreciate in value vis-à-vis the foreign currency. The freedom to operate an independent monetary policy, thus, can cause considerable instability in the economy, particularly, if that freedom is abused by resorting to profligate fiscal and monetary policies.

## 6.4.3 Managed Float Regime

A managed float regime is a compromise between a fixed exchange rate regime and a flexible exchange rate regime. Largest numbers of countries in the world have adopted this regime. Under this regime, the central bank announces that the exchange rate is market determined, but to the extent, market is not perfect, it intervenes in the market from time to time, to bring orderly conditions in the market but no target rate is fixed. The advantage of this system, principally, is that fluctuations in exchange rate are smoothened somewhat. This brings an element of stability in the exchange rates and, if properly handled, this regime can also reduce possibilities of a speculative attack on the currency. The businessman eminently desires both. On the other hand, since the central bank either does not know or does not announce a rate it proposes to target, uncertainty about the rates is not completely eliminated. The macroeconomic implications of intervention in the currency market in terms of impact on domestic interest rates and prices also remain. Uncertainty regarding the central bank's tactics or long-term intentions may also kindle speculative attacks.

## 6.4.4 Conclusion

From the preceding discussion the following points are clear:

1. If a country wants to have stable exchange rates, it cannot have an independent monetary policy.
2. If a country wants to have an independent monetary policy, it cannot have stable exchange rates.
3. If a country wants to have both stable exchange rates and an independent monetary policy, it must have capital controls, i.e., impose restrictions on inflows and outflows of capital. Thus, on domestic considerations, if the central bank decides to lower the interest rates, capital flight will not take place and the exchange rate will remain stable. Both monetary independence and exchange rate stability are achieved.

Clearly, on the first two options above, the choice is not clear-cut. We have discussed the pros and cons in detail. In the last option, the consensus view is that, besides interfering with market forces, such a proposition runs counter to the global trend towards dismantling all controls. There is also the question of how long capital controls can be sustained in an era of rapid capital movements and high degree of financial sector sophistication that the globe is going through.

Presently, most countries are, therefore, operating around a system of managed float and are in favour of limiting certain types of external capital flows.

What are the implications of the above discussion for managerial decision making? The manager should understand that when the central bank intervenes in the currency market, it also affects the money markets (unless the intervention is sterilized). Thus, domestic interest rates will be affected by central bank intervention in the currency market. Also, when the central bank allows the currency to be determined in the market place, the manager should be prepared for a certain amount of volatility in exchange rates. In a managed float, of course, the manager has to take a call on what will be the next move of the central bank. In other words, to understand foreign exchange risks and interest rate risks, the manager must understand how different exchange rate regimes work and their implications on key cost variables.

## 6.5 Fiscal and Monetary Policy Effectiveness Under Different Exchange Rate Regimes

The purpose of this section is to familiarize the reader about the relative potency of fiscal and monetary policy in influencing GDP under different exchange rate regimes and under alternative assumptions about capital mobility. We will discuss four cases.

### 6.5.1 Case 1: Fixed Exchange Rates and Complete Capital Mobility

#### *Fiscal Policy*

Let us say the government expenditure increases, that is, the government follows an expansionary fiscal policy. This will lead to an increase in GDP and increased demand for money. Since the supply of money is fixed, the increase in money demand will push up interest rates. An increase in the interest rate will attract capital inflows. There will be an upward pressure on the domestic currency. Since the central bank is committed to keeping the exchange rate fixed, it will mop up the extra supply of foreign exchange. The monetary base will rise. Money supply will increase. This will bring the domestic interest rates down. An expansionary fiscal policy in a regime of fixed exchange rates and complete capital mobility, thus, will result in maximum increase in output with little or no crowding out of private investment.

### *Monetary Policy*

Now consider, under the same regime, the central bank follows an expansionary monetary policy. Money supply will increase. This will result in a fall in the interest rates. Capital will flow out of the country. There will be a downward pressure on the currency. The central bank, to maintain the fixed rate, will sell foreign exchange in the market. Monetary base will come down. Money supply will come down. Monetary policy is ineffective in effecting a change in GDP.

## 6.5.2 Case 2: Flexible Exchange Rate and Complete Capital Mobility

### *Fiscal Policy*

Again, let us say, the government follows an expansionary fiscal policy. This will increase the demand for money. With a given supply, a rise in the demand for money will increase the interest rates. This will result in capital inflow. The demand for foreign exchange will be more than the supply of foreign exchange. Since the exchange rate is flexible, the adjustment will take place through an appreciation of the domestic currency. A rise in the domestic currency will crowd out exports. Therefore, rise in '*G*' will be offset by a fall in '*X*', the final effect depending on relative share of '*G*' and '*X*' in GDP. Fiscal policy is, therefore, not effective in influencing GDP in a regime of flexible exchange rates and complete capital mobility.

## *Monetary Policy*

Now consider an expansionary monetary policy. An increase in money supply will lower interest rates. Capital will flow out of the country. This will put downward pressure on the domestic currency. Under flexible exchange rate system, domestic currency will depreciate in value. This will result in an increase in net exports. GDP increases with no change in domestic interest rates. Monetary policy is, therefore, very effective in a regime of flexible exchange rates with free capital mobility.

# 6.5.3 Case 3: Fixed Exchange Rate and Capital Control

## *Fiscal Policy*

Under this regime, if the government follows an expansionary fiscal policy, GDP will rise but so will interest rates, as in the earlier regimes. However, since capital movements are controlled, this will not result in an inflow of capital. An increase in GDP, other things being equal, will worsen net exports since '*M*' is a positive function of GDP. As the exchange rate is fixed, the central bank will intervene in the currency market by selling foreign exchange in the market. This will reduce the money supply. While a fall in money supply will restore the balance between *X* and *M*, it will lead to a further rise in the interest rates. GDP will increase by the difference between increase in GDP on account of increase in '*G*' and fall in GDP on account of crowding out of '*I*', consequent to a rise in interest rates.

## *Monetary Policy*

Under this regime, an expansionary monetary policy will bring down the interest rates but as there are capital controls, this will not result in a capital outflow. But a higher GDP growth, consequent to a fall in the interest rates, other things being equal, will increase import demand, '*M*' being a positive function of GDP. Net exports, thus, will come down putting a downward pressure on the currency. The central bank will intervene to keep the rate fixed. Money supply will fall. Interest rates will rise again. Monetary policy is ineffective in influencing GDP.

## 6.5.4 Flexible Exchange Rates and Capital Controls

### *Fiscal Policy*

Under a flexible exchange rate system with capital controls, an expansionary fiscal policy will lead to an increase in GDP and in interest rates as in Case 3. A rise in GDP, again, will reduce net exports. However, the central bank will not intervene to fix the exchange rate. The domestic currency will depreciate, restoring the $X$ and $M$ balance. Overall impact on the GDP will be the difference between increase in GDP on account of increase in '$G$' and fall in GDP on account of crowding out of '$I$', consequent to a rise in interest rates.

### *Monetary Policy*

An expansionary monetary policy will result in a fall in interest rates and a rise in GDP but no change in capital movements. Only net exports will fall, which will lead to a depreciation of the currency to restore the $X$ and $M$ balance. Monetary policy is effective in increasing GDP by lowering the interest rates.

## 6.5.5 Discussion

The four cases discussed above show different possible scenarios. First, under a fixed exchange rate system and complete capital mobility, fiscal policy is a more potent tool than monetary policy in its impact on domestic output. Second, in a regime of flexible exchange rates and complete capital mobility, monetary policy is a better tool than fiscal policy in effecting a rise in domestic output. You should be able to see that these two conclusions corroborate our earlier finding under a fixed exchange rate regime; monetary policy loses independence while in a flexible exchange rate regime monetary policy independence is restored. Third, under a regime of capital controls, irrespective of the type of exchange rate regime, the external sector is affected only through the current account, which at all times must be in balance since a deficit cannot be financed by a surplus on capital account. Other than that, under a fixed exchange rate regime, fiscal policy appears to be more effective while under a flexible exchange regime, monetary policy is more potent in effecting a rise in domestic GDP.

The cases can also give some insight into how one country's policies affect another country. Assume two countries, A and B. They have a fixed exchange rate between themselves and capital is completely mobile between the countries. We are discussing Case 1 scenario. Let us say country A goes for an expansionary fiscal policy, which results in a rise in the domestic interest rates. This will attract capital from country B to country A. In country B, the demand for foreign exchange will increase compared to supply. Country B's currency will be under pressure to depreciate vis-à-vis country A's. But since the countries are operating under a fixed exchange rate regime, country B's central bank will have to intervene by selling foreign exchange in the market. Country B's money supply growth will come down. This will slow down country B's economy. Something like this happened during German unification. Germany decided to finance infrastructure in the erstwhile East Germany by increasing government expenditure, leading to a rise in German interest rates. This slowed down the growth of France as Germany and France had a fixed exchange rate (with a band) and capital was completely mobile between the countries. This suggests that under fixed exchange rate regime, macroeconomic policies between countries need to be in sync for the exchange rate regime to work effectively.

Under a flexible exchange rate system, however, the above problem does not arise (Case 2). If country A follows an expansionary fiscal policy, leading to a rise in the domestic interest rates and this encourages capital inflow from country B, the adjustment in country A will take place through appreciation of country A's currency and in country B, through depreciation of its currency. In fact, country A's action will stimulate economic activity in country B through a boost in exports. Domestic monetary policy remains independent.

Case 3 is close to the situation that prevailed in India prior to economic liberalization. An increase in government expenditure spilled over to a current account deficit. The $X - M$ deficit widened. That created other problems in the economy as discussed in Chapter 3. Case 4 explains the same situation under a flexible exchange rate system.

One important element left out of the above discussion is prices. This was done to enable a basic understanding of the principles involved in the transmission mechanism between macroeconomic policy moves and their impact on domestic output under different assumptions with regard to exchange rate regimes and mobility of capital. The basic principles still hold. However, the impact of variable prices can be seen as follows. In the above discussion, every time we mentioned about an increase in money supply, the reference was to real money supply growth. Or, an increase in $M/P$, where $M$ stands for money supply and $P$ for prices. Clearly, if an increase in money supply is accompanied by an equal increase in prices, there is no change in real money supply. Similarly, if an increase in money supply is accompanied by some increase in prices, which is less than the increase in money supply, we will say that money supply has increased but not by as much as it would, if prices were constant. So in this entire discussion, if prices are variable, an increase in $M/P$ will affect interest rates and exchange rates differently than if they were constant, though the transmission mechanism described above will be still relevant. For example, consider Case 2, where we have a flexible exchange rate regime with complete capital mobility. Assume the central bank follows an expansionary monetary policy. But now we assume prices to be variable. What is the difference? An expansionary monetary policy in the previous case will lead to a fall in the interest rate and capital outflow. The domestic currency will depreciate and net exports will increase. GDP will increase. The difference begins here. When we assume variable prices, we note that an increase in GDP will also lead to an increase in prices. As the prices increase, $M/P$ will fall. Interest rates will rise again, this time leading to an inflow of capital. Domestic currency will start appreciating and net exports will fall. The extent to which prices will get affected by an expansionary monetary policy will depend on the state of the economy. Nevertheless, with variable prices, the final effect on GDP will be somewhat moderated in the short run, compared to what we discussed earlier, when prices were assumed to be constant.

## 6.6 What Causes Financial Sector Collapse?

This topic has assumed great importance in the wake of Asian financial crisis of 1997, and the more recent (2007–09) U.S. sub-prime crisis. The Asian financial crisis started in Thailand and rapidly spread to other countries in the region. The crisis caused a major economic slowdown in these regions that lasted several years. Many businesses collapsed and the domestic currency suffered a severe blow. The U.S. sub-prime crisis also spread like wildfire across the globe and caused unprecedented financial and economic slowdown. While for many of the affected countries the worst may have been over, the revival process from the meltdown is still slow and painful and proving to be protracted.

The question we are asking in this section, therefore, is: what causes a country's financial sector to be vulnerable to shocks? In the light of the experience gained from Asian crises and the U.S. sub-prime crisis, can we identify certain variables, which will enable the manager to come to a judgment about the robustness of a country's financial sector before he invests in that currency? We will begin by introducing a few terms, which are essential to understand the questions we have addressed.

## *Financial Repression*

Financial repression refers to a situation where the governments follow policies vis-à-vis the financial sector, which impede the efficient functioning of the sector. Typically, these are as follows:

1. Imposition of credit controls
2. Administered interest rates
3. Barriers to entry for both domestic and foreign financial institutions
4. Interference in the day to day functioning of the financial institutions
5. Public ownership of financial institutions, and
6. Restrictions on international capital flows

All of the above factors come in the way of efficient functioning of the financial sector. For example, by imposing controls on credit allocation, the banks and other financial institutions are disallowed to lend money to those customers who offer the best combination of risk and return on the borrowed money. By administering interest rates, the banks are barred from lending money based on market signals. The interest rate ceases to represent the true value of the loan. Again, through barriers to entry, the government scuttles competition and the efficiency gain that accompanies it. Similarly, without autonomy, bankers cannot take independent decisions and cannot be held accountable for their actions. Public ownership of banks and financial institutions, besides interfering with autonomy of financial institutions, also lead to nepotism and corruption. Finally, restrictions on international capital flows deny a country an opportunity to invest more than it saves; to gain from globally competitive rates; to be able to diversify its portfolio and in general, to allow its financial sector to be globally competitive.

Many countries in the now emerging world, including India, had repressed their financial sector in the past. Why were they doing it? The answer lay in the fact that in many of these countries, the state had taken the responsibility of directing investment activities in the economy. As part of the policy, the role of private sector was relegated to the background. The state, with such major responsibilities at hand, therefore, needed cheap credit for a multitude of activities. The banking and financial system that emerged were guided more by relationship between the government and the banks than by financial prudence. Banking sector started funnelling funds to state-owned enterprises and other sectors of the economy without considering the possibility of repayment. In short, financial repression was driven primarily by the government's fiscal needs. Other considerations were unimportant.

At the time when the state-driven economic model was adopted, there was perhaps some justification for imposing financial repression. Credit markets were imperfect, for example. But in due course of time, it became increasingly clear that financial repression was not sustainable. The financial sector had become inefficient; the non-performing loans had reached dangerous proportions; interest rates were less and less based on credit risk and other typical market forces; and, all these factors severely hampered bank's risk management and prudent construction of its loan portfolio. There was, thus, a pressure to liberalize the financial sector. Financial liberalization gathered momentum as more and more economies in the erstwhile socialist/communist regimes chose to make a transition from their existing system towards a market-driven economy. Financial sector liberalization, thus, became the buzzword.

## *Financial Sector Liberalization*

Financial sector liberalization aims at policies that are meant to undo the dangers posed to the financial sector by financial repression. Thus, one by one, credit controls are lifted/eased; interest rates are deregulated; banks and financial institutions are granted more autonomy; privatization of public sector banks and financial institutions is emphasized; barriers to entry of foreign banks and other financial institutions are lifted and last, but not least, capital controls are liberalized. These policies are aimed towards achieving efficiency in the functioning of the financial sector by making them globally competitive, through adoption of international banking practices, including managerial and technical competencies. In some countries, financial liberalization has moved at a rapid pace; in others it has been more gradual.

## *Financial Sector Reforms*

Financial sector reforms, simply put, refer to creation of institutions and mechanisms, which will provide a conducive environment for a smooth transition from a repressed financial system to a more liberalized financial system. Why is it so important? There are several reasons. First, information is asymmetric. That is, when we deposit money in the bank we do so in good faith, but actually we do not know what the bank is going to do with this money. If we open up (liberalize) the banking sector and give it total functional autonomy, what is the guarantee that the bank will not misuse our funds? The temptation to misuse will be greater if the bank is in distress for, if it succeeds, it will gain but if it does not it will not lose (depositors will lose). Second, banks can also indulge in nepotism in the disbursement of loans, thus putting the depositor's money at risk. Finally, given the fact that banks operate with a high debt–equity ratio, a small loss of debt service can lead to an erosion of its net worth.

Obviously, we do not possess the resources to supervise what the banks are doing with our money. And, yet someone has to supervise to ensure that our money is safe. An important component of financial sector reforms is to put institutions and systems in place to ensure that freedom to function independently does not mean freedom to resort to unfair tactics. Thus, before opening up the banking sector, the RBI has prescribed capital adequacy norms for the banks, thereby making it compulsory for banks to maintain a certain level of capital against its loans. This provides the banks with additional equity cushion. The banks are also required to follow certain accounting norms and be more transparent in their disclosures. For capital market, similarly, RBI has constituted Securities and Exchange Board of India (SEBI) to regulate the working of the capital markets to make sure that opening up does not result in unfair competition. For insurance sector, we have the Insurance Regulatory Authority (IRA) to do the same job. Opening up the external capital flows requires particular attention since some of it (short-term capital) may be highly volatile. The central bank or whatever supervisory body the country chooses, must ensure that short-term loans are not used to fund long-term projects; there is no currency mismatch, i.e., banks do not lend in local currency money that is borrowed in foreign currency and banks do not advance too many risky loans. A sound financial system is a necessary prerequisite for financial liberalization. Here the role of the regulatory body becomes that of a facilitator of fair market play and not as a repressor in the earlier sense. Finally, it must be kept in mind that a sound financial system must go hand in hand with macroeconomic stability. If fiscal stabilization, for example, is not in place, the financial system is likely to be under tremendous pressure.

## *What Makes the Financial Sector Vulnerable?*

We are now able to put the whole story together. The financial sector of a country becomes vulnerable when it resorts to financial sector liberalization without financial sector reforms. The meaning of vulnerability has to be understood. If everything is going right in the economy, despite financial sector vulnerability, the problems may not come to the surface but if one thing goes wrong, everything goes wrong. Typically, this is how events take shape:

1. Financial liberalization with poor regulation and supervision results in lending booms.
2. The banks advance risky loans and the poor asset quality acquired by banks makes them vulnerable to macroeconomic shocks.
3. Macroeconomic shocks could come in the form of recession, high interest rates, asset price collapses, a persistent current account deficit etc.
4. The crisis results in a decline in bank lending and a sharp contraction in real economic activity.

## *Asian Economic Crisis in 1997*

The Asian economic crisis started in Thailand. The Thailand economy grew very impressively for several years in a row before the crisis set in. The rapid growth accentuated large capital inflows, which were partly encouraged by pegged exchange rates.

The macroeconomic shock came from the external sector, i.e., a widening of the gap between imports ($M$) and exports ($X$). Thailand had pegged its currency to the US dollar at a fixed 25 baht to a dollar. As $M - X$ gap widened, the Bank of Thailand started selling dollars in the market to support the baht. However, $M - X$ gap persisted and speculators and others took a dim view of Bank of Thailand's ability to go on supporting the currency. They started taking their money out. This led to a sharp increase in the demand for dollars, so much so that the Bank of Thailand had to abandon the fixed exchange rate regime. The Thai baht started floating and the exchange rate of baht plummeted from 25 baht to 54 baht per dollar in a very short span of time.

At an analytical level, what is described above for Thailand is not very much different from what happened in India at the time of 1991 economic crisis. By the end of 1990, $M - X$ gap had become unsustainable; the non-resident Indians started taking their money out; RBI ran out of foreign exchange reserves to support the currency and had to devalue the rupee by about 25 per cent.

But the similarity ended here. The Thai external sector crisis led to a financial sector crash but nothing of that sort happened in India. The reason was that Thailand liberalized its financial sector, including international capital flows, too fast and without financial sector reforms in place, while this was not the case in India. In Thailand, lack of prudential regulation led to several financial sector weaknesses. First, there was preponderance of short-term loans and FII investments in total inflows. Short-term capital exceeded the size of foreign exchange reserves of the country. Despite impressively high savings rate, debt–income ratio went up substantially. Second, short-term capital was extensively used to finance long-term investments in real estate and construction. This was partly driven by 'relationship-based banking' whereby loans were given more on the basis of relationships established than on any business criterion for allocation of credit. Third, a currency mismatch ensued in the portfolio of the banks. And, finally there was a total absence of any risk management technique such as hedging against depreciation of foreign currency loans. A pegged currency was believed to be sufficient guarantee against any such risk.

When short-term foreign currency loans are used to finance long-term projects, then, in the event of an external shock, it becomes difficult to meet the demands of the creditors when they want their money back. The fact that short-term loans can quickly be withdrawn makes these countries vulnerable to large outflows of capital when the perceived risk associated with such lending increases. Currency mismatches make things only worse. If a bank borrows 100 dollars and lends it in baht, based on the current exchange rate of say baht 25 to a dollar, this currency mismatch in the portfolio of the bank can be disastrous, if the value of baht falls due to an external shock. Assume baht now becomes 50 to a dollar. On the asset side, on this account, the amount is still 2500 baht but on the liability side it becomes 5000 baht. The bank's capital turns negative and it becomes insolvent. The fear of bank failure becomes self-fulfilling and spreads to other banks. Depositors withdraw their funds from all domestic banks and deposit them in safer investments abroad. This pushes down the domestic currency further. A financial crisis occurs when large proportion of banks and companies in the economy are insolvent (liabilities are greater than assets). Banks do not have money or are unwilling to lend to companies; companies are unwilling to spend money on investment projects. The economy goes into a prolonged recession. The impact, then, is not confined to one country alone but spreads like a contagion to other countries that have similar financial systems. This is precisely what happened in the Asian region.

You will also notice that when external shock results in a financial sector crisis, conduct of macroeconomic policies also becomes tricky. If the central bank raises the interest rates to arrest the fall in the domestic currency (Figure 6.4), the economy will go into deeper recession. On the other hand, if the central bank lowers domestic interest rates to stimulate the domestic economy (Figure 6.5), the currency will take a further beating. The macroeconomic policy choice, thus, becomes a choice between two evils.

In summary, it can be said that Thailand introduced financial sector liberalization without financial sector reforms. This made their financial sectors vulnerable to shocks, leading to banking crises and bank panics. The crisis spread to other regions that had similar financial systems. Those economies with the most vulnerable financial sectors (Indonesia, South Korea and Thailand) experienced the most severe crises. In contrast, economies with more robust and well-capitalized financial institutions (such as Singapore) did not experience similar disruptions, in spite of slowing economic activity and declining asset values.

A manager must, therefore, monitor the sequencing of financial sector reforms. Generally, the sequencing suggested is as follows[4]:

- First, liberalization of trade and FDI
- Second, fiscal consolidation
- Third, reform of the domestic banking system
- Fourth, free domestic interest rates
- Fifth, liberalize capital outflows
- Sixth, allow entry of foreign banks
- Last, liberalize short term capital inflows

[4] Fischer and Reisen. *Financial Opening: Why, How and When*, ICS Press, 1993.

The first one refers to liberalization of current account through removal of trade barriers and liberalization of FDI (long-term capital), which is considered more robust. The second measure talks about the need for macroeconomic stabilization through fiscal stabilization so that persistent fiscal imbalance does not spill over to the external sector (Section 2.1.12). The third measure emphasizes the need to have domestic banking sector reforms of the type we mentioned earlier, before opening up to the foreigners. The fourth measure suggests freeing of interest rates after the first few reforms are in place so that a rise in the interest rate, which is likely to follow from freeing the rates, does not destabilize the economy. The fifth measure pleads for opening up of capital outflows first to get a feel for the market. The sixth measure suggests opening up of the banking sector to foreigners only after the first five steps are completed. Liberalization of short-term capital inflows, according to this sequencing, has to come last. The order of sequencing, thus, suggests extra caution when it comes to liberalization of short-term capital flows.

## *Exchange Rate Regime and Asian Currency Crisis*

We close this section by highlighting the role of exchange rate regime in a currency crisis. We know, for example, that under a fixed exchange rate regime if there is a persistent current account deficit, the central bank will have difficulty supporting the currency for any extended period of time. Speculators and others will soon figure out that the currency is overvalued and will attack the currency. The central bank will then have to abandon intervening in the currency market. The domestic currency will crash.

Overvaluation of the currency occurred in Thailand because, with a fixed exchange rate system, companies and banks felt comfortable borrowing foreign exchange to finance domestic investment activities. Foreign creditors, for same reasons, also felt safe to lend. Interest due on foreign debt went up. This, along with a trade deficit, resulted in a sharp rise in the current account deficit, which, in course of time became unsustainable. Initially, the central bank did whatever it could to support the currency, but later had to give up in favour of a free float. The value of the Thai baht plummeted.

The lesson from the above story is that, when the current account deficit is persistent, it is better to either devalue the currency or allow it to float towards the starting of the problem and allow the currency to settle at a more appropriate level than wait till the end and let the currency crash. Hanging on to a pegged currency regime, in the face of a persistent current account deficit, in fact, was an important factor behind the currency crash in Thailand, which, subsequently, in the absence of reforms in the financial system, precipitated the financial sector crash.

## *The US Sub-Prime Crisis*

The starting point of US sub-prime crisis was a continuous rise in housing prices each year from mid-1990 to 2006, not supported by population or income growth. The demand for housing was triggered largely by easy availability of credit and an expectation that prices will maintain their upward trend.

Banks saw an opportunity in mortgage lending. In order to step up mortgage lending, banks relaxed lending conditions. Loans were extended without any down payments. The borrowers included so-called sub-prime customers who had a poor credit history. More than half of the loans that originated in 2006 were sub-prime. This was done on the assumption that the expected positive wealth from the rising value of the mortgage will outweigh the negative impact of any loan default by the sub-prime customers.

Further, mortgages held by banks were bundled and sold to bank-sponsored structured investment vehicles (SIVs).[5] The SIVs, in turn, converted those into mortgage-backed securities (MBS). MBS is a financial product made up of debt from a number of mortgages, which can be traded. A financial structure called collateral debt obligation (CDOs), which grouped individual loans in a portfolio, was created. These MBS were then rated by rating institutions such as Moody's, Standard & Poor. Investors bought these MBS based on their appetite for debt. Those who bought these securities received income when the original home buyers made their mortgage payments.

Since the mortgage held by the banks were securitized and sold off, the banks' capital remained intact. They utilized this to advance further loans to both prime and sub-prime customers in the housing sector. The process continued.

[5] SIVs are specialist funds, which are kept off the balance sheet of the banks. They invest in illiquid assets and fund those through sale of commercial papers (unsecured short-term loans).

Simultaneously, the leveraged buyout[6] (LBO) market was heating up. Taking advantage of soft interest regime, private equity firms were acquiring other companies and financing such deals by borrowing from banks with very high debt ratios. The same culture extended to MBS. As it is, the mortgages held by the banks were bundled in such a manner, aided by positive ratings by rating agencies, that it was difficult to assess the downward risks properly. On top of that, the investors used excessive leverage to buy into them.

Finally, to complete the cycle, MBS were 'insured' through credit default swaps (CDS). CDS refers to an agreement between two parties whereby one party pays a premium regularly to the other party in return for a protection in the event of a default on payment on an asset, in this case MBS. This market was unregulated and a large number of such 'insurers' flourished and no one bothered to ask what would happen if the 'insurer' failed to meet his part of the obligation.

The party continued till 2005–06. Two things happened subsequently. First, a revival of demand, initially, and supply side pressures (largely due to a rise in commodity prices, including oil) subsequently, put an upward pressure on domestic prices. The interest rates were, thus, gradually raised to 5.26 per cent by June 2006. Secondly, while the general price level (and the interest rate to contain it) was rising, home prices were falling because of a massive supply build up propelled by indiscriminate lending by banks, compared to demand.

The borrower was faced with a double whammy. While interest rate at which the borrower had to service the loan was going up, the mortgage prices were falling. Many of them defaulted and their homes had to be surrendered. This led to further fall in home/mortgage prices. As mortgage prices dipped, the valuation of MBS suffered heavily. The major banks, pension funds, insurance companies and hedge funds globally, who had invested in MBS, found their balance sheets eroding. The problem extended to the debt market as leading banks not only had to show their SIV debt on their balance sheets (as no one was willing to buy SIV's commercial papers) but also had to bear the brunt of over leveraging. Finally, the CDO market collapsed all the way from giants like AIG down the line. There was a financial sector meltdown.

[6] Using debt to supplement investment is called leveraging. The more one borrows on top of the funds (or equity) one already has, the more highly leveraged one is.

The credit crisis took the form of a liquidity crisis as nobody trusted anybody in the financial market. Everyone decided to invest in safe U.S. government securities rather than lending money to each other or investing in other financial instruments. This derailed many economies. United States, Japan, Euro zone and UK went into recession and have only recently come out of it.

The sequence of events leading to the financial meltdown in the developed world can be analysed as follows: Perhaps, a sharp reduction in interest rates in the wake of IT boom bust in 2000 cannot be faulted. It was necessary to revive the U.S. economy. A rise in investment demand for housing in response to falling interest rates was also normal. There was also nothing wrong with securitization per se. Securitization not only helps to diversify risks but also enables price discovery of a risky asset. The seeds of crisis were actually sown subsequently. There was no justification for such indiscriminate lending by banks. Also, the nature of securitization put the investor to additional risk rather than spreading it. Overleveraging and resorting to CDS on such a massive scale were clear examples of regulatory failure. In other words, a lot of financial innovation (liberalization) was allowed in the U.S. financial system without appropriate checks and balances.

The lesson to learn from the U.S. sub-prime crisis is the same as from Asian crisis, though the nature of shock which triggered the crisis was different in these two regions. In the Asian crisis, the shock came from a current account deficit; in the U.S. sub-prime crisis, the shock emanated from a property market crash. But the lesson is clear. Financial liberalization without financial sector reforms (read regulation) makes the financial sector highly vulnerable. When the going is good, this vulnerability does not come to the surface; but if one thing goes wrong, everything collapses like a pack of cards. Wherever such crises have taken place, either the central bank has failed to keep up with the pace of financial liberalization or has been outright lax.

Why did the regulators in the United States not do more? They probably believed that markets were efficient and self correcting. Information was not necessarily asymmetric. Hence, less regulation was better than more. But in their attempt to deregulate, they probably failed to discriminate between regulation, which scuttles competition, and regulation, which ensures fair play. The present efforts of the Obama administration to bring in selected regulation in the U. S. financial system will, hopefully, set things right.

## 6.7 Is Decoupling Hypothesis a Myth?

The decoupling hypothesis gained considerable ground in the recent global economic slowdown discussions. The main argument underlying the hypothesis is that certain countries, like Brazil, Russia, India and China (BRIC countries), which have a large domestic market, are unlikely to be affected by a global economic slowdown. These countries are, therefore, decoupled from the rest of the economies. Did this bear out in the aftermath of current slowdown? We will try to answer this question using India as an example.

A slowdown in the developed world can impact a country like India through two routes. First, it can directly impact the production sector. Since imports are a positive function of GDP, an economic slowdown in other countries also reduces their demand for imports. The imports by other countries form our exports. Thus our export growth also suffers. Since exports are a component of GDP, our GDP growth also slows down. Second, to the extent the global economic slowdown was in the nature of a financial sector meltdown, the impact could also be felt indirectly through the financial sector. Here the argument is that in a globally integrated world, a financial sector crash in the developed world will also scathe the domestic financial sector. If that happens, the production sector may have difficulty financing new investments. GDP growth may come down.

To the above possibilities, India's position was that we were largely decoupled from happenings in the developed world. Our exports constituted only 15 per cent of GDP; 85 per cent of the GDP was domestic demand driven. A back of the envelope calculation showed that even if 15 per cent of the economy (constituting the export sector) suffered a slowdown because of sluggish foreign demand, the weighted average growth would come down, at worst, from 9 per cent to 8 per cent per annum. Similarly, we argued that Indian financial sector was well regulated. Not a single Indian bank had declared insolvency; nor did any financial institution declare bankruptcy. Hence, there was no need to suspect that India's financial sector would not be able to meet the credit demands of the producing sector.

Both the arguments put forth above are factually correct. Still, the fall in India's GDP growth in 2008–09 was not 1 per cent as estimated earlier but much larger than that. In 2008–09, Indian economy grew by 6.7 per cent compared to average 9 per cent growth during the preceding five years. So what was the route through which India got affected by the global economic slowdown?

India got impacted by that component of globalization, which integrates countries through movement of international finance. The transmission mechanism can be summarized as follows:

- Foreign institutional investors (FII) retrenched their assets in the Indian market, leading to a crash in the capital market. An important source of raising money through capital market for new investments by Indian business dried up.
- Non-banking financial institutions (like mutual funds) who invest their money in capital markets to lend to various segments of the economy also suffered a setback. A second source of raising money, therefore, dried up.
- A third source of raising money by Indian businesses through external commercial borrowings also dried up because of global financial meltdown.
- Finally, Indian banks worried about their balance sheets, in general, became more cautious about lending.

It can be seen from the above that Indian economy also faced a liquidity crisis despite a robust and well-regulated financial sector. This adversely impacted private sector sentiments, thereby decelerating growth. The growth slackened particularly in the industrial sector where, hitherto, it had been largely driven by credit growth. The slowdown would have been deeper but for government's fiscal stimulation (Section 4.6). Not just India but other members of BRIC countries also went through a similar setback consequent to economic slowdown in the developed world, though the transmission mechanism may have varied.

Strictly speaking, therefore, there is nothing called decoupling. Today, countries are integrated with each other through so many different ways that it is impossible for a country to avoid being impacted by happenings in other parts of the world, albeit the developed world. The only thing we can say is that the impact will vary depending on the country's exposure to the outside world through trade and finance.

## 6.8 India's Externel Sector: Recent Trends

India's external sector underwent substantial change, albeit in a phased manner, in the wake of economic liberalization of 1991. The main policy changes introduced are highlighted below.

## 6.8.1 Trade Reforms

Four policy changes in respect of trade were initiated: (a) virtual elimination of licensing and progressive shift of restricted items of imports under open general licenses (OGL); (b) gradually lifting all quantitative restrictions on imports of goods; (c) phased reduction in peak tariff rates from 300 per cent in 1990–91 to 10 per cent in 2008–09; and, (d) simplification and rationalization of export-oriented units (EOUs) and export promotion zones (EPZs). While the first three measures were aimed at achieving better efficiency through improved access to and reduced cost of imported raw materials, the last one was meant to provide special encouragement to certain export-oriented units mainly by way of fiscal incentives.

Figure 6.6 gives the broad trends in India's exports, imports and overall trade between 2000–01 and 2008–09. Point to point, during this period, export has increased by 53 per cent; import by 102 per cent; and overall trade by 80 per cent.

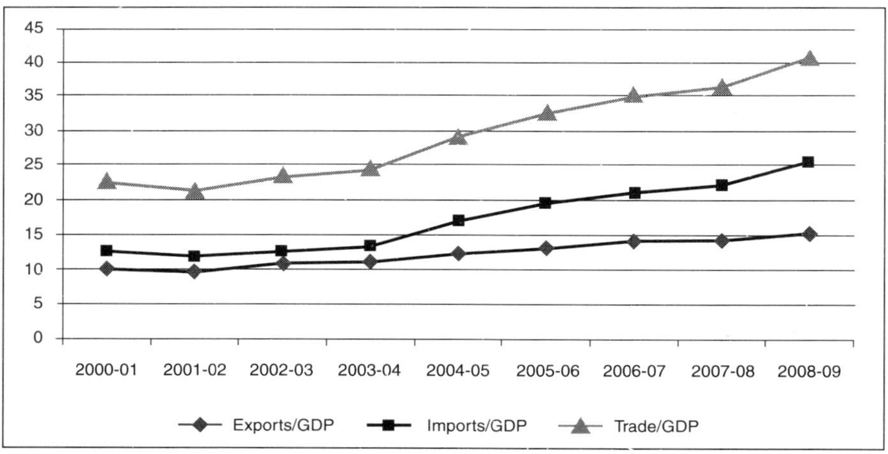


*Source*: Data culled out of www.rbi.org.in *Handbook of Statistics on Indian Economy*.

**FIGURE 6.6** *India: Trends in Foreign Trade*

These increases are substantially higher than what were achieved in the decades of the 1980s and 1990s. Not only that, recent reports suggest acceleration in pace.

Figure 6.7 shows export growth and share in world exports of India along with other select countries. While share of India's trade in GDP registered an impressive rise during the decade from 2000, its share in world exports continues to be small at 1.1 per cent. Every other country, except Indonesia and Thailand, has a higher share than India. The difference between India and China is particularly stark considering that in 1990, the share of world exports of China and India were 1.8 per cent and 0.5 per cent, respectively, and in 2008 their respective share stood at 8.9 per cent and 1.1 per cent.

In terms of growth rate (2000–08), though moderate, India seems to have done better than many other countries, except China and Russia.

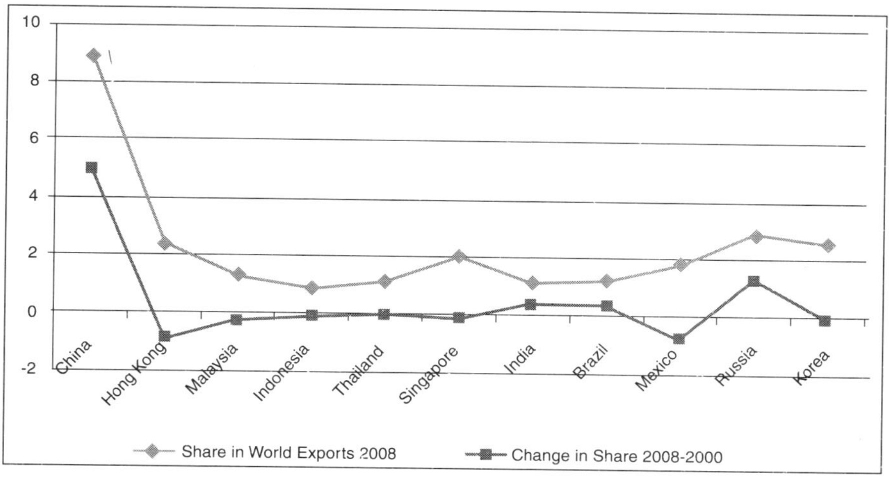


*Source*: Data culled out of www.finmin.nic.in Economic Survey, 2009–10.

**Figure 6.7** *Export Growth and Share in World Exports: India and Other Select Countries*

## 6.8.2 Liberalization of Capital Flows[7]

### *Non-Debt Capital Flows*

Non-debt capital flows include foreign direct investment (FDI) and foreign portfolio investment (FII). In respect of FDI, two routes have been specified: (a) automatic and (b) case-by-case approval. "The automatic route is currently divided into four categories. Key sectors, where 100 per cent foreign ownership is allowed under the automatic route, include power;

[7] In describing the policy changes with respect to capital flows, I have drawn from Jadhav Narendra, *Capital Account Liberalization, The Indian Experience*, New Delhi, 2003. The paper is available on NCAER website.

roads and highways; ports and harbours; mass rapid transport system; drugs and pharmaceuticals; hotel and tourism sectors; advertising and mining. Another major thrust area where up to 100 per cent FDI has been permitted under the automatic route is special economic zones (SEZs) for most manufacturing activities. The major sectors where less than 100 per cent FDI is permitted under the automatic route are telecommunications (49 per cent), airports (74 per cent) and defence industry sector (26 per cent). The financial sector also has been gradually opened for FDI in tune with the gradual liberalization initiated since the early 1990s. Currently, FDI is allowed in private sector banks (49 per cent), non-banking financial companies (100 per cent), and insurance sector (26 per cent)".[8] Additionally, foreign companies are allowed to set up 100 per cent subsidiary. FDI through merger and acquisition route has also been substantially liberalized.

There is a small list of industries where case-by-case approval is required. These include domestic airlines, petroleum sector, print media and broadcasting, postal and courier services, development of integrated township, tea plantation, defence and strategic industries, atomic minerals, establishment and operation of satellite, and investing companies in infrastructure and services sector.

Finally, there is a negative list, which includes retail trade, atomic energy, lottery business, gambling and betting, housing and real estate business and certain activities in agriculture and plantation.

As far as FII is concerned, "Investment by Foreign Institutional Investors (FII) was permitted in the early 1990s. Portfolio investments are restricted to selected players mainly for approved institutional investors. A single FII can invest up to 10 per cent in any company, while FIIs together can invest up to sectoral caps in both the primary as well as secondary market. There are currently two classes of FIIs: the first one is subject to equity: debt investment in the ratio of 70:30 and the other class pertains to 100 per cent debt funds. While the former class of FIIs can invest in debt securities, including government securities and units of domestic mutual funds in the ratio of 70:30, investments by 100% debt funds are subject to an overall cap". Investment limit for the FIIs as a group in government securities currently is US$ 3.2 billion. The limit for investment in corporate debt is US$ 1.5 billion. At present, the FIIs can also invest in innovative instruments such as upper tier-II capital up to a limit of US$ 1 billion. "The cap on investment by debt funds is based on the consideration of controlling short-term debt flows as

[8] Jadhav Narendra, OPCIT.

part of the overall external debt management."[9] There are no restrictions on repatriation of portfolio investment.

Figure 6.8 gives the trends in gross foreign investment in India between 2000–01 and 2008–09. As a per centage of GDP, total foreign investment increased from about 4 per cent in 2000–01 to 23 per cent in 2007–08. It took a dip in 2008–09 because of global economic meltdown discussed earlier. Between FDI and FII, FII surpassed FDI almost throughout the period.

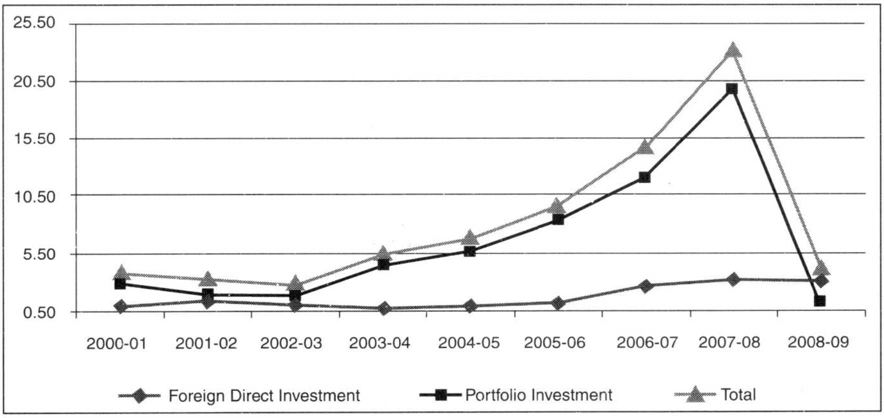


*Source*: Data culled out of www.rbi.org.in *Handbook of Statistics on Indian Economy.*

**FIGURE 6.8** *Trends in Gross Foreign Investment (% of GDP)*

## *Debt Capital Flows*

Proper management of debt capital flows is crucial to external sector stability. As we have seen, a sudden reversal of capital can wreck havoc to the economy. At the same time, external debt plays an important role in financing a country's development. It is, therefore, important to ensure that potential benefits outweigh the likely costs. India's debt management policy is geared towards achieving this balance.

Debt capital flows are of four types: (a) external commercial borrowings (ECBs), (b) non-resident deposits (NRI deposits), (c) short-term debt and (d) government account debt. While ECBs are encouraged, they are restricted to companies and development financial institutions like IDBI, IFCI etc. Banks cannot avail external commercial borrowing. ECBs are also subject to annual ceilings, maturity norms and end-use restrictions. NRI deposit

[9] Jadhav Narendra, OPCIT.

schemes have been substantially streamlined to ensure that while stable inflow is maintained, there are adequate safeguards against sudden outflow. Thus, on the one hand, interest rates on rupee-denominated deposits have been rationalized; interest rates on foreign-denominated deposits have been linked to LIBOR[10]; short-term foreign currency–denominated deposits have been de-emphasized; exchange rate guarantees are withdrawn; on the other hand, to retain the attractiveness, complete repatriation of NRI deposits has been allowed. Short-term borrowings have been subjected to severe quantitative restrictions and are essentially trade-related, i.e., to cover for the lag in receiving trade related payments. Finally, central government's own debt has been confined largely to official sources, i.e., bilateral and multilateral sources, which have a long maturity period and which are generally available on concessionary terms. State governments have not been allowed to access any form of external borrowing directly.

Figure 6.9 shows the trends in India's external debt between 2000–01 and 2008–09. On all indicators, India has done well. The total stock of external debt as a per centage of GDP has been steady or falling over the years. At about 18 per cent of GDP, India's debt stock to GDP ratio compares well with that of Brazil at 18.7 per cent, China at 11.6 per cent and Russia at 29.4 per cent. Short-term debt as a per centage of total debt, though on the rise, has been kept at a safe level of about 20 per cent compared to 16.5 per cent in Brazil, 54.5 per cent in China and 21.4 per cent in Russia. Debt–service ratio,

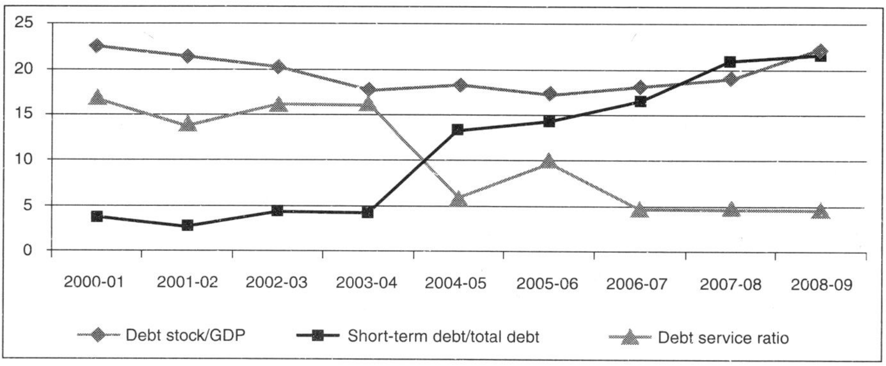


*Source*: Data culled out of www.rbi.org.in *Handbook of Statistics on Indian Economy*.

**FIGURE 6.9** *India: Trends in External Debt*

[10] London Inter Bank Offered Rate. The rate at which banks lend money to each other.

which measures the per centage of export earnings going towards servicing the debt, is also immensely manageable at about 4 per cent. India's external sector, indeed, appears to be robust today.

## 6.8.3 Exchange Rate Regime

Since March 1993, the exchange rate regime RBI is following can be characterized as a 'managed float'. The stated objective has not been to achieve any explicit or implicit target for the exchange rate but to contain volatility by ensuring orderly market conditions. Thus, the regime is 'more floating' during normal market conditions and 'managed' when the market turns disorderly. In the former case, intervention could be viewed as 'passive' while in the latter case intervention is 'active'. In other words, the objective behind passive intervention could be to avoid nominal appreciation whereas in case of active intervention, the objective is to avoid disruptive market conditions. In the more recent years, net RBI purchases of foreign exchange from the market have been positive, but the impact on broad money supply growth was moderate, as RBI intervention was largely sterilized.

Starting from 1993–94, Indian rupee has been made fully convertible on current account (Section 6.2.3). India has, however, not yet gone for capital account convertibility (CAC). The Tarapore committee, which went into the issue of CAC for India, had laid down certain conditions that needed to be fulfilled before India could go in for CAC. In respect of many of these conditions, e.g., inflation, interest rate deregulation, CRR levels, external debt–service ratio, foreign exchange reserves, disclosure norms, etc., substantial progress has been made. However, fiscal consolidation is still to be achieved. Also, some more strengthening of the financial system, particularly with regard to non-performing assets, is called for.

## 6.8.4 Foreign Exchange Reserve Management

One of the outcomes of a managed float system has been a substantial foreign exchange reserve build up by RBI. The inflows (supply) of foreign exchange, in the recent period, have persistently outpaced outflows (demand), exerting an upward pressure on the rupee. To maintain an orderly behaviour of the market, RBI has been purchasing foreign exchange from the market, thereby swelling its reserve coffer.

Figure 6.10 below shows the trends in foreign exchange reserves of RBI between 2001–02 and 2008–09. As can be seen from the table, foreign exchange reserves have grown almost six times during this brief period of 8 years. The increase has been particularly sharp in the recent years, except 2008–09, which was an unusual year.

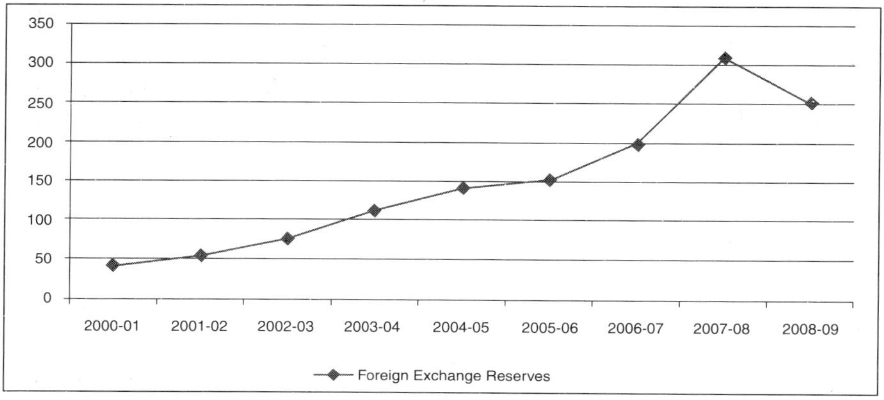


*Source*: Data culled out of www.rbi.org.in *Handbook of Statistics on Indian Economy*.

**FIGURE 6.10** *Trends in Foreign Exchange Reserves (in Billion US dollars)*

The source of accretion of foreign exchange reserves can be seen from Table 6.3.

Clearly, the foreign exchange reserves in India are built primarily out of a surplus on the capital account, which turned out to be more than the current account deficit. This is further corroborated by Figure 6.11. Except for three years when India's current account was in surplus, in all other years, it was in deficit. On the other hand, capital account surplus has been uniformly higher than current account deficit. This became more pronounced starting 2003–04.

Figure 6.12, thus, shows the source of net capital account inflows in the recent years.

The turning point in Figure 6.12 appears to be 2004–05. Starting from that year a pattern emerges. The largest source has been loans (mainly external commercial borrowings). Next is portfolio investment, followed by FDI and finally, banking capital, including NRI investments.

Why do capital inflows take place? In general, inflows take place when investors perceive that the domestic rate of return has risen relative to the international rate of return. This, in turn, depends on the perception of investors about (a) after tax yield; (b) stability of the exchange rate, at which they will be able to convert back the investment; and (c) the risk that they may not be able to convert the money.

***Table 6.3 Source of accretion of FOREX reserves in India since 1991***

(US $ million)

| 1991–92 to 2007–08 (up to end September, 2008) | | | |
|---|---|---|---|
| **Items** | | | |
| A | | Reserve Outstanding as on end-March 1991 | 5.8 |
| B.I. | | Current Account Balance | –74.1 |
| B.II. | | Capital Account (net) (a to e) | 341.8 |
| | a. | Foreign Investment | 160.8 |
| | | *of which:* | |
| | | *(i) FDI* | *72.9* |
| | | *(ii) FII* | *60.0* |
| | b. | NRI Deposits | 30.8 |
| | c. | External Assistance | 16.9 |
| | d. | External Commercial | 60.1 |
| | | Borrowings | |
| | e. | Other items in Capital Account | 73.2 |
| B.III. | | Valuation Change | 12.8 |
| | | Total (A+BI+BII+BIII) | 286.3 |

*Source*: Taken from Neeraj Kumar, "Study of Foreign Exchange Reserve Policy in India", *PGPPM Dissertation*, IIMB, 2009.

How are these perceptions formed? There are basically four factors: (a) growth in GDP (aggregate demand); (b) potential growth in GDP (expected growth in aggregate demand); (c) external conditions; and (d) credibility and content of host government's policy announcements. Inflows arising out of the first two considerations will probably be in the nature of foreign direct investment and inflows arising out of the third consideration will probably be of Portfolio Investment type. The fourth factor listed above is, of course, important for all types of capital inflows. As a rule of thumb, the

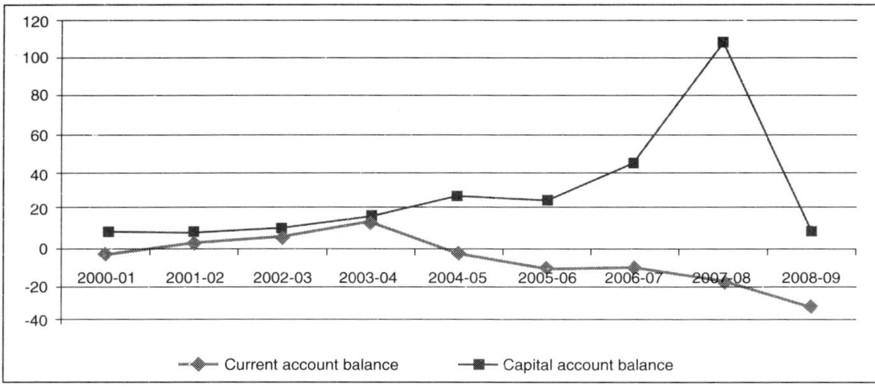


**FIGURE 6.11** *Trends in Current and Capital Account Balance (Billion U.S. Dollars)*

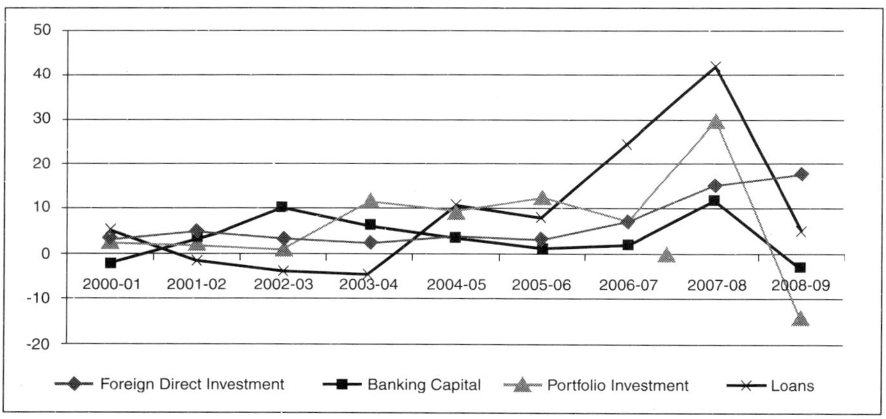


**FIGURE 6.12** *India: Trends in Net Capital Inflows (Billion U.S. dollars)*

less the inflows are related to current or future economic developments (the first two factors), more likely they are to be reversed. And, since a sizeable proportion of foreign exchange reserves in India constitute portfolio investments, let us briefly look at how robust India's foreign exchange reserves position is.

There are typically three indicators, which are monitored to assess the robustness/adequacy of foreign exchange reserves in a country. These are as follows:

1. Debt-based indicator, which says that short-term debt obligations and cumulative portfolio investments should not exceed 60 per cent of reserves held.
2. Trade based indicator, which focuses on the number of months a country can continue to support its current level of imports out of its reserves, if all other inflows and outflows cease. Typically, six-month import coverage is considered safe.
3. Monetary indicator, which looks at the ratio of net foreign exchange reserves to broad money. A high stock of foreign exchange reserves as a proportion of reserve money is considered a sign of confidence in the financial system of the country (in case residents choose to take their money out) and is, therefore, desirable. For India, it is recommended that net foreign exchange assets should be at least 70 per cent of currency in circulation.

On all the three indicators above, India's foreign exchange reserves position is not only safe but also more than safe. Reserves are in excess of what is required. On the first indicator, for example, short-term debt *plus* portfolio investments constituted only 35.81 per cent of reserves in 2007–08, as against 60 per cent allowed. Similarly, on the second indicator, foreign exchange reserves in 2007–08 were adequate to cover 15 month's imports compared to six months, considered safe. Finally, on the third indicator, net foreign exchange reserves as a proportion currency was almost 200 per cent as against the minimum requirement of 70 per cent.

This brings us to the next question: should we hold so much of foreign exchange reserves? What are the benefits and costs? A comfortable foreign exchange reserve cannot only help the central bank stabilize the exchange rate through timely intervention in the currency market but can also stem any speculative attack on the currency. As a result, confidence in the financial sector of the country can gain considerable strength.

However, foreign exchange reserves do not come without cost. There are not only direct costs of holding reserves but also indirect costs to the economy in terms of inflation and interest rate changes. The dilemma the central banker faces when the size of reserves becomes excessive are already spelt out in Section 5.5.3 of Chapter 5. Very briefly, the central bank has to take a call whether to; (a) stop accumulating reserves and let the currency appreciate; (b) keep accumulating, despite the cost of holding the reserves and its inflationary implications; and (c) accumulate and sterilize with its accompanying cost and impact on interest rates. The choice clearly is not straightforward.

As the Indian economic revival gathers momentum, import demand will increase and part of the need to build reserves will come down on its own. The government of India has also toyed with the idea of deploying a portion of the reserves for financing infrastructure development in the country. The original idea was to finance the government's deficit, on account of infrastructure investment, through borrowing from the central bank (money financed). The government then uses the money to buy foreign exchange to import goods and services for infrastructure development. Since the created money is used for importing goods and services and not for spending domestically, it is not expected to be inflationary. A modified version of this approach is being currently adopted. The government has created a special purpose vehicle, called the India Infrastructure Finance Company Limited out of market borrowings and used part of the money to buy foreign exchange (US$ 5 billion) and kept in the fund to lend for import of capital goods for infrastructure development. On the flip side, if investment in infrastructure is mostly rupee expenditure, this will not work. Also, whether this is the best way to address the problem of excess reserves is debatable.

In general, the consensus view is that rupee will be under pressure of appreciation in the near future. The reasons are twofold: (a) the revival of the Indian economy is faster than other parts of the world, except China; and (b) the interest rate differential between India and rest of the world is widening. Both these events will attract more foreign capital into the country. With inflation showing its ugly head, RBI may be constrained to conduct unsterilized intervention. On the other hand, sterilized intervention does not arrest capital inflows and is costly. RBI may closely monitor the movement of rupee vis-à-vis our competing country's currencies. It may even allow for some real appreciation of the rupee.

The other alternatives are a reduction in tariff rates to encourage more imports. Further easing of restrictions on outflows and introducing some restrictions on certain types of inflows may also slow down capital inflows and thereby the need for reserve accumulation. These are some of the issues with which RBI will be occupied with in the days to come.

## 6.9 Chapter Summary

We began by getting a feel for the place of external sector in macroeconomics. We argued that if a country followed a set of macroeconomic policies, it not only affected its own economy but also had a repercussion effect on other economies. This is the essence of the external sector discussion. The nature of impact will, of course, depend on the exchange rate regime a country is following and how mobile the capital is between the countries. A discussion of exchange rate regimes and capital account mobility was, thus, taken up next.

We first defined exchange rates in general. Then we focused on fixed and flexible exchange rate systems and their variants. Then to understand what was meant by capital account and capital account mobility, we had a discussion of balance of payment (BOP) statements. In understanding, the relationship between BOP accounts and exchange rate determination we emphasized that inflow (supply) of foreign exchange was the sum of what we earn by way of exports and what comes in by way of capital inflow. Similarly, outflow (demand) of foreign exchange is the sum of what we pay for imports and what goes out by way of capital outflow. And, exchange rate in the absence of any intervention by the central bank is given by the demand for and supply of foreign exchange. Thus, a rising rupee is compatible with a current account deficit if the total inflow is greater than total outflow. Finally, capital account and current account convertibility takes place when for all transactions on each account, the rupee is fully convertible into dollars and vice versa.

Macroeconomic adjustment under fixed exchange rate regime takes place through an increase or decrease in money supply because exchange rate stability is the paramount objective. This, in turn, affects money markets and interest rates. However, if, under a fixed exchange regime, a country cannot support its currency (in case it is under downward pressure) because it runs out of reserves or if the adjustment becomes politically painful, it can reset the price of its currency against dollar (devaluation) and vice versa. Then we moved to flexible exchange rate system and its variant, managed float. The important thing to learn here is that unlike in the fixed exchange rate system where macroeconomic adjustment takes place through money supply changes, in a purely flexible exchange rate regime macroeconomic adjustment takes place through changes in the exchange rates. Money supply changes are not required to manage the external sector. Under a managed float, we saw the management features of both fixed and flexible exchange rate systems. The central bank allows the exchange rate to be determined in the market place but intervenes if the market gets disorderly.

Equipped with all these concepts, then, we saw how macroeconomic policies under different assumptions with regard to exchange rate regimes and capital mobility work and how effective fiscal and monetary policies are in each case.

We also looked at why financial crises happen and when a currency becomes vulnerable. We ended the chapter with a discussion of external sector trends and issues in the Indian economy, including the question of management of foreign exchange reserves.

A manager must, besides understanding the analytics of external economy, track the external sector developments carefully to assess their impact on different cost and revenue variables.

# REVIEW QUESTIONS

1. Why is study of the external sector important for understanding fluctuations in aggregate demand and cost variables?
2. Distinguish between current account and capital account in a country's balance of payments. Why are these terms important?
3. Describe fixed, flexible (floating) and managed floating exchange rate systems. What are the advantages and disadvantages of each? Which exchange rate system we follow in India today?
4. Two countries, A and B maintain a fixed exchange rate system between themselves, but inflation is higher in country B than in country A. How will it affect the real exchange rate between the countries? Is h possible to maintain fixed exchange rate between the two, under the circumstances?
5. Suppose now that these countries decide to allow their currencies to float against each other. How will it affect nominal and real exchange rates? What will happen to nominal interest rates?
6. What is the difference between currency appreciation (depreciation) and currency revaluation (devaluation)?
7. What are the implications of perfect capital mobility under both fixed and flexible exchange rate systems?
8. Why are the following statements true?
   (a) Under perfect capital mobility, a country can not follow an independent monetary policy if it wants to stabilize the exchange rates

(b) Under perfect capital mobility, a country can not stabilize the exchange rates if it wants to follow an independent monetary policy and,

(c) If a country wants to stabilize exchange rates as well as follow an independent monetary policy, it must impose capital controls.

**9.** What causes financial sector vulnerability leading eventually to a crisis? What variables should be monitored to examine financial sector fragility?

**10.** In your assessment, is India globally integrated? Give reasons for your answer.

**11.** In your view, is India's foreign exchange reserve too high? What are the costs and benefits of having large foreign exchange reserves? How does management of reserves affect macroeconomic variables?

**12.** Define sterilization. What does it do? Can RBI go on with sterilized intervention for an indefinite period? Why or why not?

CHAPTER

7

# Implications for Managerial Decision Making

In the concluding chapter, we will attempt two things. First, we will bring together our learning to assess the Indian economic scenario and then go on to do the same thing for the global economy. In each case, we will draw some implications for managerial decision-making.

## 7.1 Learnings on the Indian Economic Environment

Let us begin from where we started. Consider Figure 7.1. It conveys that every company is interested in sustained growth in profits. Profit is the difference between revenue and cost. The attempt of every company, therefore, is to maximize the revenue and minimize the cost.

Revenue is a function of how much the company is able to sell its product or service, which, in turn, is a function of demand for that product or service. Ability to keep the costs low, similarly, depends on mode of financing as also on efficiency of utilization of funds.

Every company puts in lots of effort and money, internally, to find new ways of generating demand through innovative pricing and discounting policies, sales promotion efforts etc. Similarly, companies are constantly evolving cost effective ways of financing new ventures and setting up processes within the organization to minimize their day-to-day expenses.

But, in either case, companies have to bank on support from the overall economy. On the demand side companies look for stability in GDP growth and, on the cost side, stability in interest rates, tax rates, exchange rates and inflation rates. Our focus in this chapter will be on external support, which is the subject matter of macroeconomics.

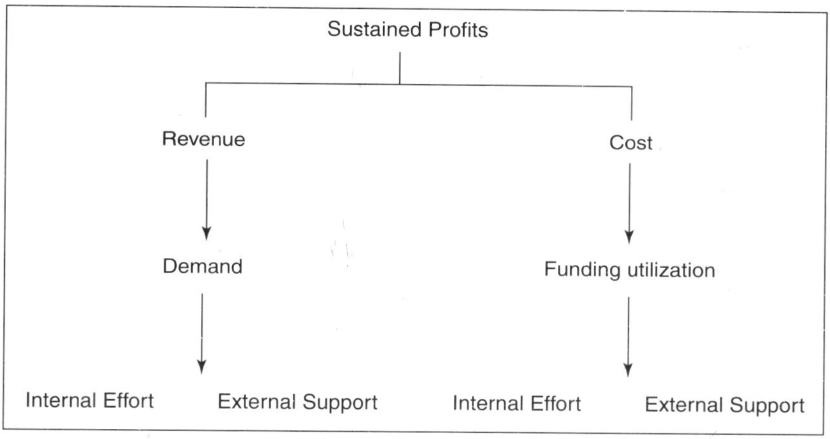


**FIGURE 7.1** *Macroeconomics and Managerial Decision-Making*

We start with GDP, which tells us about the growth of demand for goods and services in the economy at a macro level.

## 7.1.1 Overall Demand for Goods and Services

The following general points emerge from an analysis of the Indian economy:

1. India's potential GDP growth is presently estimated at 9 per cent per annum. Barring the abnormal year, 2008–09, whose effect spilled over partly to 2010–11, India has achieved a growth rate, which is close to the potential growth rate. The forecast is that 9 per cent growth will be revived in 2011–12. The Twelfth Five Year Plan starting 2012 is likely to set a higher growth target of 10 per cent per annum during the plan period. India is, therefore, poised for a rapid growth, given the right set of policies.

2. Investment in infrastructure holds the key to a sustained growth of GDP in India.
3. Investment demand is not just a function of economic variables; it also depends on the structure of the economy and expectations people hold about the future. These variables are not mutually exclusive but reinforce each other.
4. Poor governance and large diversion of investible resources of the economy can slowdown the growth of the economy. Outcomes are more important than outlays.
5. The manager needs to monitor certain key variables to assess the overall demand growth prospects in the Indian economy: (a) performance of the agricultural sector which still depends on the weather; (b) government finances, from the *revenue* side: pace of disinvestment in PSUs; speedier implementation of Goods and Services Tax (GST) and direct tax code. From the *cost* side: reduction in structural deficit, a basic prerequisite for reducing revenue deficit; (c) inflation, both supply side and demand side. This will set the direction of monetary policy; (d) revival of the global economy. This will determine export growth; and finally, (e) Investment in infrastructure; which will be crucial to the sustainability of overall growth.
6. The silver lining is that the present UPA government is stable; thus, barring exogenous shocks on account of geo-political risks, manifold rise in oil prices, failed monsoon, it may be able to make progress on all these fronts.

At a more operational level, the manager needs to keep in mind the following:

1. Understanding the state of the economy is important to be able to analyze policy effectiveness. In a period of slowdown, the state of the economy will be characterized by (a) unexpected build-up of inventories; (b) slow off take of credit; (c) fall in inflation rate; (d) soft interest rates; and, (e) high unemployment. A period of boom is a mirror view of slowdown with these factors working in the opposite direction.
2. A strong GDP growth after recession may just indicate better utilization of capacity. A strong GDP growth in a period of boom may mean addition to capacity but it can also signal a rise in prices

and, perhaps, imports. In India, as of now, we are perhaps seeing an economic (industrial) revival driven by better utilization of capacity, though in some sectors additions to capacity are in the pipeline.

3. There are leading and lagging indicators to signal changes in the economy. For example, at the earliest sign of a revival, monetary authorities may resort to a pre-emptive rise in interest rates. This is, therefore, a leading indicator that a revival is in the offing. A lagging indicator will be growth of manufacturing. Typically, in a period of revival, manufacturing capacity peaks with a lag. Again, in a period of slowdown, businessmen usually look up to the government to kick-start the economy. But in a period of revival/boom, businessmen want the government to stay away from business. This is consistent with our conceptual framework that the role of fiscal policy is inversely related to the state of the economy. The Monetary policy's primary role is price stability and exchange rate stability.
4. There is considerable merit in having a disaggregated look at GDP and in specifying demand for a product as being driven by the user industry demand rather than overall GDP. An impressive rise in GDP, propelled by service sector growth, might not signal a growing demand for industrial goods, but an increase in construction activity certainly would. Similarly, demand for consumer durables, in addition to its own price, also depends on interest rates. Any demand estimation, in today's environment, cannot ignore consumer tastes and preferences to capture changing life-styles, sentiments etc. Correct specification of demand, incorporating both macro and microeconomic variables, is vital for forecasting revenue of a firm.

## 7.1.2 Behaviour of Cost Variables

For assessing the behaviour of cost variables, an understanding of the state of the economy assumes even greater importance. Else, trends in cost variables may signal a distorted picture. For example, a manager should understand the following:

1. An increase in money supply need not lead to a depreciation of the currency, if the state of the economy is characterized by the presence of excess capacity. In that case, an increase in money supply may

stimulate the economy and perhaps attract more foreign investment in the economy, leading to an appreciation of the currency.

2. A fall in the interest rate, similarly, if it facilitates additional economic activity, may encourage more inflow of foreign capital than outflow, thereby resulting in an appreciation of currency. Again, high interest rate, if it is perceived to slowdown the economy leading to bankruptcies, may lead to capital outflow rather than inflow.
3. A current account deficit, if accompanied by a capital account surplus, does not lead to a depreciation of the currency. In fact, the currency may appreciate.
4. There is a need to make a distinction between whether the central bank is resorting to a tight monetary policy to stem a possible rise in prices or to address a current high price level. The former signals boom time ahead and the latter signals a reversal of business cycle.
5. Last but not least, as we have seen, if business sentiment is down, an increase in government deficit need not increase the interest rates and if business sentiment is upbeat, an increase in the interest rate need not crowd out private investment.

Indeed, in the short run, the manager has to be more alert about the state of the economy and, given the state, to make an intelligent judgment on how policies may impact cost variables. However, over a longer time horizon, cost variables do behave consistent with the fundamentals of macroeconomic theory. No country can sustain a persistent current account deficit or a persistent high inflation rate without paying a price.

In the light of what we have learnt so far, can we make an intelligent guess about the likely behaviour of cost variables, in the short run, in the Indian economy? Let us try that.

## *Tax Rates*

The principle governing tax rates is now well accepted. The rates should be reasonable and the procedures for tax collection should be simple but the tax base should be wide enough to cover all who should be paying taxes. It will, therefore, be unreasonable to expect any rise in tax rates, both direct and indirect. As a matter of fact with the implementation of Goods and Services Tax (GST) and Direct Tax Code (DTC), tax rates may stabilize at somewhat lower rates. But the tax base is likely to be considerably widened. Businessmen can, therefore, look for stability on the tax front.

## *Interest Rates*

Interest rates depend on demand for and supply of money. The demand may increase from two sources: (a) revival of the Indian economy which now looks more solid (back to state of the economy) and, as a result, RBI initiates a pre-emptive move to stem any rise in prices beyond the acceptable level by raising interest rates; and, (b) an increase in government borrowing from the market, primarily to finance its revenue deficit which may put upward pressure on the interest rates. The former is not bad for business as it signals an impending boom and if businessman's expectations of the future demand for goods and services are positive, a rise in the cost by way of an increase in the interest rates, at least in the short run, can be absorbed.

However, if the source of interest rate rise is the latter, there is a cause for concern, because this rise is unlikely from additional production of goods and services in the economy. It will only add to the size of the debt.

On the supply side, capital inflows may have some soothing effect on interest rates. On balance, probably, we should expect a moderate rise in the interest rates. But to assess how it will affect business environment, the manager needs to closely monitor the source of the rise — is it from monetary policy or fiscal policy?

## *Exchange Rates*

Exchange rates will depend on outflow (demand) and inflow (supply) of foreign exchange and RBI intervention in the currency market. On inflows, a surplus on the current account, if at all, is likely to be inconsequential. This is because, as industrial revival gathers momentum, import demand is likely to go up. On capital account inflows (and surplus on capital account) will depend on two factors: (a) how attractive India looks in an absolute sense; and (b) how India looks relative to other countries. The former will determine the size of FDI; the latter will determine the size of FII. The suggestion is that capital account surplus is likely to continue and, therefore, it is unlikely that there will be any pressure on the rupee to depreciate in the immediate future. What will be the stance of the RBI? Of course, we do not know. But from our previous discussions (Chapters 5 and 6), it would appear to make sense to let the rupee appreciate as long as there is not much of a relative (relative to other countries' currencies) appreciation.

### *Inflation*

In a globalized economic environment where trade is getting increasingly liberalized, it is unlikely that we will see a rate of inflation that prevailed in the pre-liberalization period or even in the early 1990s. On the other hand, to be able to compete in a globally integrated world, it will be desirable to have inflation, which is in sync with inflation in other countries. With this as the medium term objective, RBI, for now, is likely to work towards stabilization of prices at the acceptable level of around 5 per cent per annum. We may see bouts of price rise on account of certain supply side shocks. Beyond that it will depend on the trend of price rise in other countries.

From the above, it would appear that stability of macroeconomic policy induced cost variables, other than those created by state of public finances, may not pose a formidable challenge to the business in India in the short run. However, it is the effective cost, imposed by a rigid structure of the economy, discussed in Chapter 3, and unforeseen exogenous shocks, which may create the real obstacle.

Before we end this section, it is worth emphasizing again that, while no one can forecast correctly what the emerging trend is likely to be with respect to important macroeconomic cost and revenue variables, an understanding of what causes fluctuations in those helps in managerial decision-making. The above "scenario analysis" should be seen in that spirit.

## 7.2 Global Economic Scenario

In this section, we will try to understand and analyze the global economic trends and prospects. We will begin by looking at the structure of the global GDP and how it has been changing in the recent period. We will then provide a framework for analyzing the changes. Finally, we will draw some strategic implications for business.

## 7.2.1 Global Economic Trends

Based on purchasing power parity (PPP) share, United States, Japan and the Euro zone together accounted for about 44 per cent of global GDP in 2008. Of this, United States at 21 per cent and Euro zone at 16 per cent made up the bulk; the balance, about 7 per cent was Japan's share. All the three regions, however, unfolded a decline in share between 2001 and 2008 (Figure 7.2). The share of these countries in global GDP fell by 5 per cent during this period.

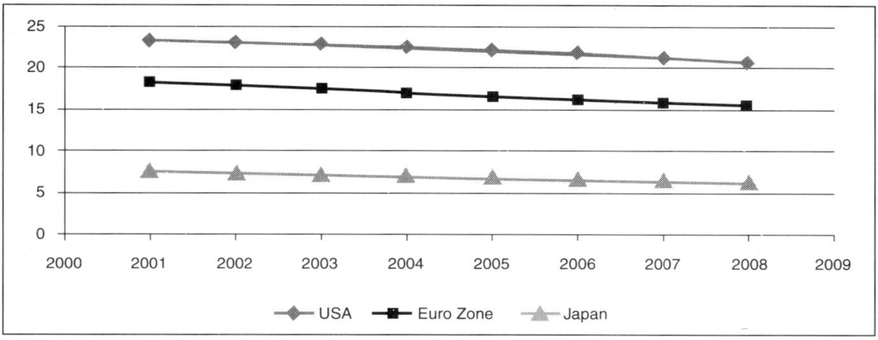


*Source:* Based on data culled out of http://www.econstats.com/

**FIGURE 7.2** *Share of USA, Euro Zone and Japan in Global GDP*

Emerging economy share in the global GDP, also weighted by purchasing power, on the other hand, advanced. Figure 7.3 shows the share of BRIC (Brazil, Russia, India and China) countries, the most talked about among emerging economies, between 2001 and 2008. All the four countries improved their share. The increase was most pronounced in the case of China, followed by India. The shares of Brazil and Russia went up only marginally. Together, the BRIC countries' share in global GDP surged from 16 per cent in 2001 to 22 per cent in 2008.

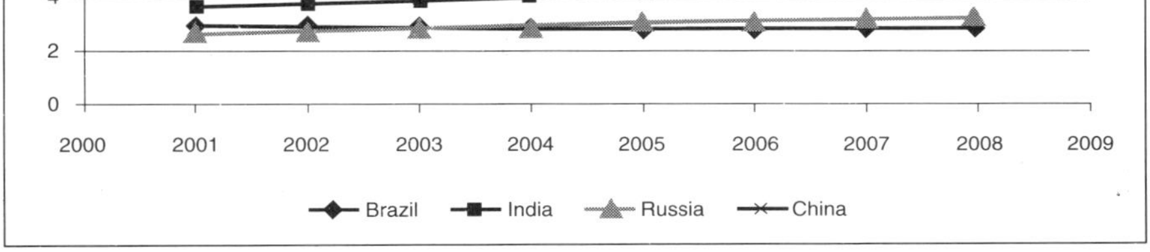


*Source:* Based on data culled out of http://www.econstats.com/

**FIGURE 7.3** *Share of BRIC Countries in Global GDP*

The fall in the share of United States, Japan and the Euro zone in the global GDP can be attributed to: (a) modest overall growth rate; and (b) within this modest growth, a tendency towards deceleration.

Figure 7.4 shows the trends in real GDP growth in the three leading economies of the world between 2001 and 2008. The US economy, after realizing a GDP growth of 3.6 per cent in 2004, suffered a major setback in the following years. The growth decelerated close to zero in 2008 and turned negative in 2009.

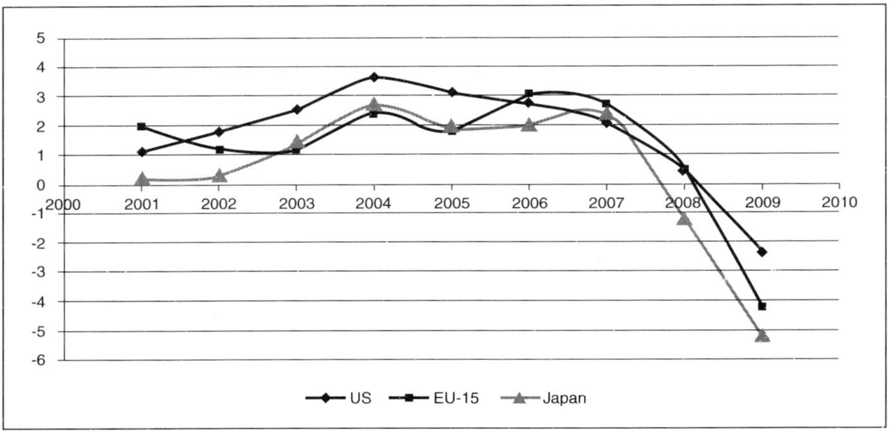


*Source*: Based on data culled out of http://www.econstats.com/

**FIGURE 7.4** *Trends in Real GDP Growth, USA, Euro Zone and Japan*

Japanese growth started slowing down from 2006. The growth turned negative both in 2008 and 2009. Euro Zone growth similarly started its downward slide in 2007 and turned negative in 2009.

In all the three regions, while the negative growth could be attributed to the 'great recession', even positive growth, it can be seen from Figure 7.4, was modest and, generally, increasing at a decreasing rate.

As against the above, the BRIC countries not only grew faster but the growth rate also appeared to be steadier. This is particularly true of China and India. As Figure 7.5 brings out that while in all four countries growth fell in 2008 and 2009 in the aftermath of global economic slowdown, China and India proved more resilient than Brazil and Russia.

Though not always accurate, forecasts of the global economy by the World Bank are viewed with considerable excitement by the press across the world.

Table 7.1 reproduces the data from a recent global economic outlook report by the World Bank. The numbers forecast similar trends in growth rates as observed above for the next several years. Though all regions are projected to recover from the levels of 2009, the growth forecasts are strongest for East Asia and Pacific and South Asia of which China and India, respectively, are the two most important countries. Europe and Central Asia of which Russia is a part and Latin America and Caribbean where Brazil occupies an important place are forecast to grow in the four per cent range, along with Middle East and North Africa. The other region which holds promise of higher growth is sub-Saharan Africa.

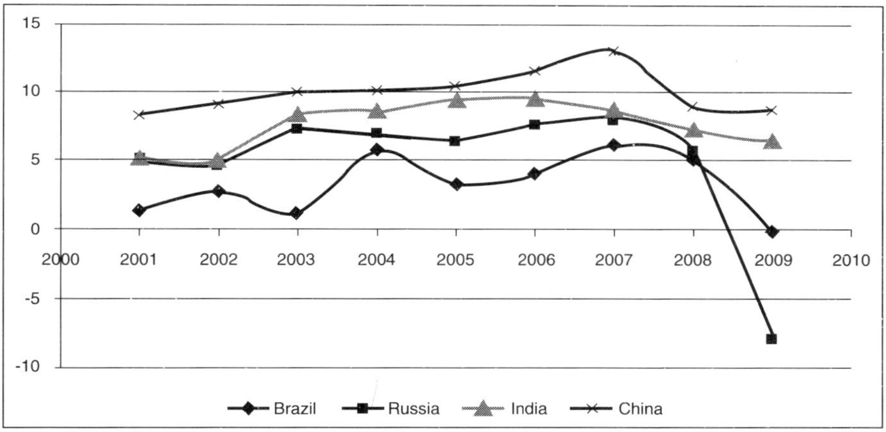


Source: Based on data culled out of http://www.econstats.com/

**FIGURE 7.5** *Trends in Real GDP Growth in BRIC Countries*

Clearly, the recovery in the leading economies of the world namely, United States, Euro zone and Japan will continue to be modest in the coming years, though in an absolute sense, they will retain an important place in the global economic arena. The rising stars will be East and South Asia. BRIC countries, in particular, are likely to gain. It will also be interesting to monitor how Sub-Sahara Africa emerges as a business destination.

## 7.2.2 Understanding Slowdowns: A Framework

A slowdown, it may be recalled, is defined as a situation where actual GDP is below potential GDP. A slowdown can be caused by:

1. regular business cycle,
2. negative sentiment,
3. financial crisis and
4. structural factors.

*Table 7.1 Global Economic Outlook*

| Regions | 2008 | 2009 | 2010 | 2011 | 2012 |
|---|---|---|---|---|---|
| Euro Zone | 0.4 | –4.1 | 0.7 | 1.3 | 1.8 |
| Japan | –1.2 | –5.2 | 2.5 | 2.1 | 2.2 |
| USA | 0.4 | –2.4 | 3.3 | 2.9 | 3.0 |
| East Asia and Pacific | 8.5 | 7.1 | 8.7 | 7.8 | 7.7 |
| Europe and Central Asia | 4.2 | –5.3 | 4.1 | 4.2 | 4.5 |
| Latin America and Caribbean | 4.1 | –2.3 | 4.5 | 4.1 | 4.2 |
| Middle East and North Africa | 4.2 | 3.2 | 4.0 | 4.3 | 4.5 |
| South Asia | 4.9 | 7.1 | 7.5 | 8.0 | 7.7 |
| Sub-Sahara Africa | 5.0 | 1.6 | 4.5 | 5.1 | 5.4 |

*Source*: World Bank. Figures for 2010–12 are forecasts.

A regular business cycle slowdown is largely confined to the real sector of the economy, where goods and services are produced. The real sector estimates demand and sets up capacity accordingly. Then it finds that the actual demand is deficient. This leads to an unintended inventory build-up. New investments are held up. Growth weakens and the downward phase of the cycle begins. In the second phase demand slowly revives, propelled by macroeconomic policies, external factors or just normal fixed investment and inventory cycles. Initially, the increased demand is met from drawing down of inventories. Then new investments ensue, which result in further increase in demand through the multiplier process (Chapter 4) and more investment. The revival phase gathers momentum. Finally a peak is reached. At the peak, supply bottlenecks emerge which drive prices and interest rates up. Output growth is pulled back and this is the turning point of the cycle in the other direction. In this phase as investments come down, more factors of production are rendered unemployed and slowdown gathers momentum. Finally a trough is reached. This, once again, is a turning point of the cycle in the reverse direction. In the trough, interest rates and prices start falling; this induces more investment and labour demand. Government's discretionary policies and automatic stabilizers both are activated. And, the process begins all over. Typically a recession lasts between six months to a year.

A negative sentiment driven slowdown is usually caused by the financial sector. In this case an initial increase in demand creates euphoria in the financial markets. Asset prices of the companies/sectors showing some promise are bid up completely out of proportion to growth of the real sector, due to noise, contagion, or simply asymmetric information. Consumers who own these assets feel richer and they buy more. They borrow money on the basis of their asset market wealth. Companies/sectors also find it easy to borrow using asset market wealth as good collateral and raise new capital. To get a piece of action, foreign investors pour money in. Meanwhile an asset market bubble is created which eventually bursts[1]. A massive erosion of wealth takes place. Sentiments turn negative. Foreign investors flee and banks tighten up. Both consumption and investment demand weaken. In situations when sentiments turn negative macroeconomic policies take longer to revive economies (Chapter 3). The slowdown is prolonged.

A financial crisis takes place when asset market collapse leads to a full-fledged banking crisis. A banking crisis occurs when large proportion of banks and financial institutions in the economy are insolvent (liabilities are greater than assets). Banks are unwilling to lend money to companies for fear that they may not get it back; companies are unwilling to spend money on investment projects for fear that they may lose more and banks will ask the money back. The sensitivity of investment to the degree of financial crisis varies from country to country. But if it persists, capital flows out, resulting in a balance of payment crisis. Foreign debt becomes difficult to service. This disrupts both trade and production. In this case, also, the slowdown is prolonged.

A slowdown driven by structural factors arises mainly out of structural rigidities in the economy. This may take the shape of inflexibility in labour and capital movements, rigid policy environment, and political paralysis and so on. In these situations, though there are opportunities for new investment and growth, the rigid structure acts as a barrier and growth continues to be sluggish.

[1]Typically, these are in the nature of a crash in the stock market or property market.

Where do U.S., Japan and Euro zone slowdowns fit into the above framework? Clearly, in none of the three regions, the slowdown can be termed as a regular business cycle slowdown. Let us look at each region a bit more closely.

## *U.S. Slowdown*

The U.S. economic slowdown in the decade of 2000s can be characterized as a negative sentiment driven slowdown. U.S. economy registered a growth of 4 plus per centage points per annum between 1996 and 2000. This was the period of boom initiated by IT revolution and subsequently driven by stock market euphoria. However, with the stock market crash in 2000, GDP growth crashed to 1.7 per cent in 2001.There was a massive erosion of wealth. Both consumer and business sentiment turned negative. The rest of the story is captured in Chapter 3.

A second shock to the U.S. economy came by way of sub-prime crisis (Section 6.6). Though the crisis had been brewing for some time, its full impact was felt during the period 2007–2009. A financial sector meltdown ensued. Negative sentiment from loss of wealth culminated into a feeling of mistrust in the financial institutions. Financial sector failed to support the growth of the real sector. Consumer spending slackened fearing uncertainty, investors cut down fearing lack of demand and banks became reluctant to lend money fearing defaults. The engine of economy got derailed. GDP growth in the United States declined sharply from 2.7 per cent per annum in 2006 to –2.4 per cent per annum in 2009. Unemployment rate during the same period jumped from 4.6 per cent of labour force to a whopping 9.27 per cent of labour force.

As discussed earlier, in a negative sentiment driven slowdown, further complicated by a financial sector crash, macroeconomic policies are not very effective in stimulating economies. U.S. policy rates, as a part of monetary policy stimulation, were brought down from 5.25 per cent in 2006 to 0.1 per cent in 2009 but the economy failed to respond promptly. Similarly, as a part of fiscal policy stimulation, U.S. fiscal deficit went up to an unprecedented 10.7 per cent of GDP in 2009, as the government, among other measures, resorted to expensive rescue of major financial firms such as insurer AIG and government mortgage agencies Freddie Mac and Fannie Mae. But the GDP did not rise commensurately. The debt/GDP ratio went up from 61.07 per cent in 2006 to 83.21 per cent in 2009.

The U.S. economic growth is estimated to have recovered to 3.2 per cent in 2010, albeit from a low base. But a sustained recovery in the short run will be constrained by persistent high unemployment rate currently estimated at close to 10 per cent of labour force. An offshoot of this is lower wages and continued depressed sentiments. Demand for houses in the United States, a major indicator of economic revival, also remains subdued.

What are the chances of a more rapid U.S. economic recovery in the medium term? On the positive side there are certain structural features of United States, which are likely to make U.S. recovery fastest among the three. Labour and product markets are lot more flexible in the United States than in Japan or Euro zone. It, therefore, does not face too much opposition in response to changes in product and labour market conditions. The institutions are stronger. Certain aspects of financial sector fragility in the economy, brought out in the wake of sub-prime crisis, are also likely to be addressed by the new banking regulation bill[2]. Finally, there is no political paralysis.

What may create problem, however, are the size of the current account deficit, and, the size of the fiscal deficit which is pushing up the debt/GDP ratio. The current account deficit of the US economy, during the five year period 2004–2008, hovered around 5 per cent of GDP, which is high. In 2009 the deficit came down to about 3 per cent of GDP, largely due to a negative growth of the economy rather than to any structural change.

As we have discussed earlier, current account deficit means that the country is borrowing from abroad to finance the gap between imports and exports of goods and services. Obviously this gap is being financed by a capital account surplus. We also saw that capital flows into a country mainly for two reasons: (a) on expectations of higher growth; and (b) to take advantage of short-term interest rate differentials between countries.

In the past, capital has been flowing into the United States for a variety of reasons. First, between mid-1990s and almost up to 2000, the U.S. economy grew at a very impressive pace, while both Japan and the Euro zone experienced a slowdown. In fact, during this period, U.S. economy was perhaps the only large economy in the world, which was growing. In the process, it was acting as an engine of growth for the rest of the world.

[2]The financial regulation bill focuses on six aspects: a) consumer protection; b) avoidance of regulatory oversight through creation of council of regulators; c) an orderly liquidation in the event of a financial crisis to avoid a ripple effect; d) stripping the banks of their proprietary trading activities; e) fine tuning the derivatives market to minimize the risk associated with a bust; and, f) hiving off of swaps businesses by banks to reduce exposure to potential losses.

Second, short-term interest rates in the United States were higher than in either Euro zone or Japan. Third, there were certain unique features of the U.S. economy, which attracted more foreign investment to the United States. For example, the sheer size which exuded confidence. Again, the fact that dollar denominated transactions still held sway and that more than half the dollar currency resided outside United States also added to demand for dollars over other currencies. Finally, investors seemed to like the flexible structure of the U.S. economy.

But some of these favourable factors have changed in the recent past. First, U.S. economy is not growing as robustly as before. Therefore, the incremental return is not perceived to be as high as before. Continued gain in productivity levels in the United States is, of course, a positive feature of the economy. But, with higher levels of investment, risk premium, or the return expected by the international investors also goes up. Second, as Figure 7.6 shows, short-term interest rates (policy rates), which had favoured the United States in the early part of 2000, have since moved close to zero. Indications are that they will remain at these levels in the near future. In fact, in all the three leading economic zones the interest rates are ruling at historic lows. Investments in these economies are no longer viewed as attractive either on account of growth prospects or for higher short-term returns. Third, certain developing country economies like India, China, Brazil and Russia are offering opportunities for growth as well as short-term investments, though their economies may not match the size of US, Japan or the Euro zone. Foreign capital inflows to some of these economies have stepped up considerably. Finally, the quality of current account deficit, besides size, in the United States has also changed for the worse. Of late, the deficit is driven more by increased demand for imported consumer rather than produced goods and services. If money borrowed from abroad to finance the current account deficit does not lead to growth, then there may be problems in servicing the foreign debt. This raises concerns about sustainability of the current account deficit and puts additional pressure on doing something about it.

The implication of the first three points raised above is that, in normal course, one can expect certain depreciation of the dollar as foreign investments move out of United States to other destinations. This is already happening. Additionally, the last point above suggests that United States may also like to engineer a fall in the value of the dollar in the interest of long-

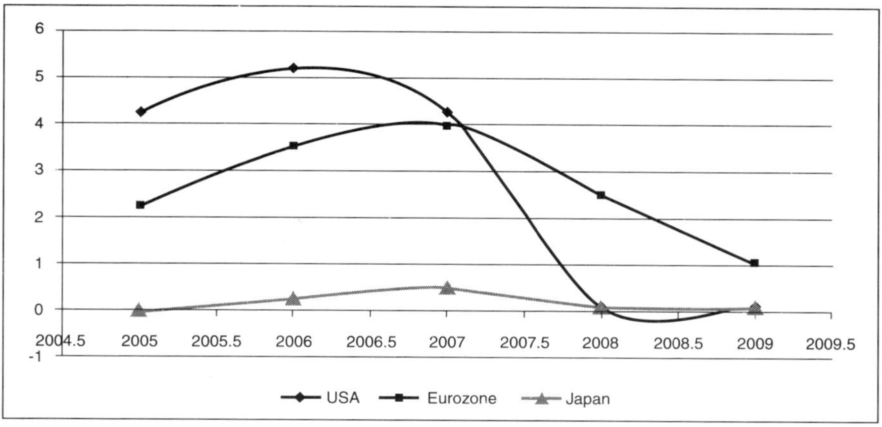


*Source*: Based on data culled out of http://gfs.eiu.com/

**FIGURE 7.6** *Policy Rates in United States, Euro Zone and Japan, 2005–2009*

term sustainability of the current account deficit. Only hope is that it does not resort to protectionism to achieve its objective. While the above analysis of recent developments in the U.S. economy would appear to be likely, it should also be highlighted that the fall in dollar will have to be gradual. This is for two reasons: First, a large part of the rest of the world grows on the basis of exports to United States. Other than China, the countries/regions that have a sizeable current account surplus with the United States are Euro area, Japan, Asia, Canada, Mexico and OPEC countries. Given the size of the U.S. economy, if the United States starts buying less of these countries' goods and services, it may result in a global recession. The only way this could be avoided would be if some other countries/regions were in a position to buy up the goods and services, not sold to the United States, from the affected countries. But neither Euro zone nor Japan is growing at a rate to be able to increase their imports to that magnitude. To some extent China is able to do it but their imports are small compared to what would be required. Second, highest current account deficit of the United States, to the extent of almost 25 per cent of the total, is with China. And, China still manages its currency vis-à-vis the dollar. Therefore, even if dollar depreciates, it does not affect trade with China, which accounts for the largest current account deficit of the United States. Of course, things would be different if China could be persuaded to revalue its currency vis-à-vis dollar. But, then, there are domestic constraints in China to resorting to such a step. At best, China may show some more symbolic gesture.

To sum up, we are probably safe in arguing that a combination of factors, cited above, will necessitate a fall in the value of dollar in the short to medium run. This will have a soothing effect on the U.S. current account deficit. But this will have to be gradual.

A second source of modest U.S. GDP growth in the short-run is not external but internal. This has to do with the size of the fiscal deficit, which has risen close to 10 per cent of GDP. A debt-GDP ratio of more than 80 per cent is also very high. While fiscal stimulation was required to bail the economy out of an unprecedented slowdown[3], such a large deficit and debt is unsustainable. A high fiscal deficit and overall debt, we have seen in Chapter 4, creates uncertainty about future course of interest rates, prices, tax rates and exchange rates depending on how the fiscal deficit is financed. It is, therefore, a matter of time before United States starts initiating measures to pull back, at least, part of the fiscal stimulation.

Finally, some exogenous shocks in the form of terrorist attacks or a sharp rise in international prices of oil may stall the growth process. While these "unknowns" should not be used as convenient working hypotheses to push one's point of view, these factors, nevertheless, cannot be completely ignored.

Let us summarize. The main points are the following:

1. The U.S. slowdown fits into our categorization of a negative sentiment-driven slowdown, culminating in financial sector crash. When sentiments are negative, macroeconomic policies become less effective in stimulating the economy. It takes longer to revive the economy.
2. While the above is true, the U.S. economy has many structural features, which enables it to come out of a slowdown faster than Japan or Euro zone.
3. There are some early signs of revival of the U.S. economy, but it has not yet changed the unemployment rate to any significant extent.
4. Even if it does, the U.S. growth rate may be tempered because of the size of current account and fiscal deficits, both of which have reached unsustainable proportions.

---

[3]In situations when private sector spending is not growing at the desired pace because of negative sentiment and export growth cannot be stimulated because of sluggish growth of the incomes of buyer countries, an increase in government expenditure is the only way to stimulate economies. In fact, whatever revival we observe in the economies across the world can be ascribed to fiscal stimulation.

5. Exogenous shocks can also adversely affect growth and,
6. In the short run, U.S. GDP growth can be expected to be stable but moderate.

## *Japanese Slowdown*

Japanese economic slowdown falls in the category of financial crisis-driven slowdown. Let us, briefly trace the events leading to the Japanese slowdown.

The Japanese economy structurally is very different from the U.S. economy. The main features of the Japanese economic structure have been the following: (a) large role of the government in investment decisions in the economy; (b) a repressed banking system; (c) dominance of enterprise groups; and (d) long-term labour contracts based on relationship rather than competition. To some extent, the structure reflected Japanese social and cultural traits, where relationships were valued more than efficiency. This structure was also necessitated by the need to mobilize resources and direct those to certain lines of activity in the aftermath of war. Japan achieved a phenomenal productivity growth of nearly 5 per cent per annum between 1960 and 1992. The productivity gain in tradable was particularly impressive both in size and composition. From being an exporter of toys and textiles in the aftermath of war, Japan quickly moved up the value chain to being an exporter of light manufactured items in the 1950s; to consumer electronics, ship building, steel and sophisticated optical products in the next two decades; to, finally, automobiles and semiconductors in the 1980s.

However, the strain of the structure started showing in the Japanese economy. The economy, which grew at 10.4 per cent per annum in the 1960s slowed down to 5.2 per cent in the 1970s. Productivity levels also declined. The economic need to mobilize resources to finance activities in the aftermath of war also diminished. Beginning in the late 1970s, Japan, therefore, started liberalizing its financial sector. Interest rates were deregulated; new financial services and products were introduced; capital flows were substantially liberalized and credit and capital market controls were by and large lifted. As a result, Japanese financial markets underwent a qualitative transformation. "Large enterprises with high credit ratings were able to raise funds from both domestic and international capital markets at interest rates much lower than those charged by banks. In fact, quite a few corporate entities availed of the opportunity to go out of the main bank system by repaying bank loans with borrowings from other sources"[4]. All this, coupled with an easy monetary policy followed by the Bank of Japan, helped sustain a boom in the Japanese economy.

However, with financial liberalization, as alternative source of funding increased, the role of Japanese banks became less important. Two things ensued: (a) the banks started lending to more risky customers, and (b) the banks started investing in more risky avenues like shares and real estates. This resulted in an investment-cum-stock market boom. As long as the going was good, both banks and others made huge profits. The vulnerability of banks never came to surface. However the asset price bubble burst in late 1980s. A sharp reversal in monetary policy in 1989, which drastically slowed down the growth of base money, aggravated the impact of the bubble burst. Banks ended up with mounting non-performing assets. Financial markets were disrupted. Many banks were declared insolvent. A fall in investment and output growth, which started in 1991, still continues. The numbers are mindboggling. At its trough in October 1998, the benchmark Nikkei average index was down to one-third its peak level recorded in late 1989. Prices of land for commercial use and residential had dropped 70 per cent and 45 per cent, respectively, from 1991 levels.[5] And, the economic growth just hovered around less than 1 per cent per annum on the average throughout the 1990s, with several years, in between, showing negative growth.

Note that Japan is another case of financial sector liberalization unaccompanied by proper financial sector reforms, particularly in respect of prudential norms and supervision. Banks could lend to risky customers because the relationship based banking and the Bank of Japan was there to protect the failing banks. Banks were also willing to finance investments in share prices and real estate because they knew that while the loss would be to depositors, the gain would accrue entirely to them. Also note that the shock in Japan, unlike in Thailand (Chapter 6), which exposed its financial sector fragility, came from an asset price bubble burst. And, the banks' vulnerability came sharply to the surface, causing immense hardship to households and businesses, which cut down their spending to repair their balance sheets. The economy has not fully recovered since 1989.

---

[4]Rakshit Mihir, "Economic Crisis in Japan: Analytical and Policy Issues" in Money and Finance, No.9. April – June 1999, page 54. ICRA Limited, New Delhi.

[5]Kwan C. H, "Revitalizing the Japanese Economy", *CNAPS Working Paper*, June 2000. The Brookings Institution, Washington D.C.

How did the macroeconomic policies react to such a slowdown?[6] Obviously, if the aggregate demand growth shrinks, the need of the hour is to follow expansionary fiscal and monetary policies. Japan's short-term interest rates were accordingly brought down to almost zero. Fiscal deficit also, in course of time, rose to its highest level in Japanese history, more than 7 per cent of GDP. However, monetary policy turned out to be ineffective for three reasons; (a) banking sector collapse which resulted in a drastic reduction in loans; (b) short-term interest rates had already turned so low that further cut was not possible. When people can hold money without any cost, as would happen when short-term interest rates are close to zero, the nominal rate of interest cannot be negative since no one, then, would extend any loan. Monetary policy, which works through lowering of interest rates to stimulate aggregate demand, is totally ineffective; and (c) if interest rates are so low, that destabilizes the financial market; hence businessmen, instead of investing more, invest less.

Fiscal policy ineffectiveness stems from the fact that people size up that fiscal stimulus resulting in massive fiscal deficit, can only be temporary and hence likely to be reversed sooner than later. They become cautious about spending.

The debate on the role of macroeconomic policies in slowdowns of the type Japan has experienced is very much alive. Clearly Japanese slowdown does not fit into standard macroeconomic policy analysis framework. One important reason for that, of course, is loss of confidence in the financial system. But there are also other considerations. A decline in birth rate and an increase in life expectancy have resulted in a rise in the proportion of aged population to working population. Current savings to provide for the longer retirement span has correspondingly gone up. These demographic changes not only adversely affect current consumption spending but also future expected returns from investment. Additionally, structural weaknesses persist, besides banking and finance, in public spending, corporate governance, industrial policy and government regulations and so on.

Japan has launched comprehensive reforms covering the entire gamut of how corporate sector should restructure to reap efficiency gains, how financial sector reforms should be effected and how taxes and government finances should be rationalized. However, the traditional egalitarian view

---

[6]Look up www.web.mit.edu/krugman/www/keynes.html for further insights into the subject.

of the society is not easy to change. Also there are vested interests, which are resisting these changes. Some of these changes are also difficult to carry out. For example, restructuring involves closing down certain units, laying off workers, mergers and acquisitions etc. These are difficult choices to make given rigid labour and product markets. In other words, political and social paralysis is more rooted in Japan than in the United States. At every stage of reform, the social and political costs have to be carefully weighed.

Japanese economic growth turned negative both in 2008 and 2009 (Figure 7.4). The forecast is that Japan may clock a positive 2.5 per cent growth in 2010 over the negative 5.4 per cent growth in 2009. Also, the growth is expected to remain in the 2 per cent range in the medium term (Table 7.1). The recovery is expected to come from a fiscal stimulation along with robust export growth.

However, one needs to be cautious about these projections. First, domestic demand in Japan continues to be weak so much so that inflation turned negative (deflation) at –1.4 per cent in 2009. Second, its ability to sell abroad is dependent on the pace of recovery of the buyer countries, which is still uncertain. Finally, Japan's fiscal deficit and debt/GDP ratio, which are estimated at 8 per cent and more than 200 per cent, respectively, do not exude optimism about any further fiscal stimulus.

## *Euro Zone Slowdown*

Euro zone has also been experiencing sluggish growth in the 2000s (Figure 7.4). In this case, the reasons can perhaps be traced to structural factors. As we all know, the Euro zone switched to a single currency, Euro, in January 1999. For some time, Euro coexisted with the national currencies of the Euro zone countries. In January 2002, Euro replaced all national currencies and Euro notes and coins came into existence. Each member country's exchange rate is irrevocably fixed against Euro and is measured as number of currency equal to one Euro. Table 7.2 gives the conversion rate of each Euro zone country currency to Euro.

The creation of Euro is seen as a means to achieve exchange rate stability in the face of highly volatile capital flows. Such stability would also reduce the cost of transactions and hedging. Euro is also expected to boost trade within the Euro zone. Finally, it opens up opportunity for a single Euro-wise capital market.

*Table 7.2 Conversion rate of each Euro zone country currency to Euro*[a]

| Country | Currency | One Euro equal to |
|---|---|---|
| Austria | Austrian schilling | 13.760300 |
| Belgium | Belgian franc | 40.339900 |
| Finland | Finnish markka | 5.945730 |
| France | French franc | 6.559570 |
| Germany | German mark | 1.955830 |
| Ireland | Irish punt | 0.787564 |
| Italy | Italian lira | 1936.270000 |
| Luxembourg | Luxembourg franc | 40.339900 |
| Netherlands | Dutch guilder | 2.203710 |
| Portugal | Portuguese escudo | 200.482000 |
| Spain | Spanish peseta | 166.386000 |

[a]From the above, conversion of 100,000 French Francs to Euros 100,000 FFr/6.55957 = 15,244.90 Euros. Similarly, for conversion of 100,000 Deutsche Marks to French Francs (so-called "Triangulation Process"): Step 1–100,000 DM / 1.95583 = 51,129.188 Euros. Step 2–51,129.188 Euros × 6.55957 = 335,385.49 FFr

But Euro did not come without a cost. The member countries are expected to abide by certain conditions as a part of "stability and growth pact" to maintain the stability of Euro. These are the following:

1. Containment of fiscal deficit to 3 per cent of GDP.
2. Containment of outstanding government debt to 60 per cent of GDP.
3. Containment of inflation within 1.5 per cent of the average of the lowest three countries' inflation and
4. Containment of interest rate within 2 per cent of the average of the lowest three member countries.

A European Central Bank (ECB) with office in Frankfurt has been set up to oversee the stability and growth pact. The decision-making body on monetary policy in the Euro zone is the ECB governing council consisting of six executive members and eleven governors of respective national central banks. The national central banks will be the implementing authorities. The ECB governing council has a stated goal of "price stability".

The logic underlying the stability and growth pact in the context of Euro has to be understood. The entire attempt is to ensure stability of Euro, followed by growth. The first two conditions of the stability and growth path are meant to ensure fiscal discipline. In Chapter 4, we have seen how fiscal indiscipline can destabilize the exchange rate. The third condition is also necessary to support a common currency. Inflation differential within the Euro zone can jeopardize the fixity of the national currency against Euro. The last condition, additionally, is important for achieving credibility in financial markets.

Clearly, the price to pay for stability of Euro is sacrifice of independent macroeconomic policies by member countries. The stability and growth pact bars the member countries from following a set of macroeconomic policies, which are at variance with the conditions laid out in the pact. Some of these arguments follow directly from what we discussed in Chapter 6 on macroeconomic adjustment under different exchange rate regimes. If member countries of Euro zone have agreed to irrevocably fix their currency in Euro, they cannot follow independent macroeconomic policies which might disturb the fixity of the currency. The macroeconomic policies of all the member countries have to be synchronized.

But what happens if certain common policy announcements affect different member countries differently? For example, one country in the Euro zone may be close to capacity output while another may be faced with a massive slowdown. How will a common interest rate regime announced by the Central Bank of Europe affect these two countries? The first country, given the state of its economy, may find the interest rate too low and may fear overheating of the economy while the other country may find the interest rate too high considering the huge slack that exists in the economy. An "optimum currency area", a term ascribed to Prof. Mundell, stipulates that in the above situation, resources from the second country, particularly labour, will flow to the first country to cool down that economy and resources from the first country, particularly capital, will flow to the second country to take advantage of higher returns. And the policy of "one size fits all" need not affect different member countries differently.

The implication of the above discussion is that for a single currency to work, not only the macroeconomic policies have to converge in terms of business cycles and policy transmission mechanism, but also there has to be perfect mobility of labour and capital across the Euro zone. Additionally, a single currency stipulates fiscal transfer to areas within the region that are adversely affected by the integration. Else, different countries will be affected differently and the growth process will stall. The question, therefore, is: does the Euro zone qualify to be an optimum currency area?

The answer is: Not yet. Cultural, linguistic and barriers to mobility of labour persists. Wages are highly rigid. Business cycles across the Euro zone do not converge. They are asymmetric. Under the circumstances how will a common monetary policy work? Let us illustrate the problem with the help of Figures 7.7 and 7.8, which show the trends in unemployment rates and inflation rates in the Euro zone in recent years.

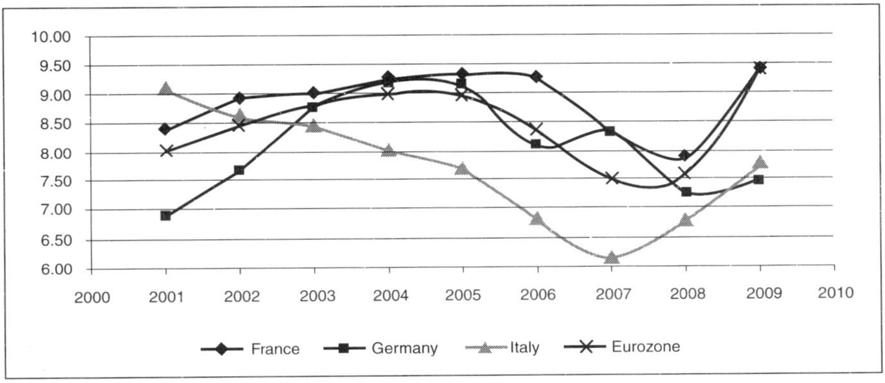


*Source*: Based on data culled out of http://www.econstats.com/

**FIGURE 7.7** *Trends in Unemployment Rates in the Euro Zone*

Unemployment rate in Germany and France has been higher than Euro zone average, though Germany seems to have faced the impact of global economic slowdown (2009) better than others. As one would expect, inflation rate in Germany and France has, accordingly, ruled lower compared to the rest of the Euro zone (Figure 7.3), barring 2009, which was an exceptional year.

Does a common interest rate policy announced by ECB, in such situations, stimulate economic growth? Clearly, given the lack of flexibility in the economic structure in the area, economies, where unemployment is high and inflation is low, can absorb a lower interest rate. What about fiscal policy? A fiscal straight jacket does not allow a rise in fiscal deficit to counter unemployment either. Nor does it allow fiscal transfers to regions, which are adversely hit by integration. Fiscal adjustment of the type implied in the growth and stability pact is particularly painful considering the fact that government expenditure as a per centage of GDP has always been high in the Euro zone, compared to, say, United States.

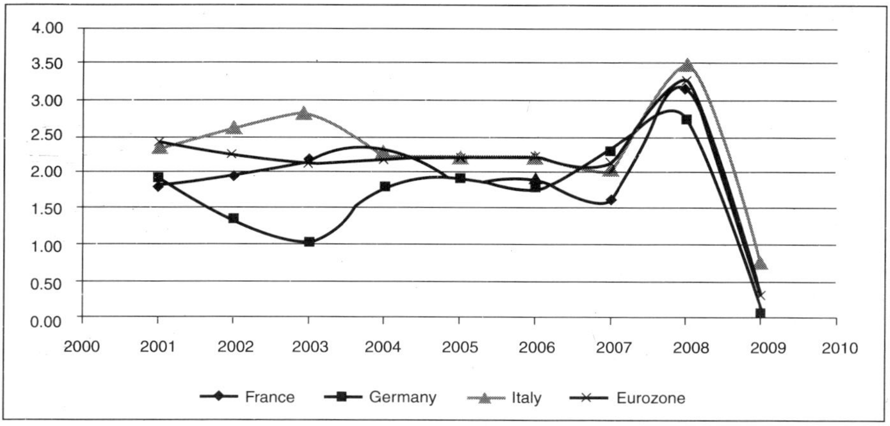


*Source*: Based on data culled out of http://www.econstats.com/

**FIGURE 7.8** *Trends in Inflation Rates in Euro Zone*

The typical answer to some of the concerns raised above is: change the rigid economic structure in the Euro region and things will fall in place. But this is easier said than done. Indeed a beginning has been made in banking and insurance. It is also extended to manufacturing. But wherever it has involved branch closures and job losses, restructuring moves have encountered resistance. We must not forget that it was resentment against high unemployment rates, which brought social democratic and centre-left parties to power in many European countries. The long and short of the Euro zone story is that while structural rigidities slow down growth, restructuring is a gradual process. Restructuring process is likely to get more complicated with more east European economies joining the Euro zone.

Euro zone's economy is projected to recover from –4.1 per cent in 2009 to 0.7 per cent in 2010 and then gradually advance to 1.3 per cent and 1.8 per cent in the following two years (Table 7.1). However, the main hurdle to growth will come from the fact that virtually all countries involved have breached their own self-imposed fiscal rules in the wake of the global economic crisis and, in some cases, even before.

Under the stability pact, as stated earlier, government debt was to be contained within 60% of GDP at the end of the fiscal year. Likewise, the annual government deficit could not exceed 3% of GDP. However, only two of the 16 Euro zone countries, Luxembourg and Finland, have managed

**Box 7.1: Debt Crisis in Greece and Euro Zone Stability**

Greece is a tiny country in the Euro zone. Its proportion of Euro area GDP is a meagre 2.6 per cent. However, Greece's importance in the stability of the Euro zone today stems not from its economic size but from the size of its debt. Greece has a debt of more than €270 billion, about 115 per cent of its GDP. The size of the debt is projected to go up to around €340 billion by 2014, which will work out to 150 per cent of its GDP.

More important, Greece's debt is not out of borrowing from within Greece but from outside. For example, as of June 2009 Greece owed €276 billion to outside investors, out of which more than 90 per cent was to other European banks, mainly French, Swiss and German.

The importance of Greece's debt for Euro zone stability arises from a possibility of default. This possibility is taken seriously because the return on the borrowed money has been consistently below the cost of servicing the debt. In fact, each additional euro debt of Greece was associated with less and less growth. Greece is the only country in the Euro zone which is still reeling under recession.

The fear is that if, indeed Greece defaults, three consequences will follow: (a) European banks, already mauled by the global financial meltdown, will turn even more fragile; (b) The other three countries in the PIGS (Portugal, Italy, Greece and Spain) who are faced with similar if not identical problems as Greece will become vulnerable through the contagion effect; and, (c) if Greece has to leave the Euro zone, a number of other countries in the zone, including some Eastern European countries, will have to follow suit. The existence of euro will be shaky.

How did Greece's debt reach such dangerous levels? What happened to the stability pact whereby each member country was expected to contain its fiscal deficit to 3 per cent and debt to 60 per cent of GDP? The fact is that it is hard to foster a monetary union without a fiscal union. The monetary union was established with the setting up of the Central Bank of Europe with a declared objective of maintaining price stability in the Euro zone. But fiscal union was left to moral suasion. Even the fiscal transfer mechanism to help member countries adversely affected by integration was not institutionalized.

True, the 2007–09 global economic slowdown may have necessitated some fiscal relaxation as fiscal stimulation, given the circumstances leading to the slowdown, appeared to be the only way to bail out economies. But fiscal profligacy has been going even before the slowdown began in some of these countries, the PIGS in particular.

Greece, for example, mismanaged and misreported its public finances for many years. Its labour costs went completely out of tune with productivity. On the other hand tax evasion became rampant. Corruption became deep rooted into the economy. The gap between revenue and expenditure, therefore, widened. The problem came to a boil when revenue from tourism, an important source of revenue for the economy of Greece, also slackened because of economic meltdown. Other countries within the Euro zone which are vulnerable have similar problems; the difference is only in degree.

What Euro zone needs to sustain is a massive structural change involving major changes in tax laws, fiscal austerity, restrained labour costs, and supply side measures to raise productivity, labour market reforms and so on. Surprisingly, the initial resistance to austerity measures has somewhat mellowed down which suggest that structural reforms may be difficult but not impossible.

Meanwhile the bailout package, worked out with IMF, of €110 billion exclusively for Greece and creation of a general Euro zone stabilization fund of €750 billion, along with monetary policy stimulation extended by European Central Bank will help in the transition. But the long-term solution is only structural reforms.

What finally turns out will impact Indian economy as well. If things go the right way India stands to gain by way of more business/capital flows. If things don't work out, the opposite will happen. The impact on oil prices, and the resultant gain or loss to India will, however, be positively related to Euro zone's recovery.

to stick to both rules. Among the top 5 countries of Euro zone, Germany's debt/GDP ratio in 2009 stood at 73.2 per cent; France's at 77.6 per cent; Italy's at 115.8 per cent; Spain's at 53.2 per cent; and, Portugal's at 76.8 per cent. Similarly, in 2009, Germany's fiscal deficit as a per centage of GDP was 3.3 per cent; France's 7.5 per cent; Italy's 5.3 per cent; Spain's 11.2 per cent; and Portugal's at 9.4 per cent. Certainly, such high deficit and debt levels raise risks of doing business in the Euro zone. It is likely, therefore, that Euro zone countries will embark on a vigorous effort towards fiscal consolidation, which, in turn, will temper the growth rates.

## *Discussion*

In this section we have used our learning from earlier chapters to analyze the performance of three leading economic regions of the world in the 1920s. All the three regions have registered modest growth. The sluggish growth of the United States, in the early part of 2000, was propelled by a stock market bubble burst, which turned sentiments negative. Subsequently, the economy faced a bigger shock in the form of sub-prime crisis, which resulted in a financial sector meltdown. The impact of this meltdown on U.S. economy and on others was unprecedented both in scope and size. Macroeconomic policies in the form of tax cuts and interest rate cuts were rendered ineffective. The U.S. economy, like many others, resorted to heavy fiscal deficit to perk up the economies. While there are some early signs of revival, the lingering worry is will the resultant debt/GDP ratio become unsustainable? Also, will it scuttle private sector growth? What is an appropriate time to pull out?

Sustained recovery may also be constrained by the size of the current account deficits. Finally, unless the recovery helps in creating jobs, consumer sentiments will remain negative. However, given the flexible structure of the economy, United States may be able to adapt to changes faster than others. Besides, borrowing in domestic currency, which also happens to be a major reserve currency[7], helps in initially managing the deficit better.

The Japanese problem began with a financial sector crash, which followed a stock market crash. Japanese recovery is contingent on how fast the fragile financial system and other parts of business can be restructured. This will not come without social and political costs. The process is slow. The changing demographic characteristics are also not helping in increasing spending in the economy. Japan's fiscal deficit and government debt is mounting. It has, so far, been able to sustain such high levels of deficit and debt because of large domestic saving pool to finance the borrowing. But there is a limit to how far it can go. The pressure to rein in deficits will gather force. At best, the economic growth in the coming years in Japan will be modest and resulting mostly from export growth.

In the Euro zone, the exacting requirements of the growth and stability pact and the rigid structure are coming in the way of faster growth of the region. The entire region is reeling under heavy deficit and debt. If the

[7]A reserve currency is a currency which is held in significant quantities by many governments and institutions as part of their foreign exchange reserves.

enhanced risk perception, as a result of this, causes the euro to depreciate against major currencies, some of the leading economies of Euro zone, notably, Germany may benefit from higher exports. Attempts at fiscal consolidation and some restructuring are also in the way and, while the progress is gradual the economies are increasingly showing less resilience to change. If this trend is continued, over time, Euro zone may pull itself out of the current difficulties. But the immediate outlook for growth is not optimistic.

In all the three regions, therefore, the GDP growth, in the short run, will be conservative, faster, perhaps in the United States than in Japan and the Euro region. This may be desirable in the interest of long-term sustained growth of these economies. But in the short-run businesses will look for opportunities elsewhere.

## 7.2.3 Strategic Implication for Business

Based on our analysis earlier, global capital will now look for countries, besides United States, Japan and Euro zone for better return. Some of the capital will flow to East Asian countries. In these countries, despite a global economic slowdown, early signs of revival, led by improved domestic spending and higher exports to China, are discernible. But the most talked about nations where more foreign investments may flow are the BRIC countries, namely, Brazil, Russia, India and China. These are all large countries and, in all the four, the investment needs are massive compared to availability of domestic savings. So here is an opportunity for these countries to tap more foreign investment for growth.

Table 7.3 provides data on key economic indicators for the BRIC countries. Row 1 shows the current economic performance as measured by GDP growth. China which already accounts for 11 per cent of global GDP is growing the fastest. India, which has an importance of 5 per cent in global GDP, is also advancing impressively. Brazil and Russia are not far behind either. Among the contributory factors, Chinese growth is supported by massive fiscal stimulus; Indian growth is due to a revival of domestic demand; same is the case in Brazil; while Russian growth is in response to a rise in oil prices.

Row 2 of Table 7.3 captures the excess capacity in these regions. With right set of policies this excess capacity can be tapped for further growth. Clearly, enough excess capacity exists in all the four regions. High inflation (row 3) is a source of worry in all the four regions. As inflation rate goes beyond an acceptable rate, central banks will try to moderate demand by signalling a rise in the interest rates. In India, inflation is particularly high. However, this high inflation is mainly due to supply side factors and is likely to ease following an improvement in agricultural production. Current account deficit (row 4), a measure of performance of the economy vis-à-vis external sector, is not a problem in both Russia and China. Even in India and Brazil, though there is a deficit, the size appears to be immensely manageable.

*Table 7.3 BRIC countries: Key economic indicators*[a]

| Item | Unit | Brazil | Russia | India | China |
|---|---|---|---|---|---|
| **1.** GDP growth | % per annum | 6.3 | 4.8 | 7.9 | 9.9 |
| **2.** Unemployment rate | % of labour force | 7.5 | 7.3 | 10.7 | 9.6 |
| **3.** Inflation | % | 5.5 | 6.4 | 11.5 | 3.1 |
| **4.** Current a/c Deficit | % of GDP | –2.8 | 5.2 | –1.6 | 4.1 |
| **5.** Three month interest rates | % | 10.16 | 7.75 | 5.37 | 2.61 |
| **6.** Ten year govt. bond yields | % | 6.16 | 5.64 | 8.2 | 2.97 |
| **7.** Fiscal Deficit | % of GDP | –1.9 | –3.9 | –5.5 | –2.6 |
| **8.** Change in exchange rate[b] | over last year | +11.05 | +1.95 | +3.88 | +0.73 |

*Source*: Taken from *The Economist*, July 10–16 2010. [a]Data relate to latest available; [b] + means appreciation.

Short-term interest rates (row 5) in all the regions are high. This is perhaps a reaction to higher inflation rates. However, what is interesting is a comparison of long-term interest rates (row 6) with short-term interest rates (row 5). In India and China, long-term rates are higher than short-term rates, thereby signifying a faster growth in the future years. However, in Russia and Brazil, the opposite is the case.

Fiscal deficit (row 7), captures the medium-term business environment in a country through its impact on cost and demand variables. In India it needs to be closely monitored (Section 4.6). In all the countries, however, the local currency is appreciating against the U.S. dollar (row 8). Foreign investors prefer an appreciating currency for two reasons. First, it signals the strength of the currency and second, in dollar terms, it brings higher returns. A stable currency, on the other hand, has its own merits as discussed in Chapter 6.

Aside from the economic variables, there are two more features which favour BRIC countries over others as a business destination. First, in a recently concluded study[8], based on ten drivers of global manufacturing competitiveness[9] China and India are rated first and second, ahead of United States, Japan and Germany; Brazil is rated fifth, ahead of Japan and Germany and Russia is rated 20 out of a total of 26 countries. The study forecasts an elevation in Russia's rating from 20 to 14 and Brazil's rating from 5 to 4 in the next five years. No change is anticipated in China and India's ratings.

Second, studies have shown a distinct change in the pattern of international trade in the recent years. Intra-regional trade has grown manifold at the expense of trade between developed and developing countries. These studies also point to the emergence of hub countries, i.e., Asia in manufacturing; Americas in agricultural products; Africa in natural resource based commodities and India, possibly in services. They also suggest that FDI strategies will increasingly get regional. The implication of these is that developing countries will become more immune to global slowdowns. The fact that Asian countries, as also Latin America, were relatively less impacted by the global economic slowdown perhaps bears this out[10].

In the light of the above, in what follows, we will briefly look at investment climate in India and China, which, as of now, are perceived to be the forerunners in attracting foreign investment in the country. Table 7.4 provides the rankings of the two countries against certain indicators. The rankings are indicative.

The table is instructive in two respects. First it provides a framework for comparison between countries in terms of investment attractiveness. Second, it brings to the fore, the importance of good infrastructure,

---

[8]Deloitte and US Council on Competitiveness - 2010. Global Manufacturing Competitiveness Index; ©Deloitte, Touche, Tohmatsu, 2010.

[9]Namely, talent driven innovation; cost of labour and materials; energy cost and policies; economic, trade, financial and tax systems; quality of physical infrastructure; government investments in manufacturing and innovation; legal and regulatory system; supplier network; local business dynamics; and quality and availability of health care.

[10]Manoj Pant, *Economic Times*, April 9, 2010; May 14, 2010; and June 11, 2010.

quality of fiscal deficit and red tapes (amount of time it takes for obtaining clearances etc.) as important discriminatory variables in investment decisions. On every other indicator, India is either better or same as China as an investment destination. This further strengthens our argument in Chapter 4 that, for a sustained growth of the economy, India must focus on infrastructure, reducing the size of revenue deficit and improving the quality of governance.

***Table 7.4 Investment climate in India and China: A comparison***

| Indicators | India | China | Advantage |
|---|---|---|---|
| **A.** Macroeconomic Stability | | | |
| 1. Fiscal Deficit | High | Moderate | China |
| 2. Current account Deficit | deficit, but manageable | Surplus | Same |
| 3. Inflation | rising | rising | Same |
| **B.** Infrastructure | Poor | Good | China |
| **C.** Institutions | | | |
| 1. Legal | Developed | Not developed | India |
| 2. Corruption | Present | Present | Same |
| 3. Red tape | More | Less | China |
| 4. Political | Stable | Stable | Same |
| 5. Openness | More | Less | India |
| 6. Financial | Robust | Fragile | India |
| **D.** Demographic | | | |
| 1. English-speaking population | More | Less | India |
| 2. Ratio of Young to Old | Favourable | Favourable | Same |
| 3. Higher Education | Better | Good | India |

Finally, we provide an outline of a framework on how an Indian company might identify business opportunities abroad. Clearly, there are many micro level decisions involved in considering such an option like dealership networks, joint ventures, taxes etc. But here we will consider only the macro variables. There are several steps involved:

1. List out all the changes that are taking place across the globe. These will include changes in GDP, life styles, connectivity, mobility, health consciousness, accounting practices etc.
2. Identify the constraints in terms of meeting some of these changes. Look for both opportunities and threats through these constraints.
3. Find out your own strengths.
4. See if the business proposition is compatible with your company's vision, ethics and social commitments.
5. See if the business is capable of scaling to global levels.

Then assess the relative attractiveness of countries (it could very well be our own country) for setting up business. The framework is provided in Table 7.5.

**TABLE 7.5** *Assessing business environment*

| Variables | Weight | Country 1 | Country 2 | Country 3 |
|---|---|---|---|---|
| Microeconomic Stability<br>Demand and costs variables | | | | |
| Infrastructure supports | | | | |
| Institutions<br>Legal, political, financial etc.<br>Politics towards FDIs, Hassel etc. | | | | |
| Social<br>Literacy, primary, secondary, higher, language demography | | | | |

On the left hand side, we have the key indicators. Based on the situation in the country we assign weights. These could be numerical or just "acceptable" or "unacceptable". Finally, we select the country, which meets your business objectives best.

Besides BRIC countries, it will be interesting to try out two more countries/regions in the above framework. These are South Korea and Sub-Sahara Africa. Swift and bold government response to economic slowdown as also sound macro fundamentals restricted South Korea's slowdown to less than six months. In fact, Korea today is rated third in manufacturing competitive index after China and India.

Similarly, investors are taking keen interest in Sub-Sahara Africa because global competition for commodities is giving a new strategic importance to resource-rich Sub-Saharan Africa. With unprecedented volumes of investment on offer, the stakes are high not only for resource companies seeking to expand in Africa but also for the region itself. The challenge for African governments will be to manage their commodities better to avoid a repeat of the boom-and-bust years of the 1970s to 1990s[11].

[11] http://gfs.eiu.com/Article.aspx?articleType=wif&articleId=219

# CONCLUDING COMMENTS: WHITHER MACROECONOMICS?

The severity and depth of the global economic and financial meltdown, in the wake of sub-prime crisis in USA, has had another casualty – the subject of macroeconomics. The questions that are being asked all over the world are threefold: (a) why macroeconomic policies failed to spot the impending crisis; (b) why are they taking so much time to revive the economies; and (c) is there a need for some rethinking on the future direction macroeconomic policies should take? In the appendix to this chapter, we briefly review some of these questions.[12]

## Monetary Policy

The goal of monetary policy in most of the developed world has been price stability. This is based on the postulate that holding prices stable at moderate levels (2 per cent inflation) contributes to broader economic goals. There is also some evidence to suggest that, over a period of time, economies with lower inflation have registered a higher real GDP growth. Thus, the price

[12]For further insights see Oliver Blanchard, Giovanni Dell'Ariccia, and Paolo Mauro, "Rethinking Macroeconomic Policy." IMF staff position note SPN/10/03, International Monetary Fund, February 12, 2010.

stability objective is also viewed as sufficient to meet the other important macroeconomic policy objective of sustained growth in GDP.

Price stability objective is achieved by focusing on general price level. Typically, each country announces a benchmark or an acceptable rate of inflation based on trends in general price level. Price stability is targeted around that level. The instrument used to achieve the target involves open market operations in government securities. If the inflation rate goes higher than the acceptable rate of inflation, the central bank resorts to open market sales of government securities and, vice versa if the inflation rate goes substantially below the acceptable rate.

The traditional way of conducting monetary policy, as spelled out above, is being reexamined in the light of the recent global financial meltdown. There are three main reasons for this. First, despite both inflation and output growth being stable, the recent experience has shown that behavior of some asset prices (property prices) or the composition of output (heavy investment in housing) can create major macroeconomic problems later on. The belief that market has all the information and thus the price of a financial asset reflects the true value of the asset is not true. The market price of an asset can be greater than the intrinsic value of the asset and remain there to form a bubble. This happens, as behavioural economists point out, because irrespective of available information, people form their own judgment about the future direction of asset prices and, even may end up being responsible for the creation of the bubble. More seriously, when the bubble bursts, the same behavioural characteristics can make people to retrench their assets in a panic and thereby amplify the fall in prices. The suggestion, therefore, is that central banks must find some ways of targeting asset prices, if not directly, at least indirectly, and not be just obsessed with targeting the general price level.

Second, because of the crucial role banks play in the money supply process, traditionally, central banks, across the world, have placed banks under their regulatory and supervisory ambit. However, other than that, central banks have paid scant attention to the rest of the financial system. This was based on three premises: (a) financial markets are efficient and can regulate themselves; (b) financial innovation benefits both the financial and real sectors of the economy; and (c) if there is a disturbance in one part of the financial system that need not cause a systemic failure as prices of different asset classes are not correlated. However, the recent events witnessed in the global financial meltdown would seem to suggest that none of the three premises put forth above could be taken for granted. The consensus view, therefore, is that while financial innovation is desirable, there should be adequate checks and balances to ensure that destructive financial innovations do not create havoc in the market. The financial regulation bill recently passed in the US attempts to do precisely that.

Third, economists are questioning the desirability of targeting inflation rate at a low 2 per cent or around, which central banks in most parts of the developed world, practice. Since one reason why interest rate exists is inflation (chapter 2), a low inflation rate corresponds to a low nominal interest rate in the economy. And, with a low nominal interest rate, in a period of slowdown or recession, the central bank is constrained to bring about sufficient reduction in interest rates to stimulate the economy. Monetary policy proves to be ineffective. In most of the developed world, policy rates are at all time low, close to zero in some cases. Probably the economies of these countries require more monetary policy stimulation, but the flexibility to reduce the policy rates substantially when the existing rates are already low is limited. After all, nominal interest rates cannot be less than zero. This constraint that central banks are facing today in the conduct of monetary policy opens up a possibility that inflation targets may have to be set at more realistic levels.

# FISCAL POLICY

In the recent economic meltdown, the role of fiscal policy in stimulating economies has been rediscovered. The logic is as follows: Actual GDP equals aggregate demand for goods and services in the economy. A slowdown or recession is caused because aggregate demand growth is deficient. In such situations, the role of the macroeconomic policies is to give a boost to demand. However, the task of augmenting demand may become difficult, if demand does not respond to policy stimulation. That can happen if the slowdown/recession is caused by a major shock in the economy. Conceptually, we know that:

$$\mathbf{AD = Pvt_D + Govt_D + Net\ Forgn_D}$$

where,

AD = aggregate demand

$Pvt_D$ = private sector demand

$Govt_D$ = government sector demand and,

$Net\ Forgn_D$ = net foreign sector demand (X – M)

In a severe slowdown/recession of the type witnessed recently, private sector demand, because of negative sentiment may not proportionately respond to interest rate and tax rate changes (chapter 3); similarly, the ability of policies to give a boost to export demand is limited by the rate of growth of GDP of the buyer countries. The only recourse open to stimulate demand then is to step up discretionary government expenditure. This is precisely what has been happening across the world. Whatever revival that we see in the global economies today is on account of massive fiscal stimulation.

Then, where is the catch? The catch is that nowhere in the world, the increase in government expenditure is met out of governments' own income (excess of revenue over expenditure). The entire increase is out of borrowed money. This has resulted in a substantial jump in the fiscal deficit and the size of the government debt. And, since initially, to have a quick effect, the increase in the government expenditure has mainly comprised consumption expenditure, the size of debt has gone up in relation to GDP. We have already discussed the problem this has caused in Greece (Box 6.1); suffice it to say, many other countries are equally concerned about their swelling debt/GDP ratios.[13]

On fiscal policy, therefore, one can think of two changes in the future. First, fiscal policy will, probably gain more importance in macroeconomic policy formulation in view of its pivotal role in stimulating economies in a period of deep slowdown/recession. But at the same time, macroeconomic policies will insist that every country works toward creating a fiscal space to accommodate the need for such fiscal stimulation without causing a sharp rise in debt. Essentially, that means building up a surplus when the economy is doing well and using it to meet the imperative of stimulating the economy in a period of slowdown. This will also mean austerity measures, reducing the fiscal lag and improving the delivery system.

## The External Sector

In advanced economies exchange rate stabilization, except when it impacted domestic inflation, has not been an exclusive objective of monetary policy. In many other economies, however, central banks have intervened in the

[13]A high debt/GDP ratio may not impact all countries equally. For example, it may be more sustainable if the borrowing is in local currency, which also happens to be a reserve currency (USA) or when the domestic saving rate is very high (Japan). However, these countries can only buy time but cannot sustain it for a prolonged period.

currency market to stabilize the exchange rate. Thus, in a period, when the supply of foreign exchange exceeded the demand for foreign exchange, central banks purchased foreign exchange from the market to tame the appreciation of the domestic currency. This went towards building up of foreign exchange reserves. Central banks played around with different tools (chapter 5) to ensure that the resultant increase in money supply was manageable.

Similarly, in a period when the demand for foreign exchange exceeded the supply of foreign exchange, central banks sold foreign exchange in the market to arrest the depreciation of the domestic currency. Once again, they employed different tools to minimize the adverse impact of reduced money supply.

This practice of intervening in the currency market has generally been viewed unfavourably by many economists. Keeping the domestic currency undervalued through purchase of foreign exchange from the market is considered unfair to the trading partner; similarly, keeping the currency overvalued can open up the risk of a speculative attack and the accompanying contagion.

However, central banks that chose to intervene in the currency market did, in the face of heavy capital movements, manage to avoid sharp downturn in export growth when their domestic currency was under pressure of appreciation. Similarly, they were able to avoid a possible disruption in the domestic financial sector when their currency was under pressure of depreciation.

The recent economic and financial meltdown has brought two points to the fore. First, capital flows can be highly volatile and second, those economies which had adequate foreign exchange reserves were able to face the massive outflow of capital in the wake of the meltdown, much better than others, though their currencies also depreciated to varying degrees.

Clearly, there is a rethinking whether intervention in the currency market is necessarily bad and whether free movement of capital is always good.

## Where does India Stand on Some of these Issues?

The Indian position can be explained best in former governor Y.V. Reddy's own words. "In India, the mandate for the Reserve Bank of India (RBI) is very broad. It was interpreted to mean the dual objectives of growth and price stability, the relative emphasis depending on the context. The RBI reinterpreted this a few years ago by adding financial stability to the objectives and by ensuring inflation of not more than 5 per cent per annum (3 per cent over the medium term) so as to be consistent with global trends. More explicitly, since 2004, price and financial stability were given greater weight because the poor are affected severely and instantly by instability while the reform-induced benefits of growth percolate to them with a time lag. Public policy did not severely counter the resetting of priorities by the RBI."

"The policy monitored several indicators, growth in credit aggregates and asset prices were among them. Similarly, both direct and indirect instruments were used, depending on the evolving circumstances."

"The management of the external sector in India is characterised by (a) a sustainable current account deficit over the medium term; (b) an exchange rate that is not excessively volatile; (c) management of a capital account that eschews short-term debt unrelated to trade; (d) a gradual process of liberalisation of the capital account; and (e) extensive recourse to prudential measures over financial intermediaries, which have the effect of an active management of the capital account."[14]

Many economists, who felt that India was regulating its financial sector too much, now see a lot of merit in what India has been doing. India was able to tide over the great recession of 2008–09 much better than others. The message is clear: text book solutions work only if markets are perfect; in real life markets are not always perfect. Thus, "reform of the financial sector globally means reregulation and improving the quality as well as the effectiveness of regulation[15]".

India's worry is on the fiscal front. Unless it is able to tame the size and quality of fiscal deficit, ultimately, it will also impact the conduct of monetary policy.

[14]Reddy, Y. V. "Financial Sector Regulation in India." *Economic and Political Weekly*, April 3, 2010, pp. 40–50.

[15]Op. cit. p. 50.

# REVIEW QUESTIONS

1. How will you explain the nature of the current global slowdown?
2. Why monitoring the financial sector in today's context, is perhaps more important than monitoring the real sector?
3. Do you take into consideration some of the issues discussed in this chapter in strategic planning? Should we?
4. Are there any strategic implications for business of what we have learnt in Chapter 7? Discuss.
5. If you looking for new business opportunities, how will you go about it?

# GLOSSARY

**Aggregate demand:** Total spending on final goods and services in an economy in a given period.

**Aggregate supply:** Value of total production of final goods and services in an economy in a given period.

**Appreciation:** An increase in the value of a currency in relation to another currency. Holds true in a flexible exchange rate regime.

**Automatic stabilizer:** A system through which government expenditure and taxes automatically provide a cushion against fluctuations in income.

**Autonomous variable:** Variables which determine aggregate demand independently of macroeconomic policies like sentiment, expectations, gut feeling, etc.

**Average propensity to consume:** Ratio of consumption to income.

**Bank rate:** The rate at which the central bank lends to the commercial banks.

**Balance of payments:** A statement, which shows all transactions of a country with the rest of the world in a given period.

**Balance of trade:** A statement showing transaction of a country with the rest of the world in respect of merchandise only in a given period.

**Balance sheet:** A record of assets and liabilities of an economic unit.

**Boom:** When the actual growth of GDP (aggregate demand) has a tendency to outpace the potential growth.

**Bubble:** When asset prices are driven up based on future expectations or speculative motive and not on fundamentals.

**Call money market rate:** The rate at which one bank borrows from the other.

**Capacity output:** The maximum level of output which can be produced when all factors of production are fully employed.

**Capital account:** Record of a country's assets transactions with the rest of the world.

**Capital account convertibility:** When for all transactions on capital account of the balance of payment the currency is fully convertible.

**Capital adequacy norms:** Norms that guide a bank's amount and funding structure depending on their assets.

**Capital controls:** Controls on the free movement of capital in and out of the country.

**Capital stock:** Stock of equipments, buildings and structure used in production at any point of time.

**Cash reserve ratio:** A requirement that banks must hold a proportion of their total deposits in the form of cash reserves.

**Central bank:** An apex bank, which is in charge of the conduct of monetary policy in the country.

**Collateral Debt Obligation:** A financial structure which groups individual loans in a portfolio.

**Consumption:** Total spending on goods and services by the consumers.

**Cost of capital:** The cost of acquiring capital, given by interest rate, depreciation and expected inflation rate.

**Credibility:** The extent to which people perceive that government's policy announcements can be believed.

**Credit Default Swaps:** An agreement between two parties for a protection in the event of a default on payment of an asset.

**Crowding out:** Decrease in private investment consequent to excessive government borrowing from the market.

**Currency deposit ratio:** Ratio of currency to bank deposits. Affects the size of money multiplier.

**Currency overvaluation:** When the exchange rate between the local and foreign currency is valued by the central bank at a level that is much higher than what would prevail if the exchange rate were market determined.

**Currency undervaluation:** When the exchange rate between the local and foreign currency is valued by the central bank at a level that is much lower than what would prevail if the exchange rate were market determined.

**Current account:** The part of the balance of payments account that records non-capital transactions.

**Current account convertibility:** When for all transactions on current account of balance of payments the currency is fully convertible.

**Cyclical Deficit:** Government borrowing resorted to at the low point of business cycle.

**Debt sustainability:** Refers to movements in debt-GDP ratio. If debt-GDP ratio is rising debt is unsustainable and vice versa.

**Deflator:** A price index that converts nominal numbers to real ones.

**Demand management:** Management of aggregate demand for goods and services in an economy consistent with the supply capacity of the economy.

**Depreciation:** A decrease in the value of one currency in relation to the other. Holds true in a flexible exchange rate regime.

**Depression:** It is a deeper recession.

**Devaluation:** A fall in the value of a currency in relation to other, effected by the central bank of the country to correct balance of payment disequilibria. Valid in a fixed exchange rate regime.

**Discretionary policy:** Where, instead of following fixed rules, the government or the central bank uses its discretion to frame policies to influence aggregate demand.

**Disposable income:** Personal income minus taxes. Divided between consumption and saving.

**Effective exchange rate:** An index that gives the weighted average value of an exchange rate against several other countries.

**Exchange rate:** The price of one currency against the other. Also called the nominal exchange rate.

**Expectation driven variables:** When consumer sentiments, business optimism/pessimism are primary drivers of aggregate demand.

**Fiat money:** Money that is valued on account of backing of government legislation/fiat rather than its intrinsic value.

**Final good:** What is sold directly to the final consumer.

**Financial crisis:** When banks become insolvent.

**Financial liberalization:** When financial sector is opened up to improve competition and efficiency.

**Financial repression:** When controls are imposed on the financial sector posing obstacles in its efficient functioning. Usually follows government's desire to raise cheap money.

**Financial sector reforms:** Setting up norms and institutions to facilitate fair competition in the financial markets.

**Fiscal deficit:** Difference between the government's total expenditure and its own receipts.

**Fiscal policy:** Has three components: government expenditure, government debt and taxes. Through changes in these, fiscal policy influences aggregate demand.

**Fiscal responsibility and budget management bill:** A bill passed in the Indian parliament to contain government's fiscal deficit within a specified limit by 2009.

**Fixed exchange rate:** When the government fixes exchange rate between countries and the rate is maintained through central bank intervention in the currency market.

**Flexible exchange rate:** An exchange rate between one currency and the other that is determined solely based on demand for and supply of the currencies in the market place.

**Flow variable:** A variable that is measured per unit of time.

**Foreign exchange Intervention:** When the central bank buys and sells foreign exchange in the currency market to tame exchange rate fluctuations.

**Gross domestic product:** Market value of all final goods and services produced in an economy over a specified period.

**Gross investment:** Addition to the stock of capital in a country during a particular period.

**Human development index:** A broad measure of welfare of the people prepared by the United Nations, which includes, in addition to GDP, indicators of health and education.

**Inflation:** A continuous rise in the general price level in an economy and a consequent fall in the purchasing power of money. Can be caused by demand pull or cost push.

**Interest rate:** It is the price charged for borrowed money. Also called the nominal interest rate.

**Leveraging:** Using debt to supplement investment.

**Kelkar committee report:** A committee set up to look into India's tax reforms.

**M1, M3:** Different measures of the aggregate stock of money in Indian economy. M1 is narrow money and M3 is broad money and is, therefore, larger in value.

**Market Stabilization Bonds:** When the government issues bonds to stabilize the foreign exchange market and not for its expenditure. The amount raised is kept with RBI in a cash account.

**Marginal propensity to consume:** Change in consumption expenditure in response to a change in disposable income.

**Monetary base:** Also called 'high powered money' or 'reserve money' consists of currency with public and banks' deposits with the central bank.

**Monetary policy:** A policy tool through which the central bank influences the aggregate demand for goods and services in the economy by changing the money supply and thereby the interest rates.

**Money multiplier:** Ratio of money stock to monetary base.

**Mortgage backed securities:** A financial product made up of debt from a number of mortgages which can be traded.

**Mundell-Fleming model:** Explores economies with free capital mobility and flexible exchange rates.

**Net investment:** Gross investment minus depreciation (consumption of capital).

**Open market operations:** Purchase and sale of government securities in the market by the central bank with the objective of controlling the money supply.

**Policy induced variables:** Refer to macroeconomic policy variables like tax rates and interest rates etc., which can induce change in aggregate demand for goods and services in an economy.

**Primary deficit:** Fiscal deficit minus interest payments.

**Prime lending rate:** Rate at which the banks lend to their most favoured customers.

**Purchasing power parity:** Parity between two currencies at an exchange rate that will give each currency the same purchasing power in its own economy.

**Real exchange rate:** Nominal exchange rate multiplied by the ratio of foreign prices to domestic prices.

**Real interest rate:** Nominal interest rate minus the expected inflation rate.

**Recession:** It is a deeper slowdown.

**Repo transactions:** Central bank's purchase of government securities from the banks with an agreement that the securities will be bought back by the banks at a later date at a specified rate.

**Reserves:** Money that banks do not lend but keep partly as vault cash and partly as deposits with the central bank.

**Revaluation:** A rise in the value of a currency in relation to other, effected by the central bank of the country to correct balance of payment disequilibria. Valid in a fixed exchange rate regime.

**Revenue deficit:** The difference between the government's revenue (current) expenditure and revenue (current) receipts.

**Reverse repo transactions:** Central bank's sale of government securities to the banks with an understanding that it will buy back the securities from the banks at a later date at a specified rate.

**Saving:** What is left out of disposable income after consumption.

**Slowdown:** When the actual growth of GDP (aggregate demand) is less than the potential growth.

**Structural deficit:** Fiscal deficit that remains through the business cycle.

**Structural variables:** Refer to rigidities in the structure of an economy which come in the way of more spending on goods and services in the economy.

**Sterilization:** A means to neutralize the inflationary/deflationary effects of central bank's intervention in the foreign exchange market.

**Sub-prime loans:** Housing loans extended to customers who are less creditworthy.

**Value added:** The value added to goods and services at each stage of production or rendering of service.

**Velocity of circulation:** The number of times the money is spent on GDP in a given period, given by the ratio of nominal GDP to nominal money stock.

**Wealth:** Sum of value of assets and money held by a household.

**Wealth effect:** A change in the aggregate demand consequent to change in the wealth of the household.

# Index

# AUTHOR'S PROFILE

Dr. Shyamal Roy is a Professor of Economics at Indian Institute of Management, Bangalore (IIMB). Before joining IIMB, Dr. Roy worked in various capacities at the World Bank in Washington DC, FAO in Rome, International Food Policy Research Institute (IFPRI) at Washington DC and the Brookings Institution in Washington DC.

Dr. Roy has many publications to his credit. The World Bank, IFPRI, Brookings Institution and leading national and international journals have published his work. His research interest is in the area of Economic Policy. He teaches Macroeconomic Theory and International Business to masters and Ph.D. level students at IIMB. Additionally, he lectures in various companies on macroeconomic issues and provides consultancy services on policy matters to the corporate sector and the government.

Dr. Roy has held key positions in academic administration, including, as Academic Dean and member, Board of Governors, IIMB.

He is an MA (Economics) from Delhi University and Ph.D. (Agri. Econ) from the University of Missouri, Columbia, USA.

# CFM Quarterly in Finance

Centre for Financial Management brings out an e-journal called ***CFM Quarterly in Finance*** edited by Dr. Prasanna Chandra.

Written in a relatively non–technical manner, ***CFM Quarterly in Finance*** has three sections. The first section, the principal section, carries short articles and cases to discuss important ideas, concepts, and state–of–the–art practices in the broad fields of finance and investments. The second section carries snippets that provide useful insights. Finally, the third section provides some wit and wisdom.

***CFM Quarterly in Finance*** is designed for two categories of readers: finance educators and finance practitioners.

***Finance educators*** will find the material useful to enrich the courses taught by them.

***Finance practitioners*** will get valuable insights and perspectives to handle their professional challenges.

You can access the ***CFM Quarterly in Finance*** at www.cfm-india.com